The be

Cotswolds

Katie Jarvis

Contents

The Guide

Foreword

Alex James

Four years ago, my wife Claire and I had a balcony in Covent Garden: now we've got 200 Cotswold acres and hundreds of sheep. The Cotswolds are still the prettiest part of England and England is the prettiest place in the world. There's the soft rolling countryside – small fields and hedgerows – and all the randomness. It hasn't all been homogenised: lovely little nestling villages, and huge piles with their formal gardens laid out.

Before we moved here, I remember going to see Dan Chadwick at Lypiatt Park in Stroud – right in *Cider with Rosie* country – who has the most beautiful house I've ever seen. The fact that he was a sculptor who could live and work in the area seemed inspirational – and maybe that got the dream started.

We went trawling round looking for houses. I didn't know if I wanted a big house or a little one, and we had this crazy car as well – like a really bad BMW that had caught fire once – and we'd turn up to look at these piles. It was when we got to the farm we eventually bought and discovered our car was nicer than the guy's who was selling the place, then I knew this was the one. There was so much space here, and all these Cotswold stone buildings with tiled roofs that were falling down; you can't build things like that anymore. It just needed investment: a place you could dream about.

Now we farm organic sheep and we make cheese. Making cheese is the least global thing you can do – and there's a real demand for the genuine local, handmade product. It's great to hear about other Cotswold cheesemakers such as Charles Martell: he's an artist; someone who wants to make something brilliant rather than to make as much of something as he can. And then there are places like the shop at Daylesford. When we bring people up from London who live in Notting Hill, even they think Daylesford is posh: it's preposterously brilliant.

Our decision to move down here was a bit crazy, and if we hadn't done it when we did, we probably never would have got round to it. But I'm really glad we did: we're both surprised at how little we've looked back. You can have lots of houses but you can only have one home, and the Cotswolds are our home.

Alex James is the multi-talented columnist, writer and musician who first found fame as the bass player in Blur. Since moving to a farm in the Oxfordshire Cotswolds with wife, Claire Neate, and their four children, life has been more Roquefort than rock, for he's now an award-winning cheese producer, too.

Introduction

Imagine your perfect country scene; the kind an artist would sketch in soft pencil and colour with vibrant oils: golden honey for the stone of a cottage; mauve for the wild orchids tumbling through the chaotic garden; mahogany for the cows grazing in the yellow-dotted cowslip meadow alongside; transparent blue for the burbling stream; and every kind of green for the sides of the gently-sloping valley that opens out below. It's so ridiculously perfect – so idyllically bucolic – that surely it has to be confined to the pages of a child's picture book... But if you were to stand atop the Evenlode Valley, or above Laurie Lee's Slad, or in any of 100 other breeze-swept Cotswold spots, that same scene would stretch out before you.

If that sounds too much like the sort of thing a guide book would say, then you can put it to the test. You can stand in a spot, unchanged since the 18th century, breathing in pure air, perhaps lightly scented by honeysuckle, feeling nothing but the warm wind and the mossy grass beneath your feet, and hearing – nothing. At night, there's true blackness, unbroken by artificial light; and in the morning, the only thing that wakes you is your own internal body clock. No wonder this unspoilt area has attracted celebrities such as Alex James, Elizabeth Hurley, Kate Moss and Stella McCartney.

So what – and where – are the Cotswolds? They're hills, of course: gently sloping hills in the heart of England; cultivated hills with none of the craggy bleakness of mountains, but which nevertheless offer giddy views from their rolling, tumocky heights, sometimes over 1,000ft up; part of a band of oolitic limestone that sweeps from Dorset to the Humber. The dramatic escarpment to the west, the Cotswold Edge, looks out over the Severn Vale – with its flowing rivers, playful brooks, fertile low-lying fields and bustling towns – across the Forest of Dean to the Welsh mountains beyond. The east is more approachable, more gentle: a rolling profile of deep valleys and sheep-grazed slopes.

Indeed, it's a place where the landscape has influenced every aspect of this glorious region – the sheep that grazed here and created the wealth that built the manor houses and churches; the streams that powered the mills; the food that defines the Cotswolds – Gloucester beef, Old Spot pork, Single Gloucester cheeses, apple juice from ancient varieties such as Ashmead's Kernel and Arlingham Schoolboys.

The Cotswolds stretch across six counties – Wiltshire, Somerset, Worcestershire and Warwickshire, with their heartland in Gloucestershire and Oxfordshire. Here you will see the characteristics that help define them: drystone walls built by craftsmen of yore without the aid of mortar; golden-stone cottages and manor houses that look as if they've not been built but have arisen organically from the ground they stand on; villages with mellow houses gathered around greens as if idly passing the time of day; market towns that seem barely to have noticed the passage of time; woodland of ancient beech trees with buzzards mewing high above; limestone grassland that's never been fertilised or ploughed, where scabious, harebells, cowslips and wild orchids thrive. Indeed, it was this natural beauty that led to the Cotswolds being designated an Area of Outstanding Natural Beauty back in 1966.

There's Bourton-on-the-Water, the Venice of the Cotswolds, where the River Windrush passes through; the lovely Slaughter villages; towns such as medieval Tewkesbury, Regency Chel-tenham and Georgian Bath. The nation's favourite places, from Laurie Lee's Slad, Bibury's Arlington Row and Sir Peter Scott's Wildfowl & Wetlands Trust at Slimbridge to Castle Combe and Bath's Royal Crescent, are in there.

But there's more to this place than just looks. There's culture in the form of festivals galore – literature, science, music; top horse-racing at Cheltenham. It's an area that will make you laugh with its quirky customs (rolling cheeses down hills; shin-kicking at the Cotswold Olimpick Games); intrigue you with its mysteries (the legend-rich Rollright Stones in Oxfordshire; the unfinished Woodchester Mansion near Stroud); and charm you with its eccentricities (Snowshill Manor, packed to the rafters with a collector's ephemera). The Cotswolds also have a water park – where you can sail, bird-watch or swim.

Listen to the locals speak in their rich burr and you will hear sounds of a world where time moves more slowly. You can't rush the Cotswolds, and nor should you. Visit, relax, enjoy.

Unmissable highlights

01 Westonbirt Arboretum

Experience the most glorious gold and russet autumn you've ever seen, at Westonbirt, The National Arboretum; its collection of Japanese maples is world famous – and then go back for winter, spring and summer, too, p. 96

02 Laurie Lee's Slad

Wander the slopes of the Slad valley,
along the road from Stroud to Birdlip,
a copy of *Cider with Rosie* in hand;
here are the Cotswold places beloved
by the poet and author, Laurie Lee, p. 61

03 Stroud Farmers' Market

Indulge your senses at Stroud Farmers' Market, which takes place every Saturday: local cheeses, meats, luscious fruit juices, gleaming vegetables, and brimful of atmosphere. It's recently been judged best in the country by the National Farmers' Retail & Markets Association (FARMA), p. 72

04 Slimbridge, One Wildfowl & Wetlands Trust

Take the family on a bird-watching canoe safari at the internationally-renowned Wildfowl & Wetlands Trust at Slimbridge, a wildfowl haven created by the late artist and conservationist, Sir Peter Scott, p. 77

05 Cheltenham Races

Enjoy a flutter at Cheltenham Racecourse – and hats off to you if you manage a win on Gold Cup day, p. 281

06 Blenheim Palace

Take in the vista at Blenheim Palace: Blenheim Lake, spanned by Vanbrugh's Grand Bridge. American-born Lady Randolph Churchill (Sir Winston's mother) declared it *'the finest view in England'*, p. 206

07 The Severn Bore

Stand on the banks at Stonebench, wait for the birds to fall silent and the very air to quieten around you – then listen, amazed, as the Severn Bore tidal wave rushes up the river like an express train, p. 297

08 Roman Bath

Admire the Roman Baths – among the most splendid in Britain – where the natural spring produces more than a million litres of water a day at 46°C, p. 243

09 The Slaughters

Walk from Upper Slaughter to Lower Slaughter, two of the most gorgeous villages in England, and decide whether even Walt Disney could have done a better job, p. 147

10 Shakeseare's Stratford

Visit the Shakespeare houses at Stratford-upon-Avon and see some of the sights the Bard himself would have seen more than four centuries ago – followed by a drink with the actors at the famous Dirty Duck, p. 187

Secret
Cotswolds
Local Recommendations

01 A Cotswold beach

Sunbathe on a Cotswold beach (a manmade one, anyway) – At Keynes Country Park, there's a super child-friendly beach where you can take your inflatables – and the sand is tiptop castle-making material

02 The Ships' Graveyard

For a unique – and free – experience, head to Purton for majestic and moving sight: the old ships' graveyard. These old boats that lie beached along the shore are the Severn trows that once plied their trade along the river

03 Minchinhampton Common

Fly a kite among the tufted dilly dumps of Minchinhampton Common, where cows roam freely all summer and multicoloured butterflies – including the rare Duke of Burgundy – flit between wild orchids

04 William's deli

Shop for lunch at William's Fish Market and Food Hall in Nailsworth. Locals know how outstanding this delicatessen truly is. Even so, the town's mayor was astonished to discover visiting MP Jack Straw was a fan. Bet he'd like to know they now have an oyster bar, too

05 The Cotswold perfumery

The Cotswold Perfumery in Bourton-on-the-Water is a fragrant outlet in a beautiful village. This unusual shop and perfumery offers factory tours and special courses under the watchful nose of perfumer John Stephen

06 Mysterious Woodchester

Take a look at Woodchester Mansion, Gloucestershire's most mysterious house – an architectural masterpiece of the Victorian age, strangely abandoned by its builders before it was completed

07 Giffords Circus

Travel back to the showmanship of the 1930s with Giffords Circus. Its summer season takes it round the village greens and commons of the Cotswolds with a traditional, musical, arty, polished and enormously fun show – even the family geese do a turn.

08 Bibury trout

Feed the fish (and greedy ducks) at Bibury Trout Farm, one of the oldest trout farms in the country; then sample the fresh or smoked trout from the fish counter

09 Bath: view from on high

Glimpse the beauty of Bath from Beechen Cliff – just go up to Alexandra Park and take a look. Jane Austen was a frequent visitor and remarked on the view.

10 Cirencester's Corinium Museum

Visit Cirencester's award-winning Corinium Museum, where children can play Roman games (of a peaceable nature) and dress as Roman soldiers

Factfile

01 The Cotswolds were designated an Area of Outstanding Natural Beauty (AONB) in 1966, which means they have the same landscape quality and status as a National Park; The Cotswolds are the largest AONB in England and Wales, covering 790sq miles

02 The AONB has 10% of the country's breeding horseshoe bats and the UK's only population of the snail *Lauria sempronii* (it's found on two short stretches of drystone wall at Edgeworth); while the rare Cotswold pennycress is only found as a native plant in this region

03 Over half of the country's flower-rich limestone grassland is found in the Cotswolds

04 Around 80% of the Cotswolds is farmland

05 Cotswold stone is made up of layer upon layer of sand and shell fragments, bound together like a bull's eye sweet; it was formed during the Jurassic Age, around 200 million years ago, when the area was covered by a warm, shallow sea and dinosaurs roamed the earth

06 There are more than 4,000 miles of drystone walls in the Cotswolds AONB; put together they'd be the same length as the Great Wall of China

07 The Cotswolds contain two World Heritage Sites – Bath, with its well-preserved Roman remains, baths and Georgian architecture, and Blenheim Palace, Churchill's birthplace

08 Cheltenham is England's most complete Regency town, and Tewkesbury is one of the best-preserved medieval townscapes in the country

09 The Cotswold Lion isn't a fierce jungle beast, but the name of the area's native sheep which, at one time, provided wool for more than half of England's cloth

10 The Forest of Dean is one of England's few remaining ancient forests, covering over 110sq km; while the AONB has internationally important beech and yew woods

THE FACTS

WHEN TO GO

It may sound like stating the obvious, but the Cotswolds are very rural – in fact, much of the area is still farmland. What that means is that you can visit in spring and see a landscape green with leaves, and fields covered in wild flowers, then visit the same spot six months later, russetted and burned orange by autumn, and feel you've entered a completely different universe. It's one of the joys that makes this an all-year-round destination.

Spring

Wild flowers are in profusion all over the Cotswolds each spring. Particularly famous are the snowdrop displays at **Painswick Rococo Garden**, originally laid out in the early 18th century (p. 61). During weekends in February, you can visit the **Colesbourne Estate**, which *Country Life* called '*England's greatest snowdrop garden*' (p. 277). In the Forest of Dean, **Dymock** is renowned for its wild daffodils, and the village of **Kempley** organises a daffodil weekend in March, with guided walks.

Many farms are open to the public, and children will love watching chicks hatch and giving lambs their bottles at numerous places, among them **Butts Farm** in South Cerney (p. 132) and the **Cotswold Farm Park** near Guiting Power (p. 154). In spring, many breeding birds return to the **Cotswold Water Park**, such as the little ringed plover; you might even hear the song of a nightingale (p. 123).

There are some iconic Cotswold events – as well as the quirky! **Badminton Horse Trials** take place in May, while on Spring Bank Holiday – the last Monday – there are the **Tetbury Woolsack Races**, where teams run in relays carrying 60lb woolsacks up and down Gumstool Hill with its 1 in 4 gradient (p. 101). As if that's not enough, there's the cheese rolling involving chasing a Double Gloucester cheese – which can reach speeds of up to 70mph – down Coopers Hill near Gloucester (p. 310); and a few days later, the **Cotswold Olimpicks** take place at Dovers Hill, Chipping Campden, complete with competitive shin-kicking (p. 176).

Shakespeare's Birthday Celebrations are held in Stratford-upon-Avon on the weekend nearest to 23 April, with traditional dancing and street entertainment (p. 189). But perhaps the event that pulls the largest crowds of all is Cheltenham's famous **Gold Cup Week** at the racecourse, one of the biggest events of the racing calendar (p. 281).

Summer

This is the time to enjoy the outdoors, whether walking some of the Cotswolds' 3,000 miles of public footpaths, including the 102 mile **Cotswold Way** that stretches from Chipping Campden to Bath, or visiting outstanding gardens – the Arts and Crafts masterpiece at **Hidcote Manor** (p. 171) for example. You can admire Rose Week in June at **Sudeley**, dubbed England's most romantic castle (p. 150); enjoy an al fresco concert at **Blenheim Palace** (p. 206); or opera in a garden at **Longborough** (p. 177). **Minchinhampton** and **Rodborough Commons** are delightful in the summer, dotted with wild orchids and grazed by free-roaming cows (p. 58).

There's plenty of organised activity going on, from top **music** events, such as the internationally-renowned festival at Cheltenham in July (p. 275), to the **cricket** at Cheltenham College (p. 282). **Gatcombe Horse Trials**, at the home of the Princess

Royal, is another event that draws people from many miles away (p. 59).

This is the time to enjoy some of the fruits of the land in the form of pick-your-own strawberries. You can't beat **Primrose Vale Farm Shop** near Cheltenham (p. 288) or **Hayles Fruit Farm** at Winchcombe (p. 161). Or take home some fresh fish from **Bibury Trout Farm** (p. 114).

Autumn

Several autumns ago, no fewer than 18,000 visitors turned up in one day to admire the colours at **Westonbirt Arboretum** near Tetbury (p. 96). Its collection of Japanese maples, which glow iridescently plum, crimson, saffron and scarlet in autumn, is well on the way to becoming the best in Europe, if not the world.

This is the time of year when the **Forest of Dean** is spectacular, too, of course. One section, between Wenchford picnic site and the Dean Heritage Centre in Soudley, is nicknamed the Golden Mile because of its rich colours at this time of year (p. 301). And each autumn, Bewick's swans return to the **Wildfowl & Wetlands Trust** at Slimbridge (p. 77).

Bath celebrates its **Jane Austen** connections in September with a fun festival based around the writer and her time in the city (p. 255). And literary buffs should look out for the **Cheltenham Festival of Literature** (p. 281).

Winter

It can, of course, be pretty chilly up in those hills in winter, especially in elevated towns such as '*Stow-on-the-Wold where the wind blows cold*', as the old rhyme goes. Cold – but beautiful and archetypally English: the winter scenes for *Bridget Jones's Diary* were filmed in and around the north Cotswold village of Snowshill.

The reward is that most of the pubs in the area will have roaring real fires. And if you put on your wellington boots and fleeces and walk there, you will feel justified in sampling the comfort food that awaits on many a traditional menu. Just remember that it gets dark early – before 4pm in the depths of the season – so set out in plenty of time, if you don't want to have to use a torch.

Many visitor attractions close for the winter – though not all, by any means. But you will find a plethora of shopping events and fairs, especially featuring beautiful craft work. Bath has a popular **Christmas market** next to the abbey in December (p. 256), and youngsters will have plenty of opportunities to meet Santa, including on the **Gloucestershire Warwickshire Railway** (p. 281) and in **Clearwell Caves** in the Forest of Dean (p. 304). A Christmas service at **Gloucester Cathedral** or **Tewkesbury Abbey** is something to remember for life. For a magical December experience with a difference, you need to do Westonbirt Arboretum's **Enchanted Christmas**, a mile-long evening trail through illuminated woodland (p. 97).

GETTING THERE

One reason why so many high-profile people live in this area is its sheer accessibility and excellent communications in all directions.

By car

By and large, the main routes into the Cotswolds are easily accessible and free-flowing at most times of the day. The M4/A419 via Swindon will get you to and from the centre of London in around two hours, bar hold-ups, and the M40 provides access to the north Cotswolds from the capital. The M5 motorway runs north/south through the Cotswolds, albeit to the west side, which serves those arriving from the north, including Birmingham/the Midlands, or the south-west: Bristol, Devon and Cornwall.

Once you exit the motorway, there are good trunk roads; but at some point, you will probably have to venture on to the smaller roads. Many of them, especially around

10... Cotswold gardens

1 Hidcote Manor Garden, Hidcote, Bartrim Chipping, Campden – influential 20th-century Arts and Crafts garden, p. 171

2 Abbey House Garden, Malmesbury – one of Britain's largest private collections of plants, owned by the 'Naked Gardeners', p. 99

3 Painswick Rococo Garden – rare example of flamboyant and sensual 18th-century design, p. 61

4 Sudeley Castle, Winchcombe – historic and romantic, p. 150

5 Kiftsgate Court Gardens, Chipping Campden – home to the famous Kiftsgate Rose, p. 172

6 Westbury Court Garden, Westbury-on-Severn – rare and beautiful Dutch water garden, p. 303

7 Mill Dene Garden, Blockley – a stream runs through it, p. 174

8 Sezincote Garden, near Moreton-in-Marsh – pools, Indian temple and grotto, p. 176

9 Rousham House, near Steeple Aston – described by Monty Don as the best garden in Britain, p. 202

10 Lydney Spring Gardens, Lydney Park – secluded wooded valley with views over the Severn Estuary, p. 302

the villages, are only wide enough for one car. You could easily find yourself behind the odd tractor, and there could be some muddy byways to boot. There may not be the level of lighting that you are used to at night. And one of the most important things to remember is that animals will often roam free, especially in summer. Sheep 'own' the roads in the Forest of Dean; cows – some of which are black and very difficult to see at night – wander freely around some of the commons, such as Minchinhampton and Rodborough near Stroud; and it's not unusual to find a family of ducks or geese waddling across the highway. Stay patient – these places were not built for modern life; you will just have to think of all this as part of the area's quirky charm!

If you are coming by car, don't rely 100% on GPS systems. It's not unusual, especially in very rural areas, for them to be misleading. Make sure you have good directions – backed up by landmarks – and an up-to-date map. It's also a good idea to check the availability of parking at your chosen destination. In some of the market towns in particular, there aren't enough car spaces to go round.

By train

Rail connections to the Cotswolds from all over the country are direct and frequent. From central London (Paddington), you can get to the Cotswolds in around an hour-and-three-quarters. Train travel is not always cheap: book in advance, if you can, and avoid business hours when the prices rise steeply. Because so many London escapees to the Cotswolds commute back to the city, trains can be extremely busy first thing in the morning. Frequent services are operated by First Great Western (www.firstgreatwestern. co.uk) from stations at:

- Cheltenham Spa and Gloucester in the west
- Stroud, Stonehouse and Kemble (which serves Cirencester) in the central region
- Moreton-in-Marsh and Stratford-upon-Avon in the North Cotswolds
- Kingham for the Oxfordshire Cotswolds
- Bath Spa to the south

Other useful websites are www.national rail.co.uk and www.thetrainline.com.

A cheaper option is to arrive by coach, though it does take a lot longer (☎08717 818181; www.nationalexpress.com). To be frank, public transport isn't fantastic within the Cotswolds themselves. If you do come by train or coach, you might want to consider hiring a car once you're here. National car-hire companies include www.hertz.com and www.avis.co.uk.

Great Escape Classic Car Hire (www. greatescapecars.co.uk, ☎01527 893733) in Redditch, 20 minutes north of Broadway, offers luxury in the form of an Alfa Romeo Spider or a Jensen Interceptor, among others; and to the south, **Cotswolds Classic Car Hire** (☎01225 703377, www.cotswoldsclassiccarhire.co.uk)

GREEN TOURISM

Choosing the Cotswolds in the first place is a pretty green thing to do. But if you want to ensure you make some good sustainable choices while you're here, there are two separate but complementary 'green' schemes. The Green Tourism Business Scheme judges businesses that have performed well in a wide list of categories, including energy efficiency, reducing waste, recycling, buying local and promoting public transport. 'Step into the Cotswolds' is a visitor payback scheme being trialled in the Oxfordshire Cotswolds. Participating businesses will ask customers to make a small voluntary contribution, which will be invested into projects to conserve the area, to make it more accessible, and to promote awareness of its special features. Simply look out for the logos.

in Melksham proffers such delights as a Jaguar E-Type or, for Inspector Morse fans, a Jaguar MK II, and an Austin-Healey 3000.

ACCOMMODATION

One of the hardest decisions you're going to have to make is where to stay, never mind choosing the type of accommodation. Do you want an isolated rural, small village, a busy market town, bigger town or even city centre? There's the full gamut within the Cotswolds. Then there are canal boats, working farms, B&Bs, campsites, luxury lodges, or even a yurt eco-camp on the edge of Cirencester.

Top 10 lists are, by their very nature, subjective and specific; but there are Cotswold hotels that crop up again and again in the listings, which has to say something about their quality and style. Lords of the Manor in Upper Slaughter provides the height of luxury in a rural setting, while American readers of Condé Nast voted Lower Slaughter Manor

10... places to avoid in the Cotswolds

1 **Hesters Way, Cheltenham** – often in the papers, not always for the right reasons

2 **Smug weekender villages** – deserted Monday to Friday, followed by an influx of people who think cocks shouldn't crow and roads should be kept clean of mud

3 **Minchinhampton Common** – in summer at night (black cows wandering in the dark)

4 **The retail barns** on Gloucester's ring road

5 **Fast food restaurants** – this is the place to really savour the slow food movement

6 **Horsley tip, near Nailsworth, on a Sunday** (and the B4048 running past it) – locals' idea of a day out

7 **The 'Air Balloon' roundabout,** near Birdlip, at rush hour

8 **Quedgeley** Sorry, Quedgeley – what were the planners thinking of?

9 **Cromwell** Street, Gloucester – where many of Fred and Rosemary West's victims were buried – the house is now demolished

10 **Stow-on-the-Wold** – if you're AA Gill, that is. The rest of us rather like it

the second-best hotel in the whole of the UK (p. 148); Cowley Manor near Cheltenham is the epitome of contemporary chic (p. 287); Calcot Manor near Tetbury offers a great spa experience (p. 103); and Whatley Manor near Malmesbury was recently voted one of the best hotels in the world (p. 103). Elizabeth Hurley and Arun Nayar partied at Barnsley House in the village of Barnsley near Cirencester, and hired the Village Pub next door to accommodate wedding guests, who included Elton John and Hugh Grant (p. 137). You can't have much more of a recommendation than that!

You will find options for all budgets within this book, but bear in mind that this is only a snapshot of what is available. Most of the tourist information centres offer an accommodation-booking service, and all the major tourism websites have suggested accommodation sections, with clear ratings. You might like to try www.cotswolds.com, www.visitstratforduponavon.co.uk,www.oxford shirecotswolds.org, www.visitbath.co.uk or www.visitforestofdean.co.uk which, between them, cover the whole Cotswolds area and offer excellent suggestions on where to stay.

10... eco-friendly destinations

1 **The Yurt Eco-Camp, Abbey Home Farm, Cirencester** – compost loos, wood-fuelled hot water, and situated on the edge of a wood with lovely views: this is a real eco-camp run by a first-class organic farm – so no plugs for hair straighteners or tiled shower blocks, plus you warm your own water on the fire, p. 104

2 **The Greenshop, Bisley** – set in a new eco-building in Bisley, near Stroud, this low-energy shop sells a massive range of sustainable and low impact products, which are interesting and thought-provoking, p. 70

3 **The Forge, Churchill** – winner of a 'Gold' award in the Green Tourism Business Scheme, here's a B&B in the Oxfordshire Cotswolds that uses environmentally-friendly and energy-efficient products wherever possible, p. 213

4 **The Living Green Centre, High Street, Bourton-on-the-Water** – situated next to a bus stop; this is a shop and show garden packed with ideas for sustainable 21st century living, p. 146

5 **Gateway Centre, Spine Road East, South Cerney** – this spectacular building is literally the gateway to the Cotswold Water Park and its numerous lakes; a visitor centre with café, it's made from green oak, has one of the largest solar roofs in the region, and uses rainwater to flush the loos, p. 125

6 **Westonbirt Arboretum, Westonbirt, near Tetbury** – sustainability is high on the agenda at the arboretum, which is leading research into the effect of climate change on trees; even its famous Enchanted Christmas walk in December, where the forest is lit up, is eco-friendly, p. 96

7 **Woodruffs Café, Stroud** – in the high street of one of the greenest places in the Cotswolds – among other things, Stroud is home to the Biodynamic Agricultural Association. Woodruff's was Britain's first fully organic café and serves fabulous fresh food, p. 62

8 **The Veg Shed, near Tetbury** (GL8 8SE; look out for the orange signs on Cherington Lane, just off the A433) – you can buy vegetables fit for a prince (Prince Charles, of course) here, all grown organically on Duchy Home Farm, a short tractor ride away; it's open Wednesdays from 8am to 5pm, p. 105

9 **Daylesford Organic, Daylesford near Kingham** – there's not much you can't get in organic version at this incredible shop, which proves that going green can be very posh indeed, p. 212

10 **Wildfowl & Wetlands Trust, Slimbridge** – a world-famous conservation centre, this trust is leading the way when it comes to saving wetlands; the grounds provide a safe haven for many rare and endangered birds, and the trust is involved in breeding and conservation programmes to protect them and their habitats around the world, p. 77

The best... Cotswold places to stay

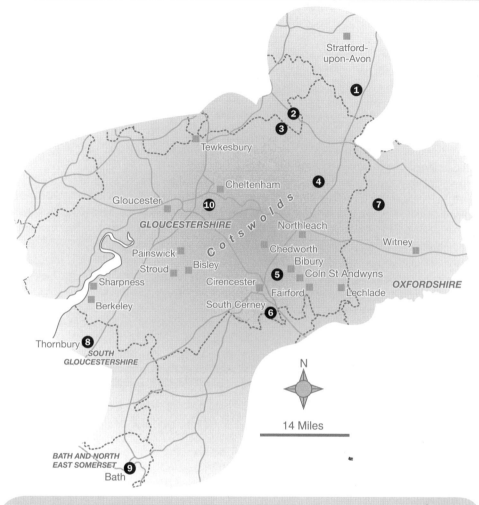

❶ Ettington Park, near Stratford-upon-Avon – in the Stour Valley, 6 miles from Stratford; expect warmth and hospitality, p. 194

❷ Lygon Arms Hotel, Broadway; rich in history and charm – and Bill Bryson's stayed here, p. 178

❸ Buckland Manor, Buckland – a real English treat, which makes the most of produce from the Vale of Evesham next door, p. 180

❹ Lords of the Manor, Upper Slaughter – a gorgeous place to unwind, set in more than 8 acres of garden, lake and parkland, p. 160

❺ Barnsley House, near Cirencester – former home of the late gardener Rosemary Verey, this is Elizabeth Hurley's hotel of choice, p. 135

❻ Hoburne Cotswold, South Cerney – the perfect camping experience, based around lakes teeming with wildlife, p. 135

❼ Bruern Holiday Cottages near Chipping Norton – there's a games room, wonderful Wendy houses and warm swimming pool, p. 213

❽ Thornbury Castle, Thornbury – a 500-year-old palace that even produces its own wine, p. 86

❾ The Royal Crescent Hotel, Bath – set in Royal Crescent itself, one of Europe's finest 18th-century masterpieces, p. 258

❿ The Greenway Hotel, Cheltenham – luxury country house experience just a short drive from the town centre; a favourite stop-over of the late Queen Mother in Gold Cup week, p. 287

Self-catering

Of course, many national companies have plenty of idyllic Cotswold cottages on their books, such as Country Holidays (☎0845 268 0773; www.country-holidays.co.uk); and Premier Cottages (☎0114 2751477; www.premiercottages.co.uk). The National Trust rents out some of the most beautiful examples of vernacular architecture, particularly in the quintessential north Cotswold village of Snowshill (☎0844 8002070; www.nationaltrustcottages.co.uk). The building preservation charity, The Landmark Trust, has some highly interesting and unusual properties: it restores historic and interesting buildings and gives them a new lease of life by letting them out for holidays (www.landmarktrust.org.uk). Rural Retreats provides stylish holiday cottages throughout the country, though it operates from near Moreton-in-Marsh (☎01386 701177; www.ruralretreats.co.uk)

Companies based in the Cotswolds that deal specifically with properties in the area know the Cotswolds extremely well. Examples are:

· **Manor Cottages** – ☎0870 9500404; www.manorcottages.co.uk
· **Discover the Cotswolds** – ☎01386 841441; www.discoverthecotswolds.net
· **Cottage in the Country** – ☎01608 646833; cottageinthecountry.co.uk; has properties just outside the area, too.

Camping

There's an impressive number of Cotswold camp sites that made the top 100 in the country, as compiled by *Practical Caravan's* website: www.practicalcaravan.com.

If you think that camping means roughing it, then you need to get up to date. 'Glamping' (a mix of glamorous and camping) means luxury beneath a designer canvas. After all, there's nothing like a retroprint tent to put the 'camp' back into camping. One of the joys of opting for a holiday under canvas is

particularly apparent if you enjoy outdoor sports. Hoburne Cotswold in South Cerney (01285 860216; www.hoburne.com), for example, is even popular with people who live just a few miles away because it's right in the middle of the Cotswold Water Park. They'll go and camp for a weekend, simply to get the most out of the surrounding massive area of open water, where you can do everything from sail to waterski.

FOOD AND DRINK

Although the Cotswolds are well known for their outstanding food and drink producers – everything from ice cream to pick-your-own strawberries – traditionally local fare is simple: simple, but tasty and full of natural goodness. You will find all of the region's delicious food and drink at farmers' markets, farm shops and good local butchers.

One of the most iconic of the region's offerings is **Gloucestershire Old Spot** pork. These pigs have a layer of flavoursome fat that was once an essential source of energy and nourishment for farm workers out working long tiring hours in the depths of winter. Nowadays, the pigs are carefully rationed and don't get as huge as they once did, but the flavour is still superb. The pork makes particularly tasty sausages.

Cotswold sheep were originally developed for their quality wool, which was ideal for hand-spinning; the most valuable fleece came from a castrated male in its first year. It's a mutton sheep, which had gone out of fashion, but recently people such as Prince Charles have been working to persuade people to go back to eating it.

Gloucester cattle were developed as triple-purpose animals. They're very docile and strong – which was necessary for the one-time walk to Smithfield Market – and they were used as draught oxen. The cattle are black-brown – people refer to it as mahogany – but most important is the white tail and white stripe down the back, which usually starts at the hips. They were kept

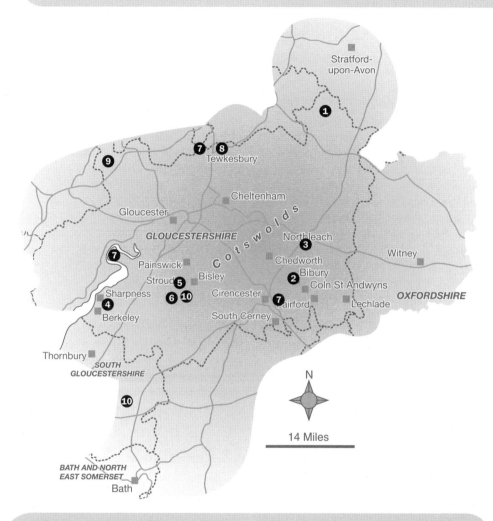

Stratford-upon-Avon

Tewkesbury

Cheltenham

Gloucester

GLOUCESTERSHIRE

Cotswolds

Northleach

Witney

Painswick

Chedworth

Bibury

Stroud

Bisley

Coln St Andwyns

Sharpness

Cirencester

OXFORDSHIRE

Berkeley

Fairford

Lechlade

South Cerney

Thornbury

SOUTH GLOUCESTERSHIRE

N

14 Miles

BATH AND NORTH EAST SOMERSET

Bath

1 Asparagus from the north Cotswolds and the Vale of Evesham – look out for Haïnes asparagus in Sainsbury's and Waitrose, p. 179

2 Bibury Trout – from the trout farm in the heart of Bibury, p. 114

3 Cotswold Ice Cream – fairtrade and made on Hill House Farm, Farmington, from organic milk, p. 119

4 Organic Old Spot pork at Adey's Farm near Berkeley – where the piglets roam free, p. 87

5 Single Gloucester cheese from Godsell's Church Farm, Leonard Stanley – fifth generation dairy farmers, p. 72

6 Uley Old Spot – you can't go home without downing a pint of this iconic brew from Uley, p. 88

7 Arlingham Schoolboys, Tewkesbury Baron, Ampney Red – the names of old varieties of Gloucestershire apples resound with rich social history, p. 26

8 Minchew's Cyder, Tewkesbury – made from fruit that's hand-picked, hand-washed and milled in an old-fashioned scratter, p. 291

9 Even Wallace and Gromit love Stinking Bishop – a fine cheese from Charles Martell in the Forest of Dean, p. 314

10 Hobbs House bread in Chipping Sodbury and Nailsworth is made without chemicals or improvements – just extra-added time and TLC!, p. 72

25

for their beef, but milk and cheese as well. Gloucester milk has a very small fat globule and it's rich in solids, so there's a lot of substance to it for cheese.

Only farms that are registered as having Gloucester cattle are entitled to make **Single Gloucester** cheese. It's made from a combination of semi-skimmed and full cream milk. Traditionally, the farmer would skim the evening milk to make butter, then mix it with the full cream milk the next morning to make the cheese. You won't find many cheese makers specialising in this delicious cheese, but those who do make it exceptionally well.

Double Gloucester – one of the county's most famous cheeses – is made with full fat milk, and coloured deep orange with a natural dye made from the seed of the Annatto tree. Although some superb Double Gloucester is made in the Cotswolds, it isn't protected in the same way as Single: it was already being so widely made by the time regulations came in, it was impossible to impose restrictions.

Nowadays, there are other quality cheeses made here – such as: Charles Martell's **Stinking Bishop**; Simon Weaver's **Cotswold Brie**; and Alex James and Juliet Harbutt's **Little Wallop**, to name but a few. Traditional? No. Delicious? Absolutely.

Apples, pears and plums are another very 'Cotswold' treat. The Severn Vale is famous for **Blaisdon Red plums and perry pears**. If you were to eat only **Gloucestershire apple** varieties, you could feast on the fruit from late July to well into November. There are the early varieties, such as Beauty of Bath, George Cave and the Discoveries; there's the nutty, crisp Severn Bank in mid-September; Taynton Codlin in early to mid October (all Codlin apples will cook to a light fluff; in fact, some say this is where the phrase 'to mollycoddle' originates because, when you've been ill, all you can cope with is stewed fluffy apple!); and Ashmead's Kernel: highly recommended as a late dessert apple, this is one of Gloucestershire's best.

You can eat and drink these apples, for many are made into juice and sold at farmers' markets over the region. Varieties such as Arlingham Schoolboys, Foxwhelp from the Forest of Dean, and the Kingston Black – a dark red apple with high sugar levels – are used for cider. You can get more information on local apples from the Gloucestershire Orchard Group: www. orchard-group.org.uk/glos.

Finally, believe it or not, fish feature on the Cotswold menu. **Elvers** from the River Severn were once a staple of the local diet, but now many of them are exported. The purity and low temperatures of the region's rivers, however, make them ideal spots for **trout** farms, such as at Bibury and Donnington. As well as fresh, you can try smoked trout and pâté.

As far as drinking goes, this is real ale country. The number of microbreweries offering their own distinctively character-filled nectar is heart warming. If you want an unusual way to explore the area, then follow the **Gloucestershire Ale Trail** through pubs and outlets where you're guaranteed to find a draught Gloucestershire beer. See www. glosaletrail.org.uk.

LOCAL FESTIVALS

Something that always surprises visitors to the Cotswolds is just how much there is going on – especially when it comes to events of an international standard. This is no cultural backwater, and that's not flannel. Professor Lord Robert Winston hails Cheltenham as '*undeniably and undoubtedly the best science festival in the country*'. The horse trials at Badminton and Gatcombe are highlights of the equestrian calendar and attract record-breaking crowds, whereas Gold Cup Week at Cheltenham Racecourse has become a legend in its own right.

But don't let these goliaths dwarf the other, more idiosyncratic events. If you've never seen grown men (and women) chasing

The best... Cotswold places to eat

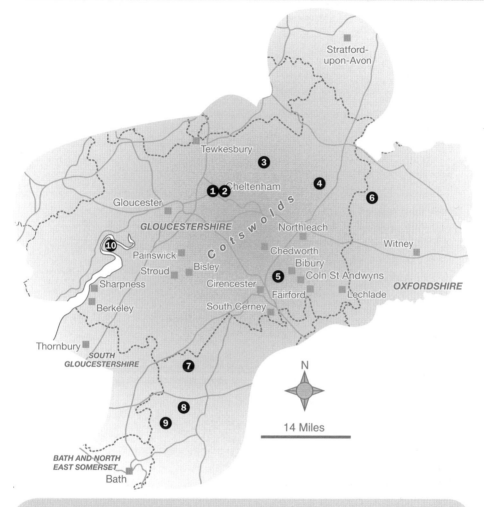

1. Le Champignon Sauvage, Cheltenham – owned by the Cotswolds' only two-star Michelin chef, David Everitt-Matthias, p. 290
2. Curry Corner, Cheltenham – local produce combined with Bangladeshi and Indian cuisine, p. 290
3. 5 North Street, Winchcombe – charming, accomplished and admired by top food critics, Kate and Marcus Ashenford's small restaurant punches well above its weight, p. 163
4. Lower Slaughter Manor, Lower Slaughter – complete with historic provenance, it's quite simply one of the most chic restaurants around, p. 163
5. Village Pub, Barnsley – you've read the hype – Elizabeth Hurley loves it – now see why; onstantly changing menu based on seasonal, fresh ingredients, p. 137
6. Kingham Plough, Kingham – bump into Alex James and Jeremy Clarkson who love Emily Watkins' cooking, using produce that's often so local it could walk here, p. 216
7. Whatley Manor – among glorious gardens, this restaurant is in the top 30 of the *Which? 2009 Good Food Guide*, p. 103
8. Manor House, Castle Combe – this is a lesson in how to provide luxury, yet still make your diners feel totally relaxed, p. 258
9. Lucknam Park, Colerne – on a 500 acre estate where herbs from the garden and the best organic ingredients go into the dishes, p. 261
10. Old Passage Inn, Arlingham – it mightn't be by the sea (though it is a riverside inn) but it's won numerous accolades for its wonderful fish, p. 315

Double Gloucester cheese down a 1-in-1 hill, or racing through Tetbury with 60lb woolsack on their back then your life has been far too sheltered. Help is at hand...

Calendar of events

January
- New Year Meeting at Cheltenham Racecourse, Prestbury Park, p. 281

February
- Cheltenham Folk Festival, p. 283

March
- Bath Literature Festival
- National Hunt Festival (Gold Cup Week), Cheltenham Racecourse
- Kempley Daffodil Weekend, p. 304

April
- Forest of Dean Outdoors Activities Festival
- Shakespeare Birthday Celebrations
- Cheltenham Jazz Festival, p. 281

May
- May to September, Giffords Circus tours the Cotswolds
- Traditional Gypsy Horse Fair (also held in October)
- Stroudwater Textile Festival
- Badminton Horse Trials
- Cheltenham Jazz Festival
- Tewkesbury Festival of Food and Drink
- Bath International Music Festival
- Cheese Rolling at Coopers Hill
- Tetbury Woolsack Races, p. 101

June
- Cheltenham Food and Drink Festival
- Robert Dover's Olimpick Games and the Scuttlebrook Wake
- Cheltenham Festival of Science
- Longborough Festival Opera, p. 177

July
- Cheltenham Music Festival
- Tewkesbury Medieval Festival

- Royal International Air Tattoo
- Cheltenham Cricket Festival, p. 282

August
- Festival of British Eventing, Gatcombe Park
- Three Choirs Festival (rotating between the cathedrals of Worcester, Hereford and Gloucester)
- Festival of the Tree at Westonbirt Arboretum, p. 101

September
- Moreton-in-Marsh Show
- Blenheim Horse Trials
- Jane Austen Festival, p. 255

October
- Cheltenham Festival of Literature, p. 281

November
- Cheltenham Races: the Open, p. 281

December
- Enchanted Christmas, an illuminated trail through Westonbirt Arboretum, p. 97

TRAVELLING WITH CHILDREN

The Cotswolds are a perfect destination, particularly for younger children. Here they can do what children tend to love best: connect with wildlife and farm animals, and experience huge open spaces and the freedom that goes with them. It's a very safe place. You can easily get well away from traffic, on the many footpaths, commons and cycle routes. And don't think there's nothing for the teenagers here. Depending on personalities, you might want to consider holidaying in a busy market town, or in the Cotswold Water Park or Forest of Dean, where there are water sports and outdoor activities galore.

You shouldn't need to travel huge distances once you're in the Cotswolds, and you can plan your route via small roads,

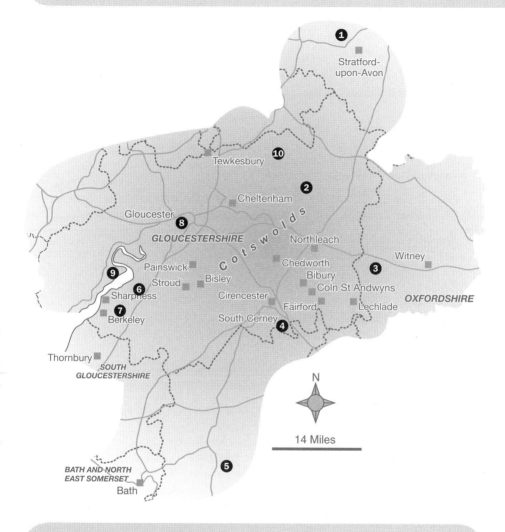

1. Mary Arden's Farm, near Stratford-upon-Avon – see a Tudor family tending their farm in this living history experience, p. 189
2. Cotswold Farm Park, Guiting Power – meet rare-breed farm animals, p. 154
3. Cotswold Wildlife Park, Burford – white rhinos, big cats, primates, bats and more, p. 227
4. Keynes Country Park, South Cerney – lakeside walks, fossils and Britain's largest inland beach, p. 126
5. Lacock Abbey near Chippenham – former medieval cloistered abbey where *Harry Potter* was filmed, p. 249
6. The Wildfowl & Wetlands Trust, Slimbridge – feed the birds in this wildlife haven, p. 77
7. Cattle Country, Berkeley – farm park adventure with animals and activities, p. 84
8. Soldiers of Gloucestershire Museum – follow the lives of soldiers in war and peace, p. 296
9. Go Ape, Forest of Dean – high wire forest course, p. 308
10. Gloucestershire Warwickshire Railway – steam train fun, p. 152

where you can stop whenever you need to. If you want regular public conveniences, you should plan your route in advance, taking in child-friendly cafés, of which there are many, and some of the plentiful attractions children will love.

OUTDOOR ACTIVITIES

Walking in the Cotswolds

There's really only one way to explore the Cotswolds– pull on your wellies and adjust your senses to maximum sensitivity. You need to see the colours, smell the scents, hear the birdsong, touch the flowers (but don't pick them), and even eat the fruits you can identify safely – wild blackberries being the favourite in late summer.

Gloucestershire has 3,400 miles of footpaths and other known public rights of way. You can, of course, plan your own route; just remember to take a bottle of water and sun cream in summer, and in winter wrap up with waterproofs, take a warm drink and snack, and make sure your ramble leads you to a pub with a toasty open fire. A mobile phone is always useful, but you can't rely on getting a signal.

As Gloucestershire County Council's Public Rights of Way Team Manager, Alan Bently, explains:

- Anyone can use a public right of way. Dogs are allowed, though they absolutely must be under close control, especially near live-stock, and not foul or stray from the path.
- Public footpaths are for foot or wheelchair-use only. The roadside sign-arms say 'Public Footpath', and there are yellow arrows marked on stiles and gates.
- Public bridleways are for foot, wheelchair, horseback and bicycle use. These road-side signs say 'Public Bridleway', with blue arrows on gates.
- Byways are open to all traffic – but don't expect a smooth tarmac surface. There'll be a 'Byway' sign at the start, and red

arrows, but there are only a few miles of these in Gloucestershire.
- Restricted byways: the rights are the same as for a bridleway, except that you're also allowed to use a horse-drawn carriage. However, private vehicular rights may exist. You will find 'Restricted Byway' signs at roadside and purple arrows on gates and gateposts.
- These paths are all shown in detail on Ordnance Survey *Explorer* maps (the orange-covered ones), as green broken dashes – the short dashes are footpaths; longer ones are bridleways; dashes with dots depict restricted byways.

There are three National Trails (or parts thereof) in Gloucestershire: the Cotswold Way (which runs from Bath to Chipping Campden, a total of 102 miles), the Thames Path (from the source of the Thames, near Coates, to Greenwich in London) and the Offa's Dyke Path (from Sedbury in the Forest of Dean to Prestatyn on the north Wales coast). Look at the website www.nationaltrail.co.uk for further information about these routes.

Compass Holidays, based at Cheltenham Spa Railway Station, is a tour operator offering cycling walking and garden tours in the Cotswolds. It runs a service along the whole of the Cotswold Way moving luggage between accommodation stops, allowing people to walk freely either from end to end or in short breaks, between Easter and October, delivering the bags between 10am and 5pm, seven days per week. The costs are from £8.50 per bag, with a minimum of two bags per booking (with concessions for six-plus). Compass Holidays also offers a planning and accommodation booking service along the way (☎01242 250642; www.compass-holidays.com).

There are a large number of important recreational routes, including:

- **The Severn Way** – all the way from Avonmouth to the source of the river at Plynlimon

The best... things to do with water

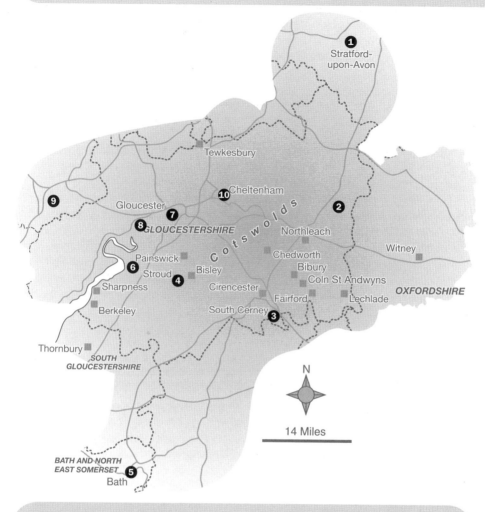

1. See Stratford-upon-Avon from the water: either hire rowing boats, motor boats or take a 45-minute cruise, p. 185
2. Watch the wildlife at the Greystones Farm Nature Reserve at Bourton-on-the-Water, along the banks of the Rivers Eye and Dikler, where water voles and otters live, p. 146
3. Waterski at the Cotswold Water Park (where you can also do wakeboarding, cable ski towing and fun inflatable rides), p. 124
4. Learn about Stroud's wool heritage, powered by the area's many streams, by visiting the mills on one of the regular open days, p. 62
5. Shop at Pulteney Bridge, Bath; designed by Robert Adam, it's one of only four bridges in the world lined with shops, p. 256
6. Have lunch at The Stables Café on the canal bank at Saul, followed by a trip on the Perseverance on the Gloucester & Sharpness Canal, p. 316
7. Explore Gloucester Docks with their award-winning National Waterways Museum, p. 296
8. Listen to the birds go quiet and the air fall still and wait for the Severn Bore tidal wave to come rushing up the river like an express train, p. 297
9. Canoe on the River Wye in the Forest of Dean, p. 308
10. Swim in Sandford Lido, Cheltenham, one of the top 10 lidos in Britain, p. 280

- **The Gloucestershire Way** – from Tewkesbury to Chepstow via Stow-on-the-Wold,
- Many **shorter routes**, which are totally within the county, for example the Windrush Way in the Cotswolds and the Daffodil Way in the Dymock area.

There is a list of walks on Gloucestershire County Council's website (www.gloucestershire.gov.uk/prow); you can also find out more about walking in the region through the Cotswolds Conservation Board (www.cotswoldsaonb.com), the Forest of Dean's online information service, www.active.visit forestofdean.co.uk, and at www.walkweb.org.uk. Tourist information centres stock walk leaflets.

There are some great walks to follow in the Oxfordshire Cotswolds, detailed at the county council website (www.oxfordshire.gov.uk), particularly the Oxfordshire Way, a 68-mile walk across the county. Many of the market towns such as Newent, Fairford and Lechlade have also put together their own walking booklets – ask at tourist information centres or the town council offices.

Alternatively, you could join one of the many guided walks that are organised throughout the year by groups such as the Cotswold Voluntary Wardens. Again, look at the various websites mentioned above, but remember that, on the whole, dogs are not allowed on walks. Westonbirt (www.forestry.gov.uk/westonbirt) and Batsford Arboreta (www.batsarb.co.uk) put on guided walks, as well as being picturesque places to wander freely.

Cycling in the Cotswolds

You can't thank the much-maligned Beeching for much, but his axing of many branch lines means there are some first-rate cycle trails in the country along former railway routes, and the Cotswolds are no exception. A lovely route is the 6 mile Stroud Valleys Pedestrian Cycle Trail between Nailsworth and Stonehouse. The quietest stretch is from Dudbridge to Nailsworth: you can hear the birds singing, and see squirrels and other wildlife. A leaflet on the trail is available from Stroud Tourist Information Centre, call ☎01453 760960.

There's cycling for everyone in the Forest of Dean. Whether a serious down-hiller, a cross-country fanatic or a disabled cyclist, you will find a suitable route. For children, the 17km Family Cycle Trail is traffic-free, beginning by the Pedalabikeaway bike-hire centre at Cannop Valley near Coleford (GL16 7EH; ☎01594 860065).

Gloucestershire Rural Community Council has produced a series of five circular cycling routes in Bourton-on-the-Water, Moreton-in-Marsh, Kingham, Bibury and Kemble. Packs are available from visitor information centres, tourist attractions, businesses along the routes and train stations or by emailing glosrcc@grcc.org.uk. There are plans for a new cycle route via Cheltenham, Gloucester, and Warwick. See the Sustrans website for further information (www.sustrans.co.uk).

Other activities

Horse riding is a top Cotswold activity. There are hundreds of miles of bridleways, as well as quiet lanes where you can ride safely away from much of the traffic. In most areas, there are riding stables that will take out everyone from beginners to experienced riders on suitable hacks – it's a wonderful, leisurely way to explore the region. And then there are the open spaces, which give such a sense of freedom. Among them, is the Forest of Dean, where horse riding is actively encouraged. Riders are welcome to enjoy bridleways, forest roads and riding trails; if you want to find out exactly where you can ride, you can ring the Forestry Commission during office hours on 01594 833057.

If you're bringing your own horse, then the Cotswolds commons provide wonderful opportunities for riding. Again, it's worth checking these out beforehand. On Cleeve Common, for example, four miles north-east of Cheltenham, all riders may use the bridleways that skirt the edges, but a hacking licence is required elsewhere, which costs £20 per year: www.cleevecommon.org.uk.

You can obtain The Cotswolds on Horseback (Road Safety & Travelling), price £2, from the British Horse Society, www.britishhorse.com. The society also publishes information on The Sabrina Way, a 200-mile riding route with 44 miles crossing Gloucestershire from Forthampton to Great Barrington. The illustrated leaflets include maps and a list of B&B accommodation. Find out more from www.ride-uk.org.uk, which also keeps information about B&Bs for horses!

You can find out more about riding, including the location of stables, from Gloucestershire County Council's website www.gloucestershire.gov.uk and from www.active.visitforestofdean.co.uk. Defra also has a useful database on walks and rides throughout the region at countrywalks.defra.gov.uk

Golf, of course, is a hugely popular pastime. The Manor House Golf Club at Castle Combe (see p 263) is considered one of the best in the country; there are Minchinhampton's golf clubs, one of which is on the common and grazed by cows (see p 59); the Cotswold Hills near Cheltenham (see p 292); and Puckrup Hall, set between the Cotswolds and the Malvern Hills (see p 292), to name but a few.

Gliding is a sport enjoyed by many, and there are clubs at Aston Down, Minchinhampton (see p 75); Nympsfield (see p 90); and Stratford (see p 198).

If you're after a really active holiday, though, this is the place for you. The **Cotswold Water Park** and the **Forest of Dean**, in particular, offer fantastic opportunities for all sorts of sports including caving, rock climbing, windsurfing, sailing, windsurfing, waterskiing, wakeboarding, ringo rides and angling. You'll find out more from www.waterpark.org and www.active.visitforestofdean.co.uk.

ORGANISED HOLIDAYS AND COURSES

For holidaymakers who fancy coming to the area to explore a specific activity, there are all sorts of organised holidays and courses taking place.

For amateur **artists**, this is the place to pick up art supplies and, perhaps more importantly, beautiful views to transfer to canvas. Andalucian Adventures is a specialist holiday company based in the heart of the Cotswolds, which organises short residential painting courses in Rodborough (staying, incidentally, at The Bear of Rodborough, an 'Arts and Crafts' remodelled hotel). You can do the same with photography: the winter light around Stroud's Five Valleys provides some unusual opportunities for pictures: www.andalucian-adventures.co.uk.

Food and walking are, it would seem, an essential combination. The Three Ways House Hotel at Mickleton – home of The Pudding Club, which aims to preserve the Great British pudding – specialises in walking breaks (www.puddingclub.com; 01386 438429). Never was there a better excuse to eat Spotted Dick with impunity.

Rob Rees – known as the Cotswold Chef – prefers to concentrate on eating! He offers 'insider' food tours, focusing on his expert knowledge of local food, visiting the best outlets for produce and finishing with a cookery lesson or demonstration. Food tours are for from one to six people, with prices (excluding VAT) starting at £199 per person or £300 per couple for a full day including a Champagne breakfast basket, light lunch and demonstration (01285760170; www.robrees.com).

For those who want to have a hand in the cooking themselves, Bath's Bertinet Kitchen is owned and run by French chef and baker, Richard Bertinet. The kitchen offers a range of relaxed and fun courses for food lovers of all abilities: www.thebertinetkitchen.com.

10... Cotswold things to do for free

1 **Fly a kite on the top of the world** – or at least the giddy heights of Minchinhampton Common – where wild flowers bloom and cows roam free (in summer), and the wind guarantees a great lift-off, p. 59

2 **Sail the Seven Seas** as captain of your own ship on the Purton Hulks; all you need supply is imagination. These old boats that lie beached along the shore are the Severn trows that once plied their trade along the river, p. 84

3 **See behind the scenes with the greatest classical theatre company** in the world. The RSC offers free tours of The Courtyard Theatre that last approximately 45 minutes; you can even stand on the same stage as David Tennant (though, sadly, not at the same time), p.192

4 **Go badger-watching** in the evening with Tony Dean, from the end of April to the beginning of September; because Tony is 'one of the family' to the badgers, you will see them begin to emerge as soon as he whistles. It's free, though donations are welcome, p. 67

5 **Have a stroll round Bath** with someone worth their salt! There's a free walk provided every day except Christmas Day that lasts around two hours, leaving from outside the main entrance to the Pump Room, p. 241

6 **Go cycling in the Forest of Dean.** The 17km Family Cycle Trail is a circular route that takes you around the heart of the forest: suitable for all ages and abilities, it's away from the dangers of the roads. It's also a great way to explore the area's industrial past, for it takes you alongside former coal mines, collieries and railway stations, p. 307

7 **Gloucester City Museum** is free and an ideal way to learn more about the area, with Roman and medieval displays, dinosaurs, fossils, paintings and the stunning Birdlip mirror; look out for free children's activities too, from craft tables to storytelling, p. 298

8 **The children's playground at Chalford** near Stroud (accessed off the High Street) is one of the most popular summer destinations for locals; it's the perfect place to take a picnic, get wet in the stream, and let off steam. Donkeys are used in this village for deliveries!, p. 67

9 **Wander through Cirencester Park** (the main entrance is on Cecily Hill in the town) and spot wildlife galore. There are around 3,000 acres of parkland on this wonderful estate, which is home to the Bathurst family, p. 93

10 **Cotswold geology truly rocks;** in fact, you won't begin to understand the area if you don't look under your feet. At Huntsman's Quarry near Naunton you can see footprints from a 150 million year-old dinosaur. If you want to splash out, spend £2 on a geology trail leaflet from www.glosgeotrust.org.uk, p. 46

And don't forget that Gloucestershire produces some excellent **wine**. The Three Choirs Vineyard in Newent is the ideal base from which to explore the Cotswolds and the Forest of Dean; it also caters for wine-tasting weekends with guided tours of the vineyard (www.three-choirs-vineyards.co.uk).

There are plenty of other options. Stanton Guildhouse, an Arts and Crafts manor near Broadway, holds courses throughout the year, and summer schools, in **crafts** such as stained glass and stone carving (www.stantonguildhouse.org.uk); and the beautiful Farncombe Estate nearby – 300-acres of privately-owned parkland – runs weekend leisure breaks based around a programme with a wide range of subjects from Art to Zen: www.farncombeestate.co.uk.

FURTHER INFORMATION

There are a great many useful websites for the Cotswolds, some commercial, others produced by tourist boards, and all offering different perspectives. Just make sure that the ones flagging up accommodation offer some kind of rating scheme you recognise, so you can be sure of the quality you can expect. All the visitor information centres in the area will help you with places to stay, and some provide an accommodation booking service on your behalf. A good site for finding reasonable deals is www.laterooms.com, a national service which nevertheless covers the Cotswolds well.

The South West Tourist Board has a useful website at www.visitsouthwest.co.uk. You can find out more about 'Stratford' country at www.heartofenglandtourism.com; and the Oxfordshire area is detailed in www.visitsoutheastengland.com. One of the best internet services is www.cotswolds.com, which is friendly, useful and packed full of information. But do look at the visitor information at the end of each section of this guide book for more local sites and the addresses of visitor information centres, which will be able to provide you with specific help.

When you're visiting a smaller town or village, look at the parish or town council websites – either Google them, or the relevant county or district council should provide a link (www.gloucestershire.gov.uk; www.oxfordshire.gov.uk; www.warwickshire.gov.uk; www.bathnes.gov.uk). Some towns will have council offices, where they often keep books of walks and other useful information, and the clerks will have a good knowledge of the area. It's worth calling in.

Local newspapers

There's nothing like a good local 'rag' for giving you the feel for an area. If the lead crime story is 'Man parks on double yellow lines', you know you can sleep easy at night. In the central Cotswolds, there are established papers such as the *Stroud News & Journal* (www.stroudnewsandjournal.co.uk), the *Dursley Gazette* (www.gazetteseries.co.uk) and the *Wilts & Gloucestershire Standard* (www.wiltsglosstandard.co.uk). Further north, papers include the *Cotswold Journal* at www.cotswoldjournal.co.uk, the *Stratford Observer*, www.stratfordobserver.co.uk and the *Stratford-upon-Avon Herald*. In the west, there's the *Gloucestershire Echo*, *The Citizen* and *The Forester* (www.thisisgloucestershire.co.uk); and there's the *Tewkesbury Admag* (www.tewkesburyadmag.co.uk). West Oxfordshire has the *Witney Gazette* (www.witneygazette.co.uk), while in Bath there's the *Bath Chronicle* (www.thisisbath.co.uk).

If you're confused about the areas, the simple rule is that you will only be able to buy a relevant newspaper in the local newsagent. The most established regional glossy is the monthly *Cotswold Life* magazine (www.cotswoldlife.co.uk), with its celebrity interviews, articles about attractions, towns and villages, and unbiased, sometimes searingly honest restaurant reviews (I should know; I write them).

Local radio stations

The main broadcasters for the area include:

- BBC Radio Gloucestershire (www.bbc.co.uk/gloucestershire) 95 (Stroud), 95.8 (Cirencester), 104.7 (Gloucester, Cheltenham & Tewkesbury) FM and 1413 in the Cotswolds & Forest of Dean AM. You can also listen via the internet.
- Gloucestershire's Star 107.5FM (www.star1075.co.uk)
- Severn Sound (www.severnsound.co.uk) 102.4 FM (Gloucester), 103FM (Stroud)
- Stroud FM 107.9 (www.stroudfm.co.uk)

- North Cotswolds Community Radio (NCCR) (www.northcotswoldonline.com) is available online.
- Forest of Dean community Radio (www.fodradio.org) 1521/1503 AM
- BBC Radio Oxford, covering Oxfordshire (www.bbc.co.uk/oxford) 95.2 MHz VHF FM
- BBC Somerset (www.bbc.co.uk/somerset) 95.5 FM and 1566 AM
- BBC Coventry and Warwickshire (www.bbc.co.uk/coventry) 94.8, 103.7 and 104 FM
- Stratford Community Radio (SCR) (www.myscr.co.uk) is available online.

THE BACKGROUND

HISTORY

The mists of time

Picture this: it's dark – just an hour before sunrise as the people make their way by the light of flaming torches to the sacred site. Dressed in animal skins, they're well wrapped up against the early morning cold. The landscape, with its hills and valleys, is recognisably Cotswold. In fact, the sacred site itself looks familiar to the modern eye. Today, you can only see the outline of this long barrow that, 5,500 years on, has left its impression on **Nympsfield**, near Stroud (p. 79). In Neolithic times, it was a magnificent structure, sited to take advantage of far-reaching views over the river valley. Yesterday, the bones of the honoured dead were brought up to the barrow. They've been lying in the woods for weeks, picked over by birds and animals.

Today, in a sacred ceremony held on the entrance forecourt, they'll be laid to rest in the chambers, along with precious objects they owned in life.

Of course, although based on archaeological evidence, much of this is speculation. Indeed, one of the great mysteries of the late Neolithic period (2500–2000BC) are the **Rollright Stones** in West Oxfordshire (p. 202). The truth is that little is known about Neolithic man's life in the Cotswolds. What is certain is that 5,500 years ago, something amazing happened. Up until then, the hunter-gatherers had chased beasts over many miles of countryside and relied on whatever the bushes had to offer. But around 3500BC, the first farmer was born.

To begin with, flint was the main material for tools but, later, metal took over; the Iron Age landscape was just as busy as that of today, scattered with shrines, temples, field systems and hillforts, such as those still to be seen at **Little Sodbury** (p. 265) and **Crickley Hill** (p. 276). Alongside practical realities, there was still room for creativity. The art produced in Britain during the pre-Roman Iron Age is usually defined as Celtic. There were chariot mounts – one beautiful example with enamel inlay was found near Sudeley and is now in the British Museum; there were intricately worked harness mounts, such as the one discovered near South Cerney and on display in the **Corinium Museum in Cirencester** (p. 93). One of the most stunning examples of all from this area is the complex bronze mirror – a Celtic masterpiece – found in a woman's grave near Birdlip, now with the **Gloucester City Museum** (p. 298). The craftsmen who made them would have been respected and honoured for their skills.

Indeed, the Romans who arrived in Cirencester in AD43 did not find an insular, savage people; they walked into a well-ordered and sophisticated society with European links. In fact, influences between Roman conqueror and Britons were mutual.

Romans

Soon after the Roman army arrived in the south of Britain in the summer of AD43, a 500-man cavalry unit made its way to Cirencester – one of only 20 in the army.

The effect on the economy was dramatic. The largest army group had ended up in one of the smallest provinces – ie Britain – and it was the natives' job to feed them. Around Cirencester, the local Dobunni tribe had to find 7lb of oats a day for each of 750 horses; hay to cut; grazing to be requisitioned; not to mention men and their servants to be satisfied. On the plus side, here were

500 men with money to burn, looking for women, for servants, for drink, for native goods. Quite quickly, the local population started to identify there was a market. They began drifting down, bringing corn, furs, wool, horses to trade... Brothels were set up, inns, gambling dens. There were niches for brooch-makers, and for craftsmen who decorated swords.

As the new province settled down – the army pulled out around 25 years after they'd arrived – plans for the new town began to be drawn up. Another 25 years later, huge public buildings were being laid out in Cirencester. The forum complex was a large, open meeting area, not unlike a modern-day stock exchange in business terms, but where people would chat, stage political hustings and public ceremonies. You can still see the remains of a huge **amphitheatre** on the outskirts of the town (p. 93).

The fourth century was the period of Cirencester's greatest importance. Up until then, it had been a tribal capital; but when the Emperor Diocletian reorganised the whole empire, it was transformed into a tremendous seat of power. Everything south west of a line from Chester to Southampton Water was ruled from this once muddy valley. And it's quite possible that the all-important governor lived in a villa in the small village of Woodchester, near Stroud. Although the villa remains are no longer on public display, you can see a replica of the magnificent **Great Orpheus Roman Pavement** found there, on display at Prinknash Abbey near Painswick (p. 64).

You can see Roman remains in Glouce-ster, both in the street outside Boots and in Gloucester City Museum (p. 298). Of course, **Bath's Roman remains** are still among the most splendid in Britain, and the baths are considered the best-preserved Roman religious spa in the world. They surround the original sacred spring, which produces more than a million litres a day at a temperature of 46°C.

Anglo-Saxons

The Anglo-Saxons are often overlooked. Yet when the Romans left early in the fifth century – too busy struggling to protect other borders to bother with Britain – it was the Angles and the Saxons who stepped into the power vacuum. This period is the most formative of all when it comes to 'Englishness'. It's the time when the quintessential English countryside we know and understand today was created. The shires, for instance – Gloucestershire itself – were a mid-Saxon invention; our law derives from theirs; the language of Shakespeare, the language of Chaucer is derived from these early settlers. Indeed, the very concept of being English didn't exist before the Saxons' arrival.

If you'd like to see a genuine time traveller from this period, then visit the Anglo-Saxon gallery of the **Corinium Museum in Cirencester** (p. 93). Here, you will find a real face from the past; a meticulously researched forensic reconstruction of the skeletal remains of a human being who breathed, ate and slept in the Cotswolds 1,500 years ago.

In 1985, a team from the Oxfordshire Archaeological Unit started digging on a piece of farmland known as Butlers Field in Lechlade. The astonished archaeologists began to uncover bodies, buried over hundreds of years. And not only bodies but the treasures that, more than 1,000 years ago, were mournfully placed beside them. Of the 219 bodies discovered in 199 graves, quite the most incredible was the 6th-century woman whose bone structure was the basis for the reconstruction. Affectionately nicknamed Mrs Getty after the oil mogul, this wealthy individual was discovered with 500 objects, ranging from gilt bronze brooches and silver rings to amber beads and ivory purse rings. In Anglo-Saxon terms, this woman was the equivalent of a princess.

It was during this time – coinciding with St Augustine's mission of AD597 to recon-vert the heathen English – that churches

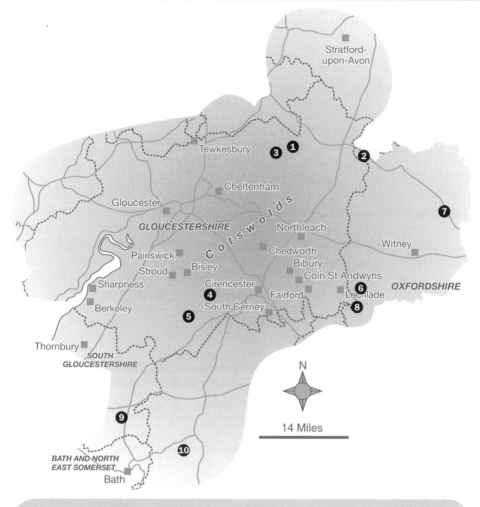

1. Snowshill Manor near Broadway – a very English piece of eccentricity, packed with a collector's ephemera, p. 175
2. Chastleton House near Moreton-in-Marsh – one of England's finest and most complete Jacobean houses, p. 205
3. Stanway House, Stanway, near Winchcombe – its water garden boasts a 300ft fountain, the tallest in Britain, p. 153
4. Rodmarton Manor near Tetbury – magnificent Arts and Crafts country house, p. 68
5. Chavenage House, Tetbury – an Elizabethan manor, still very much lived in by the Lowsley-Williams family, p. 96
6. Kelmscott Manor, near Lechlade – William Morris spent many of his summers here, delighting in its natural setting, p. 131
7. Blenheim Palace, Woodstock – Churchill's birthplace and a World Heritage Site, p. 206
8. Buscot House, Faringdon – home to The Faringdon Collection, including paintings by Rembrandt, Murillo, Rossetti, and the Briar Rose series by Burne-Jones, p. 132
9. Dyrham Park near Bath – unchanged mansion with ancient deer park, elegant gardens, woodlands and lakes to explore, p. 250
10. Corsham Park, Corsham – with one of the most distinguished collections of Old Masters in the country, p. 248

began to spring up around Gloucestershire. **Odda's Chapel at Deerhurst** (p. 280) is a simple two-room structure retaining its original chancel arch and a number of Saxon windows. **St Mary's Church**, (p. 279) also in Deerhurst, was founded around AD800, and is one of the finest remaining Saxon churches.

Another great building that owes its origins to this period is **Cirencester Parish Church** (p. 92). During the late Saxon period, the town became a royal village for the important Kings of Wessex, the old realm which covered the whole of the south-west. Although ruling from Winchester, the King would have visited Cirencester and probably had the church built for his own use: hence its status and, ultimately, the fine architecture we see today.

Middle Ages

The sheep that grazed the sparse slopes of the Cotswold hills were, in medieval times, a simple way to get rich quick. Sheep had long been a part of the Cotswold landscape – after all, it was ideal sheep country. The soil was thin and infertile up on the hills – certainly not good for arable farming – and the slow-flowing rivers were ideal for wool washing. The undemanding sheep thrived there, grazing in 'cots' or enclosures up on the 'wolds' – the hills: in other words, they even provided the area with a name.

The breed known as the Cotswold Lion was a particularly fine one. Sturdy, white-faced and long-fleeced, this animal produced high-quality wool in abundance. As news of its excellence travelled, the fame of the Cotswolds went with it. In the 14th century, Cirencester and the towns round about were known as far away as Florence and Venice. Wool from this area was even traded in Constantinople. In fact, wool had become so important to England's economy that, during Edward III's reign, The Woolsack – the seat stuffed with wool – became the symbol of the office of the Lord Chancellor.

Successful merchants started trying to outdo each other – with a touch of altruism to boot – and many fine manors and beautiful churches were constructed, such as those at **Northleach** (p. 113), **Chipping Campden** (p. 170) and the abbey church (the parish church) of **Cirencester** (p. 91). In fact, at one time, Cirencester Abbey was the richest of its kind in England, thanks to the vast tracts of sheep-rich land that it owned in eight counties. **St Mary's Church**, **Fairford** (p. 128) is the only church in the country with a complete set of medieval stained glass windows.

Although the ordinary Cotswoldians saw little in the way of riches, many cottage industries boomed: weavers, carders, combers. After shearing, long wool was combed and the short wool was carded, before being oiled and mixed to loosen the fibres. The spinning took place in the Cotswold stone cottages – once the home of humble workers – that are so often snapped up by wealthy incomers today.

Mills began to form part of the Cotswold landscape. The earliest was in Guiting Power in the 12th century; others followed in places such as Cirencester and Winchcombe, as well as the **Stroud Valleys** (p. 62), rich in their cascading streams and the constant supply of water from the River Frome. These waters provided power, and their natural salts were essential for cleaning and dyeing. Specialised guilds emerged for each stage of the process, and many towns had their own wool markets.

Tewkesbury, with its half-timbered buildings and overhanging upper storeys, has one of the best medieval townscapes in Britain (p. 277); while **Berkeley Castle** is renowned as being 'possibly the most outstanding example of medieval domestic architecture in the country' (p. 81).

Civil War

The Civil War was a turbulent time, not just for the Cotswolds but for the whole of

Great Britain. Cotswold towns and villages feature time and again in this story, not only as battlegrounds but as places of refuge. **Moreton-in-Marsh** was a Royalist centre (p. 167), and the King stayed at the White Hart Royal in the town on his final march from his Oxford HQ; the former George Inn at Burford was another of his resting places. Indeed, **Burford's church** bears witness to the violent end of a group of Levellers who had supported Parliament throughout the Civil War (p. 221).

Perhaps the most famous battle in this area was that of **Stow-on-the-Wold** in 1646 (p. 148). The Royalist, Sir Jacob Astley, had raised 2,000 loyal fighters in Wales and was trying to make his way to join up with King Charles's troops at Oxford. But as Astley approached Stow, a huge Parliamentary force met them and a terrible battle ensued. Astley's men did their best, but they were no match. The streets, they say, were so full of blood that the ducks bathed in it, hence the name of Digbeth – Ducks' Bath – Street. Certainly, this defeat was a bitter blow for Charles; two months later, he surrendered to the Scottish army in Nottinghamshire. **Sudeley Castle** at Winchcombe (p. 150), was the headquarters of Prince Rupert, Charles I's loyal nephew; Cromwell later destroyed it. **Chavenage House**, Tetbury, was the home of Nathaniel Stephens, one of the signatories to the death warrant of Charles I (p. 96).

The Georgians

The social whirl of 18th-century Bath was a giddy, dizzyingly exciting experience. The season ran from September to May and anyone who was anyone was there.

Imagine the scene: in the hub of the city, at the **Assembly Rooms** (p. 243), the candlelight from glittering chandeliers falls onto the beautiful young ladies dancing by in their peacock-coloured silks, glancing coquettishly into the eyes of rich young dukes and rakish army officers. Carefully watching over them are their staid mamas, full of boastful chatter about their daughters' accomplishments, while the older men stand idly by, bettering each others' extravagant gambling stories. It's hard to believe, isn't it, that a few short years before, Bath had been just another provincial town, still confined by its Roman walls and medieval street plan, its only claim to fame a medicinal one? At that time, the healing spring bubbling up from the earth below, had turned Bath into the urban equivalent of paracetamol – to be taken when aches and pains demanded it. In fact, at one time it was so full of invalids and beggars hoping for cures that the Bath Acts had to be introduced, effectively banning visitors who didn't have money in their pockets and a doctor's note legitimising their stay in the city.

It was a series of medical 'miracles' among the great and good that turned its reputation around. Firstly, Queen Mary, the barren wife of James II, came to take the waters in the hope of conceiving; and right on cue, the ancient spring worked its magic, much to the delight of the King. Then it was the turn of Queen Anne, who visited the city in 1702 to try to improve her life-long ill health. The Lady Di of her age, Anne was stylish and fashionable, surrounding herself with such celebrities as the dazzling Duke and Duchess of Marlborough. England was looking for diversions. Agriculture was flourishing, the Empire was growing; the glitterati had both leisure and money, and they wanted to socialise. Wherever Anne went, the elite followed. London was becoming a little too predictable, my dear; a touch passé. The beau monde was on the look-out for somewhere new.

If you want to see where the moneyed gentry stayed, then visit the museum at **Number 1 Royal Crescent** (p. 244). This might have been the most prestigious address in Bath, but it was nevertheless a boarding house. Admittedly, though, the guests were always persons of rank and quality – and they certainly needed deep pockets to rent this house – an astounding £110 for the season.

10... special Cotswold churches

1 Gloucester Cathedral Pilgrims have been worshipping at the Norman cathedral for more than 900 years. Not only an architectural gem, it contains the beautiful tomb of King Edward II, described by Pevsner as *'a work of genius'*. On a less elevated note, the cloisters were transformed into Hogwarts School for the *Harry Potter* films, p.299

2 St John the Baptist, Cirencester Cirencester's parish church is a fine example of a building added to and adorned by the proceeds of the wool trade, which came from the rich abbey lands stretching over eight counties. The church has a unique porch built in the 15th century by the abbot as a place where he could conduct business, p.91

3 St James' Church, Chipping Campden – one of England's greatest wool churches, its benefactor was one William Grevel, possibly the inspiration for the merchant in Chaucer's *Canterbury Tales*, buried in front of the altar in 1401 under a splendid memorial brass naming him 'The Flower of the Wool Merchants of All England', p.170

4 St John the Baptist, Burford – built from around 1175, it was described as 'queen of Oxfordshire' by Simon Jenkins in his *England's Thousand Best Churches*. Its violent history includes the imprisonment and execution of rebels by Cromwell in 1649, p.221

5 St Mary's Church, Fairford – the only parish church in the country to have managed to preserve a complete set of medieval glass windows; this set of 28 was made by the master glazier to King Henry VII, p.128

6 Odda's Chapel, Deerhurst – this tiny, very plain chapel, is a remarkable survival from Saxon times, retaining its original chancel arch and a number of Saxon windows. Against the odds, this village is home to another Saxon gem: the parish church of St Mary, p.280

7 St Peter and St Paul, Northleach – another rich wool church, this one dates from the early 12th century; as you walk round, you will see magnificent memorial brasses on the floor, dedicated to the wool merchants and their wives, depicting sheep and woolpacks along with their woolmarks, p.116

8 St Mary's Church, Kempley – the most complete set of Romanesque frescos in northern Europe is to be found in the chancel of this small church in the Forest of Dean, p.304

9 Tewkesbury Abbey – medieval architecture is predominant in beautiful Tewkesbury Abbey, which has, according to Pevsner, probably the largest and finest Romanesque tower in England; the chancel retains 14th-century windows; only Westminster Abbey contains more medieval monuments, p.277

10 All Saints Church, Selsley – architect G F Bodley gave the commission for the stained glass windows to his friend William Morris; his first ever such ecclesiastical project, Morris worked on the stained glass alongside Rossetti, Webb, Madox Brown and Burne-Jones, p.68

Cheltenham is a wonderful Regency townscape, its period houses characterised by ornate ironwork balconies and painted stucco facades (p. 270).

Modern times

As James Watt was putting the finishing touches to his rotary-motion steam engine – with its multi-purpose circular motion – unsuspecting hand-weavers were finishing the last of their days beavering away in their honey-stoned cottages. At the start of the 1800s, there was still plenty of money to be made as a highly-skilled hand weaver. But as the 19th century wore on, things began to change. While England celebrated the Battle of Waterloo and Napoleon slunk off to St Helena, the woollen weavers must have felt more ambivalent about the victory. For with the cessation of war went a large part of their income making uniforms. On top of that, the Yorkshire woollen industry began to see the benefits of churning out poorer-quality material, and became a strong competitor at the cheaper end of the market. Finally, in the 1830s, came a serious blow indeed: the British East India Company lost its monopoly, and with it went Stroud's easy route to trade in the exotic East. As a consequence, there were few 'Luddites' in the Stroud area as the new machinery began to roll in; for this mechanisation marked the way forward for a failing industry. Suddenly, men, women and children were once again required in the surviving mills.

Grateful as the locals were for work, their jobs were hardly a picnic when it came to conditions – as noted by the factory inspectors of the time. Edward Barnard ran Nailsworth Mills, where Somerfield now sits. Asked whether or not the mill was heated, he blithely replied that there was warmth enough generated by the moving belts and the workers' busy movements fetching and carrying materials.

It was partly thanks to the inventiveness of Stroud clothiers that this new age of mechanisation was coming into being. John Lewis of Brimscombe patented a revolutionary rotary shearing machine in 1815 that sold over the country in its thousands. In fact, it was when this machine was being manufactured at the Phoenix Iron Works in Thrupp that Edwin Budding saw its potential for a different application and used its principles to invent the world's first lawnmower. You can learn more at **Stroud's Museum in the Park** (p. 62).

By the 1850s, **the mills of the Stroud Valley** were almost entirely mechanised, from the fulling stocks to the power looms (p. 63). But far from dispensing with workers, they gobbled them up – though many of the tasks they had to perform were far more humdrum than in the past. No wonder accidents happened. One over-enthusiastic 8-year-old, who hadn't long started at Lightpill near Stroud, pushed not only fibres into a carding machine, but his hand with them. His skin was stripped by the wires within.

Some entrepreneurs were a cut above the rest, and when it came to improving the conditions of workers, no name in the Stroud area stands out more than those of the Holloway brothers, George and Henry. They were the first people in Britain to attach a sewing machine to a steam engine, which allowed them to branch out into ready-made clothing. In 1875, George established the Stroud Working Men's Benefit Society, which provided workers with sickness benefit, free medical attention and a pension, all for a penny a day. He built brick terraces for his workers in Horns Road at the top of Stroud, allowing tenants to buy their homes through mortgage-type schemes. You can see his statue in Russell Street, Stroud.

In 1834, Stroud businessmen invited a certain Isambard Kingdom Brunel, the newly-appointed chief engineer of the Great Western Railway, to attend a meeting. The idea was to promote a line from Swindon to Cheltenham. The route wasn't an easy one, for the hilly terrain meant tunnels had to be dug and bridges built, and even then, two steam engines would be needed to pull a train out of the Stroud Valleys. But the businessmen pitched their idea and sold it: the resultant railway line, which opened in 1845, connected Stroud directly to London and brought the possibility of travel to many more people.

Go to Stroud Library today and you will see one of the town's most historic relics: the Town Time clock, made in 1858 by watchmaker, Robert Bragg. His clock, which he helpfully kept on display in the window of his shop, showed Greenwich Mean Time as a reminder to townsfolk. For up until the arrival of the railways, each town in England had kept its own time. At eight minutes 50 seconds behind Greenwich, Stroud was the last town in England to conform to the new standard.

Arts and Crafts

There's a rare photograph of Ernest Gimson on a leaflet published by the **Cheltenham Art Gallery and Museum** (p. 273). Gimson was a leading practitioner of Arts and Crafts, a movement that not only concerned itself with aesthetics, but with the need for social reform. Arts and Crafts was one of the few artistic movements to start in England. Difficult to define as a style, it was more a movement of ideas about using natural materials and tools, and taking inspiration from nature as a source for pattern. But above all, it was about art and the working man; looking at how art could play a role in revitalising the dignity in the work and lives of ordinary craftsmen and women.

As a young architect, Gimson went to work at the London office of J D Sedding, which was next door to William Morris's 'Morris and Co' shop. Here he met important figures such as Ernest Barnsley – who went on to build **Rodmarton Manor** (p. 68) – and fellow architect Detmar Blow. Gimson's growing fascination with the Arts and Crafts Movement, and his concern for rural

craftsmen, led him to move to the village of **Sapperton** (p. 68), outside Cirencester, in the late 19th century, where he founded a workshop for them to design furniture and practise their architecture.

At that time, the Cotswolds were very rundown. People were losing their income from wool and textiles, and there was a crisis in agriculture. Others had also been attracted by the destitute quality of the towns and villages. When C R Ashbee moved from the East End of London to set up his Guild of Handicrafts in Chipping Campden in 1902, the mill he occupied had last been used for making silk stockings nearly 60 years previously. You can still see craft work going on today at the **Old Silk Mill in Sheep Street** (p. 171). Cheltenham Art Gallery and Museum has an internationally recognised Arts and Crafts Collection (see www.artsandcraftsmuseum.org.uk).

For a child's eye view, there's a new computer game designed to introduce 7–11-year-olds to the Cotswold landscape via a virtual sheep which gambols through four periods in the region's history. Various attractions take it in turn to host a kiosk where the game can be played. For the latest locations, visit www.wonderfulwolds.org.uk.

GEOGRAPHY AND GEOLOGY

A glorious sun shines down on a land that's a holidaymaker's paradise. The warm, shallow sea – only metres deep – laps against white shores and low sandy islands, reminiscent of the Caribbean or the Persian Gulf. Huge dolphin-like creatures – some up to 16m long – glide by, dwarfing the smaller forms of sea life, some of which look vaguely like squid; on the bottom of the seabed lie thousands upon thousands of oysters. This is the Cotswolds around 200 million years ago, during the Jurassic Age. It's one of the most defining geological periods of all for this area, for it was the time when the

10... spooky places in the Cotswolds

1 **The Ram Inn, Wotton-under-Edge** – built in 1145 and reputedly the most haunted house in Britain; a child's grave was found under the stairs, and crying is frequently heard around that area; to cap it all, the inn was built on an old pagan site used for human sacrifices, p.81

2 **Woodchester Mansion, near Stroud** – half-finished mansion with headless horseman and a floating coffin; two spiritualists made contact on live television with spirits who told them murders had been committed on site, p.64

3 **Prestbury, Cheltenham** – home to the black-hooded Black Abbot who walks from the churchyard to a 16th-century cottage on Deep Street, supposedly once the burial ground for monks. He also occasionally shops in the High Street, p.291

4 **Owlpen Manor, near Dursley** – Margaret of Anjou stayed here before the disastrous (for her) Battle of Tewkesbury; after the battle, Margaret was imprisoned and her son killed. Always a snappy dresser, she drifts through various rooms in the house, p.79

5 **Chavenage House, Tetbury** – Nathaniel Stephens undoubtedly died of guilt after dobbing on Charles I; the moment he died, a black coach and horses driven by a headless coachman pulled up at the door, and the ghost of Nathaniel climbed in, p.96

6 **The Falstaff's Experience, Stratford** – the 500-year-old Shrieve's House barn is often stayed in by paranormal groups; spirits include a Tudor archer, a little girl pickpocket, the victims of a serial killer and a dark hooded figure with red glowing eyes. Put it this way – it scared Derek Acorah..., p.192

7 **New Inn, Gloucester** – Lady Jane Grey walks in a long robe through the Queen's Suite; she was pronounced Queen of England while staying here, a job she didn't want. She was beheaded, aged 17 (elsewhere), p.295

8 **Berkeley Castle** – King Edward II doesn't appear but screams loudly, forgivable given that his death was precipitated by an unpleasant experience with hot pokers; a pretty atrocious ruler, he'd been committed to the custody of Lord Berkeley, owner of said castle, p.82

9 **Ragged Cot, Hyde, near Minchinhampton** – home of Mrs Clavers and her child; in December 1760, the poverty-stricken landlord of the pub, Bill Clavers, decided to hold up the midnight stage coach to London. His horrified wife, holding their child, tried to stop him, but he drunkenly pushed her out of the way, killing both, p.71

10 **Lodge Park** – former owner, the inveterate gambler John 'Crump' Dutton refuses to leave; one housekeeper, who repeatedly heard footsteps down a phantom staircase, was so convinced by his ghost, she always laid a place for him at the dinner table, p.112

distinctive honey-coloured **Cotswold stone** was being formed. Even today, if you study a piece of Cotswold limestone, there are visible clues as to how it was created.

Cotswold stone is also known as **oolitic limestone**. 'Ooid' means 'eggs' and refers to the tiny particles which make it up. The limestone started with a grain of sand or perhaps a shell fragment; then the movement of the sea would have gathered more and more particles around it, until the end result was the size of a pinhead. These are the particles that went to make up the stones. The paleness of the stone reflects the colour of the shells and the sand as they were being deposited. The variation in the depth of colour – for example between the honey stone of the north Cotswolds or the greyer stone of Stroud – is the product of differing amounts of iron oxide.

As it began to be used for building, the very properties of the stone dictated design. The weight of the roof tiles, for example, called for a certain pitch of roofline – and so, by this process, the distinctive architecture we so love today evolved. Of course, there are differing qualities of stone. The most beautiful has been admired throughout the ages – and by no means can it just be seen in this area. Cotswold limestone was chosen as part of the construction of some of England's most lovely buildings, including **St Paul's Cathedral** and the **Houses of Parliament**.

At **Leckhampton Hill** and **Cleeve Common** (p. 276) are the thickest and most complete sections of Middle Jurassic rocks, all clearly exposed; you can obtain interpretation leaflets from the Gloucestershire Geology Trust (www.glosgeotrust.org.uk). In more craggy pieces of stone, you can see burrows and tracks made by creatures millions of years ago; in other parts, there are concave indentations, where the stone is encrusted with the shells of the oysters which once lived there.

If you visit **Huntsman's Quarry**, **near Naunton**, you will discover casts of large dinosaur footprints that were found there from the 150 million year old dinosaur Megalosaurus. Dig in a Cotswold garden and you might unearth a devil's toenail – a large oyster – or even the backbone of a belemnite, a squid-like creature.

Hills and valleys

All the above doesn't explain why we have the deep valleys and rounded hills of today. That was the result of a later phenomenon when the sea level dropped dramatically. Since then – for the last 100 million years – it's erosion that's been eating away at the rock to create the rolling landscape we now know. Easy targets were the softer rocks, which were gradually worn down to create valleys; the harder, higher rocks remain as the hills.

The way limestone weathers is by being dissolved – because it's soluble – and carried away by streams. That's why the water here has a high lime content, which furs up kettles. It's also why the Cotswolds are very infertile. The erosion only leaves a thin soil cover, which is where the sheep come in as being ideal for this sort of land.

Area of outstanding natural beauty

The big question, of course, is: where do the Cotswolds begin and end? The great thing is that no one has a definitive answer. The Cotswolds Conservation Board, which is the guardian of this area, has a useful map on its website (www.cotswoldsaonb.org.uk), reaching from just above Chipping Campden in the north, to below Bath in the south. In the west, it stops just short of Gloucester; to just east of Chipping Norton in the Oxfordshire area – though other definitions (including this guide book) are more creative.

When the Cotswolds AONB was drawn up, the basic premise was to include areas that demonstrated Cotswold characteristics, such as drystone walls, Cotswold stone buildings and ancient woodland. It's a designation that's worked well: Cotswold features must be among the most distinctive in the world. Today, at 790sq miles (2,038sq km), it is the second largest protected landscape in Britain.

WILDLIFE AND HABITATS

One of the key features of the Cotswolds is 'unimproved' limestone grassland that's lain untouched for hundreds of years: no fertilisers or pesticides have been added to its sparse soil; no plough has ever churned up its layers. At **Elliott Nature Reserve** at Swifts Hill near Stroud, for example – one of more than 70 nature reserves managed by Gloucestershire Wildlife Trust – you will find 11 species of orchid, as well as scabious, harebells and cowslips, which only grow in these sorts of conditions; you will also come across the 'small blue' butterfly – no longer a common sight – and snails, adders, small mammals, bugs and beetles. In the 1940s, 40% of the Cotswolds was covered by this type of grassland; nowadays, there's just 1.5% of that 40% left.

There are many other nationally important sites in the area, such as Minchinhampton and Rodborough Commons. In spring, you will find these amazing habitats being grazed by free-roaming cattle – just as they have been for hundreds of years. The animals that steadily munch their way across the land have helped create a unique habitat that not only supports an incredible diversity of grasses and other plants – including the rare pasque flower – but nearly 50% of all British species of butterfly find a haven here.

The Cotswold Water Park south of Cirencester – Britain's largest man-made group of lakes – is the ideal place to see birds. It has 12 Sites of Special Scientific Interest, and welcomes 20,000 wintering waterbirds each year, as well as gulls, breeding warblers, nightingales, little ringed plover and common tern. It's an important stop-over for migrating birds during both spring and autumn. It's also the spot to see otter, water vole, bats, dragonflies and wild-flower meadows. The Wildfowl & Wetlands Trust at Slimbridge, of course, is a fantastic venue for introducing children (and adults!) to birds at close quarters. It's known for the Bewick's swans that visit each year from Arctic Russia.

The Cotswolds are famous for their beech woods, and a prime example is Buckholt Wood, 3 miles north east of Painswick, where flowers include dog-violet, wood anemone, primrose, lords and ladies and woodruff. It's been designated a National Nature Reserve – an internationally important area (www.naturalengland.org.uk). The Forest of Dean – Britain's premier oak forest – is becoming a diverse area for wildlife, and a project to restore heathland is beginning to attract species such as the nightjar, especially around Tidenham, in ever-increasing numbers. Wild boar live in its depths, as do many deer. Peregrine falcons can be viewed from Symonds Yat Rock, goshawks from the New Fancy viewpoint and buzzards throughout the woodlands.

For more on wildlife, visit Gloucestershire Wildlife Trust's website (www.gloucestershire wildlifetrust.co.uk). West Oxfordshire's nature reserves are managed by Berks, Bucks & Oxon Wildlife Trust (www.bbowt.org.uk).

CULTURE

Vibrant Stroud doesn't have the mellow stone of Stow-on-the-Wold or the rich history of Tewkesbury, but it does have more artists per capita than almost anywhere else in Britain. That influx of talent started in Victorian times with William Morris, whose followers made their homes in nearby Sapperton and round about, and it still continues today: Damien Hirst has a studio at Chalford, just down the road.

Of course, this phenomenon isn't confined to Stroud, nor to art itself. Artists thrive all over the Cotswolds, which are packed full of top-notch art galleries. There's also a noble tradition of writers, right from J Arthur Gibbs, whose *A Cotswold Village* could be said to be the first 'popular' Cotswold book, to Bisley-based Jilly Cooper, whose best-selling novels always have a Cotswold theme in them somewhere.

Music thrives, too. What's incredible is the way even relatively small villages, such as Guiting Power (www.guitingfestival.org), can sustain their own festivals. Equally exciting are the village green performances by Giffords Circus, which has put the culture back into this skilful art form (www.giffordscircus.com). And you simply can't pigeonhole Tewkesbury's wide-ranging Awaken the Senses festival, intertwined with the town's Roses Theatre, with its music, dance, and art of all kinds (www.awakenyoursenses.org).

And don't forget the crafts. The survival of true craftsmanship in the area is one of the elements that attracted the Arts and Crafts proponents such as the architects Ernest Gimson, brothers Sidney and Ernest Barnsley, and C R Ashbee to the area in the late 19th and early 20th centuries. Silversmiths, calligraphers, ceramicists, designers, furniture makers, photographers, textile artists and more still thrive here; but you can also find traditional rural crafts such as hedge-laying, drystone walling, blacksmithing, hazel hurdle-making and ploughing – skilful and intrinsic to the area.

Art

Art plays an extraordinarily important part in Cotswold life, both in a professional and amateur sense. Places such as Stow-on-the-Wold and Broadway are well known for the quality of their art galleries. If you want to take back a painterly souvenir – a fine Cotswold view – you will be spoilt for choice. It's not surprising that Broadway has such riches; in the 19th century, it became an important centre for the arts, attracting artists, writers and composers such as John Singer Sargent, J M Barrie, Ralph Vaughan Williams and Edward Elgar.

Stroud has an arts festival that runs throughout the year (www.stroudartsfestival. org), a visual arts festival in June, where 100 artists or more open the doors of their studios and welcome the public in (www. sitefestival.org.uk) and the International Textile Festival, offering a programme of activities connected to textiles and textile-related arts, culminating in the main festival in May (www.stroudinternationaltextiles.org.uk). The sculptor Daniel Chadwick is planning in the near future to open the Lynn Chadwick Sculpture Park, dedicated to the work of his late and celebrated father, on land in the Toadsmoor Valley outside Stroud. It's a large-scale venture, designed to attract around 60,000 visitors a year. Importantly, it will be the UK's only permanent showcase of its kind dedicated to one artist.

Cheltenham is another centre for artists, with an open air art exhibition held in the Imperial Gardens (www.cheltenham-art.com) each summer, as well as an open studios

THE RURAL CAPITAL OF CULTURE

Forget Liverpool! The Cotswolds and Forest of Dean have named themselves Britain's Rural Capital of Culture. *'The Cotswolds' image may be of sleepy villages, country pubs and historic houses and gardens, but we're just as proud of the amazing range of cultural events that bring the area to life, day-by-day and week-by-week,'* says tourism manager, Chris Dee. From now until 2011, www.cotswolds.com will be bringing a full range of events to the public's attention through the website and a dedicated brochure.

event in June. And of course, the town has the riches of Cheltenham Art Gallery and Museum (www.cheltenham.artgallery. museum).

During Oxfordshire *Artweeks,* there are open studios in May and June, as well as exhibitions www.artweeks.org; and artists in West Oxfordshire are supported by West Ox Arts (www.wospweb.com/site/West-Ox-Arts/index.htm), with a gallery on the first floor of a Grade II listed building, Bampton Town Hall.

You can find out more about open studio events – Gloucester and the Forest of Dean have them, too – from www.southwestopen studios.org and www.forest-of-dean-open studios.org.uk. Don't miss the Forest of Dean's Sculpture Trial – open from dawn to dusk – which shows 17 permanent works by international artists, with free access, in a woodland setting, beginning at Beechenhurst Lodge (www.forestofdean-sculpture.org.uk).

An unusual venue with a unique, intimate atmosphere, is Prema in Uley, near Dursley. A small independent rural arts centre, in a former Baptist chapel, it hosts all sorts of diverse and unusual exhibitions, as well as offering workshops and live events (www. prema.demon.co.uk).

Photography is another important art, of course. The first photographic gallery to have opened in the north Cotswolds is 6HQ Photographic Gallery in Chipping Campden's High Street (www.6hq.co.uk).

Crafts

This section needs breaking down into two areas: there are the designer crafts, and you will find many workshops dotted about the place, as well as regular markets, where you can buy outstanding jewellery, wood products, glass, woven baskets and much more. The Princess Royal hosts a crafts event at Gatcombe Park near Minchinhampton in the autumn, as does Blenheim Palace in Woodstock near Christmas (www.living crafts.co.uk).

The Gloucestershire Guild of Craftsmen has a permanent gallery in Bisley Street, Painswick (www.guildcrafts.org.uk). The Cotswold Craftsmen, a rich cross-section of craftsmen, designers and artists who value traditions and skills, hold three main events a year: at Malvern in the spring and autumn, and at Bishops Cleeve near Cheltenham at Christmas (www.cotswold-craftsmen.org).

The area is blessed with so many hubs for the arts, and none more valued than the New Brewery Arts in Cirencester (www. breweryarts.org.uk). With exhibitions, classes and performances, it hosts resident makers in 12 world-class craft studios, including glass, jewellery, furniture and cloth. In Chipping Campden, Ashbee and his 150 East End workers set up shop in the Old Silk Mill in the early 20th century; today it's occupied by gold and silversmith, David Hart, whose grandfather was one of those original Londoners (www.hartsilversmiths.co.uk), and there's a guild of craftworkers, The Gallery@ The Guild (www.thegalleryattheguild.co. uk). One of the biggest events is the Celebration of Craftsmanship and Design held at Cheltenham College each August, an incredible pool of talent from all over the country, where makers sell their own designs and accept commissions (www. celebrationofcraftsmanship.com). You will find superb contemporary furniture here.

As far as rural crafts are concerned, there's an interesting picture. For where some crafts are naturally dying out, others are flourishing. When it comes to greenwood industries, forge work, withy work and drystone walling, craftsmen are alive and well. You've only got to look at the fact that the Cotswolds are criss-crossed by over 4,000 miles of drystone walls to realise the need there is for these traditional skills to continue. Indeed, drystone walling is one of the best-known Cotswold crafts. It started as a very practical measure, simply to keep the livestock in. There was plenty of stone in the hilly areas, and building walls was both cheap and a good way of clearing rocks from the fields. Many of today's walls date back to Victorian times. You can see demonstrations of these crafts at country fairs such as the Cotswold Show at Cirencester Park in July (www.cotswoldshow. co.uk) and Frampton Country Fair in the Park at Frampton-on-Severn in September (www. framptoncountryfair.co.uk).

If you fancy learning one of these traditional arts, you can join a course run by the Royal Agricultural College's Rural Skills Centre (rsc.rac.ac.uk) or the Cotswolds Conservation Board (www.cotswoldsaonb.org. uk). Tourist information centres, libraries and arts venues should have a copy of *Artists and Craftspeople in Gloucestershire and the Cotswolds*, listing galleries and shops.

Music

The Cotswolds' rich tradition of music is astonishing: Ralph Vaughan Williams, Gustav Holst, Ivor Gurney, Herbert Howells, Gerald Finzi, and Edward Elgar, who was born just over the 'border' in a village near Worcester. It was this connection that led to cellist Julian Lloyd Webber buying a cottage in the north Cotswolds: '*Any musician who has seen where Elgar lived is at a huge advantage,*' he says. '*The chief characteristic of Elgar's music is that it is very influenced by the countryside and landscape: I'm absolutely convinced of that. And I think if he had not been brought up around Worcester and Malvern and had not spent his youth walking on the Malvern Hills, his music would be very different.*'

Today, the composer Colin Decio (www. colindecio.com) is writing a host of new works, including the recent *Gloucester Symphony*. Ollie Baines, a member of opera-meets-pop group Blake (www.blakeofficial. com), is from near Malmesbury. And Sarah Connolly, one of the foremost British mezzo sopranos, might sing with English National Opera, Glyndebourne, Welsh National in Milan, Paris, New York or San Francisco – but she always comes home to her cottage high in the hills above Stroud (www.sarah-connolly.com).

There are first-class music festivals in abundance, but the first thing to remember is the quality of music you can get for free – in the churches. Go to evensong at Tewkesbury Abbey, for example, and you will hear soaring music without having to spend a dime, in a 900-year-old building (www. tewkesburyabbey.org.uk).

Many opportunities to hear music are detailed in the body of this guide, but do look at websites such as Cheltenham Town Hall's (www.cheltenhamtownhall.org. uk). There's Cheltenham's Jazz Festival in early May and the town's famous Music Festival in July (cheltenhamfestivals.com). The newly constructed Centaur at Cheltenham Racecourse is the perfect venue for concerts: among other events, it hosts the Wychwood Music Festival in May (www. wychwoodfestival.com), with more than 80 live acts, comedians and workshops; and Greenbelt, the UK's largest Christian arts festival (www.greenbelt.org.uk), in August.

The north Cotswold town of Chipping Campden holds its own music festival in May (www.campdenmusicfestival.co.uk); there's The Three Choirs Festival (www.3choirs. org), which takes place in August at each of the three cathedral cities of Gloucester, Worcester and Hereford in turn; Gloucester Festival (www.gloucester.gov.uk/festival) and the Gloucester International Blues Festival in the summer (gloucesterblues.co.uk); and Tetbury Music Festival in October (www. tetburymusicfestival.org.uk). And that's not even going into other events such as Longborough Festival Opera, the Cotswolds' own Glyndebourne (www.lfo.org.uk); and the contemporary Cornbury Music Festival at Cornbury Park in West Oxfordshire, which has recently featured acts such as Paul Simon, Crowded House and KT Tunstall (www.cornburyfestival.com).

Literature

Of course, we lay claim to Shakespeare, and a visit to Stratford is de rigeur for all Bard fans; Jane Austen dallied in Bath; and we take as our own J K Rowling, born in Yate. But there are many others more rooted in a distinctive Cotswolds tradition.

In 1934, the chartered accountants Randall & Payne in Stroud received a resignation note. It was from a humble clerk who explained, '*I am not suited to office work*'. The note was signed 'Laurie Lee'. His *Cider With Rosie* is one of the most famous of Cotswold books: evocative, poetic, redolent with the sights and scents of the Stroud Valleys. The poets Ivor Gurney (again – he was a musician, too) and F W Harvey belong here; and Jenny Joseph, famous for her many literary achievements including the poem *Warning*, which begins, '*When I am an old woman, I shall wear purple/ With a red hat which doesn't go, and doesn't suit me...*', lives in Minchinhampton, where novelist Joanna Trollope was born. The wonderful Jilly Cooper and Katie Fforde both colour their novels with local scenes and characters. M C Beaton, who lives in the very real Blockley, places her detective Agatha Raisin in the fictional Cotswolds village of Carsely.

The Forest of Dean has its literary connections with playwright Dennis Potter, who often incorporated the Forest into his work (*Blue Remembered Hills*, *Pennies from Heaven* and *The Singing Detective*), and the Dymock Poets, who lived around the village of Dymock in 1914: Lascelles Abercrombie, Wilfrid Gibson, John Drinkwater and Robert Frost, with Rupert Brooke as a visitor. The early chapters of Lady Edna Healey's autobiography, *Part of the Pattern: Memoirs of a Wife at Westminster,* paint a delightful picture of growing up in Coleford. And who can visit Gloucester without thinking of Beatrix Potter's tailor, commemorated in a city centre museum and shop?

Wander back into the past with *Portrait of Elmbury* by John Moore, a fictionalised account of Tewkesbury; *The Diary of a Cotswold Parson* by F E Witts; and Ablington, immortalised by the 19th-century squire and social commentator J Arthur Gibbs in his book, *A Cotswold Village.* Nancy Mitford drew on her eccentric and isolated West Oxfordshire childhood for *The Pursuit of Love.* More loose connections include Victorian author Mrs Craik, who wrote *John Halifax Gentleman* at Rose Cottage in Amberley, and centred the action (or rather lack of it) in Tewkesbury. And P G Wodehouse's Blandings is thought to be Sudeley Castle.

If you visit Stanway House in the north Cotswolds, you can see stamps on the ceiling, playfully flicked there by J M Barrie, who donated the thatched pavilion to the village. And many more... One of the best ways of exploring literature of any kind is at Cheltenham Literature Festival in October (cheltenhamfestivals.com) and Bath Literature (www.bathlitfest.org.uk) in early March. The city also dedicates a literature festival to children each September (www.bathfestivalofchildrensliterature.co.uk).

LOCAL HEROES

Celebrities, as one wit put it, spend the first half of their lives trying to become famous; and the second half trying to avoid being recognised.

And perhaps that's why you can find so many of them queuing up to buy homes in the Cotswolds. For the Cotswolds are the geographical equivalent of a pair of D&G sunglasses and an NY baseball cap pulled low over the forehead. Celebrities love it here because it affords them a degree of privacy they can't find in many other places.

It's extraordinary that, until fairly recently, there were no fewer than three Royal households based in the Cotswolds: **The Prince of Wales** is at Highgrove in Tetbury; **The Princess Royal** is at Gatcombe Park, Minchinhampton; and until 2006, **Prince and Princess Michael of Kent** lived at

10... great historical figures

1 William Shakespeare – arguably the world's greatest dramatist, he was born in Stratford-upon-Avon in 1564 probably on 23 April, and that's when his home town celebrates with its annual Shakespeare Birthday Celebrations

2 Winston Churchill – the inspirational war-time prime minister was born in a small room in Blenheim Palace, Woodstock, in 1874 after his mother went into labour early while on a visit. His grave is just down the road in Bladon Churchyard

3 Laurie Lee – the poet and writer put the Stroud Valleys on the literary map with his beautiful autobiographical novel, *Cider with Rosie*. His lyrical descriptions of the Cotswold countryside in the early 20th century, and his young passion for Rosie, have brought many flocking to the village of Slad where his childhood haunts are still easily recognisable

4 The Mitford sisters Unity, Pam, Diana, Nancy, Jessica and Deborah were the talk of the 20th century with their glamorous exploits and political extremes. Their early lives in the Oxfordshire Cotswolds were satirised in Nancy's novel, *The Pursuit of Love*

5 Jane Austen – the novelist arrived in Bath towards the end of the 18th century, and used it as the setting for *Persuasion* and *Northanger Abbey*.-

6 Edward 'Bill' Wilson – this polar explorer, born in Cheltenham, reached the South Pole on 17 January, 1912, only to find the Norwegian explorer Roald Amundsen had got there first. Wilson perished with Captain Scott and other members of the party a few weeks later in their attempt to return to base

7 Gustav Holst – the composer of *The Planet Suite*, which includes the tune of *I Vow to Thee My Country,* was born in a Regency terrace in Cheltenham. In 1974 on the centenary of his birth, his former home was turned into the Holst Birthplace Museum

8 Edward Jenner – thanks to this outstanding doctor, who set up a practice in Berkeley in the 18th century, smallpox is the only disease to have been eradicated from the world

9 William Morris – the founder of the Arts and Crafts Movement used both Broadway Tower and Kelmscott Manor (after which he named his Kelmscott Press) as his country bases, and helped reinvigorate craftsmanship in the Cotswolds

10 W G Grace – born in Downend in 1848, this great test cricketer played in the first ever Cheltenham Festival match, still held annually at Cheltenham College.

Nether Lypiatt. For a long time, the area was known by the sobriquet 'The Royal Triangle'. If you want to see Wills and Harry, just visit a local polo ground. **Zara** – who lives at Gatcombe with **Mike Tindall** – is sometimes spotted riding out in the lanes around Minchinhampton. **Peter and Autumn Phillips** also have a house here. But while the royals are happy to give out their addresses and postcodes and even to have the public round on the odd occasion, celebrities can be more tricky to track down.

In 2002, **Kate Winslet and Sam Mendes** paid £3.3 million for their Grade II listed manor in Church Westcote, near Stow-on-the-Wold. They reportedly beat off competition from stars such as Sir Elton John to secure the property. **Elizabeth Hurley**, and television prankster **Dom Joly**, have settled in villages near Cirencester, though he's so far kept his mobile turned off in local libraries. **Jilly Cooper** (Bisley), **Fiona Fullerton** (Fairford-way), **Pam Ayres** and **Anne Robinson** (also Cirencester) all have long associations with the area, and all have immortalised it in print. In fact, this region is a mecca for celebrities: **Willie Carson**, **Laurence Llewelyn-Bowen**, **Gary Kemp**, **Sharron Davies**, **Tina Hobley**

and **Tony Adams** also call it home. Further north there's **Steve Winwood** and **Julian Lloyd Webber**, and into Oxfordshire, you will find **Alex James**, **Rory Bremner**, **Jeremy Clarkson**, **David Cameron** and **Ruby Wax**.

It doesn't stop there: model **Kate Moss** has a place at Little Faringdon and enjoys a night out at her local, The Swan at Southrop; controversial artist **Damien Hirst** has a studio in Chalford; and **Richard Ashcroft** of The Verve enjoys life in South Gloucestershire. Pershore way, you've got **Stella McCartney**, Conde Nast MD and author **Nicholas Coleridge**, and **Toyah Willcox** and her husband, **Robert Fripp**. **Simon Pegg** was born in Gloucester – his dad, John Beckingham, has his own jazz band, which you can catch playing at the Daffodil restaurant in Cheltenham.

Bridget Jones's Diary was filmed at Snowshill and Johnny Depp stayed in Chipping Campden while filming *The Libertine*. Chavenage House, near Tetbury, is the manor in *Lark Rise to Candleford*. No wonder a national newspaper once named Waitrose in Cirencester as one of the top 10 places to be seen.

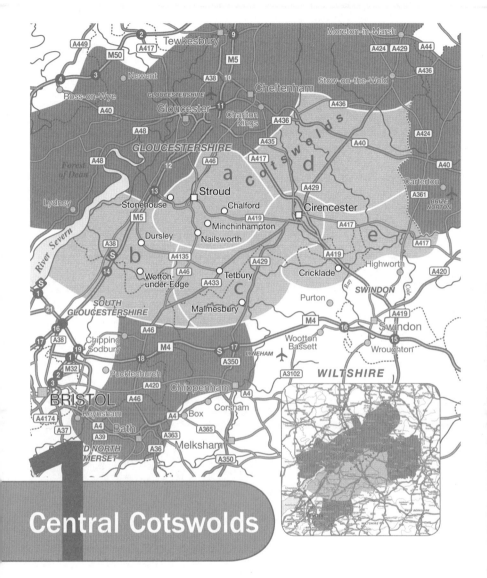

Central Cotswolds

a. The Five Valleys

b. Dursley, Wotton and the Vale of Berkeley

c. Cirencester and the south

d. Bibury, Coln Valley, and Northleach

e. The Cotswold Water Park

Unmissable highlights

01 Down a pint of Uley bitter at the Woolpack, Laurie Lee's old haunt in Slad. You might even be served by actor Keith Allen, who does stints behind the bar, p. 73

02 Do your food shop at Stroud Farmers' Market. With between 45 and 50 stalls, it's recently been judged best in the country by the National Farmers' Retail & Markets Association, p. 72

03 Hug a tree at Westonbirt, The National Arboretum; its collection of Japanese maples is world famous – and dogs love the fact that they can explore Silk Wood off the lead, p. 96

04 Wills and Harry play polo in the estate grounds of Cirencester Park, and at the Beaufort Polo Club. You can see some first-class matches during the season at both venues, from April to September, p. 102

05 Take the family on a bird-watching canoe safari at the internationally-known Wildfowl & Wetlands Trust at Slimbridge, p. 77

06 Take back some exclusive souvenirs: in 2008, Prince Charles opened the only high-street 'Highgrove' shop, right in the heart of Tetbury, p. 102

07 For a unique – and free – experience, head to Purton: the old ships' graveyard. These old boats that lie beached along the shore are the Severn trows that once plied their trade along the river, p. 84

08 Elizabeth Hurley loves Barnsley House hotel; you can dine here and then enjoy the outstanding gardens designed and once owned by Prince Charles's friend, the late Rosemary Verey, p. 135

09 Sunbathe on a Cotswold beach! (A man-made one, anyway). At Keynes Country Park, there's a super child-friendly beach where you can take your inflatables–and the sand is tip-top castle-making material, p. 126

10 Feed the fish (and greedy ducks) at Bibury Trout Farm, then sample the fish other people have fattened up for you by buying fresh or smoked trout from the fish counter, p. 114

CENTRAL COTSWOLDS

There's much more to the Cotswolds than honeyed stone, sheep and rolling hills, as this central area wonderfully exemplifies! If you're dining on delicious local fare at the New Inn at Coln St Aldwyns, where the view could come straight from a Cotswolds picture book, you'd feel you'd found the heart of this area. Yet just a few miles south lies the Cotswold Water Park, the largest area of open water in Britain, which attracts rare and beautiful wildlife. You can enjoy glorious walks in one location and, just a few minutes later, be water-skiing in the other.

Cirencester, the late Princess of Wales's favourite town, is as traditional as they come; but don't miss out on its close neighbour, Stroud, where 'green' doesn't just describe the colours of the hills that surround it: it's one of the most forward-thinking, environmentally friendly and artistic towns in England – and full of fascinating characters. In nearby Slad, where once Laurie Lee held sway in the Woolpack, you will now find the actor Keith Allen propping up the bar. There are the villages down by the River Severn, with their maritime heritage; the manicured and cultured hamlets of the Coln Valley; the flat plains of the vale and the giddy heights of the wold.

However, this region isn't simply about views and climbing over stiles. The family attractions are world famous. Beautiful Westonbirt Arboretum hosts the National Collection of Japanese Maples; Slimbridge – the Wildfowl & Wetlands Trust – cares for world's largest collection of swans, geese, and duck; there's Berkeley Castle, with its jousts and re-enactments, which has been lived in by the same family for over 900 years; and Painswick's Rococo Garden, world-famous for its snowdrop displays, to name but a few.

Best of all, you can eat the delicious views. The food produced in this area is ethically grown by people who really care. Artisan cheeses, rare salt-marsh lamb, Old Spot pork, sparkling wines, award-winning ales – all available from some of the best farmers' markets you will find in the country (and that's official: just look at the awards).

THE FIVE VALLEYS
INCLUDING STROUD, PAINSWICK AND NAILSWORTH

The Five Valleys are startlingly beautiful. If you like your countryside perfectly manicured, you must head further north; if, on the other hand, you prefer a little more ruggedness, this is the place for you: steeply wooded hillsides tumbling down into deeply secret valleys. You climb over a wooden stile, round a corner – and suddenly, unexpectedly, the unbelievably green slopes of a hidden vale open up before you, carpeted with soft blue scabious and harebells, and yellow-flowering cowslips.

So what are the Five Valleys? **Golden Valley**, named for the riches it brought Middle Ages wool merchants who grazed their picturesque (and lucrative) sheep on its slopes, is dotted with the old mills that once proliferated, turning fluffy white fleeces into valuable cloth. **Nailsworth Valley** is still presided over by a friendly, forward-thinking market town. **Toadsmoor Valley** is different again, with its wild garlic scented woods and lake offering secluded walks. Laurie Lee immortalised the **Slad Valley** in his autobiographical novel, *Cider with Rosie*. And finally, the **Painswick Valley**, where its eponymous town – known as the Queen of the Cotswolds – reigns supreme. Here you will find 'Paradise'.... According to local lore, Charles I stood high up on the famous Painswick Beacon and declared the valley to the east 'must be paradise' and the spot he admired was named accordingly. These five valleys, where industry and artistry have flourished for many centuries, all meet in **Stroud**. It's a working town, not a twee village, brimful of character; the area is home to more artists and craftsmen than almost anywhere else in the country. If you love the countryside, walking, history and art, you will find outlets for all your passions within the Five Valleys.

WHAT TO SEE AND DO

Around Minchinhampton

High up on the hills around Stroud, you will find **Minchinhampton**, **Rodborough** and **Selsley Commons**. This is the ideal spot to begin a visit to the Five Valleys: for one thing, it affords you a breathtakingly panoramic view of the area.

Here, on hundreds of acres of land that have remained largely untouched by the plough, cows roam freely all summer long while the multicoloured butterflies – including the rare Duke of Burgundy – flit between wild orchids. Minchinhampton is also one of the most important archaeological sites in Britain. Those bumps you can see are a combination of prehistoric field systems, a Neolithic long barrow, medieval roads, quarries and military defences from the Second World War.

Stile at Minchinhampton

The tufted dilly dumps are perfect for flying kites, playing ball games, having picnics and letting off steam. Cool down afterwards with an ice cream from **Winstone's** (☎01453 873270; www.winstonesicecream.co.uk), who have been making delicious ices on Rodborough Common since 1925. Minchinhampton Common is also home to one of the earliest **golf** clubs in the West of England (☎01453 832642), and there are two 'new' courses, too, one of which (Cherington) was the venue for the Open qualifier for six years (☎01453 833840). Just one word of warning: remember, when you're driving (cars or golf balls), that those free-roaming cows have as much interest in road safety as their Cotswoldian neighbour, Jeremy Clarkson...

Minchinhampton itself is definitely worth a stroll around (there's a choice of great tearooms and pubs). It's one of the Cotswolds' less-discovered towns, yet its 17th-century Market House, held up by pillars, gives a clue that it was once one of the most important cloth centres of the area. The novelist **Joanna Trollope** spent much of her early childhood at the Priest House in Butt Street, when her grandfather, Rex Hodson, was rector. 'He always delivered parish magazines on horseback... and on hunting days often took communion services with his boots and spurs plainly visible below his cassock!' she recalls.

The Princess Royal lives at **Gatcombe Park**, on the edge of the town, where, every August, she hosts the Festival of British Eventing, familiarly known as Gatcombe Horse Trials (www.gatcombe-horse.co.uk). The event offers a rare glimpse of the Princess's lovely 18th-century Bath stone house, as well as a chance to see top riders in action – including, in all likelihood, her daughter Zara Phillips. Actually, you might catch sight of Zara riding out in the quiet lanes round about.

You can easily slip down to the village of **Avening** from here, which has connections with two (rather different) leading ladies: Queen Matilda, who commissioned the 11th-

The Gatcombe Horse Trials held at the home of the Princess Royal, Gatcombe Park

century church in remorse for murdering her lover, Battrick; and Holby City's **Tina Hobley**, who, with her husband Oli Wheeler and children, has a cottage in the village. '*We sleep so well here,*' she says. '*If there wasn't a reason to get up, I'm sure we'd sleep for 10 years. We get woken up by the birds or the horses coming past.*'

Painswick, Queen of the Cotswolds

There are so many pretty villages in this area – such as **Eastcombe**, **Amberley**, **Woodchester**, **Bisley** and **Chalford**, where an age-old means of transport has been reintroduced for delivering groceries and newspapers: donkeys (check out chalford donkeyproject.blogspot.com) – but don't miss out on **Painswick**, up the A46 north of Stroud. Dubbed the 'Queen of the Cotswolds', this fine town – built on the proceeds of the wool trade – is a network of quaint narrow streets: its 'New Street' was constructed in around 1428, and it boasts the oldest village rugby club in England. The 11th -century parish church of **St Mary** bears the battle scars of bullets and cannons, fired in 1644 when the Royalists advanced on

The beautiful scenery in Painswick's Rococo Garden

Parliamentarians who had taken refuge there. In the churchyard, there are 99 yew trees because – so legend has it – the Devil won't permit a hundredth. Also keep your eyes peeled for one of the most unusual graves in England: a pyramid, commemorating a stonemason.

> **PAINSWICK ROCOCO GARDEN:** Painswick GL6 6TH; ☎01452 813204; www.rococogarden.org.uk. Entry: adults £5.50; seniors £4.50; children £2.75; family £15; open daily Jan to Oct, 11am–5pm; restaurant serves light lunches.

Most famous of all, however, is Painswick's flamboyant **Rococo Garden**, a unique masterpiece of 18th-century design, particularly celebrated for its snowdrops. Whatever time of year you visit, you will be captivated by the beauty, fragrance and tranquillity of these 6 acres, which can take nearly an hour to wander around.

Laurie Lee's Slad

Foot or horseback – both are perfect ways to explore the extraordinary natural beauty of the Five Valleys, the most famous of which is **Slad**, along the road from Stroud to Birdlip. It's still possible to wander these slopes, a copy of *Cider with Rosie* in hand, and identify the places the poet and author, Laurie Lee, so vividly described: the honey-coloured village school where Miss Wardley gave lessons on local wildlife; the cottage where the chaotic Mrs Lee held sway. The late Jim Fern, one of Stroud's great characters and an old school-friend of Laurie, used to recall the scene with fondness: *'Mrs Lee was very eccentric. She didn't have any money, but she couldn't resist buying odds and ends from the sales. At times, you'd look round for somewhere to put your mug, but the table would be so full of stuff you couldn't find room.'* And there's the church where Laurie once sang in the choir and now lies buried in the older, lower graveyard.

The **Elliott Nature Reserve** on Swifts Hill in Slad is a mecca for wildlife. You can wander freely round the 25 acre site, which is home to 11 species of orchid, as well as butterflies, snails, adders, small mammals, bugs and beetles. You can also glimpse a dizzy 170 million years of geological history on the rock face of the hill's former quarry. It's one of more than 70 reserves managed by the Gloucestershire Wildlife Trust. Find out more at www.gloucestershirewildlifetrust.co.uk.

Pyramidal Orchid in the Elliott Nature Reserve

Stroud

Stroud's been described as Notting Hill with wellies – but locals know well that Notting Hill is simply Stroud without wellies. This eclectic, vibrant, alternative and surprising town has been the backdrop for a best-selling Katie Fforde novel; it has seen roof-top protests, determined sit-ins and high-street marches on global ethical issues. It had the first green-controlled council in the country and the first fully organic café in the form of Woodruff's on the High Street. Its weekly Saturday farmers' market has been voted the best in the country; it's a fantastic place to sit and enjoy a coffee at one of the pavement cafés. Art is also all-important in this town. Catch up with the latest exhibitions, shows and artistic events at www.the-space.org.

In the graveyard of St Laurence, just off The Shambles in Stroud, there is an inscription: '*Here lie the remains of Joseph Francis Delmont, Lieutenant, of his Majesty's 82nd Regiment, born 28th November 1785, died 18th August 1807*'. This 21-year-old lad is unforgotten, even after 200 years – but for reasons few would envy: the last man to die in a duel in Britain.

Further up the High Street is The Cross, where you will find a sculpture of a ram with a bolt of cloth and a waterwheel – a tribute to the town's industrial past. At the beginning of the 19th century, demand for cloth produced in the Stroud Valleys was huge. In fact, you'd have seen the green fields of the valleys turned multicoloured as the different cloths were stretched out on tenters to dry: Stroud Scarlet for the army; Uley Blue for the Royal Navy; 'drab' yellow, as it was known, for Lord Berkeley's livery – a colour that was later adopted by the Prince of Wales and his fashionable followers.

During the Civil War, Oliver Cromwell commandeered the area's entire stock of 'Stroud Scarlet' to make uniforms for his New Model Army. It can still be seen today, worn by the Guards regiments. You can learn about Stroud's wool heritage through the Stroudwater Textile Trust, which holds regular mill open days (www.stroud-textile. org.uk). There's a major project underway to reopen the canal system that was once the lifeblood of Stroud's many industries (visit www.cotswoldcanals.com for the latest canal news).

For a fun and fascinating tour of the past, visit the **Museum in the Park**, a 17th-century wool merchant's mansion set in the grounds of Stratford Park in Stroud. Here you will see history from the dinosaurs to the world's first lawnmower, invented by local engineer Edwin Budding in 1830. He had his light-bulb (or, presumably, gas-lamp) moment while watching the action of a machine trimming cloth in a local mill.

THE MUSEUM IN THE PARK: Stratford Park, Stroud GL5 4AF; ☎01453 763394; www. museuminthepark.org.uk. Entry: free; open Apr to Sept, Tues–Fri 10am–5pm, Sat/Sun and bank holidays 11am–5pm; Oct to Mar, Tues–Fri 10am–4pm, Sat/Sun 11am–4pm; open every day in Aug; closed Good Friday; call ☎01453 763394 for December arrangements; open New Year's Day.

Still on the subject of history, 10 minutes south-west of Stroud (2 miles south-west of Stonehouse) is **Frocester Tithe Barn**, in the centre of Frocester village, one of the most important and best preserved in England. Dating back to the 13th century, it's open daily all year round during daylight hours, free of charge, though donations are welcome. Phone first on 01453 823250.

South of Stroud on the A46, is **Nailsworth**. If you want to know about its

The Museum in the Park is housed in a 17th century wool merchant's mansion in Stroud

personality, look at the shops – there are still two ironmonger's, as well as outstanding food shops, interior designers, clothes, gifts, flowers and books, to name but a few. But if you want to understand its past, look at the mills. Egypt Mill – now an hotel and restaurant – was so named because the waters around it once ran red with cloth dyes emptied into the local stream, transforming it into the 'Red Sea'.

RUSKIN MILL: Old Bristol Road, Nailsworth GL6 0LA; ☎01453 837537; www.rmet.org.uk Entry: open 11am–4pm daily.

Ruskin Mill is another example of creative new uses for these historic buildings – literally. Inspired by the work of John Ruskin, William Morris and Rudolf Steiner, it offers cultural events, workshops, exhibitions and has a lovely organic and biodynamic garden, and a coffee shop.

At the top of the town is The New Lawn, home to Forest Green Rovers, the excellent local football team (www.forestgreenroversfc.com). Watledge – a hamlet of Nailsworth – is where poet **W H Davies** once lived: '*What is this life if full of care, We have no time to stand and stare?*' You can see a plaque over the door of his cottage, Glendower.

You can **cycle** the Stroud Valleys Pedestrian Cycle Trail, along the old railway line from Nailsworth to Stonehouse via Stroud; maps are available from tourist information centres.

Woodchester Mansion

Woodchester Mansion, near the village of Nymspfield outside Nailsworth, is Gloucestershire's most mysterious house – an architectural masterpiece of the Victorian age, strangely abandoned by its builders before it was completed. Work began on the mansion in the mid 1850s, but stopped in the 1870s. When Stroud District Council stepped in to save it in 1987, they found workmen's ladders still in place, and tools lying where they'd been left on the ground. Indeed, paranormal groups often visit the mansion for its 'ghosts'.

No one really knows why the mansion was abandoned. Some think the owner, William Leigh, ran out of money, others that there was a murder on the building site, and the workmen refused to return.

Interior of Stanley Mill in Nailsworth

Perhaps the truth is more prosaic. One of William Leigh's descendants – a lady who has since died – revealed it was his doctor who'd warned him that building in that particular spot would lead to chest complaints as it was so damp. Today, the mansion is owned by a charitable trust that holds regular open days. Surrounding it is a secluded 400-acre park, with an abundance of wildlife and rare-breed cattle, owned by the National Trust. The grounds themselves are open, entry free, every day from 9am to dusk.

WOODCHESTER MANSION: Nymspfield, Stonehouse GL10 3TS; ☎01453 861541; www.woodchestermansion.org.uk. Entry: adults £5.50, concessions £4.50, children under 14 free; open 11am–5pm Easter to Oct, Sun and 1st Sat of month, bank holidays, including Mon; Sat/Sun in July/Aug.

🌂 Wet weather

In 1793, Gloucestershire archaeologist Samuel Lysons was working in the grounds of a church in Woodchester, near Stroud, when he unearthed a treasure: one of the largest and finest **Great Orpheus Roman Pavement** mosaics ever to be found in northern Europe. Made by skilled craftsmen in AD325 from 1,500,000 small stone tiles, it had once been the centre-piece of an enormous 64-room villa, belonging to an important Roman – possibly the Governor of Britain himself.

GREAT ORPHEUS ROMAN PAVEMENT: Prinknash Abbey, Gloucester GL4 8EX; ☎01452 812066; www.prinknashabbey. org. Entry: adults £3.50, children (12–18) £1.75; open Wed–Sun, 10am–4pm; on-site café and shop.

LOCAL KNOWLEDGE

Romantic novelist **Katie Fforde** used to work during the day in the kitchens of Stroud whole-food store Mother Nature, and scribble away in the evenings at home. That persistence paid off: readers loved her first novel, *Living Dangerously* (in which Stroud features heavily). You will recognise many other local features in her chart-busting books. She and her husband, Desmond, live in Rodborough, on the outskirts of Stroud.

Best view: To the left of Rodborough Fort (an 18th-century folly) on Rodborough Common. From there you can see the Severn, the Forest of Dean and, on very clear days, the Black Mountains and the Sugar Loaf. It is constantly inspiring.

Best-kept secret: The kneelers in St Mary's Church, Painswick, made by members of the congregation. All are different, individual and enchanting.

Favourite pub: I'm very fond of the Prince Albert just up the hill in Rodborough. In winter, I particularly like the Old Fleece along the A46 at Rooksmoor because of the open fires. And the Weighbridge Inn on the road from Nailsworth to Avening is good if you're very, very hungry; the cauliflower cheese is my favourite.

Best Cotswold ingredient: Asparagus, served with melted butter, which I buy in season from Stroud Farmers' Market or from Malcolm who's in The Shambles, a general market in Stroud, on a Friday and Saturday.

Best Cotswold read: Miss Read books; she's more Oxfordshire, but she evokes a lovely old-fashioned rural feeling.

Iconic Cotswolds village: I'm very fond of Woodchester with its church and two pubs. There's South and North Woodchester, though I never know which is which. One of the reasons they're lovely is because there's a lot of parkland with grazing animals.

Favourite restaurant: In Stroud, it would be HK House in Gloucester Street. If further afield, I'd recommend 5 North Street in Winchcombe, run by Gus Ashenford. I interviewed him while researching my novel, *Thyme Out* – it was fascinating to talk to someone so passionate about food.

CELEBRITY CONNECTIONS

Jilly Cooper is a well-loved part of the Stroud community. As well as campaigning for local causes, such as the fight to keep the town's maternity hospital up and running, she's given the Cotswolds a role in many of her novels. 'Riders *was a love affair with the Cotswolds – though, actually, if you read most of my books, the houses are findable because I need a geographical location,*' she says.

In 1982, Jilly and her husband Leo popped from London to Longleat to stay for the weekend with Alexander Bath. During lunch, a fellow guest happened to mention that a certain house in Bisley, a village near Stroud, was for sale. '*Leo went to look at it and came back very pale, saying, "Darling, it's the loveliest house I've ever seen"*' she recalls, '*so I went and looked too. When I discovered the train fare from Stroud to London was the same as a taxi from Putney to London, that settled it.*'

Since then, the house they bought – which was once a dormitory for a brotherhood of monks – has become their beloved home. Bisley, Jilly says, is a '*sweet, sweet village – an incredible village. I was so pleased when I heard it described as "vibrant". It's full of intellectuals and painters and sculptors, and everyone's incredibly kind. I adore the Cotswolds.*'

If you ask Jilly to name a favourite local place, she has no hesitation in recommending a visit to Woodchester Mansion near Nympsfield (www. woodchestermansion.org.uk). '*You should go in November at dusk; it's haunted beyond belief,*' she says. As for favourite people, there's one in particular she misses terribly: Laurie Lee, who died in 1997. '*He was the best companion, who used to regale me with anecdotes about literary people he knew. He was so funny. I remember he'd once been to a party and came back with a bag loaded with food. He offered it to me and I pulled out a bone. He'd eaten the chicken and put it back in the bag!*'

Although the original is no longer on display, it was meticulously recreated over 10 years by two brothers, Bob and John Woodward; their perfect replica is now on view at **Prinknash Abbey**. Covering more than 2,200sq ft, it shows pheasants, a hunting dog, an elephant, leopard and gryphon. Most wonderful of all is Orpheus who, according to Greek mythology, captivated the natural world with music from his lyre.

What to do with children...

Prinknash Bird and Deer Park is right next to the Orpheus Pavement, making a perfect family day out (though a bit of sunshine is ideal for a visit to the bird park). Peacocks and waterfowl provide a noisy welcome on the way to the Love Bird Aviary and the Golden Wood – full of golden pheasants – leading to the haunted Monks' Fish Pond, teeming with large fish. There's a two-storey Tudor Wendy house, a lake, many more birds, as well as surprisingly tame fallow deer. The Abbey shop and tearoom are on the same site.

Children will not only enjoy **Thistle-down Centre** in Nympsfield, they'll learn from it, too. This inspiring environmental centre, in a lovely Cotswold setting, is designed to help people understand more about the countryside and people's impact on it.

There's also fun to be had for free. Try the huge play area just off **Chalford** High Street (4 miles from Stroud on the A419), with picnic tables to eat at, and a river to splash in. It's the locals' best-kept secret (or rather, it was).

Stratford Park, a shortish walk from Stroud centre, has an on-site leisure centre (☎01453 766771) offering splash time and roller-skating on a Saturday (though double-check first in case the hall is being used for an event), and families come from miles around for the

The mysterious Woodchester Mansion

PRINKNASH BIRD AND DEER PARK: Cranham GL4 8EX; ☎01452 812727; www.prinknash-bird-and-deerpark.com. Entry: adults £5, seniors £4.50, children £3.50; bird food 25p per bag; open daily 10am–5pm summer, 10am–4pm winter.

play park. Younger children can feed the ducks; everyone can picnic. Stroud also has a **cinema** (www.apollocinemas.co.uk) and **bowling alley** (☎01453 762200). The Reverend Wilbert Awdry, creator of **Thomas the Tank Engine**, lived in Rodborough on the outskirts of Stroud, from 1965 until his death in 1997. He and Thomas are depicted in a stained-glass window at Rodborough Church.

For a real rural treat for older children (or younger, if they can keep still and quiet), there's **badger-watching** with

THISTLEDOWN CENTRE: Tinkley Lane, Nympsfield GL10 3UH; ☎01453 860420; www.thistledown.org.uk. Entry: adults £3.50, concessions £2.50, children £1.50; open daily, 10am–5.30pm.

Stroud expert Tony Dean (☎01453 750164) from the end of April to the beginning of September. It takes place in the evenings, and sessions last about an hour-and-a-half. It's free, but donations are welcome.

The Rodmarton Manor was built in the traditional style by the Cotswold Group of Craftsmen

✄ ... and how to avoid children

Do an **Arts and Crafts** trail around the area. In 1893, the architects Ernest Gimson and brothers Sidney and Ernest Barnsley moved to the Cotswolds with the intention of leading 'a simple life' and set up furniture workshops in **Sapperton**, between Stroud and Cirencester. Ernest Barnsley and the Cotswold Group of Craftsmen went on to build and furnish **Rodmarton Manor**, one of the last country houses to be built and furnished in the old traditional style, by hand using local materials. **Selsley Church** at Selsley near Stroud boasts the first ecclesiastical glass commission for William Morris & Co.

RODMARTON MANOR: Rodmarton GL7 6PF; ☎01285 841253; www.rodmarton-manor. co.uk. Entry: adults £7, children £3.50 (garden only £4/£1); open Easter Monday, then May–Sept, Wed/Sat.

Fit in a meal at the excellent **Bell at Sapperton** pub (GL7 6LE; ☎01285 760298) on the way, renowned for its use of local food. Find out more about Cotswold Arts and Crafts at www.artsandcraftsmuseum.org.uk. Two leaflets on walks taking in Arts and Crafts buildings on Minchinhampton and Rodborough Commons are available from the area's tourist information centres.

🎭 Entertainment

Special events

Stroud abounds with special events that highlight its culture and heritage. In May each year, the **Textile Festival** (www.stroudwatertextiles.org.uk) draws people from all over the world, while the June 'Site' arts festival includes an **Open Studios** trail, frequently with 100 or more artists inviting the public into their workplaces around the valleys (www.sva.org.uk). **Lynn Chadwick**, who died in 2003, was considered one of the greatest sculptors of the 20th century. He established a sculpture park at Lypiatt Park, his home near Stroud, which his son Daniel – also an artist – is hoping to open to the public in 2009 (visit www.lynnchadwick.com and www.pangolin-editions.com).

In July, **Stroud Show** in Stratford Park celebrates its rural, agricultural and industrial heritage. In fact, the town is set to become the festival capital of the south-west in September when music, walking, food and drink are combined within a new **Stroud Festival Fortnight**. More information is available from www.stroud2020.org.uk.

Writer and broadcaster Sue Limb is patron of **Nailsworth Festival**, which runs in April: a heady combination of art, literature, music and 'Nailstock' celebrating local bands (www.nailsworthfestival.org.uk).

The best way to see the Five Valleys is on foot. If you come in September, there's the exhausting but worthwhile fundraising 21-mile **Five Valleys Walk**, organised by the Meningitis Trust, on the last Sunday (www.meningitis-trust.org).

So far, so normal. But if you're looking for something a bit more quirky, you've come to exactly the right place. Here are some of the oddest customs to be found in this part of the world. **Bisley Well Dressing** ceremony began in 1863 to give thanks for Bisley's pure water. Nowadays, it's held on Ascension Day, and begins with a church service, after which there's a procession to the wells, accompanied by a brass band and led by pupils from Bisley Blue Coat School, carrying flowers; the two oldest boys and the two oldest girls wear 19th-century-style uniforms.

Local legends: the Bisley boy

Ever heard the tale about Elizabeth I really being a man? Just before he died, the Reverend Thomas Keble, vicar of Bisley, 5 miles east of Stroud, made a strange confession to his family. During building works at Overcourt in Bisley in 1870, an old stone coffin had been unearthed. Within it, Keble had discovered the body of a young girl, aged around 9, distinctively dressed in Tudor clothing. He immediately had his suspicions as to who this might be, so ordered that the remains be secretly reburied nearby to preserve anonymity. Those who knew the reverend – a most serious character – never doubted his story.

So why did the reverend think this could have been Elizabeth I? Well, in 1542, King Henry VIII went off to hunt at nearby Berkeley. Worried about the plague that was rife, he left his 9-year-old daughter, Elizabeth, at Overcourt, a one-time royal hunting lodge, believing her to be safer there. To the horror of her hosts, the little girl fell ill and died. Panic-stricken and fearful for their lives, there was but one solution: to substitute the village's red-haired boy of similar age for the dead child.

It's easy to pick holes in the legend, but there are strange anomalies which, to this day, remain unexplained. The Virgin Queen refused to marry – unheard of in her position; she was bald and wore a wig; and she decreed that, on her death, her body should remain unviolated by any post mortem... Dracula author Bram Stoker wrote more about the legend in his book *Famous Imposters*.

Randwick Wap, on the second Saturday in May, includes the dunking of the Wap Mayor in the village pond. Some say it all began 700 years ago when one of the workmen needed freshening up after imbibing a little too much ale. Others link it to a Saxon word 'Wappenshaw', when the men gathered to show they were ready for battle. **Painswick Clypping Ceremony**, held on Feast Sunday on or around September 19, derives from the Saxon word *ycleping* or 'embracing'. Children carrying nosegays join hands around the church to form a chain, while singing the Clypping Hymn during an open-air service. The custom dates back to 1321 and represents a re-dedication of the church.

🛒 Shopping

Stroud enjoys a well-earned reputation for its green principles, as well as an above-average number of individual traders. Try the **Made in Stroud** shop in Kendrick Street for interesting and ethically sourced goods (☎01453 758060; madeinstroud.org). The Friday and Saturday markets in The Shambles (with their 16th-century Market House) offer a variety of stalls, from food to DVDs.

A fascinating and unusual shop at Bisley, along the road to Cheltenham, on the site of Holbrook Garage (which sells a range of traditional and environmentally friendly fuels), **The Greenshop** only stocks what it believes to be true 'environmental products' and is full of advice on how to run a sustainable home. **Miserden Nursery** – 800ft up in the Cotswold hills – is based around the Edwardian glasshouses of Misarden Estate, and specialises in hardy perennials (GL6 7JA; ☎01285 821638). You can combine shopping here with a visit to the estate gardens (www.misardenpark.co.uk; open Tues–Thurs, 10am–4.30pm from April to the end September).

> THE GREENSHOP: Cheltenham Road, Bisley GL6 7BX; ☎01452 770629; www.greenshop.co.uk. Entry: open Mon–Fri 9am–7pm; Sat 9am–6pm; Sun and bank holidays 9.30am–1pm.

Shopping in Painswick is a pleasure, for similar reasons. The **Gloucestershire Guild of Craftsmen** gallery at the Painswick Centre in Bisley Street (☎01452 814745) is dedicated to promoting contemporary designer crafts; for fantastic woodware by Dennis French, visit **Painswick Woodcrafts** in New Street (☎01452 814195).

The best... **PLACES TO STAY**

BOUTIQUE

Cotswolds 88 Hotel

Kemps Lane, Painswick GL6 6YB
☎ 01452 813688
www.cotswolds88hotel.com

This is a cool, stylish boutique hotel in a traditional building; the 18th-century classical mansion is a spectacular example of a late Palladian house. Altered over many decades by a variety of architects, it combines delightfully crooked doors and windows with a very 21st-century interior. Despite the contemporary feel, a good old afternoon tea here is fantastic.

Price: £155 for a double (with full English).

HOTEL

The Bear of Rodborough Hotel

Rodborough Common, Stroud GL5 5DE
☎ 01453 878522
www.cotswold-inns-hotels.co.uk

The Bear stands surrounded by outstanding countryside, high above Stroud on Rodborough Common. Originally built in the 17th century, this former coaching inn provided a much appreciated resting-place on the coaching route from Gloucester to London. The building you see today was remodelled in 1925 in Arts & Crafts style.

Price: from £75/£120 single/double.

Burleigh Court Hotel

Burleigh, Minchinhampton GL5 2PF
☎ 01453 883804
www.burleighcourthotel.co.uk

If you think you've seen the best views already, you might have to think again after visiting Burleigh Court, which overlooks Stroud's Golden Valley. All of the bedrooms enjoy an outlook, either over the valley or the lovely grounds. Pets allowed in the Coach House rooms.

Price: from £85 for a single; £130 for a double.

Egypt Mill

Nailsworth GL6 0AE
☎ 01453 833449
www.egyptmill.com

The beauty of Egypt Mill lies in the fact that it's so unusual. It's been converted in a way that retains its corn-mill characteristics; and its setting on the edge of the Frome is full of charm: rusticity complemented by well-chosen antiques and furnishings. There's a good restaurant, too.

Price: from £80 for a single; £90 for a double.

INN

The Ragged Cot

Minchinhampton GL6 8PE
☎ 01453 884643
www.theraggedcot.co.uk

In spite of the fact that it's been beautifully done out, wellies, children and dogs are welcome – in fact, there are dog baskets dotted all over. The paint is Farrow & Ball, the atmosphere is friendly, and there's free quiche and biscuits for those peckish moments. The chef gets rave reviews too.

Price: from £75 for a single; £90 for a double.

B&B

Cardynham House

The Cross, Painswick GL6 6XX
☎ 01452 814006
www.cardynham.co.uk

Cardynham House is a 15th–16th-century Grade II* listed house with a wealth of character, each room decorated in a style of its own. Bedrooms have a four-poster or half-tester bed and an en suite bathroom. There's also a bistro for lunch and dinner (not Mondays). There is a pool exclusively for guests.

Price: from £55/£70 single/double.

The best... FOOD AND DRINK

▶ Staying in

Award-winning **Stroud Farmers' Market**, every Saturday in the Cornhill market place from 9am to 2pm, is the best way of sourcing and meeting tip-top local producers. There are between 45 and 50 stalls each week, an excellent café, and take-away food using local produce. Look out particularly for cheese from **Birdwood Farmhouse**, Minchinhampton, and **Godsell's Church Farm** cheese, Leonard Stanley; also pork from **Forager Free Range** who keep their rare-breed pigs in the Woodchester Valley, organic veg from **Stroud Slad Farm Community,** and mulling syrup, chutneys, mustards, syrups and preserves from **Selsley Herb & Spice Company**.

Frocester Fayre at Church Farm Frocester (GL10 3TJ, ☎01453 822054, www.frocesterfayre.co.uk) sells Severn Vale farm-fresh pork, beef and lamb as well as homemade ready-to-eat meals.

Many local food shops have earned a reputation for quality. In Painswick, there's **Olivas Delicatessen** (Friday Street, GL6 6QJ, ☎01452 814774); while in Minchinhampton, it's traditional butcher **Taylor & Sons** (The Cross, West End, GL6 9JA, ☎01453 882163) which draws shoppers from miles around for its friendly service and excellent-quality meat.

'Outstanding' is the only word that can be used for two Nailsworth food shops in particular. The town's mayor was astonished when he picked up visiting MP Jack Straw from Stroud Station once. The Labour stalwart told him, '*I must stop by William's Kitchen*'. The fame of this fish shop and delicatessen has even reached the capital. It's still run by William Beeston but is now known as **William's Fish Market and Food Hall** (3, Fountain Street, ☎01453 832240); it also has a superb oyster bar, Monday to Saturday, from opening time until 4pm weekdays, 3pm Saturday.

One of Rick Stein's 'Super Heroes,' **Hobbs House Bakery** (4, George Street, Nailsworth GL6 0AG; ☎01453 839396) is another food emporium whose fame has spread. Tom Herbert is a fifth generation baker: his family has been baking in Gloucestershire for over 100 years. His secret? '*We use time where others use chemicals and improvers,*' he says. '*In fact, a lot of older people tell us, "This is how bread used to be!"*' There's a great café, too.

If you see any **Cotswold Handmade Meringues** for sale, grab them (gently) for pudding. They're made in Nailsworth according to a secret family recipe, and sold in food shops throughout the area. **Kitchen Garden**, based in Stroud, has also come a long way since Barbara Moinet cooked up her first batch of blackberry and apple jam in her kitchen at home. The company's excellent jams, chutneys, marmalades and condiments are still made carefully by hand in open pans in small batches and sold in independent shops. You can find many other excellent producers at **Nailsworth Farmers' Market** on the fourth Saturday morning of each month.

EATING OUT

FINE DINING

Stonehouse Court Hotel
Bristol Road, Stonehouse GL10 3RA
☎ 0871 871 3240
www.stonehousecourt.co.uk

Awarded two AA Rosettes, Henry's restaurant is named after the vengeful ghost of a murderous butler. The food at 'his' restaurant is relaxed, stylish and contemporary: modern European with eastern influences; dinner around £30. If it's on the menu, the roast rack of Forest of Dean lamb is the ticket.

RESTAURANTS

HK House
12a Russell Street, Stroud GL5 3AB
☎ 01453 768833

Food writer and television personality Matthew Fort (who lives near Stroud) is a fan of this Chinese restaurant which offers excellent friendly service alongside a range of quality dishes. Meals are around £22 per head.

Oldstone Restaurant
3, Old Market, Nailsworth GL6 0DU
☎ 01453 832808

This warm, intimate restaurant is full of character. Dinner: Tuesday to Saturday from 7pm and the fixed-price two or three course menu (around £26) changes twice weekly.

St Michael's Restaurant and B&B
Victoria Street, Painswick GL6 6QA
☎ 01452 814555
www.stmickshouse.co.uk

Owners Matt and Magda use the best of the Cotswolds in their meals by sourcing their produce from first-class farms, bakeries and market gardens, including Butts Farm in Cirencester, and Hobbs House Bakery in Nailsworth; set price menu from £28.

The Woolpack Inn
Slad GL6 7QA; ☎ 01452 813429
www.woolpackslad.com

Laurie Lee was once a regular fixture and it is beloved by locals for its real ale and fearsomely good food. Three courses cost around £22. Don't miss the sweetbreads with mustard and caper sauce.

CAFÉ

Mills Café
Witheys Yard, High Street,
Stroud GL5 1AS; ☎ 01453 759880

Café culture is very much alive in Stroud, and there's an eclectic choice of venue. A great place to gossip the day away is Mills Café. John and Maggie Mills were inspired to open by the fine coffees and home-cooked food they found in continental Europe.

EAT IN/TAKEAWAY

The Passage to India
Old Market, Nailsworth GL6 0DU
☎ 01453 834063
www.thepassagetoindia.com

Award-winning tandoori restaurant and take-away which serves a wide variety of traditional, authentic Indian cuisine. High standards of food and service with traditional dishes, such as a murgh jafrani – chicken with tomato and tamarind – for around £11.

⊡ Drinking

Nailsworth Brewery uses water drawn from its own spring to brew ales of quality, distinction and flavour (☎07878 448377; www.nailsworth-brewery.co.uk). And there's **Stroud Brewery**, an award-winning craft brewery using whole hops and malting barley grown on the Cotswolds (☎07891 995878; www.stroudbrewery.co.uk).

In the non-alcoholic department, **Bottle Green**, known nationally for its elderflower pressé in particular, runs from an old mill in South Woodchester. When the company began in 1989, they used flowers from the hedgerows all around Stroud. You'll find the ales in local pubs, and the pressé almost everywhere you go. Just ask for them!

The annual **Frocester Beer Festival** is run in conjunction with the outstanding Frocester Cricket Club in Frocester, near Stonehouse, every August bank holiday weekend (www.dursleylions.org/frocesterbeerfestival.htm). (And do watch a summer cricket match, too.) Because there are good breweries around, pubs take their local ales seriously. Possibly the highest pub in the area is **The Rose and Crown** at Nympsfield (GL10 3TU; ☎01453 860240), between Stroud and Dursley. You can admire views over the Severn while enjoying traditional draught ales. **The Kings Head** in France Lynch (GL6 8LT; ☎01453 882225) and **The Lamb Inn** at Eastcombe (GL6 7DN; ☎01452 770261) are both delightful village pubs.

The Black Horse at Amberley (GL5 5AL; ☎01453 872556) also offers views that are so good, you'll be in danger of forgetting the pint you came here for; and **The George Inn at Newmarket** outside Nailsworth is well thought of (GL6 0RF; ☎01453 833228), as is the **Crown Inn at Frampton Mansell** (GL6 8JG; ☎01285 760601). If you're keen on history, visit **The Falcon Inn** in New Street Painswick (GL6 6UN; ☎01452 814222): the world's oldest bowling green, which dates from 1554, is in the grounds of this pub where the first floor was once the court house for the region. In the Civil War, cannon balls were fired at the church from the inn – you can still see the marks where they hit. And underneath the Falcon there were pits where cock fighting went on.

ⓘ Visitor Information

Tourist information centres:
Stroud Tourist Information Centre, The Subscription Rooms, George Street, Stroud GL5 1AE, ☎01453 760960, www.cotswolds.com, www.visitthecotswolds.org.uk, open Mon–Sat 10am–5pm; Nailsworth Town Information Centre, 4 The Old George, Fountain Street, Nailsworth GL6 0BL, ☎01453 839222, www.nailsworthtown.co.uk, open Mon–Fri 9.30am–5pm (5.30pm in summer), and Sat 9.30am–1pm.

Hospitals: Stroud General Hospital, Trinity Road, Stroud GL5 2HY, ☎01453 562200; Cirencester Hospital, Tetbury Road, Cirencester GL7 1UY, ☎01285 655711; (both 24-hr A&E).

Supermarkets include: Tesco, Stratford Road, Stroud, GL5 4AG, ☎0845 6779633; Waitrose, London Road, Stroud GL5 2AP, ☎01453 757067; Sainsbury's, Dudbridge Road, Stroud GL5 3HG, ☎01453 755749; Somerfield, George Street, Nailsworth GL6 0AG, ☎01453 833499.

Sports: Stratford Park Leisure Centre, Stratford Road, Stroud GL5 4AF, ☎01453 766771, www.leisurecentre.com; Burnt Ash Farm Riding Stables, Minchinhampton, ☎01453 882266, www.burntashfarm.co.uk; Camp Riding Centre near Stroud, ☎01285 821219, www.campridingcentre.co.uk; Cotswold Gliding Club, Aston Down Airfield, Minchinhampton, ☎01285 760415, www.cotswoldgliding.co.uk; The Bristol and Gloucestershire Gliding Club, Nympsfield GL10 3TX, ☎01453 860342, www.bggc.co.uk; Ballooning in the Cotswolds, ☎01285 885848, www.ballooninginthecotswolds.co.uk.

Bike rental: Slimbridge Boat Station, Shepherds Patch, Slimbridge GL2 7BP, ☎01453 899190; Stonehouse Accessories Ltd, 18 High Street, Stonehouse GL10 2NA, ☎01453 822881 (24 hours' notice required).

Taxis include: A & A Taxis Stroud Ltd in Station Road GL5 3AP, ☎01453 767777.

DURSLEY, WOTTON AND THE VALE OF BERKELEY

Visitors to Gloucestershire often feel they're getting the true 'Cotswold' experience amongst the chocolate-box hamlets of the north. Yet where those honey-stone cottages give way to half-timber and brick houses, you'll find a grittier reality. The very fact that Dursley, Wotton and Berkeley aren't quite so mind-numbingly stunning has, oddly, protected them in many ways. House prices in these areas have climbed in recent years, but they're not as steep as elsewhere in the Cotswolds. As a result, the streets are still full of families who can trace their roots back generations. But don't for one moment think you're entering a land of backwaters. Dursley, Wotton and Berkeley are thriving towns, with character, heritage and strong community spirit. What's more, there's so much going on: bustling high streets, festivals, fascinating snippets of history, and an above-average number of attractions well worth visiting, particularly for children: the magnificent Berkeley Castle; the Jenner Museum commemorating Dr Edward Jenner who helped eradicate smallpox; and, of course, Slimbridge, where the Wildfowl & Wetlands Trust runs its magnificent bird sanctuary.

Purists will inform you that the Vale of Berkeley is not the Cotswolds. There's a distinction between the wold and the vale – the rise of the Cotswold escarpment and the flat lands that border the Severn. But they are neighbourly areas that are inextricably linked. And if you're keen to taste all that the region has to offer, you can't miss out on the salt-marsh lamb grazed on the unique and fertile fields that are lost under the river waters for a period each winter.

WHAT TO SEE AND DO

Dursley

Ever heard of those lost years when no one knows what **William Shakespeare** was up to? Well, rumour claims the answer lies in Dursley. After leaving school, so the story goes, young Will got into serious trouble, poaching deer in Charlecote Park, near Stratford. Fearing prosecution, he made himself scarce – in Dursley of all places – where he's reputed to have taught in a local school. Certainly, the area is knowledgeably mentioned in *Richard II*, where Berkeley Castle crops up as 'the castle by yon tuft of trees', which indicates he might have spent time here. Moreover, *A Midsummer Night's Dream* was written for the Berkeley family and first performed here.

Other writers are more securely associated with the town, such as **Evelyn Waugh**, who lived in Piers Court in nearby Stinchcombe, and JK Rowling, who grew up in Yate, half an hour's drive away. She, of course, named a whole family after the town (though probably the less said about that the better).

Berkeley Castle, where Edward II met his death

It's well worth popping into Dursley, which nestles just below the Cotswold edge, to have a look round. The Market House, with its statue of Queen Anne, is dated 1738, and the upper part is supported by pillars and has a bell turret. By contrast, the town also boasts a modern sports centre with a pool ideal for children (☎01453 546441). Dursley was the one-time home of Mikael Pedersen, the Danish inventor of the famed 19th-century Pederson bike (see www.dursley-pedersen.net). On the contemporary side, the delightful curate of St James the Great (the parish church), Skye Denno, wears a dog collar and a nose ring.

You'll probably find much of your enjoyment in the vicinity of Dursley. North-west, there's **Stinchcombe Hill**, with its views along the escarpment towards the Severn. There have been longstanding rumours that Hugh Grant has bought a house round here but it turns out he just loves the golf club (☎01453 542015; www. stinchcombehillgolfclub.com).

What makes the area internationally famous, however, is **'Slimbridge': The Wildfowl & Wetlands Trust**. Ducks, geese, swans and flamingos are among the sights in store at this wildfowl haven, created in 1946 by the artist and conservationist, the late Sir Peter Scott. It's particularly known for the annual arrival from arctic Russia of Bewick's swans. Soon after visiting the area in 1945, the Scotts realised they could identify Bewick's swans individually

THE WWT SLIMBRIDGE WETLAND CENTRE: Slimbridge GL2 7BT; ☎01453 891900; www.wwt.org.uk. Entry: adults £7.95, children £4.35, family £22.15, plus concessions; open every day, year round.

Carlos and Fernando, those pretty flamingos

Gloucestershire is a forward-thinking area, where civil partnerships are accepted in every walk of life... and in every waddle, too, as Carlos and Fernando go to prove. True emblems of pink power, the Slimbridge flamingos formed a same-sex partnership in 2001; but that wasn't enough for the love birds who desperately wanted to start a family together. They began by stealing eggs from fellow flamingos at the Wildfowl & Wetlands Trust. Despite the illegal nature of these adoptions, the authorities were impressed with Carlos and Fernando's sitting and hatching skills. So when a nest was abandoned in 2006, they were chosen as the perfect foster parents.

The 'orphan' egg found in the nest was first put in an incubator, where a healthy chick hatched. But an important part of the process would have been missing had the chick simply been handed over to its new family, because bonding begins when the chicks 'call' from inside the egg. So Slimbridge staff placed the chick in an old eggshell, which they taped up, before returning it to Carlos and Fernando's nest. The ruse worked a treat, and the happy family took to each other like – well, ducks to water.

by their bill patterns. If you want to see precisely how hard it is, there's a chart of hundreds of different bill patterns in the main building, each belonging to real one-time 'visitors' such as Emu, Y-Front, Fuddle and Handel. The centre is dedicated to preserving wetlands and their wildlife, and borders the banks of the Severn; there's an excellent visitor centre and restaurant, a wet-activity 'Welly Boot Land' for children, plus lots of exciting events, such as canoe safaris and downy duckling days.

Flamingos caring for an egg at the Wildfowl & Wetlands Trust

Uley

If you're keen on deeper, darker pursuits (and there's a literal element to this), then Hetty Pegler's Tump – 3.5 miles north-east of Dursley on the B4066 – is calling to you. Its proper title is **Uley Tumulus,** a late Stone Age (Neolithic) burial mound, dating from about 3000BC. During 19th-century excavations, a total of 23 skeletons were found here. It is fairly deep and dark – take a torch; generally, you can take a look inside, for free, all year round, though due to ongoing conservation work, the chamber may not be open at all times (☎0117 9750700; www.english-heritage.org.uk). (And by the way, Hetty was not, of course, a cavewoman, but the 17th-century owner of the field, along with husband Henry.) There's also an Iron Age hill fort, **Uley Bury,** with wonderful views of the Severn Vale, 750ft up on a spur of the Cotswold escarpment just outside Uley; while **Nympsfield Long Barrow** is nearby, 1 mile north-east of Nympsfield on the B4066. Because the mound is missing, you can see its internal burial chambers, where Bronze Age artefacts and Roman pottery have been found. There's a picnic area next door with the most stunning views over towards the Brecon Beacons.

Just over half a mile's walk from the centre of Uley, along Fiery Lane, is **Owlpen Manor** often described as the loveliest house in England. Bathed in romance, it has nestled among the bluebell woods of Uley since Tudor times. Some visit to see one of the finest examples of Arts and Crafts architecture: the house was restored by Norman Jewson in 1926 after an abandonment of 100 years. Others come to admire the unique painted cloth wall-hangings of the Great Chamber,

> OWLPEN MANOR: near Uley GL11 5BZ;
> ☎01453 860261 (estate) or 860816 (restaurant); www.owlpen.com
> Entry: adults £5.50, children £2.50, family £15.25; open from beginning of May to end Sept, Tues, Thurs, Sun (no bank holiday opening), restaurant and gardens 12 noon–5pm, house 2–5pm (last admission 4.30pm).

showing scenes from the life of Joseph and his brothers, which date back over 300 years. And though not everyone would admit to it, many are hoping for a haunting glance of the ghost of Queen Margaret of Anjou, wife of Henry VI, who stayed at Owlpen in 1471. It was her last happy night before an ignominious defeat at the Battle of Tewkesbury. Owners Karin Mander and her husband, Nicholas, have lived at the manor since 1974. Their family of five children are thought to be the first to have been born and raised in the manor house since the early 18th century.

In this area, there's plenty of beauty to be enjoyed for free. Mike Barton is in charge of 470 miles of footpaths in the South Cotswolds on behalf of Gloucestershire County Council. Recently, he completed the nine-month

Owlpen Manor in Uley is often described as 'the loveliest house in England'

task of walking every single one. '*I think my favourite stretches have to be in Kingscote and Ozleworth,*' he says. '*They're beautiful areas: you can hear the birds singing; you've got the valleys rising up on either side; and in Kingscote, particularly, there's a lovely wooded area that gives you about an hour's circular walk.*'

To experience some of that peace and rurality, you can't do better than to visit atmospheric **Newark Park** in Ozleworth, a Tudor hunting lodge on the edge of a 40ft cliff, with outstanding tumbling views of rocks, streams and trees. It was later converted into a fashionable Georgian country house; an eclectic art collection can be viewed inside, while outdoors there's a romantic garden with countryside walks.

Wotton-under-Edge

Almost halfway between Dursley and Wotton is North Nibley, with its 111ft tall **Tyndale Monument** in honour of William Tyndale, an early translator of the Bible. It's thought his birthplace was at Hunts Court in the village. Poor William suffered for his efforts – he was martyred at just 46 years of age in 1536. But his legacy was a Bible in English to improve the mental and spiritual health of the common people, and the tallest of monuments to test their physical prowess. There are lovely walks around the monument and you can enjoy spectacular views from the top. There's a notice board at the bottom of the lane with details of where to get a key.

From there, it's a lovely walk, past the Brackenbury Ditches Iron Age hill fort, to one of the most charming towns of all. Tucked under the Cotswold escarpment and surrounded by rolling hills lies Wotton-under-Edge. You can buy just about everything you need within its shops, the majority of which are individual and thriving.

Wotton's Heritage Centre charts the town's history back to Saxon times – the parish church of St Mary was established around 940AD; the organ here is said to have been played by Handel. And Sir Isaac Pitman, the inventor of shorthand, lived in a side road off Long Street. Overseas visitors often make a special trip to trace family trees, to access the

NEWARK PARK: Ozleworth, Wotton-under-Edge GL12 7PZ; ☎ 01453 842644/01793 817666 (infoline); www.nationaltrust.org.uk/newarkpark. Entry: adults £5, children £2.50, family £13; restricted opening (consult website) but generally open Wed/Thurs, Apr to Oct plus weekends Jun to Oct, 11am–5pm.

Newark Park, a Tudor hunting lodge on the edge of a cliff in Ozleworth

THE HERITAGE CENTRE: The Chipping, Wotton-under-Edge GL12 7AD; ☎ 01453 521541; www.wottonheritage.com Entry: open 10am–4pm/5pm (closed 1–2pm), winter/summer, Tues–Fri, and 10am–1pm Saturday; also open throughout the year on the first Sunday in the month 2.30–5pm.

centre's collection of photographs and postcards, or to buy the intriguing leaflets which include 'Wotton's Cruel Vicar' and 'Lord Leycester's Legacy'.

Another particularly beautiful and charitable reminder of the past is still visible in the form of **almshouses**, some of which were founded in the 17th century by merchant Hugh Perry, native of the town, and Alderman and Sheriff of the City of London.

Local legends: most haunted – the Ancient Ram Inn

The Ancient Ram Inn in Wotton-under-Edge is reputed to be the most haunted house in Britain. There are photographs of wispy smoke hovering over rooms; of a column of cloudiness descending the stairs; even a grandfather clock with the face of Richard Waite, a former innkeeper, strangely reflected in the glass.

Mediums claim to have communicated with spirits whose tales of woe alone send shivers down the spine. There's innkeeper's daughter, Nora, murdered in the weavers' attic in the 16th century; and a woman named Elizabeth and a ghostly Cavalier who also met violent deaths.

Dating back to the 1100s, this Grade II* listed house was built as an early community centre, and went on to accommodate the stonemasons who constructed nearby St Mary's Church. Wattle and daub – cow dung and twigs – make up the ancient walls; and there are beams still marked with the Roman numerals which helped the builders piece them together. John Humphries bought the inn from a brewery 40 years ago. Almost as soon as he moved in, he says, he started to feel presences. Upstairs is the most haunted part of all – the Bishop's Room, once reserved for visits from the Bishop of Worcester. Ghost hunters queue up to spend the night here where beds have been reported to rise off the floor, strange winds rip pictures off the walls, and where evidence of witchcraft was found amongst the stones of the chimney breast.

John has got various theories as to why it's so haunted. *'There are two ley lines that cross here,'* he says. *'One runs from here under the church tower and carries on past Hetty Pegler's Tump and Gloucester Cathedral; the other comes from London and goes into Wales. It's believed that ghosts and spirits travel up ley lines.'* His main battle today, however, is not with ethereal spirits; it's with saving this historic building. Money from tours – which must be booked in advance – go into the restoration fund. He can be contacted on 01453 842598 or at www.theancientraminn.com.

A drive round the area is definitely in order, visiting villages such as **Kingswood,** once the site of an important Cistercian abbey, **Hillesley**, **Wortley**, and **Alderley**, where the grange was home to the diarist **James Lees-Milne** – his writings provide an entertaining alternative glimpse of Gloucestershire.

Berkeley

Cross the M5 and venture nearer the Severn and you'll find the ancient town of Berkeley sitting on a hill, surrounded by the marshy river's flood plain. It was once a busy port, loading and unloading coal and timber from the Forest of Dean, wool and cloth from the mills, as well as wine, cider, oil, salt and cheese. A group of 17th-century emigrants from the town founded Berkeley in California.

The churchyard contains a monument to the last court jester in England, who died in 1728 after falling from **Berkeley Castle**'s minstrels' gallery. Rumour has it

The interior of Berkeley Castle

that he was pushed, possibly because of bad jokes. If so, at least he finished on an outstanding punch line.

Of course, Berkeley's greatest claim to fame is that same castle. Notorious for the brutal murder of Edward II (who's reputed to scream in September on the anniversary of his fascinatingly unpleasant death) but admired for its beauty, this castle, with its terraced Elizabethan gardens, butterfly house, and the famous Berkeley silver, has been the family home to 24 generations of Berkeleys. There are some excellent events throughout the year, from banquets to ghost hunts; Berkeley Agricultural Show each August, and the Castle by Candlelight in December.

BERKELEY CASTLE: Berkeley GL13 9BQ; ☎01453 810332; www.berkeley-castle.com Entry: adults £7.50, children £4.50, seniors £6, family £21 for entry to castle, gardens and butterfly house; open Mar to Oct, every Sunday and all bank holiday weekends 11am–5.30pm, and 7 days/week July/Aug; see website.

Charles Berkeley is heir to the castle. '*I particularly enjoy the weekend events we stage at the castle, such as the Civil War re-enactment with The Sealed Knot Society,*' he says. '*The Sealed Knot visited when my brother and I were 11 and 12. You could see the look on the soldiers' faces as they were storming the castle; you could feel the anger among the Parliamentarian troops. I remember my mother reassuring me at the time: "Don't worry; they're not really going to blow up the castle!"*'

🌂 Wet weather

A short walk from the castle is the **Edward Jenner Museum & Conference Centre**, dedicated to the memory of Edward Jenner who discovered a vaccination against smallpox. Children are fascinated by diseases and this is well thought out – one of those museums you approach thinking, 'Shall we bother?' and leave saying 'Glad we did'.

Jenner noticed that milkmaids who caught cowpox – not a particularly serious illness – never caught smallpox, which was one of the killers of the age. With brilliant insight, he took infected material from Sarah Nelmes, a milkmaid suffering from cowpox, and scratched it into the skin of James Phipps, his gardener's son. As soon as James recovered, Jenner tried to give him smallpox: the boy was immune. Thanks to Jenner, smallpox is the only human infectious disease to have been completely eradicated. The museum is set in the Georgian house and gardens where he lived for 38 years.

> EDWARD JENNER MUSEUM & CONFERENCE CENTRE: The Chantry, Church Lane, Berkeley GL13 9BN; ☎01453 810631; www.jennermuseum.com. Entry: adults £4.25, concessions £3.50, children £2.50, family £10.75; joint value ticket available for Berkeley Castle; open Apr to Sept, Tues–Sat 12.30–5.30pm, Sun 1–5.30pm; open 7 days July/Aug; Oct, open Sun only 1–5.30pm, plus bank holidays 12.30–5.30pm.

The Jenner museum, dedicated to the memory of Edward Jenner

What to do with children...

Local children will tell you one of their favourite days out is **Cattle Country** in Berkeley. It's pretty popular with adults, too, who, in fear and trembling, dare each other to try the infamously high (but perfectly safe) drop slide. Best known for its indoor and outdoor play equipment, Cattle Country has a whole range of things to do; there's also a café and restaurant.

But if you're after something unique, then head to Purton for a majestic and moving sight: the old ships' graveyard. Kids (of all ages) will be enthralled by the **Purton Hulks** that lie, like half-buried dinosaurs, their skeletons bleached and weathered. These are old boats – the Severn trows that once plied their trade along the river, schooners, barges and lighters – telling a story that delights interested sightseers and naval historians alike. They first began to be left here in 1909 when the canal was rebuilt after storm damage; unwanted vessels were used as a protection against the tides eroding the bank. Paul Barnett (barnadillo@aol.com) is in the process of researching the history of these craft; he also leads fascinating guided tours.

The old ships' graveyard, Purton Hulks

CATTLE COUNTRY ADVENTURE PARK: Berkeley Heath Farm, Berkeley GL13 9EW; ☎ 01453 810510. Entry: £7.50 for all; seniors £5; children under 3 free; open every weekend and all public and Gloucestershire school holidays.

Wotton Auction Rooms

✉ ... and how to avoid children

If you'd like to bag your own bit of history, your best bet is at the **Wotton Auction Rooms**, which holds regular Tuesday and Wednesday sales each month, but do check the website (www.wottonauctionrooms.co.uk). Writer Sue Limb, who lives nearby, is a big fan: 'Country people, history, ancient furniture, past lives, woodworm, paintings of dogs and horses, splendid old threadbare carpets, silver glinting dimly, all in an old church on a sunlit hill,' is how she describes the experience.

⚡ Entertainment

The **Lister Tyndale Steam Rally** (www.lister-tyndale-steam-rally.co.uk) takes place each June in the grounds of Berkeley Castle, and it's a great chance to see steam-powered vehicles, classic cars and all sorts of demonstrations.

The arts are particularly strong in Wotton-under-Edge – and that's not just because renowned poet U A Fan-thorpe and her partner Dr Rosie Bailey are enthusiastic residents. The well-supported Wotton Arts Project (www.undertheedgearts.org.uk) organises events for adults and children. There's also a community cinema, the Electric Picture House in Market Street, with a regular programme (see www.wottoneph.co.uk). Dursley has a world-famous male voice choir, which performs all over the area as well as further afield. It's a must if you're into music (see www.dursleymalechoir.org.uk). Other events include the **Nibley Music Festival** at North Nibley (www.nibleyfestival. co.uk) and Dursley Town Festival (www.dursleytownfestival.co.uk), both in July.

The best... **PLACES TO STAY**

HOTEL

Thornbury Castle Hotel

Thornbury BS35 1HH; ☎ 01454 281182
www.thornburycastle.co.uk

This 500-year-old palace once accommodated Henry VIII and Anne Boleyn. Today, Thornbury Castle, with its beautiful oriel windows, Tudor hall and historic parkland, is a luxury hotel, which even produces its own wine from a vineyard as old as the walls that surround it.

Price: from £150/£190, single/double.

Tortworth Court Four Pillars Hotel

Tortworth Wotton-under-Edge GL12 8HH
☎ 01454 263000
tortworth-court-hotel.four-pillars.co.uk

Tortworth Court has been wonderfully restored after a fire in 1991: you can still enjoy the house's character through the impressive wooden staircase, the library, the panelling, the fireplaces and, especially, the stunning grounds; plus there's a leisure club with pool and an excellent restaurant.

Price: double rooms from £75.

B&B

7 Prospect Place

Off May Lane, Dursley GL11 4JL
☎ 01453 543445
www.dursleybedandbreakfast.co.uk

This B&B is in a listed terrace, an original building of old Dursley. The accommodation offers one double bedroom, one twin and one single room. Breakfasts are cooked on an Aga using local farm products, and the marmalade and jams are homemade. Right on the Cotswold Way, it's perfect for walkers. Children are welcome but the stairs are steep.

Price: £28 per person per night.

SELF-CATERING

Owlpen Manor Estate Holiday Cottages

Near Uley GL11 5BZ; ☎ 01453 860261
www.owlpen.com

Marlings End and Woodwells are traditional weaver's and keeper's cottages, sleeping five or six. Grist Mill is a watermill of 1728 with a cupola which sleeps eight. The Court House is a gabled banqueting house of 1620, sleeping up to five. Manor Farm sleeps four, and Over Court sleeps five, while Peter's Nest, Summerfield and Tithe Barn are romantic retreats for two.

Price: from £295.

Stouts Hill Cotswold Holiday Resort

Uley GL11 5BT; ☎ 01453 860134
www.stoutshill.co.uk

This country house holiday resort is housed in a castellated Strawberry Hill Gothic mansion, sympathetically restored, within a 27 acre parkland setting. In addition to general lets, there are special interest stays – fishing, rambling, golf and bird-watching. The luxury apartments are one bedroom (sleeping four) or two bedroom (sleeping six). (Incidentally, this was once a prep school where Stephen Fry was a pupil.)

Price: from £295 for a week.

Ormond House

13 Bull Pitch, Dursley GL11 4NG
☎ 01453 545312

There's a self-contained annexe – the Garden Flat – in this Grade II listed town house, which provides excellent accommodation for two (or, at a push, three). Children are welcome.

Price: from £28 per person per night.

The best... FOOD AND DRINK

There's a particular speciality of this region that's rare indeed: **salt-marsh lamb**. You might never have heard of such a thing, but that's because this is a delicacy that's not readily available in England. One of the few places it can be produced is down by the River Severn where the marshes have never been touched – neither ploughed nor fertilised.

▶ Staying in

Every spring, father-and-son team John and Jamie Cullimore wait for the waters of the great River Severn to recede from their low-lying land in Slimbridge to reveal the salt marshes – those transitional areas between land and water that you find along the inter-tidal shores of estuaries. The grasses that grow on these ancient marshes are not like others – wild aromatic grasses that established themselves many hundreds of years ago, without the help of human hand. '*The sheep and the cattle love being on there*,' Jamie Cullimore says. '*Given the choice between grazing there or on normal ground, they'll go for the salt marshes every time*.'

Scientists would tell you that the salty waters keep the grazing animals healthy by destroying harmful bacteria and parasitic worms. The grasses have to be hardy to survive the extreme conditions they find themselves in, and even the beetles and the snails that thrive are an unusual collection. Jamie's specialism lies not in the science, but in the practical advantages these rare lands have to offer. '*Meat from animals grazed around here has a unique flavour*,' he says. '*People who've never tried it before often ask if the meat is salty. Strangely, it isn't at all – in fact, it's sweet. The beef is absolutely excellent, but it's the lamb that people comment on most*.'

Cullimores Organics farm shop at New House Farm, Ryalls Lane, Cambridge, is open Fridays 2–6pm and Saturdays 9am–1pm, or by appointment on ☎01453 890747. Or you can catch them every Friday at Gloucester Farmers' Market, where they also cook their own burgers.

Another ethical farm is **Adey's** down at Breadstone near Berkeley. Organic beef, lamb, pork, bacon, gammon, sausages and occasionally goose and chicken are sold directly from the farm (☎01453 511218) or, among other places, at Stroud Farmers' Market every Saturday. '*Here, the pigs have freedom*,' explain farmers Caroline and Tim Wilson. '*As well as their arks, each family has an eighth of an acre, with room to root and run about.... The babies are able to get under the wires, so they join up together and scout around the whole field. It probably means they mature more slowly because they spend their time charging around in a gang... But then they each go back to their mum to suckle*.'

Other great producers include cheese from **Wick Court** (☎01452 740117), a farm on the banks of the Severn at Arlingham; organic beef and honey from **Whitfield Farm** in the Berkeley Vale (☎01454 261010); organic vegetables (particularly potatoes) and eggs from rare breed hens from **Newark Farm**, 600ft above sea level, at Ozleworth (☎01453 842144), all of which you'll also find at Stroud Farmers' Market.

Dursley has its own farmers' market on the second Saturday of the month, 9am–1pm, held under the historic town hall. Look out for cheese from **Wharf Farm Dairy** (☎01453 890383) and **Old Isaacs** homemade preserves (☎01452 740401).

You'll also find some superb local food shops in the district. **Relish** is a popular delicatessen (with moreish flapjacks), and **AC Partners,** a good traditional butcher, both in Wotton's Long Street; while there are excellent farm shops, such as **Wotton Farm Shop** (GL12 7DT; ☎01453 521546) owned and run by the Grimes family, who have lived in and around the town for many generations; and **Puddleditch**, famous for homemade cakes, jam and chutney, in the Vale of Berkeley (GL13 9EU; ☎01453 810816). **Tortworth Estate Farm Shop** (GL12 8HF; ☎01454 261633) is universally praised for its huge variety and quality of stock. To enjoy all this fare al fresco, then head for **Coaley Peak Picnic Site,** four miles south-west of Stroud on the B4066 to Uley, with its picnic tables and panoramic views over the Severn Vale.

🍺 Drinking

Uley Brewery (www.uleybrewery.com) is well known for brewing beer with personality – and that's probably because of the personalities that brew those same beers. Refounded by Chas Wright in 1984, Uley uses traditional methods dating back to the 17th century to produce its famous pints. One of the most important elements of the taste is the spring water used, which runs underneath the site. The most famous brew – Old Spot – could well not be in existence now, if it wasn't for an accident of fate. The brewery was approached to do a special beer for Frocester Beer Festival ('*I was told by a colleague that Old Spot was a stupid name for a beer*,' says Charles, of this now legendary title.) As a one-off brew, no-one bothered much about specific measurements. So when it won a surprise first prize at the Great Western Festival in Bristol, there were many furrowed brows in Uley, as they tried to remember exactly how to produce some more. They succeeded and the rest, as they say, is brewing history. *'God preserve us from blandness!'* is Chas Wright's motto. *'And God bless all our drinkers!'*

There are other good breweries in the area, including **Wickwar** (www.wickwarbrewing. co.uk), and the **Severn Vale Brewing Company** (www.severnvalebrewing.co.uk) based on a farm on the edge of the village of Cam.

You can enjoy these ales at the **Old Spot Inn**, Hill Road, Dursley (GL11 4JQ; ☎01453 542870); www.oldspotinn.co.uk. It's been described as '*A Pub of a Thousand Locals*', and CAMRA, the Campaign for Real Ale, certainly thinks it's got something: it voted the Old Spot **Inn** the National Pub of the Year 2007, saying it was '*a great example of how successful a well-run community pub can be*'. It's on the Cotswold Way, too – a great watering hole for walkers.

Other welcoming locals include **The Swan** in Wotton's Market Street (GL12 7AE; ☎01453 843004), and **The Tudor Arms** at Slimbridge (GL2 7BP; ☎01453 890306), ideal for the Gloucester-Sharpness Canal and the Slimbridge Wildfowl & Wetlands Trust.

Also for walkers: various charities throughout the year often serve tea at Wotton Town Hall on a Sunday.

EATING OUT

FINE DINING

Tortworth Court Four Pillars Hotel
**Tortworth,
Wotton-under-Edge GL12 8HH;
☎ 01454 263000
tortworth-court-hotel.four-pillars.co.uk**

Produce comes from surrounding farms and all the breads are baked by Hobbs House Bakery in Chipping Sodbury. In the orangery, you'll pay just under £20 for dishes such as brill wrapped in crisp potatoes with a fondue of leeks.

RESTAURANT

The Cyder House Restaurant
**Owlpen Manor, Owlpen GL11 5BZ
☎ 01453 860816; www.owlpen.com**

The beautiful old Cyder House is open for a bistro-style meal (£28) on a Friday night during the 'Owlpen Manor' season (May–Sept) and on a Saturday night when the house itself is closed (though do book; it's essential). On the menu is seasonal produce from the estate, including game and traditionally reared Owlpen beef and also the produce of Owlpen's Elizabethan garden. Also open for lunch on Tues/Thurs/Sun in season.

The Pepper Pot
**Lower Wick, Dursley GL11 6DD
☎ 01453 810259
www.thepepperpotrestaurant.co.uk**

Much of the meat used here is from Tortworth Farm Shop, and other local butchers; the Charolais/Hereford beef is matured for four weeks, giving maximum flavour; the pork (Tamworth/Old Spot) and lamb (Suffolk/Jacob) is, as far as

possible, from their own stock at Green Farm, Fretherne. A mid-range three-course meal is around £26.

CAFÉ

McQuigg's
**44 Long Street,
Wotton-Under-Edge GL12 7BT
☎ 01453 844108**

Basic food such as omelettes, jacket potatoes and all-day breakfasts are supplemented by on the board specials, which usually have an international feel. They do good Sunday lunches too.

PUB

The Old Crown
**Inn, 17 The Green, Uley GL11 5SN
☎ 01453 860502
www.theoldcrownuley.co.uk**

The food at this 17th-century inn is not fussy, but it's high quality and good value, with real ales and a good selection of wines to go with it. The pretty gardens are ideal for al fresco eating in summer.

Black Horse
**1 Barrs Lane, North Nibley GL11 6DT
☎ 01453 543777
www.blackhorsenorthnibley.co.uk**

All the food is cooked from fresh in this attractive village pub, ideally situated for the Tyndale Monument. Starters begin at £4, main meals at £7.95; try the spectacular dessert for two, which incorporates every pudding on one plate.

ⓘ Visitor Information

Tourist information centres: Stroud Tourist Information Centre, The Subscription Rooms, George Street, Stroud GL5 1AE, ☎01453 760960, www.visitthecotswolds.org.uk, Mon–Sat, 10am–5pm; Three Parishes Tourism Group, The Clock Tower, High Street, Chipping Sodbury BS37 6AH, ☎01454 888686, www.cotswolds.com, Mon–Sat, 10am–5pm.

Hospitals: Stroud General Hospital, Trinity Road, Stroud GL5 2HY, ☎01453 562200. Gloucestershire Royal Hospital in Great Western Road, Gloucester GL1 3NN, ☎08454 222222; both 24-hour A&E.

Supermarkets include: Somerfield, Kingshill Road GL11 4EJ, ☎01453 542127, and Parsonage Street, Dursley GL11 4AA, ☎01453 542138; Tesco, Cam GL11 5LE, ☎0845 6779876; Co-op, Long Street, Wotton-under-Edge GL12 7BT, ☎01453 842112.

Sports: Dursley Pool & Sports Centre, Castle Street, Dursley GL11 4BS, ☎01453 546441 (pool), 01453 543832; Summerhouse Education and Equitation Centre, Hardwicke GL2 2RG, ☎01452 720288, www.summerhouseec.co.uk; Bristol and Gloucester Gliding Club, Nympsfield GL10 3TX, ☎01453 860342, www.bggc.co.uk.

Bike rental: Slimbridge Boat Station, Shepherds Patch, Slimbridge GL2 7BP, ☎01453 899190.

Taxis include: Al's Taxis, Dursley, ☎01453 519354; Hop-In & Travel, Wotton-under-Edge ☎01453 521444.

CIRENCESTER AND THE SOUTH
INCLUDING TETBURY AND MALMESBURY

Cirencester is the place that's turned Gloucestershire into Poshtershire – where you've got a 50/50 chance of bumping into either a farmer or Elizabeth Hurley down at your local. The actress moved to her 400 acre farm near Cirencester in 2003 so that her young son, Damian, would have a childhood *'climbing trees instead of inhaling pollutants in London.'*

This pretty market town was the favourite shopping destination of the late Diana, Princess of Wales; indeed, its branch of Waitrose has been named as one of the top 10 places in England 'to be seen' simply because of the number of celebrities who shop there. Among the stores, you'll find gentlemen's outfitters, purveyors of the accoutrements of country pursuits, a good choice of café and restaurant, and skilled artists' workshops. The beautiful town-centre Abbey Grounds lie behind one of the most impressive churches in the Cotswolds, St John the Baptist. There's plenty of action to be had, too: Wills and Harry often play at the polo grounds in the estate grounds of Cirencester Park, an elongated stone's throw from their home at Highgrove, in Tetbury, 15 minutes away.

The Prince of Wales, of course, settled in Tetbury in 1980. Like many other incomers, he was taken by a combination of the sheer cultivated prettiness of the area, and its easy access: London might seem a lifetime away, but it's a mere 90 or so minutes by train. In 2008, Prince Charles opened the only high-street 'Highgrove' shop, right in the heart of Tetbury. Nearby Malmesbury is a charming town, over the border into Wiltshire. It might, technically, be just outside the Cotswolds, but with its historic abbey and wonderful central gardens, boundaries need to be stretched.

WHAT TO SEE AND DO

Cirencester

If Painswick is known as the Queen of the Cotswolds, then Cirencester is her capital city. For many, it's their favourite Cotswold town – pretty much unspoiled over the years with few ubiquitous chain stores. It is the perfect town in which to window shop, to stroll, and to while away an afternoon.

Perhaps that's because Cirencester's identity is woven into the very fabric of her buildings. Take the extraordinarily beautiful church of **St John the Baptist** as an example. Standing in the Market Place, its great tower visible from all around,

The main street in the ancient market town of Cirencester

it's often referred to as the Cathedral of the Cotswolds. When its three-storey porch was built, it would have housed various guilds and traders – the world's first office block. Certainly, it's one of the largest parish churches in the country, built on the proceeds of the wool trade. '*The best wool in England comes from the Chondisgualdo (Cotswolds),*' wrote the 14th-century Italian merchant Francesco Datini; '*and the best wool of the Cotswolds comes from Northleccio (Northleach) and the great Abbey lands of Cirencester.*' The only part of the wealthy abbey still to exist is the Norman arch in the **Abbey Grounds** behind the church, which – complete with lake – are a lovely place to wander. Among the objects on display inside the church is a silver-gilt chalice, once the possession of Henry VIII's ill-fated queen, Anne Boleyn. Some believe the bells, cast by Rudhall of Gloucester, form the oldest peal of 12 in the world.

The funny thing is that no one really knows why Cirencester came to be where it is in the first place. When the Romans first marched to the spot on which it now stands, they found a boggy, slightly flooded river valley, overlooked on all sides – not the most auspicious location for what was to become Corinium Dobunnorum, their most important settlement in Britain after London. For reasons which haven't survived and which can't easily be guessed at, they nevertheless founded the town on this spot, soon after the great invasion of the British Isles in 43AD. It was even mentioned by Ptolemy in around 150AD, who called it 'Korinion'.

According to legend, Cirencester was wrested from the Britons by the Saxons in a spectacularly cunning way. Gormund, the leader of the Saxons, fixed lighted straws to the tails of sparrows, which carried them back to the thatched roofs, setting fire to the town. For this reason, the town was known as Urbs Passerum – Sparrow Town – in medieval times.

Learn about Cirencester's Roman past at the Corinium Museum

Just to the south-west of the town, in an area known as Querns, you can see the earthwork remains of a huge **amphitheatre**, which would have seated up to 12,000 people. Here the games were savage: criminals were not infrequently 'introduced' to ravenous beasts captured from Europe. You're free to wander around the spot, which is on open ground. In the centre of town, there's the superb **Corinium Museum,** where children can play Roman games (of a peaceable nature) and dress as Roman soldiers, as well as learning about other periods in the town's history – Cirencester has had a significant part to play in every century since.

CORINIUM MUSEUM: Park Street, Cirencester GL7 2BX; ☎01285 655611; www.cotswold.gov.uk. Entry: adults £12, seniors £9, children £6, family £30; open Mon–Sat (including bank holidays), 10am–5pm, Suns 2–5pm.

On Cecily Hill, one of Cirencester's most lovely streets, is the faux-medieval castle, marking the entrance to **Cirencester Park**, home to the Bathurst family. The poet Alexander Pope helped design the parkland, which is perfect for walking or riding – an experience you'll share with a plenitude of wildlife, including the shy deer that call it home. It's open to the public free of charge, on foot and horseback, from 8am to 5pm daily. And by the way, separating the town centre from the park is Europe's tallest yew hedge, planted in 1720.

Source of the Thames
You'll need the car for the next leg of the journey, along the A433 between Tetbury (5.7 miles) and Cirencester (2.8 miles). In the countryside here, you find the birth

of a legend. Park near the **Thames Head Inn** (GL7 6NZ; ☎01285 770259) and walk into the field where there's a stone inscribed: '*The Conservators of the River Thames 1857–1974. This stone was placed here to mark the source of the River Thames*'. This is where the mighty Thames – all 215 miles of it – can officially trace its origins. Depending on time of year and rainfall, this is a dry basin, but it is the start of a riverside walk that can take you all the way to London. The Ramblers' Association classifies the walk as 'easy', but you can also add the word 'long'. To complete the Thames Path, you'd walk 154 miles back to London Bridge. Alternatively, you could settle for a drink at the Thames Head itself and mull over the fact that not everyone agrees this is the river's birthplace; another school of thought claims the true source to be at Seven Springs, near Cheltenham. But they haven't got the plaque.

Tetbury

It's a pleasant drive along the A433 on to Tetbury, a town named by *Country Life* magazine as one of Britain's most desirable locations. The judges loved the 'golden Cotswold limestone', the higgledy-piggledy lanes and notable buildings. It's also, of course, a royal town; Prince Charles's house, **Highgrove**, isn't visible from the road, but it lies just over a mile outside Tetbury, along the Bath Road to Doughton.

Before Prince and Princess Michael of Kent sold their beautiful 18th-century manor at Nether Lypiatt, there were three royal households in a small area of Gloucestershire known as the Royal Triangle – with the Princess Royal at Gatcombe Park, Minchinhampton, and the Prince of Wales at Tetbury. '*Prince Charles thought that three lots of family in Gloucestershire might put too big a strain on the security services. But I said: I saw my house long before you saw your beautiful Highgrove!*' Princess Michael once joked.

Highgrove House has been the private residence of the prince since 1980. Built in the late 18th century for the wealthy Paul family of Stroud, it is here that he and the late Princess of Wales brought up William and Harry. Those lucky enough to be invited to visit the organic gardens will see the teetering tree house where the young princes once played. The Prince entertains many at his home – and not just friends and family. He is a great supporter of local organisations (Camilla is a member of the town's WI), especially food producers who work to the traditional principles he values.

The Prince's outstanding organic gardens include wild, formal, and walled kitchen areas. There are plants chosen for their scents – wisteria, honeysuckle, jasmine, holboellia, lilies and thyme; for their rarity – ox-eye daisies, yellow rattle, common spotted orchid, meadow crane's bill and ragged robin; and for their delicious taste – Charlotte potatoes and Happil strawberries, leeks, spring cabbage, Brussels sprouts and carrots. Details of how to visit, which is possible in pre-arranged groups of up to 25, are on the website (www.princeofwales.gov.uk). The waiting list is two years. Walking round the town itself is a treat, with its 17th-century market hall built on pillars. **St Mary's Church** is the oldest site of Christian worship in Gloucestershire, and claims the fourth highest spire in England.

LOCAL KNOWLEDGE

Poet **Pam Ayres** lives just outside Cirencester, in a rambling Georgian house. Here, on a 20 acre smallholding, she and her husband, Dudley Russell, keep their animals: Dexter cattle, Cotswold sheep, Old Spot pigs, and numerous hens. Pam performs her poetry all over the world but, she says, no matter how much she enjoys her travels, her heart always lifts as she approaches Cirencester.

Best pub: We go to the Hare and Hounds Inn at Foss Cross, affectionately known as The Stump because there's a tree stump outside. I like the good food and the friendly welcome.

Best Cotswold view: From the road at Sheepbridge, near Eastleach, up a great, curving valley. My husband has always loved it, so it's known to us as Dad's Valley. In the winter, there's a stream all along, and it's always dotted with sheep.

Favourite walk: From Bibury to Coln St Aldwyns. On the way, I'd stop off for a pint at the Keepers at Quenington where you can sit on the green.

Top event: The Cotswold Show at Cirencester Park every July. It's a good place to see all the different people who live and work in the Cotswolds, with lots of interesting things thrown in, like Spitfires flying overhead.

Best Cotswolds souvenir: A picture by a local artist such as Bryn Miles, who has sadly died. My son loves to go fishing so I bought him a Bryn Miles picture of the Coln at Fairford for his 21st.

Tastiest Cotswold produce: I'd buy some Gloucester Old Spot bangers from Cirencester butcher Jesse Smith; some bread from that nice lady at the farmers' market; some smoked trout; lots of salads and fruit.

Essential shop: I was going to be worthy here and say the farmers' market, but I'm going to be honest and say Bernard Griffiths, the hairdresser in Cirencester. I go in looking like a banshee and come out looking serene.

On the outskirts of Tetbury, to the west, **Chavenage House** (☎01666 502329) is an historic Elizabethan manor that you might recognise: it 'plays' Candleford House in the TV adaptation of *Lark Rise*. One of the joys of this warm and atmospheric house is that it's still very much lived in by the Lowsley-Williams family. David, the owner, often conducts the tours himself. His daughter, Caroline says, '*Upstairs, one of our tapestry rooms is reputed to be the most haunted in the county, and no one in the family has ever slept there. It's where a former owner of Chavenage, Colonel Stephens, died. Colonel Stephens was a supporter of the Parliamentarian cause during the Civil War, but he refused to be implicated in the death of the King. However, Cromwell sent his son-in-law, General Ireton, here and persuaded Stephens to change his mind. Almost immediately, Stephens fell ill. It became obvious there was no hope and, legend has it, as the family gathered round to say "Adieu", a coach drawn by four black horses pulled up. Colonel Stephens' body rose off the bed, drifted down the stairs, and was greeted by the headless driver who wore the Star and Royal Garter of Charles I...*'

The interior of the Elizabethan manor, Chavenage House

CHAVENAGE HOUSE: Chavenage, Tetbury GL8 8XP; ☎01666 502329; www.chavenage.com. Entry: adults £7, children £3.50, including a guided tour; open May to Sept, Thurs/Sun 2–5pm, also bank holidays, Easter Sunday and Easter Monday.

Rhododendrons at Westonbirt Arboretum

But perhaps the most famous attraction of all in this neck of the woods, so to speak, is **Westonbirt – The National Arboretum**. It doesn't matter which time of year it is, there's always something to see: in the autumn, it's the world-famous Japanese maples glowing iridescently plum, crimson, saffron and scarlet (the collection is well on the way to becoming the best in Europe, if not the world). Then come the brightly stemmed dogwoods and conifers that light up

WESTONBIRT – THE NATIONAL ARBORETUM: Tetbury GL8 8QS; ☎01666 880220; www.forestry.gov.uk/westonbirt. Entry: adults £5–£8, concessions £4–£7, children £1–£3; open daily, 9am–5pm.

the winter; the pinks, vivid blues and reds of the big tree magnolias, camellias, rhododendrons, and azaleas, the wood anemones and glades of flowering cherries, the bluebells that carpet the spring; and, to complete the cycle, there are the wildflowers, the lime trees, and the horse chestnuts which perfume the summer air with honey. And don't forget the exotically rare species, like the Wollemi pine, newly discovered in Australia, so ancient it once rubbed shoulders with the dinosaurs.

There are dog-friendly and dog-free areas, places to picnic, a restaurant and a café, as well as a plant centre and a shop. At Christmas time, there's an especially lit walk – Enchanted Christmas – which, once experienced, is never forgotten.

Westonbirt's creator, the Victorian entrepreneur Robert Holford, inherited a vast fortune made by piping drinking water to the city of London, and lived in what is now **Westonbirt** (www.holfordtrust.com), the famous girls' school. A new charity – The Holfords of Westonbirt Trust – is aiming to restore the house and its grounds, with the full backing of the school, to its former glory. Both will be open to the public on certain days throughout the year.

On a different but charming scale are the gardens at **Trull House**, near Tetbury GL8 8SQ (☎01285 841255; www.trullhouse.co.uk): 8 acres featuring a sunken lily pond, rockery, wild gardens, walled gardens and lawn. Open 11 am – 5 pm from April to August, generally, Wednesdays, Saturdays, Sundays and Bank Holidays; check the website for details. Entry costs £4 for adults, children under 16 free.

Westonbirt House is undergoing a massive restoration

CELEBRITY CONNECTIONS

He might normally be a trendsetter, but celebrity designer **Laurence Llewelyn-Bowen** was a late starter as far as the Cotswolds are concerned. Long after Kate Moss and Stella McCartney had moved here and made it fashionable, Laurence decided to pitch up, too. But once he'd arrived – in the working village of Siddington outside Cirencester in early 2007 – he made up for lost time. He and his wife, Jackie, have won the hearts of locals by supporting good causes, starring at fêtes, opening their gardens for charity.

When they first stumbled across their part-16th century farmhouse, it was unloved and, supposedly, haunted. In true *Changing Rooms* style, Laurence has designed his own wallpaper for the couple's swanky black and red bedroom and on the wall of another bedroom, he's painted a countryside mural of hills, copse and follies. *'It's like a fantasy football league of all the best bits of our landscape. Then we went over to Cirencester Park for tea with Lady Apsley, and I thought: hang on a second... There, in real life, were all the bits from my landscape.'*

Malmesbury

If you're visiting the Cotswolds, then you ignore Malmesbury at your peril. For one thing, it enjoys a place in the Guinness Book of Records as the oldest borough in England. A hilltop town, it's surrounded by rivers on three sides. No offence to Cirencester, but one might assume that a bit more thought went into choosing this particularly good defensive position.

Malmesbury Abbey, which dates from around 1180, stands on the site of a Benedictine monastery, founded by St Aldhelm in the 7th century (www.malmesbury abbey.com). It's a fraction of the size it once was; the church that now stands is the original nave. There are three parts you should study in particular: the south porch, renowned for its Norman sculptures depicting Bible scenes; the tomb of the town's great benefactor, and the first king of all England, King Athelstan (though it's an empty tomb; his remains are thought to lie beneath the vegetable bed of the neighbouring Abbey House) and, possibly most important of all, there's Eilmer's window.

The story of Eilmer's derring do is still told around the town nearly 1,000 years later. In 1010, this young brother from the abbey fashioned a pair of wings and, brimming with confidence, launched himself from the top of the old abbey tower in an attempt to fly. For 200m, it looked as if he had almost beaten the Wright brothers to it; but he came down to earth with a bump. Although Eilmer survived, both his legs were badly broken, and he's reputed to have been left crippled for life.

In the churchyard, you'll see a stone dedicated to Hannah Twynnoy who, in the 18th century, laid claim to the title: '*the last known person to be eaten by a tiger in England*', (which seems disappointing for the second-to-last person); the fate of the tiger is unclear.

In St John's Street, you can see the **Old Courtroom** and the **St John's Almshouses**. And there's the **Market Cross**, which dates from around 1500, and is decorated with figures of saints and the Crucifixion. It was said to be built '*for poore folkes to stande dry when rain cummeth*' – a useful addition for any English town. If it isn't raining, then the River Walk, along the banks of the Avon and Ingleburn, is a must. Geese once used to be driven over Goose Bridge to graze in the water meadows.

Another marvellous place for a stroll is **Abbey House Gardens**, home to Ian and Barbara Pollard. Thanks to their habit of gardening in the nude, they've earned the moniker 'Naked Gardeners' and have been the focus of numerous television programmes and articles. Most visitors to their town-centre gardens keep their clothes on to see the 10,000 different species of plants, including a fabulous display of more than 2,000 roses and the river gardens. But due to popular request, the Pollards do run the occasional clothes-optional day on their 5 acre site.

> ABBEY HOUSE GARDENS: Malmesbury SN16 9AS; ☎01666 822212; www.abbeyhousegardens.co.uk. Entry: adults £7, concessions £5.75; children £2.50, family £15; open mid-Mar to end Oct, 11am–5.30pm; also charity days.

There's also the **Athelstan Museum** in the Town Hall in Cross Hayes (☎01666 829258), open daily, entry free. It's filled with fascinating relics and facts – including

Abbey House Gardens in Malmesbury

an even less successful pilot than Eilmer. Walter Powell, a local MP, disappeared out to sea in a balloon in 1881, and was never heard of again. Rather more successfully, the entrepreneur James Dyson established his vacuum cleaner factory in the town in 1995; though 'manufacturing' was later transferred overseas, the Tetbury Hill site is where research and development takes place.

Wet weather

It would be criminal to miss out on Tetbury's **Police Museum**, which may not be huge but which is fascinating. Based in the old police office and cells, it includes a collection of photographs and historic artefacts, including the world-renowned Alex Nichols collection of restraint equipment! Just make sure you don't wake violent 'Fred', one of the prisoners who permanently occupies one of the cells.

POLICE MUSEUM: The Old Courthouse, Long Street, Tetbury GL8 8AA; ☎01666 504670 Entry: free; open 10am–3pm Mon–Fri, excluding bank holidays.

What to do with children...

BRISTOL AERO COLLECTION: Kemble Airfield, Kemble GL7 6BQ; ☎01285 771204; www.bristolaero.com. Entry: adults £4, concessions £3, children £2 (aged 4–12), family £10; open Easter to Oct, Sun/Mon 10am–3.30pm (last entry); Nov to Easter, Mon 10am–3.30pm (last entry); Fri–Mon over Easter, summer bank holidays, and most Kemble Airfield event days; closed between Christmas and New Year.

Teenagers of an aeronautical bent should especially enjoy the **Bristol Aero Collection** at Kemble Airfield (entry is via the main gate on the A429). As well as aircraft, engines, missiles, spacecraft and road transport, there are many other exhibits related to the aviation industry in South Gloucestershire.

The good news is that **Cirencester Open Air Swimming Pool**, dating back to 1870, is one of the oldest in the country and filled by spring water – the even better news is that it's heated. There's a 28m main pool and a children's paddling pool, tuck shop and hot showers.

Abbey View Alpacas in Malmesbury (SN16 9DA; ☎01666 823124) is great fun for the whole family with its alpaca, llamas, rare pigs, rescue goats and other animals. Open by appointment, entry is free but donations are welcomed for animal rescue service.

... and how to avoid children

Take a course at the **Royal Agricultural College, Cirencester** – an institution of which the town is justly proud. Not only does it offer an outstanding education but, founded in the 1840s, it is also the oldest agricultural college in the English-speaking world. The Rural Skills Centre runs day courses in such pursuits as drystone walling, blacksmithing, shooting and fly fishing, from £59 upwards. Most courses can be arranged throughout the year. Phone ☎01285 889873 or log onto www.rac.ac.uk for more details.

CIRENCESTER OPEN AIR SWIMMING POOL: Riverside Walk, Thomas Street, Cirencester GL7 2BA; ☎01285 653947; www.cirenopenair.co.uk. Entry: adults £3.20, children/seniors £1.80; family £9, spectators £1; open end of May to early Sept, Mon–Fri (and bank holidays) 8am–7pm, Sat 9am–6pm, Sun 11am–6pm.

Entertainment

One of the Cotswolds' strangest events, **Tetbury Woolsack Races**, takes place every May Spring Bank holiday on Gumstool Hill (which, by the way, was where nagging wives were once dunked in the pond on a gumstool, to dissuade them from their garrulous ways). In a tradition that goes back at least to the 17th century, the town's wool heritage is heavily celebrated: teams of four run in relays carrying a 60lb woolsack (or 35lb for the ladies) up and down this hill, which has a 1 in 4 gradient. It's a charity fund-raiser which also includes entertainment and a fete. Some say it was started by young drovers, showing off to their girlfriends; though quite what they

The tradition of woolsack races in Tetbury dates back to the 17th century

would be capable of after racing is open to question (www.tetburywoolsack.co.uk).

Tetbury has an outstanding classical music festival in October (www.tetbury musicfestival.org.uk); while Cirencester hosts an annual **Cotswold Early Music Festival** in July (www.cirencester-emf.fsnet.co.uk). There's an eclectic programme of **open-air concerts** each summer within the magical surroundings of Westonbirt Arboretum, usually incorporating classical, jazz, rock and every type of music in between (www.forestry.gov.uk/westonbirt). The arboretum also holds a series of festivals and family events throughout the year, such as the **Festival of the Tree** in August – a massive event when craftsmen and women from all over the UK gather to sell and give demonstrations; there are loads of wood-based family activities, from making a willow sculpture to being winched to the top of a tree!

Even if you don't know the rules, you'll enjoy watching **polo**. To bluff it as a pro, just throw in phrases such as 'That was a good ride-off' or 'What an air shot!' and no one will know. Nowadays, polo clubs don't have airs and graces – all are welcome – though they do have Heirs and Graces. You might well catch Wills and Harry on the field. The polo season runs from late April until September; there are various fixtures,

CELEBRITY CONNECTIONS

Don't think celebrities are immune from disaster. In 2007, TV prankster **Dom Joly** and his Canadian wife, Stacey, got caught up in the worst flooding to hit the region within living memory. They were on holiday in Canada when they received a phone call telling them their home, near Cirencester, was 18 inches deep in sewage. The damage was the sort experienced by families all over Gloucestershire: it was the insurance claims that were unique. *'I had some costumes that had got damaged – one of them was a squirrel. When the loss adjuster was going through the stuff, she asked, "What's in that blue bag?" I said, "A squirrel costume." She didn't bat an eyelid even though she clearly didn't recognise me!'*

The experience hasn't put them off living here one bit (especially now the drains have been upgraded). *'I had quite a schizophrenic upbringing,'* Dom says. *'I went to school in Lebanon and came to boarding school here; so it was really important that my kids grew up in one place. Although kids in London are incredibly sophisticated and street smart, they grow up so quickly. I just want my kids to be kids for as long as possible.'*

but a Sunday is always a good bet. You can visit Beaufort Polo Club at Westonbirt (GL8 8QW; ☎01666 880510; beaufortpoloclub.co.uk) and Cirencester Park Polo Club in Cirencester Park (GL7 1UR; ☎01285 653225; www.cirencesterpolo.co.uk) where supermodel Elle Macpherson has been spotted among the crowd.

Kemble Air Day in June (www.kembleairday.com), featuring flying and static displays on the air field, is always a Cotswold classic, pulling in thousands of visitors each year.

🛒 Shopping

There are two unique shopping opportunities in this area. The first is the **Highgrove Shop** in Long Street Tetbury (www.highgroveshop.com) – the only high-street shop of its kind. It sells food, drink and gifts to appeal to everyone. And whether it's china decorated with Highgrove hens, or baskets made from willows collected from the estate's hedgerows, it all has a Highgrove theme. The town also enjoys a far-reaching reputation for its many antique and specialist food shops.

The second rather special experience is **New Brewery Arts** in the Brewery Courtyard, Cirencester (www.breweryarts.org.uk), with 12 world-class craft studios, numerous events and classes, and an excellent café. There's also the Craftman's Market in Cirencester's Corn Hall in the Market Place on the first and third Saturday of each month, from 10am to 4.30pm. But perhaps the best shopping tip in this area is to visit the charity shops – particularly in Tetbury. Rumour has it that when Highgrove and other large local houses have a clear-out, this is where the wardrobe contents end up. After all, it's not every charity shop that sells second-hand polo sticks...

Interior of the Highgrove Shop, the only high-street branch of Prince Charles' shop

 The best... **PLACES TO STAY**

HOTEL

Whatley Manor

Easton Grey, Malmesbury SN16 0RB
☎ 01666 822888,
www.whatleymanor.com

Bang & Olufsen sound systems are just one of the finishing touches put to the 15 rooms and eight suites at this sophisticated hotel: understated luxury down to the finest detail. There are two restaurants – a formal dining room and the more relaxed Le Mazot. A particular feature of Whatley are the gardens, leading on to rolling countryside. Children from 12 are welcome.

Price: doubles from £290 with breakfast and use of spa.

Calcot Manor

Near Tetbury GL8 8YJ
☎ 01666 890391,
www.calcotmanor.co.uk

Calcot sits in its own 220 acre estate, and is constantly listed in various nationals as one of Britain's best country hotels. It's a former farmhouse set around a pretty courtyard of lime trees and ancient stone barns and stables (dating back to the 14th century), but with an added twist of contemporary charm. For fine dining, there's the Conservatory; there's also the relaxed Gumstool Inn. The hotel is recognised as one of the most child-friendly in Britain. Dogs welcome by prior arrangement.

Price: for doubles from £230, including breakfast.

The best... **PLACES TO STAY**

Hare & Hounds Hotel

Westonbirt, Tetbury GL8 8QL
☎ 01666 881000, www.
hareandhoundshotel.com

Just down the road from the arboretum, this is a traditional English country hotel, praised both for its green credentials and the warm welcome it extends to families. There are four rooms that accommodate up to three adults and/or two children, and there are good children's meals – half portions of all menu dishes are available on request.

Price: double rooms from £120 including breakfast.

Hotel le spa

Gloucester Road, Cirencester GL7 2LA,
☎ 01285 653840, www.lespa.com

Elegant and luxurious, Hotel le spa is part of a superb health club – and all the facilities are available to guests. After a hard day shopping in Cirencester, just over a mile away, you can relax in the gym, sauna, whirlpool spa, swimming pool, steam room or take a class. The Orchid Restaurant uses local produce and comes 'Les Routiers' recommended.

Price: from £99 for doubles including breakfast.

SELF-CATERING

Berkeley House & The Orangery

4 The Chipping, Tetbury GL8 8ET
☎ 01666 500051, www.
lenaproudlockescapes.com

Berkeley House really is rather special: this eight-bedroom Georgian town house in Tetbury was created by designer/photographer Lena Proudlock and has been featured in numerous publications, including *Vogue* and *The Sunday Times*. There are seven bedrooms in the main building; a 24ft drawing room and snug, and the dining room seats 14–16. You can also rent the Orangery and coach house, plus two/three bedroom apartments nearby.

Price: Berkeley House from £1,500 a night; apartments from £200 a night.

Folly Farm Cottages

Tetbury GL8 8XA
☎ 01666 502475, www.gtb.co.uk

There are 12 self-catering cottages (and also B&B accommodation). The most spacious cottage accommodates eight people. Within walking distance of Tetbury, all the cottages have been converted from period farm buildings and boast exposed oak beams, vaulted ceilings and wood-burning stoves.

Price: from £400 for a week for two.

FARMSTAY

Abbey Home Farm

Burford Road, Cirencester GL7 5HF
☎ 01285 640441, www.
theorganicfarmshop

There are various 'roofs' you can sleep under at the wonderful organic Abbey Home Farm, including tents, yurts or Lower Wiggold Cottage in the depths of the countryside. The four yurt eco-camp is on the edge of a wood with lovely views. It's a wonderful environment, and perfect for self-catering. The farm has an award-winning organic farm shop and café, of which even Elizabeth Hurley is a big fan.

Price: cottage from £500 a week for up to four people; four yurts from £495, 18 people max; single yurt from £90 for two nights for two.

The best... FOOD AND DRINK

▶ Staying in

There's definitely a case for calling Tetbury the 'Gloucestershire Ludlow'. Once it was known for antiques: now it's food as well. There have long been excellent hotels, restaurants and cafés, as well as food shops in the town – take **Jesse Smith's**, the fabulous butcher, and the House of Cheese in Church Street as examples. But recent arrivals to the town centre include acclaimed chef Michael Bedford and his wife, Sarah, who have opened **The Chef's Table** at 49 Long Street (☎01666 504466; www.thechefstable.co.uk), a delicatessen/food shop/fishmongers with a small café/bistro. **Quayles** is another fine delicatessen at 1 Long Street (☎01666 505151; www.quayles.co.uk). You can meet producers at the town's newly established annual food festival in September.

A couple of miles outside the town, on a Wednesday from 8am to 5pm, you'll find **The Veg Shed** (at GL8 8SE – look out for the orange signs on Cherington Lane, just off the A433). This is where to buy vegetables fit for a prince (Prince Charles, of course). For they're all plucked from the ground of Duchy Home Farm, a short tractor ride away. Of course, you'll want to indulge a little too, which is where **Westonbirt Home-made Ice Cream** can help. Made from organic shorthorn milk along with the best quality local and ethical ingredients, this delicious dessert is created at **Home Farm** in Westonbirt (☎01666 880468).

Chesterton Farm shop, near Cirencester, (☎01285 653003; www.chestertonfarm.co.uk) is highly thought of. It sells fruit, vegetables, cakes and preserves, and also has a specialist butcher on site (☎01285 642160) for rare-breed meat, including Lord Apsley's Gloucester beef from the farms round the Cirencester Park estate. **The Organic Farm Shop,** Abbey Home Farm, Burford Road, Cirencester (☎01285 640441; www.theorganicfarmshop.co.uk has won awards for its organic fresh veg, meat, dairy produce and general groceries. It has a café and accommodation (see 'Where to stay').

Taylerson's Malmesbury Syrups (☎01666 577379; www.malmesburysyrups.co.uk) produces flavoured syrups made in the old fashioned way, including apple and cinnamon, chocolate, hazelnut, and vanilla; it also produces salad dressings, balsamic vinegar and olive oil. **The Tracklement Company** at Easton Grey, Malmesbury (☎01666 827044; www.tracklements.co.uk) creates all sorts of relishes, pickles, chutneys, mustards, sauces and more. 'Most of our recipes have an historical provenance,' says Guy Tullberg of the family business. 'In fact, my father started with a mustard recipe he found in John Evelyn's 17th century diaries.'

Malmesbury holds its farmers' market around Market Cross on the second and fourth Saturdays in the month, 9am–1pm.

 EATING OUT

FINE DINING

Rectory Hotel
Crudwell, Malmesbury SN16 9EP
☎ 01666 577194
www.therectoryhotel.com

Chef Peter Fairclough is a member of the prestigious Master Chefs of Great Britain. He and his team put in as much thought to the children's menu – which includes Gloucester Old Spot sausages – as they do to the superb adult meals, where mains start at around £14.50.

RESTAURANT

The Old Bell Hotel
Abbey Row, Malmesbury SN16 0BW
☎ 01666 822344
www.oldbellhotel.com

The Old Bell Hotel was originally the guest house for Malmesbury Abbey. In fact, so ancient is its lineage, it's thought to be the oldest building in England to have been used without pause as a guest house since its construction. Executive chef Tom Rains, who trained with Anton Mosimann, gives a contemporary twist to classics.

The Priory Inn
London Road, Tetbury GL8 8JJ
☎ 01666 502251
www.theprioryinn.co.uk

This is a place that's passionate about using local, seasonable produce in its excellent menus; simple, well-cooked and well-sourced ingredients are the key. You'll find wood floors, exposed beams and an open fire with a contemporary design and feel, and an exceptionally friendly welcome. Have full dinner, or an excellent pizza for under £10.

The Ormond at Tetbury
23 Long Street, Tetbury GL8 8AA
☎ 01666 505690
www.theormond.co.uk

Head chef David Cameron (no, not that one) is a regular sight at local farmers' markets. The restaurant's website is not only reassurance that the best local ingredients are used; it's also a ready-made shopping list for anyone eating in. You can't beat cider-roasted Gloucester Old Spot pork belly – many mains well under £15.

Harry Hares
3 Gosditch Street,
Cirencester GL7 2AG
☎ 01285 652375
www.harryhares.co.uk

This is a fantastically popular Cirencester restaurant and brasserie, especially with the Ladies who Lunch. Housed in an historic building just behind the parish church, it has a kitchen led by Nigel Harding who has worked alongside Gary Rhodes and Phil Vickery. Sunday roasts with Hereford beef at £11.50.

Tatyan's
27 Castle Street, Cirencester GL7 1QD
☎ 01285 653529
www.tatyans.com

This up-market Chinese restaurant is beloved by many local people, including top woman polo player Nina Clarkin. '*Mr Tatyan is a super guy and always looks after us very well. If we go as a family somewhere, we always go to Tatyan's,*' she says. Take the family and enjoy a set menu from around £22.

EATING OUT

Jesse's Bistro
The Stableyard, Blackjack Street, Cirencester GL7 2AA
☎ **01285 641497**
www.jessesbistro.co.uk

Having gained an excellent reputation for their first-class meat in Jesse Smith the butcher's, they went on to open the bistro. Inevitably, the meat served is superb: Aberdeen Angus beef, Old Spot Pork, Cotswold lamb; and there's fresh fish from Newlyn in Cornwall. Menus vary daily but eat a great three courses for £30.

Café
New Brewery Arts
Brewery Court, Cirencester GL7 1JH
☎ **01285 657181**
www.breweryarts.org.uk

Artists at New Brewery Arts aren't just confined to the workshops; for some say that those who work in the café kitchens are artists too! This arts centre is well known for its home-made food, from breakfasts and afternoon teas, to the wholesome lunches in between: salads, quiches and soups are especially good.

Drinking

For a superb cup of coffee – buy in or take out, call into **Keith's Coffee Shop** in Blackjack Street, Cirencester (☎01285 654717). You don't need a GPS; just head for that delicious aroma. For something a bit stronger, pop into **Bow in the Cloud Vineyard** in Malmesbury (SN16 9NS; ☎01666 823040; www.bowinthecloud.co.uk) for their award-winning wines, still and sparkling. Keith Willingale began planting this modern-day vineyard in 1992. '*The Cotswolds in general are too high for wine production,*' he says. '*This means the average temperature is lower, and there is greater susceptibility to frost. The Malmesbury area was quite well known for producing wine in the Middle Ages, when there were up to five vineyards here, probably run by monks – today I'm the only one. One of the difficulties is that the soil in the Avon Valley is clay, and good drainage is a key issue for healthy vines. But I happen to be on a patch of cornbrash – limestone that's been naturally broken up by weather – with a thin layer of top soil over oolitic limestone. The fractures in the limestone allow the roots of the vines to grow down, and mean the ground is well drained. My vineyard is also sheltered by the woodland around it.*'

There are plenty of good drinking pubs around, including the **Cat and Custard Pot** – 'The Cat' to locals – in Shipton Moyne (GL8 8PN; ☎01666 880249); the **Twelve Bells** in Cirencester (GL7 1EA; ☎01285 644549); the **King's Arms** at Didmarton (GL9 1DT; ☎01454 238245); the **Royal Oak** at Leighterton (GL8 8UN; ☎01666 890250); and the lively, friendly **Rattlebone Inn** at Sherston (SN16 0LR; ☎01666 840871).

ⓘ Visitor Information

Tourist information centres: Cirencester Visitor Information Centre, Corinium Museum, Park Street, Cirencester GL7 2BX, ☎01285 654180, www.cotswold.gov.uk/go/tourism, Mon–Sat 10am–5pm, Sun 2–5pm and bank holidays; Tetbury Tourist Information Centre, 33 Church Street, Tetbury GL8 8JG, ☎01666 503552, www.visittetbury.co.uk, Mar to Oct, Mon–Sat 9.30am–4.30pm, Nov to Feb, Mon–Sat 9.30am–2.30pm; Malmesbury Tourist Information Centre, Malmesbury Town Hall, Cross Hayes, Malmesbury SN16 9BZ, ☎01666 823748, www.malmesbury.gov.uk, Easter to autumn, Mon–Thurs 9am–4.50pm, Fri 9am–4.20pm, Sat and bank holidays 10am–4pm, closed Sun and winter/spring bank holidays.

Hospitals: Cirencester Hospital, Tetbury Road, Cirencester GL7 1UY, ☎01285 655711; Great Western Hospital in Marlborough Road, Swindon SN3 6BB, ☎01793 604020 (both 24-hr A&E).

Supermarkets include: Waitrose, Sheep Street GL7 1SZ, ☎01285 643733; Tesco, Farrell Close GL7 1HW, off Castle Street, ☎0845 6779183; Tesco Extra, Cricklade Road Tetbury GL7 1NP, ☎0845 6779160, Cirencester; Tesco Superstore, London Road GL8 8HZ, ☎0845 6779667; Somerfield, Long Street, ☎01666 502685, Tetbury; Somerfield, Gloucester Road SN16 0AL, ☎01666 824948; Co-op, High Street SN16 9AU, ☎01666 823309, Malmesbury.

Sports: Cotswold Leisure Centre, Tetbury Road, Cirencester, ☎01285 654057; Tennis courts, St Michael's Park off King's Street, Circencester ☎01285 659182; Cirencester Golf Club, Bagendon, ☎01285 653939; Tetbury Sport & Leisure Centre, Sir William Romney's School, Lowfield Road, Tetbury GL8 8AE, ☎01666 505805; The Activity Zone Leisure Centre, Bremilham Road, Malmesbury SN16 0DQ, ☎01666 822533; Westonbirt Golf Club GL8 8QG, ☎01666 880242; Chippenham Golf Club, Malmesbury Road SN15 5LT, ☎01249 652040; Woodbridge Park Golf Club, Brinkworth SN15 5DG, ☎01666 510277; South Cerney Riding School, Cerney Wick Farm, Cerney Wick, near Cirencester, ☎01793 750151, cerneyridingschool.com.

Taxis include: Cirencester Radio Cars ☎01285 650850; Express Taxis of Tetbury ☎07858 450098; Abbey Taxis near Malmesbury ☎01666 826072.

BIBURY, COLN VALLEY, AND NORTHLEACH

Bibury is where the icons of the Cotswolds are to be found in abundance: drystone walls, glorious churches, picture-postcard villages, droolingly lovely mansions, burbling rivers, and hedgerows and trees burgeoning with greens of every hue.

Of course, this is also a tourist hotspot. While you might find you have some of the other 'central' regions to yourself, you'll probably (at least in summer) be dodging cameras and coaches when you stop to explore around here. But you'll instantly see why. **Arlington Row** in Bibury has become a symbol for all that's best about this region – one of the most photographed rows of houses in England. In other words, visit this area and you are entering the quintessential Cotswolds. Here, lying within the **Coln Valley**, are to be found the sorts of villages featured in picture books: Winson, Coln St Dennis, Coln St Aldwyns and Hatherop. No wonder they've earned the moniker 'the Chelsea of the Cotswolds'.

Northleach, on the other hand, is one of the area's secrets. It *is* a town because King Henry III said so: he granted it a charter in 1227, decreeing a market could be held each week, and a fair each June. But it's a small town, which manages to balance looks with personality: tourism has not swamped its community spirit. There are attractions around here (a world-famous Roman villa, for one) but, truth be told, you'll probably find yourself just as contentedly enjoying the activities that come for free: outstanding views, a picnic by a stream, a walk along overgrown paths, a quiet read in a patch of sunlight.

WHAT TO SEE AND DO

Bibury

Artist and writer William Morris, the great pioneer of the Arts & Crafts Movement who spent his summers in nearby Kelmscott Manor, called Bibury 'the most beautiful village in England'. He may well have been right (though plenty of other Cotswold villages could probably take a punt at the title); it's certainly one of the most popular. The River Coln runs alongside the main road, occupied by swans on the surface and trout beneath.

In fact, Bibury is actually two villages – Bibury one side and Arlington the other – separated by the river. If you haven't heard of Arlington itself, you've almost certainly heard of **Arlington Row** – one of the most beautiful rows of houses in the whole of England, and still lived in today. Yet these architectural icons, now owned by the National Trust, had a humble start in life. In the late 14th century, they were built as monastic wool barns; nearly 300 years later, they were converted to house the weavers of the 17th century. Once the cloth they produced was dried on Rack Island, the small water meadow beside the river.

Arlington Row, the famous row of houses owned by the National Trust

The great American car manufacturer Henry Ford took rather a fancy to Arlington Row and attempted – during a Cotswold holiday – to buy the terrace, with a view to rebuilding it in the States. When his offer was spurned, he turned to more modest ambitions and, in 1930, bought a 17th-century cottage in Chedworth for the princely sum of $5,000. Rose Cottage, once owned by a family of Cotswold stonemasons named Smith, now resides at Greenfield Village, Michigan, surrounded by a Victorian flower garden.

Bibury's Saxon **Church of St Mary** is home to a stained glass window designed in 1927 by Karl Parsons and featured on Royal Mail Christmas stamps.

Around Bibury and to the north, the gentle slopes play host to some of the most picturesque villages and hamlets. There's **Ablington**, which was once home to the 19th-century squire and social commentator J Arthur Gibbs, who immortalised it in his book, *A Cotswold Village*. This, he said, was a place '*of golden sunshine and silvery trout streams, the land of breezy uplands and valleys nestling under limestone hills*'. Other places offer unexpected treats. In the idyllic hamlet of **Calmsden**, there's a rare 14th-century stone cross – a Christian symbol undoubtedly, but it's likely that pagans once worshipped at the spring that gurgles munificently between ancient banks.

Chedworth

St Andrew's Church in **Chedworth** boasts a tower which dates from 1100, a south porch from 1300 and a magnificent 15th-century pulpit. There is also a copy of the Breeches Bible, first published in 1560, which got its name because Genesis 3:7 reads, '*Then the eyes of them bothe were opened, and they knewe that they were naked, and they sewed fig tree leaves together, and made them selves breeches*'.

Tokyo dreaming

Some of the tourists you'll see in Bibury will be from among the estimated 50,000 Japanese visitors who come to the Cotswolds each year. For them, this is one of the villages that sums up the magic of the history and countryside they come to discover. Freelance journalist Marino Matsushima came here from Tokyo with her mother, Tamako Mihira. 'She was amazed by the houses,' Marino says. 'My mother knew most of them were made of stone or brick, but she didn't realise how much you preserve old buildings. She loves the homes of honey-coloured stones with their tiny windows, but it was only when she saw a light on in one of them that she began to believe someone really did live there!'

For Japanese people, part of the fascination lies in the fact that the Cotswolds represent a way of life startlingly different from their own. 'In Japan, most people live in the cities of Tokyo, Osaka or Kyoto,' explains Marino. 'The only people who live in the countryside are those who have to be there for their jobs – farming, fishing, or maybe they are officials who govern the rural areas. Generally, people don't visit the countryside in Japan. The main reason why they'd go to a rural area is for hot springs – but even then they'd stay in their hotel rather than go out and walk around.

'When we see the Cotswolds, the scenery is just like a picture out of a book or a painting you'd see in a museum: it's so perfect. In Japan, there are important old buildings, such as the temples in Kyoto. But when you see the whole scene, there is always something that kills the view such as a big electric pole or an advertising hoarding. There are not the same strict planning laws like there are over here.'

One of the largest Roman villas to be discovered in Britain, Chedworth Roman Villa

Just north of Chedworth, at the village of Yanworth, lies **Chedworth Roman Villa**, one of the largest Roman villas ever to be discovered in Britain, set in a beautifully wooded combe where you can find out so much about the way of life in Roman times: there are the remains of two bathhouses and a hypocaust – an underground heating system – more than a mile of walls, several fine mosaics, a

CHEDWORTH ROMAN VILLA: Yanworth GL54 3LJ; ☎01242 890256; www.nationaltrust. org.uk/chedworth. Entry: adults £5.70, children £3.35, family £14.80; open Mar to Nov Tues–Sun (and bank holidays) 10am–4pm; light snacks and drinks for sale in shop; tea tent serving hot drinks and sandwiches open at weekends and during school holidays.

water-shrine and latrine. It was discovered and excavated in 1864, after being found by a gamekeeper digging for a ferret. The building covers several distinct phases – each one grander than the last – with the original part dating back to the first half of the second century. Interestingly, many of the mosaics were made down the road by a workshop in Cirencester. The British 'touch' is particularly obvious in the mosaic representing the seasons: the figure of Winter is wearing a woollen Birrus Britannicus cloak – the British national dress. The site is now owned by the National Trust: a museum houses objects from the villa, and a 15-minute audio-visual presentation gives visitors an insight into its history.

Look out, as you walk around, for some giant snails, which have been happily living here since the Romans introduced them. They loved these delicacies and would feed them on milk until they were so fat, they couldn't fit in their shells. Delicious (but now protected)!

Yanworth itself has a small, hidden 11th-century church which holds its secrets well. Here, centuries ago, six Cromwellian soldiers were discovered, dead and stripped of their arms; you'll find their grave surrounded by a Victorian iron fence.

Sherborne

Between Bibury and Northleach lies the village of **Sherborne**, which is mainly owned by the National Trust. The must-see here is Lodge Park and the Sherborne Estate, created by John 'Crump' Dutton in 1634. This inveterate gambler was a canny Civil War politician, known for his hunched back and his extravagant banqueting. He indulged his passions by creating a unique deer park with deer course and grandstand, where he could place bets with friends to his heart's content. Crump's house is not open to the public but, thanks to reconstruction work by the trust, you can see the interior of the grandstand as it would have been way back in Dutton's time. Ironically, this gambler died as a result of a horse accident, though no one is sure whether he was thrown from his horse or knocked down when he stopped to open an estate gate. Betty Hall was housekeeper to the seventh Lord Sherborne, who died in 1982. She said she would often hear 'Crump's' impatient footsteps pounding up and down a wooden staircase, but whenever she went to look, she'd find nothing. Interestingly, researchers later discovered there had indeed been a wooden staircase there – later removed – during Crump's time. Betty was so convinced of his presence, she would even lay a place for him at the dinner table.

LODGE PARK AND SHERBORNE ESTATE: Aldsworth, Near Cheltenham GL54 3PP; ☎01451 844130; www.nationaltrust.org.uk Entry: grandstand, adult £5, child £2.80, family £12.50; open Mar to Nov, Fri–Sun; estate free (£1 donation per car to support work on the estate), open daily all year round.

Gloucestershire's County Record Office has catalogued the papers of the Dutton family, the Lords Sherborne, who once owned these sweeping hills and valleys. You can browse through this fascinating archive, held in Alvin Street, Gloucester (☎01452 425295), which contains such gems as letters detailing the financial negotiations between Edward Lenox Dutton, 4th Baron Sherborne and his intended bride, Baroness Emily de Stern. It took seven years for the nuptials finally to be concluded in 1894!

The best of... COTSWOLDS BY WATER

A GOLDEN-STONE BRIDGE REFLECTED IN THE CLEAR WATERS OF A TROUT STREAM
RUNNING THROUGH A VILLAGE; AN OTTER FROLICKING IN THE RIVER DICKLER
WHERE THE WILD ORCHIDS BLOOM; A NIGHTINGALE SINGING BESIDE A DEEP STILL
LAKE; CHILDREN KAYAKING DOWN THE WYE; AND BURBLING STREAMS THAT FALL
FROM THE HILLS INTO DEEP GREEN VALLEYS BELOW...

Top: View across the Forest of Dean in the morning mist; Bottom: Village of Fairford

Top: Houses in Upper Slaughter; Middle: Boats on the River Avon in Stratford;
Bottom: Roman Baths in Bath

Top: Blenheim Palace, declared 'The Finest View in England'; Middle: Miry Bridge;
Bottom: Sunset in the Cotswolds Water Park

Top: Pulteney Bridge over the river Avon in Bath;
Middle: Ducks on stepping stones in Upper Slaughter;
Bottom: Fishing on the River Eye at Greystones Farm Nature Reserve, Bourton on the Water

Much of the countryside around Sherborne is encompassed within the Sherborne Estate's 4,000 acres, tumbling down towards the River Windrush. You can pay to go into the grandstand, or enjoy the estate for free, with its many walks and sweeping views.

Northleach

A peasant from the 16th century, spirited into the town centre, wouldn't feel completely out of place in Northleach because the town has changed so relatively little over the years. In and around the Market Place are architectural gems, varying from rows of late-medieval cottages to half-timbered Tudor houses. The medieval property boundaries – burgage plots – are in evidence: each family was granted a frontage on to the square and a long back garden for growing vegetables and keeping animals. Many of the 'cow passages', which served a number of houses, are still to be seen. It's a fascinating pursuit, simply wandering round the small alleys that lead off the market place. Rumour has it that a maze of tunnels runs underneath, though no one quite knows why – or even if – they exist.

Other interesting buildings include the **Dutton Almshouses**, built for women in 1616; and where the High Street meets the Fosse Way is the former **House of Correction** for petty offenders. When it was built in the 1790s – the brainchild of High Sheriff Sir George Onesiphorous Paul – it represented a radical new approach to prisons. Up until then, petty offenders had been housed with hardened criminals. In fact, Northleach's design was copied on a larger scale for Pentonville Model Prison in London in 1844. You can see the original court room – without charge (as it were) – which looks as it would have done in the 1850s. Most people who ended up here would have broken highway or game laws, or thieved. According to records, one man – Anthony Lathe – was brought in after setting up camp on the road one night – not recommended nowadays.

The Coln Valley

The River Coln rises at Severnhampton near Cheltenham and winds through the Cotswold hills towards Lechlade, where it joins the River Thames. Its clear waters support brown trout and bullheads – and through its valley are some of the most lovely villages in the Cotswolds, including Coln St Dennis, Calcot, Coln Rogers, and Coln St Aldwyns, where the church windows commemorate the 19th-century reformer John Keble and his father. There's a delightful walk from here, along the river to Bibury.

Wet weather

Keith Harding runs a highly unusual shop-cum-museum from the High Street in Northleach. At his **World of Mechanical Music** you'll discover one of the world's best selections of musical boxes and musical collectors' items, along with a large range of books on clocks and mechanical music, and recordings – among other things. While the shop is the perfect place to find unusual gifts, some of them going for a

CELEBRITY CONNECTIONS

The novelist **Joanna Trollope** was associated with the picture-perfect village of Coln St Aldwyns for more than 20 years, until, in 2005, she decided the time had come to up sticks and move closer to London. Joanna has always been a realist – and she's turned that realism to good use. While many believe Gloucestershire to be a wholly wealthy county, full of the well-fed and well-off, she knows differently, and has stated so publicly. '*It has got me into terrible hot water. People hate having their balloon of a dream punctured – for practical reasons: they don't want the value of their property to go down. But my aim has been to try to make the idyll as good as it looks.*' As a result, during her time in the county, Joanna worked dedicatedly for local charities. '*A village which has an exquisite façade may harbour a run-down council estate of utter deprivation,*' as she pointed out.

'*Diana Organ (the former MP for the Forest of Dean) told me about taking Tony Banks to her area, which is deprived in an historical way. He said to her, "At least they have clean air," and she said, "But that's all they do have!"*'

But there's no sentimentality about the past, either – the realism extends in all directions. '*We need to remember all the negative things that have disappeared,*' she says. '*The standard of health in the '40s was hideous. There were women with goitres that they got in the limey valleys; people with the agony of arthritis from those damp cottages. They worked in a beautiful landscape, but one must always call to mind that scene in Tess when she's on the land picking turnips – not a great thing to have to do. Think of living in Arlington Row in 1812, when you were old and probably toothless by the age of 30.*'

KEITH HARDING'S WORLD OF MECHANICAL MUSIC: High Street, Northleach GL54 3ET; ☎01451 860181. Entry: adults £8, seniors £7, children £3.50, family £19; open every day, 10am–6pm, except Christmas Day and Boxing Day.

song (prices from pence to pounds), the museum houses a huge variety of self-playing instruments and automata. It was this sort of music that households would have listened to before the advent of regular broadcasting in the 1920s. Entry to shop free.

LOCAL KNOWLEDGE

Stowell Park, near Northleach – a 6,000 acre estate, with house dating back to the 14th century – is home to **Lord Vestey**. Among other honours, Lord Vestey is Master of the Horse, the senior officer responsible for the Royal Mews, and the carriages and horses of the Sovereign, and Chairman of Cheltenham Racecourse.

Best view: From Stowell Park – they knew where to build houses in the old days. Like many Cotswold views, the colours change depending on the time of year. As I look out now, everywhere is green; later, the corn will change to brown; in autumn, the woods will be turning. At other times, there's wheat, barley, and the yellow of oilseed rape; it's beautiful.

Favourite village: Yanworth, our own village, is lovely. It's in its present position because of the Black Death – the church is about half a mile from the village. We don't know how many people died when the plague broke

out – there are no records to tell us – but in those days, the way they cleared disease was to burn all the houses. They then re-sited Yanworth, in about 1380, on the top of a hill where the wind could blow germs away. The one thing they wouldn't burn was the church; in fact, when there's digging around Yanworth church, they often find remnants of the original houses.

Favourite walk: Down the Coln Valley from Fossebridge to Withington: it's absolutely lovely. You've got the river; you've got the woods; you walk past the Roman villa, down past Compton Cassey and into Withington where there's a very nice church and a very popular pub which gets quite crowded in summer.

Must-see event: We open the garden at Stowell Park three times a year – in May, June and July; and of course there's the car boot sale in September, which is a rather high class one! It's all in aid of charity.

115

What to do with children...

Bibury is home to one of the oldest trout farms in the country, situated in the centre, next to Arlington Mill. Founded in 1902, **Bibury Trout Farm** is a working farm with a gift shop, fish counter (including fresh and smoked trout), delicatessen, plant sales, picnic and play area. Feeding trout – as well as the greedy ducks – might not be a familiar pursuit, but buy a cup of special fish food and the children will be hooked. Which is exactly what they can do with the fish, afterwards, at the beginners' fishery.

> BIBURY TROUT FARM: Bibury GL7 5NL; ☎01285 740215; www.biburytroutfarm. co.uk. Entry: adults £3.50, seniors £3, children £2.50, family £10; open Mar to Oct Mon–Sat 8am–6pm, Sun 10am–6pm; Nov–Feb open daily 8am–4pm; closed Christmas Day.

... and how to avoid children

To discover how important a town was in the Middle Ages, you only have to look at its church. Northleach has one of the most impressive wool churches in England: the 15th-century **Church of St Peter and St Paul**. Although parts date back to at least the 12th century, it was the wool barons of the 15th century who beautified it – indeed, there's a collection of memorial brasses inlaid in the nave floor, signifying the tombs of those very merchants who endowed it. For a 'themed' tour of the Cotswolds, buy Simon Jenkins' book, *England's Thousand Best Churches*, (which covers the whole country, though the Cotswolds are well represented), and plan your route via the most beautiful.

Many other towns such as Winchcombe and Chipping Campden boast magnificent churches funded by the proceeds of the woollen trade. In the latter is a memorial brass to William Grevel, 'The flower of English Woolstaplers'.

Entertainment

Every September, **the world's poshest car boot sale** takes place in the grounds of Stowell Park in Northleach in aid of the NSPCC. The car booters are by invitation only – which means the sort of people who'll be clearing out their attics vary from royalty and landed gentry to some of the many local celebrities. Who knows: if you rummage among the cardboard boxes, you might even find that famous safety-pin dress whose owner lives just down the road. There's also great entertainment, and a marquee of designer clothes. You'll find the date on the NSPCC's events pages of their website (www.nspcc.org.uk).

There are events throughout the year on the Sherborne Estate, including open-air Shakespeare; but perhaps the most evocative spectacle – reminiscent of times past – is a **deerhound day**, where you can watch these noble creatures racing down the deer course. Visit www.nationaltrust.org.uk for details. **Bibury Court Hotel** stages open-air opera in the summer, performed by leading opera companies. The 6 acres of gardens and grounds are edged by the River Coln – a perfect setting (www.biburycourt.com).

This is also the area where a unique outdoor sculpture exhibition takes place every other year (the 'odd' years!). **Fresh Air** is set in the garden and grounds of Quenington Old Rectory and aims to promote and sell the work of local, national and international artists working with materials such as bronze, metal, ceramics, wood and stone (www.freshair2009.com).

🛒 Shopping

It's always a pleasure to visit the many art galleries around the Cotswolds, especially if you're keen to take home a lasting reminder of your stay, which could also prove an excellent investment; the quality is generally superlative, and dealers know their market well. An unusual gallery is **Jonathan Poole** at **Compton Cassey Gallery**, set in a beautiful building in equally beautiful countryside. Featuring contemporary paintings and sculptures from artists throughout the UK and Europe, there are also works from the estates of Miles Davis and John Lennon.

> JONATHAN POOLE: Compton Cassey Gallery, Compton Cassey House, Near Withington GL54 4DE; ☎01242 890224; www.jonathanpoole.co.uk Entry: open by appointment.

Former coaching inn, the Swan Hotel

The best... PLACES TO STAY

BOUTIQUE

Bibury Court Hotel

Bibury GL7 5NT; ☎ 01285 740337
www.biburycourt.com

This Jacobean house, with its wonderful mature grounds, is one of Jilly Cooper's favourite hideaways. All 18 bedrooms have views, and are full of original features and antique furniture. The gardens, with their nooks and crannies, are made for hide and seek.

Prices: from £160, including breakfast.

The Swan Hotel

Bibury GL7 5NW; ☎ 01285 740695
www.cotswold-inns-hotels.co.uk

This 17th-century former coaching inn is probably one of the iconic sights of Bibury, visible almost as soon as you enter the village. It couldn't be more convenient for a stay, and sits right on the banks of the River Coln. The food is good, too (dinner £32.50 for three courses).

Price: B&B from £155 for a double.

SELF-CATERING

Cotteswold House

Market Place, Northleach GL54 3EG
☎ 01451 860493
www.cotteswoldhouse.com

This former barn, which dates back more than 400 years, has been completely renovated to provide lovely accommodation for four people. There's a double and a twin room (the latter with open beams), each with its own shower room. It's conveniently positioned in Northleach Market Place.

Price: from £250 a week.

Bibury Holiday Cottages

Bibury GL7 5NE
☎ 01285 740314
www.biburyholidaycottages.com

This is a collection of four stone cottages, two minutes' walk from the centre of the village. But a word of warning – they are very popular so book early. One of the cottages is disabled-friendly.

Price: from £250 per week.

The National Trust Holiday Cottages

Holiday Booking Office, PO Box 536, Melksham Wiltshire SN12 8SX
☎ 0844 8002070
www.nationaltrust.org.uk

There are two holiday cottages, both former lodges, on the Sherborne Estate. One stands at the edge of the village, and the other sits beside the former entrance gates to Lodge Park; they sleep two to four people and are available for short breaks and week bookings.

Price: West Lodge (two people) from £275; Deer Park Lodge (four) from £367.

Sherborne House

Sherborne GL54 3DZ; ☎ 01386 701177
www.ruralretreats.co.uk

A beautifully-furnished apartment is available within this elegant stately home, formerly owned by Lord Sherborne. Guests have the use of all facilities, which include a heated indoor swimming pool and sauna (small charge), hard tennis court and 10 acres of landscaped gardens.

Price: from £203 for a two-night stay.

The best... FOOD AND DRINK

▶ Staying in

One of the most famous foods this area has to offer has already been mentioned: delicious **Bibury trout**. You can buy fresh and smoked trout from the shop on site at Bibury Trout Farm, in the centre of the village – or, of course, catch your own (☎01285 740215/740212). But there's another product, probably equally well known and certainly as well respected. **Cerney Cheese** is the award-winning goats' cheese founded by Lady Angus at North Cerney in 1983. It's on the menu at many restaurants in this area and beyond, and has won a plethora of awards. Cerney Pyramid is made by hand, using unpasteurised goats' milk and vegetarian rennet – a full fat, Valencay-type cheese, coated with an oak ash/sea salt mix from France. Cerney Pepper is a soft goats' cheese, rolled in the finest coarse ground black pepper.

You can also get Cerney jams, chutney, jelly, oil, honey and quail. For details of stockists, how to order direct, or to visit Cerney House Gardens, the home of Sir Michael and Lady Angus and their family, log onto the website at www.cerneycheese.com.

Two miles from Northleach, in the village of Far Peak, just off the Fosse Way is the **Coln Valley Smokery** (GL54 3JL; ☎01285 740311; www.colnvalley.co.uk), which specialises in salmon and trout, among other products. One of the few genuine traditional smokeries in commercial production, it uses time-honoured methods and updated versions of the original 'London Smokeholes' which give its products their distinct flavour.

Recipe for Success in Far Peak produces a range of first-class ready meals, such as beef bourguignon – beef marinated in red wine overnight; chicken with a leek and white sauce; fish pie; and blackberry and apple crumble. All are cooked as you would at home, using ingredients from many top local suppliers. You can buy directly from the kitchen near Northleach (1, The Apple Store, Far Peak, Northleach GL54 3JL, ☎01285 720685, Mon–Fri, 9am–5pm); from outlets such as Northleach's The Cotswold Stores, Coln Stores and Post Office in Coln St Aldwyns, and the Bibury Trout Farm Shop; or you can mail order (there is a minimum amount) from www.recipeforsuccess.uk.com. There's a perfect way to round off this feast – at Farmington near Northleach, where the Slatter family has started making 'artisan' ice cream using milk from their organic herd; they aim to get from cow to carton in just one day! You can currently get vanilla bean, strawberries and cream and double chocolate (plus passionfruit and mango any time now), using Fairtrade products. **The Cotswold Ice Cream Company** is at Hill House Farm (GL54 3HN; ☎01451 861425; www.cotswoldicecream.net) and open every weekend and bank holidays from 11am to 4pm.

WJ Castle at The Green in Northleach (☎01451 860243) is a first-class butcher. And you'll find a good farm shop in Chedworth: **Cotswold Farm Fayre** at Denfurlong Farm (GL54 4NQ; ☎01285 720265).

EATING OUT

FINE DINING

Bibury Court Hotel
Bibury GL7 5NT
☎ 01285 740337
www.biburycourt.com

Even if you don't book a room here, you should still eat in the restaurant: it's food with flair, made from the best ingredients on offer, and served in an idyllic setting. You'll get the best high teas here, too. In season, you can get sauté of Aldsworth venison from down the road. Expect to pay around £35 for dinner.

CAFÉ

Blades
Fosse Way, Northleach GL54 3JH
☎ 01451 860715

This coffee shop – with internet access – serves coffee, tea, wine, beers, hot snacks, a daily special and a selection of cakes. Owner Felicity Blades attracts families, businesspeople and tourists with her local food. You can also get access from here to Northleach's historic courtroom, located in the same building.

INN

The Hare & Hounds
Foss Cross Chedworth GL54 4NN
☎ 01285 720288
www.hareandhoundsinn.com

Gerry Ragosa is a winner of a *Cotswold Life* magazine Chef of the Year award; and his partner Angela Howe is a warm and welcoming 'front of house'. Pan-fried MacSween haggis on a bed of sweet corn and sweet potato puree with a whisky and honey sauce... What more could you ask! Mains cost around £17.

The Inn at Fossebridge
Near Cheltenham GL54 3JS
☎ 01285 72072
www.fossebridgeinn.co.uk

The French chef here works alongside the Prue Leith school graduate Liz Jenkins, who owns the inn with her father, Robert. Enjoy your meal by the fire or in the restaurant. Roasted best end of Cotswold Lamb with a herb crust, fondant potatoes, and fine beans wrapped in bacon, garlic and rosemary is the signature dish at around £16.

EAT IN/TAKEAWAY

The Puesdown Inn
Near Compton Abdale GL54 4DN
☎ 01451 860262
www.puesdown.cotswoldinns.com

The Puesdown has some prestigious fans, including John Williams, chef at The Ritz, who says he makes for there whenever he can get out of London for a few days. There's now a new pizza restaurant with takeaways from around £5.

☐ Drinking

If you're looking for pure and simple goodness – something you can give the children with complete confidence – you need **Bensons fruit juices** at Stones Farm, Sherborne (GL54 3DH; ☎01451 844134; www.bensonsapplejuice.co.uk). Jeremy Benson and his wife Alexia pride themselves on their policy of no added sugar, water or preservatives. Their juice is suitable for diabetics and loved by children. In every 75cl bottle, there are 15 whole apples turned into juice within a mere 24 hours of picking. Their latest product is the Chilly Billy, a 100% pure fruit iced lolly, named after one of their children! You can buy from farmers' markets, including Woodstock and Witney (there's a full list on the website), various pubs, National Trust properties, or order online and by phone.

As for pubs, the 16th-century **Catherine Wheel** in Bibury (☎01285 740250; on the B4425 as you enter the village) is extremely popular, with its open fires in winter, its oak beams, and the real ales. This is a place packed with Cotswold charm. **The Bathurst Arms** in North Cerney (GL7 7BZ; ☎01285 831281; www.bathurstarms.com) does serve food – and it's good – but it also has a pretty flower garden which runs down to the River Churn: a superb setting for a summer evening's drink. And one of the friendliest pubs around is the **Red Lion** in Northleach's Market Place (☎01451 860251), a 15th-century former coaching inn.

Heading out towards the Oxfordshire border, the **Fox Inn** is one of the Cotswolds' prettiest, on the banks of the River Windrush at Great Barrington with fishing rights available with all the rooms. There's regular live music throughout the year, and you can enjoy Donnington real ale, brewed near Moreton-in-Marsh.

The lost Souls

When journalist Michael Walsh took a wrong turn on his way to Bourton-on-the-Water, he ended up in Great Rissington, where he casually glanced inside the church. There, on the war memorial, a series of faces peered out of old photographs at him – 13 young men from a village of just over 240, who had died in the First World War. But what struck Michael Walsh was the fact that five of these men shared the same surname: Souls. His subsequent research unearthed a fascinating and tragic story.

The Souls family lived in a farm workers' cottage in Great Rissington, a little village that consists of not much more than a main street. Albert and Walter Souls were the first of the brothers to join up when the Great War broke out – they enlisted with the 2nd Worcesters in 1914. The other three eligible lads – Fred, Alf and Arthur – joined the 16th Cheshires.

Albert was the first to be killed, in action on the Somme on 14 March 1916. He was only 21 years old. The next knock on the door for his mother, Annie, concerned Walter. He'd been wounded, and was operated on at a hospital in Rouen. Everyone thought he was doing well, but he died from a blood clot on 2 August 1916 at 24 years of age. Fred's body was never found. He was killed in action in France on 19 July 1916, aged 32; but his disbelieving mother kept a candle burning in the window of the family home, convinced it would guide him home.

Arthur and Alfred were identical twins, born an hour apart. They died in April 1918 within days of each other, aged 31, one in Flanders, the other in France. The last son – known as Bodger – died after the war of meningitis, so Annie lost every one of her boys. You can still see those photographs at St John's, Great Rissington.

ⓘ Visitor Information

Tourist information centres: Cirencester Visitor Information Centre, Corinium Museum, Park Street, Cirencester GL7 2BX, ☎01285 654180, www.cotswold. gov.uk/go/tourism, Mon–Sat 10am– 5pm, Sun 2–5pm and bank holidays; Bourton-on-the-Water Visitor Information Centre, Victoria Street, Bourton-on-the-Water GL54 2BU, ☎01451 820211; Burford Visitor Information Centre, The Brewery, Sheep Street, Burford OX18 4LP, ☎01993 823558, Mar to Oct, Mon–Sat 9.30am–5.30pm, Nov to Feb, Mon–Sat 10am–4.30pm.

Hospitals: Cirencester Hospital, Tetbury Road, Cirencester GL7 1UY, ☎01285 655711; Great Western Hospital, Marlborough Road, Swindon SN3 6BB, ☎01793 604020; (both 24-hour A&E).

Supermarkets include: Waitrose, Sheep Street, Cirencester GL7 1SZ, ☎01285 643733; Tesco, Farrell Close GL7 1HW off Castle Street, Cirencester, ☎0845 6779183; Tesco Extra, Cricklade Road, Cirencester GL7 1NP, ☎0845 6779160; Tesco, Fosse Way, Stow-on-the-Wold GL54 1BX, ☎0845 6779630; Somerfield, High Street, Bourton-on-the-Water, ☎01451 820375; The Co-Op, Station Road, Bourton-on-the-Water GL54 2EP, ☎01451 821858.

Sports: Bourton-on-the-Water Leisure Centre, The Avenue GL54 2BD, ☎01451 824024; Cotswold Leisure Centre, Tetbury Road, Cirencester, ☎01285 654057; Tennis courts, St Michael's Park off King's Street, Cirencester, ☎01285 659182; South Cerney Riding School, Cerney Wick Farm, Cerney Wick, near Cirencester, ☎01793 750151, cerneyridingschool.com; Bourton Vale Equestrian Centre, Bourton-on-the-Water, ☎01451 821101.

Bike rental: Bibury Trout Farm, Bibury, ☎01285 740215.

Taxis include: Cirencester Radio Cars ☎01285 650850; CVC Taxis and Private Hire ☎01285 750070.

THE COTSWOLD WATER PARK
INCLUDING FAIRFORD AND LECHLADE-ON-THAMES

The Cotswolds are well known for their streams and rivers – the driving force behind the wool trade that shaped almost every aspect of the area we know today. But as far as the Cotswolds and water is concerned, that's it... Isn't it? Well actually, no. The Cotswold Water Park, with its 140 man-made lakes, is currently enjoyed by anglers, walkers, naturalists and water-sport enthusiasts – but in relatively small numbers. There are many even in the Cotswolds who know almost nothing about it. Yet roughly speaking, it occupies 40sq miles – from Poole Keynes to Lechlade and from just south of Cirencester to just south of Cricklade. In short, here is the largest area of open water in Britain (half as big again as the Norfolk Broads), which attracts rare and beautiful wildlife.

It's one of the aspects of the Cotswolds which make them an outstanding family destination: something for sports enthusiasts, nature lovers, walkers, historians, artists, architecture aficionados.... And that's particularly true of this part. Close to the attractive market town of Fairford is the US air base, RAF Fairford, which each July plays host to the Royal International Air Tattoo, the world's biggest military air show. If you want to see cutting-edge aviation, you'll find it here. Yet at the other end of the history spectrum, the town is also well known for the 15th-century church of St Mary with its 28 windows made by the master glazier to King Henry VII. Recently the entire set was loaned to the V&A for a 'Gothic' exhibition – they're now safely back in place.

To return to a watery theme, 4 miles east of Fairford is Lechlade-on-Thames. For anyone exploring the Thames – one of England's major waterways – this is an obvious port of call. The town stands at the river's highest navigable point before it flows on through Oxford, and from there towards London and the sea.

WHAT TO SEE AND DO

Cotswold Water Park
It's not often that nature and humankind work hand in hand to create something that's useful to both members of the partnership... But welcome to the Cotswold Water Park! To be fair, nature probably did the lion's share. The Cotswold Water Park is the catchment area of the Upper Thames. Over millions of years, rainfall here eroded the land, as it flowed down to the river; and that erosion was laid down in vast deposits of sand and gravel. Construction firms woke up to the bounty beneath the fields in the 1930s and began a process of extraction that threatened to leave the area scarred and

ugly. But nature once again took the matter in hand: the pits filled up naturally with water, turning themselves into freshwater lakes where large numbers of waterfowl flocked to breed and winter. More recently, this process has been managed and the area is turning into a first-class eco-tourist site.

Water voles are found in the Cotswold Water Park

As a result, the Cotswold Water Park is now home to a fast-growing population of water vole, and it's hoped bittern will begin breeding here in the next few years; there are also otters in many of its streams. Nightingales, bats, dragonflies and rare plants have settled here; and around 200 species of birds overwinter from all parts of the world.

Of course, it also attracts overwintering (and over-summering) people, too. For the outdoor opportunities here are plentiful: aerial adventure, angling, birdwatching, camping, cycle hire, nature reserves, picnic areas, playgrounds, walking – and that's before you get out onto the lakes. For those interested in water sports, this is heaven. You can hire a boat, canoe or kayak; sail, swim, do wakeboarding, waterskiing or windsurfing... And there's even a (manmade) Cotswolds' sandy beach!

There's a way-marked trail featuring art installations, from a willow biodome to a stunning bird hide on the edge of Cleveland Lakes. The hide looks out over a newly

Sailing at South Cerney Outdoor Education

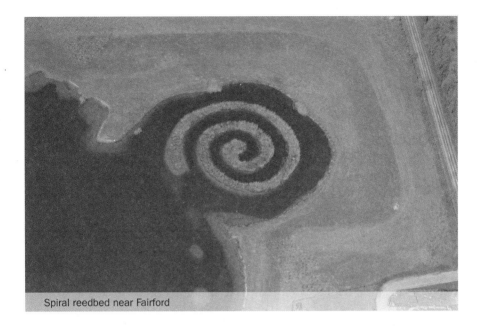
Spiral reedbed near Fairford

planted reed bed and the largest heronry in the south-west. From a bird's eye view, the wooden spiral roof and round shape of the building do not resemble a traditional bird hide, but inside it has all the familiar elements with viewing benches and excellent aspect over the lakes. You can find out exact locations from the Cotswold Water Park website (www.waterpark.org), or call in to the CWP Gateway Centre, Spine Road, South Cerney for a map.

Country parks

The best way to start exploring this whole area is to call into the **Gateway Centre** in South Cerney. This sustainable oak building is heated and cooled by lake power, and the loos are flushed using rainwater! It's also the information hub of the park, with maps and guides to the area (and there's an outdoor gear shop and good café on site). Because of all the extraction that's taken place in the area, some astounding finds have been made here, including a mammoth skull, which is on display – one of only two ever found in England.

GATEWAY CENTRE: Spine Road East, South Cerney GL7 5TL (just off the Swindon-Cirencester A419); ☎01285 862962; www.waterpark.org. Entry: free; open 9am–5pm daily.

The centre is a good starting point for walkers, cyclists and ornithologists, as the canal, footpath and cycleway network are easily accessed from here. Parking is free.

It's easy to be confused about what the Cotswold Water Park actually is – it's not one big park enclosed by a fence. Many of the lakes are privately owned by individuals and clubs. The most fun way for families to explore is to visit one of the two country parks within its boundaries.

KEYNES COUNTRY PARK: Spratsgate Lane, Shorncote, Cirencester GL7 6DF; http://keynescountrypark.com. Entry: adults £1–£4 (depending on season), children up to 50p; open daily; Oct to Mar 9am–5pm, Apr/Sept 9am–7pm; May 9am–8pm; Jun to Aug 9am–9pm.

Keynes Country Park at Shorncote is a pretty good showcase for what this area is all about. Based around two large lakes, there's a super child-friendly bathing beach, where you can take your inflatables – and the sand is tip-top castle-making material. During the summer, there's a lifeguard on duty most of the time (though adult supervision is still essential). There are imaginative playgrounds – a cut above the ordinary – and free barbecue facilities (first come, first served). This place is also hot for dogs, who have their own designated swimming area (though no paws, please, on the bathing beach or in the children's play areas). There is a lakeside café selling light snacks in summer; and a shop with hot drinks and cakes throughout the year.

Those with higher ideals can head for high ropes action at **Head for Heights** (☎01285 770007; www.head4heights.net) or for water sports with **Waterland Outdoor Pursuits** on the country park lake (☎01285 861202; www.ukwatersports.co.uk) but you must book in advance. Holiday and day tickets are also available for some excellent lake fishing (www.ashtonkeynesanglingclub.info).

The nature lover's paradise

Orchids, dragonflies, nightingales, Daubenton bats (which eat insects and hunt over open water), and snakeshead fritillary thrive in this area. There are four nature reserves in the water park, all free of charge. **Coke's Pit** is just along the road from Keynes Country Park; a 20-minute walk from the north-west corner of Lake 31 will take you to Shorncote Reedbed where there's a bird hide for viewing the winter waterbirds and summer migrants. **Clattinger Farm**, between the villages of Oaksey and Minety, is like stepping back into a rural England of 60 years ago when the fields would be carpeted with wildflowers; it's noted for a spectacular orchid show with many different varieties. It's one of the finest examples of hay meadows in the country. Visit late April to the end of June to see it at its best.

Right beside Clattinger Farm is the entrance to **Swillbrook Lakes**, one of the best spots for birdwatching. Wildflowers, willow scrub, marsh and reed beds provide habitats for a range of wildlife; warblers are the first to arrive in April; by May, the sounds are absolutely trilling: blackcap, nightingale, great crested grebe, coot, mallard and many more, with dragon and damselfly accompaniment.

For more information on these and other nature reserves in Wiltshire, visit the wildlife trust's website (www.wiltshirewildlife.org). There's also a Natural England reserve nearby. **North Meadow** (www.naturalengland.org) on the outskirts of Cricklade is another beautiful flower-rich hay meadow, often flooded by the Rivers Thames and Churn in winter. The largest population of snakeshead fritillary in Britain grows here. Look out for the organised walks around late March.

Keynes Country Park

CELEBRITY CONNECTIONS

Overwintering birds are not the only exotic creatures to fly into the Cotswold Water Park in search of a cool place to nest. **Jade Jagger**, designer daughter of Mick and Bianca, is a not-infrequent visitor. She's been working near Lechlade on a second-homes development called 'the Lakes by Yoo', a private 650-acre estate of lakes and woodland. She and business partner Tom Bartlett were brought in by the Yoo design studio to create individual floor plans and furniture for the 160 homes that are being built here.

The Cotswolds, Jade says, have always been an area she loves, partly because she has friends here, and partly because there's *'a real sense of community'. 'Ever since my late teens, I have either lived in the English countryside or in Ibiza. People often assume that I live this rock and roll city lifestyle but it couldn't be farther from the truth. I am very much a laid-back, country girl at heart.'*

The Lakes is one of several second-home developments in the area, including Lower Mill Estate (www.lowermillestate.com). Many people consider it an excellent use of land – and also a means of helping to keep traditional villages free of 'weekenders'. For Jade, this development is a way of introducing country pursuits to a wider audience. *'It is about creating a safe and secure haven for families to enjoy time away from their urban life; where families can indulge in the many local activities such as fishing, canoeing, sailing, swimming or just climbing a tree or going for a walk,'* she says.

So what is Jade Jagger's own home style? *'Very laid-back with a hint of funk and glamour,'* she says. *'I have two children and four dogs and I have always had an open-door policy wherever I am so there is always a lot going on around me. I've tried to create a place where all are welcome.'*

Neigh Bridge Country Park near Somerford Keynes (signposted off the main road) is free all year round and has a picnic area, play equipment and a lakeside walk. The Thames Path runs next to the park; and there are facilities for disabled anglers. More information is available from Ashton Keynes Angling Club (www.ashtonkeynesanglingclub.info).

Fairford

On the drive from the Cotswold Water Park to the small town of Fairford, which lies on the River Coln, is **Down Ampney**. It was here, at the Old Vicarage, that the composer Ralph Vaughan Williams was born in 1872. He paid tribute to the village by naming the tune for the hymn *Come Down, O Love Divine* in its honour. Vaughan Williams was one of the first people to travel around the countryside, noting down folksongs and carols for posterity.

There are two names that spring to mind when it comes to Fairford. The first is John Tame of Fairford Manor, a wealthy wool baron who commissioned the magnificent windows of **St Mary's Church** in the 15th century. The 28 windows were almost certainly created by the master glazier to King Henry VII, Bernard Flower, from the Netherlands: the upper half of the magnificent 30ft west window shows Christ in the glory of heaven surrounded by a rainbow, while the carryings on of hell are enjoyed by the Devil below. These windows are the only complete set in England to have survived from this period. During the Reformation, they were whitewashed to disguise them, and were removed completely during the Second World War.

Look out for another memorial in the churchyard – that of Tiddles the tabby cat, who adopted the church from 1963 until she died in 1980. She'd often visit during services and sit on various worshippers' knees. A local stonemason felt she needed a permanent memorial, which he carved himself.

The second name associated with Fairford is that of John Keble, leader of the Oxford Movement, who was born in Fairford in 1792. He went on to become rector of the pretty village of **Eastleach St Martin**, which is separated by the River Leach from its 'twin' **Eastleach Turville**, and connected by the old stone Keble's bridge.

Lechlade

In September 1815, Percy Bysshe Shelley, one of the world's finest lyric poets, took Mary Godwin (then his mistress; later his wife) on an expedition to discover the source of the Thames. Along with Mary's stepbrother, Charles Clairmont, and the satirical novelist Thomas Love Peacock, they stopped at The Swan in Lechlade. In most people's books, that few days' stay would have been long enough to buy a tea towel and send a few postcards. Shelley achieved rather more. He used the time to visit the town's 15th-century **Church of St Lawrence** where he wrote his stanzas, entitled *A Summer Evening Churchyard*; thus he managed to secure a place in the town's history, a bit more space in English anthologies, and get a slice of Lechlade named after him to boot. The path through the churchyard is now known as Shelley's Walk.

Lechlade-on-Thames stands at the river's highest navigable point before it flows on through Oxford, and thence towards London and the sea. **St John's Lock**, over the

CELEBRITY CONNECTIONS

You're more likely to catch **Sharron Davies** in a Gucci suit than a swimsuit nowadays. *'After swimming for six hours a day for so long, it's not something I do very often now,'* she admits. Instead, the former golden girl of the pool is now an all-round ambassador and a highly successful businesswoman. She and her family – husband Tony Kingston, an airline pilot, and children Fin, Grace and Elliott – live in a huge town house in Fairford, a place they adore.

It was an Olympic moment – Munich, 1972 – that first set Sharron on the path to stardom. She was only 10 years old when American swimmer Mark Spitz set a record for winning seven gold medals. *'I thought: Wow! That's what I'd like to do!'* A year later, she took part in her first ever international – in Cheltenham, of all places. Sharron then went on to achieve two gold medals at the Commonwealth Games and a silver at the 1980 Olympics in Moscow. Though she works hard to campaign to improve sporting facilities for children, she also maintains a very balanced approach: her own children enjoy a wide range of sports, including rugby, swimming, skiing, scuba diving and running. *'The nice thing with sport nowadays is that we've grown up a little bit,'* she says. *'We realise we don't have to push our kids so hard so early.'*

fields past Halfpenny Bridge, is the first of many locks between the Cotswolds and London, and is guarded by a statue of 'Old Father Thames', created for the Crystal Palace exhibition of 1851. The stone bridge here, which was originally made of wood, was put up in the 13th century and cared for by monks from the local priory. To explore on foot, buy a copy of the **Fairford and Lechlade Book of Walks** – an easy-to-use guide to 11 walks in and around the two rural towns. It's available, priced £4.95, from local shops or by calling 01285 712344.

The **Riverside Park**, just south of the Thames at Lechlade (via the A361; ☎01793 771419) is a 19 acre flood plain site, often under water during the winter. With access to the banks of the Thames, and to the Thames Path, the site has picnic tables, and is a perfect spot for nature lovers. In summer, the large area of reed beds in the north-east corner is home to many species of birds; and you'll also see fish, including trout, bream and perch, along with insects, notably dragonflies and damselflies.

From early April to the end of September, you can take to the river on the **luxury Edwardian-style river boat**, the **MV Inglesham** from here. Trips last about 30 minutes and may include a commentary on the Thames and Severn Canal, as well as local river history. In the summer, you should see kingfishers, swans, various breeds of duck, moorhen, coot and heron. Although the herons are timid when you approach them

MV INGLESHAM: ☎01367 252401/ 01367 252352; www.cotswoldcanals.com
Entry: adults £3, children £2; trips last 30min; weekends and bank holidays, Apr to Sept 11am–5pm; no need to book, though there may be a wait at busy times.

on foot, they're much less cautious of boats, which means you can get up close and personal. The roundhouses you'll see are the old lengthmen's cottages – lockkeepers, responsible for looking after a length of the canal.

Other great places for fishing are the **Lechlade and Bushyleaze Trout Fisheries**, just east of Lechlade. Both are beautifully landscaped, peaceful places to while away a half-day or day, and regularly stocked with rainbow and brown trout.

LECHLADE AND BUSHYLEAZE TROUT FISHERIES: Lechlade GL7 3QQ; ☎01367 253266; www.lechladetrout.co.uk.

At Filkins, near Lechlade, there's a sweet little museum: **Swinford Museum** (☎01367 860209) is only open on the first Sunday of the month from May to September, 2–5pm, but it is free. This Cotswold cottage displays craft tools of the area, pints and pipes from the local pub; and pottery, clothes and toys from the cottage – an interesting diversion.

CELEBRITY CONNECTIONS

Former actress **Fiona Fullerton** is still bringing the house down – but nowadays it's as a clever property expert and developer. She can tell you what to buy, what to avoid, where's hot, and where the perfect property location might be – which, of course, is the Cotswolds, where she now lives with husband Neil Shackell and their children, James and Lucy. When Fiona and Neil were house-hunting, they were determined to avoid any stereotypical image of the Cotswolds. They settled on an old vicarage on the River Thames in the southern-most corner of Gloucestershire – but in their village, the picture postcard honey-stone cottages are conspicuous by their absence. It's a real living, working environment.

There are many spots Fiona loves in the area, but a particular favourite is St Mary's Church, Kempsford. '*Although Norman in origin, it was considerably enlarged in the late 1300s by John of Gaunt whose wife, the Lady Blanche, was from Kempsford. It has statues that were defaced by Cromwell's men,*' she says. '*I love that sense of history.*'

Kelmscott Manor

Three miles east of Lechlade is the village of Kelmscott, which sprang to public attention as the home of William Morris, who signed a joint lease on the manor with his friend the Pre-Raphaelite painter Dante Gabriel Rossetti in 1871. This pioneer of the Arts and Crafts movement, which extolled fine workmanship, lived by his philosophy: '*Have nothing in your house that you do not know to be useful, or believe to be beautiful*' – and Kelmscott Manor exemplifies that. This Grade I listed farmhouse, next to the Thames, dates back to the 16th century and is built of local limestone. Morris spent his summers here, delighting in its natural setting, almost as if it had 'grown up out of the soil'.

KELMSCOTT MANOR: Kelmscott, Lechlade GL7 3HG; ☎01367 252486. Entry: house and garden, adults £8.50, children and students with card (8–16) £4.25; open Apr to Sept every Wed 11am–5pm and the first and third Sat of each month; the garden also open Thurs, 2–5pm, in May/Jun; shop/licensed restaurant.

The manor contains a superb collection of the sorts of possessions Morris surrounded himself with, and some of his work, and that of his associates, in the form of furniture, ceramics, textiles and carpets. The house has limited capacity and admission is by timed ticket not bookable in advance.

Kelmscott Manor, the home of the Pre-Raphaelite painter William Morris

Wet weather

Buscot House

The fine 18th-century house at **Buscot Park** (☎0845 345 3387), Faringdon, could tell a story or two. It was built for Edward Loveden Townsend, who earned the nickname Old Father Thames for his work improving the river from Staines to Lechlade.

> BUSCOT PARK: Faringdon, Oxfordshire SN7 8BU; ☎0845 345 3387; www.buscotpark. com; www.national-trust.org.uk. Entry: adults £7.50, children £3.75 (grounds only £5 and £2.50); open Apr to Sept (open during Mar if Easter falls early); tearoom.

Subsequent owners include the Australian tycoon, Robert Tertius Campbell, who turned Buscot into a model agricultural estate, and the city financier, Alexander Henderson, whose descendants continue to live here. Today, Buscot Park is administered by Lord Faringdon on behalf of the National Trust, and the contents of the house are owned by a separate charitable trust, The Faringdon Collection. This fabulous collection includes paintings by Rembrandt, Murillo, Rossetti, and the Briar Rose series by Burne-Jones. If it is fine, you'll enjoy a bonus: the extensive parklands offer delightful walks, and the landscaping includes a spectacular water garden designed by Harold Peto, and the Four Seasons walled garden created by the present Lord Faringdon.

Buscot Park, an 18th century house in Faringdon

What to do with children

The joys of the Cotswold Water Park are obvious in this context, too. But a particular local favourite for youngsters is the **Butts Farm** (3 miles east of Cirencester on the old A419) where you can rub shoulders with some real 'country dwellers': you can feed

LOCAL KNOWLEDGE

Over the past decade, **Catherine Elliott** has been one of the movers and shakers at Fairford's Royal International Air Tattoo. As deputy director of ground operations, she was involved in the planning and building of the showground which welcomes more than 150,000 visitors each July. In 2009, she'll be at the air tattoo for the first time ever as a visitor! The arrival of baby Harriet means she's decided to hand over the reins – at least for a while.

Best tearoom: 7a Coffee Shop & Delicatessen in Fairford, which is probably also the shop I could least live without. They're very baby-friendly, and their hot chocolate and brownies are the best in the world.

Top tip: Come to the air tattoo, of course! People know it's the biggest military air show in the world, but they don't always realise what a great all-round day out it is. You could fill a whole weekend without even looking at an aircraft if you wanted to. When Harriet is

older, I'm most looking forward to taking her round on an open-top bus; you get such a good view of the show.

Best pub: We've got out of the habit of pubs because we've such nice local restaurants in Fairford, such as Allium and The Bridge.

Favourite produce: Gloucester Old Spot belly pork from Chesterton Farm Shop in Cirencester. In May or June, I'd serve it with local asparagus.

Favourite view: Out of my upstairs window, looking out onto Fairford's water meadows across to the mill bridge. At certain times of year, there'll be wild flowers and cattle; I've seen nesting swans and little egrets. Nothing about that view ever sits still.

Best local event: Fairford Festival, which takes place each June, because of all the bonhomie and fun. There's a ball on the Friday night, a dog show and activities on The Walnut Tree Field on the Saturday, and the 10 and 3km fun runs on the Sunday.

133

pigs, lambs, and goat kids, watch chicks hatching, cuddle a bunny, have a pony ride (Thurs/Sun at 2pm) and a tractor safari (Sat 2pm). It's a real hands-on experience and a perfect place for animal lovers of all ages.

For a more macho outdoor adventure, **Cotswold Forest School** has a survival programme (minimum group size of five), with fire lighting, shelter building and tracking skills.

THE BUTTS FARM: South Cerney, Cirencester GL7 5QE; ☎01285 869414; thebuttsfarmshop.com. Entry: adults £5, children £4, concessions £4.50, family £16; open Tues–Sun 10.30 am–5pm Feb half term to Oct half term.

COTSWOLD FOREST SCHOOL: Clayhill Copse, Spine Road East, Ashton Keynes; ☎07738 708880; www.cotswoldforestschool.co.uk

Entertainment

Each July, the Cotswolds play host to the biggest military air show in the world – **Fairford's Royal International Air Tattoo**, which regularly attracts crowds in excess of 150,000 over the weekend. But as its spokesman Richard Arquati explains, there's something for everyone: *'Even though it is the biggest event of its kind in the world, the Air Tattoo is so much more than just an air show. There are so many things to see that it is almost impossible to do everything in one day.'* The flying display itself runs from 10am to 6pm.

Details change each year, though parking and entry for under-16s is free; for more information, visit www.airtattoo.com.

The Red Arrows at the Fairford Air Tattoo

In August, **Fairford Steam Rally** in Fairford Park, with its classic vehicles and arena displays is always a good family event (www.fairfordsteamrally.com). The Cotswold Water Park Society runs an annual programme of events including **guided walks, workshops, events for children, fossil hunts** and many more activities, which aim to encourage people to discover the rich variety of wildlife. They vary each year, but you'll find details at www.waterpark.org.

The best... **PLACES TO STAY**

BOUTIQUE

Barnsley House

Barnsley, Cirencester GL7 5EE
☎ **01285 740000**
www.barnsleyhouse.com

This is Elizabeth Hurley's hotel of choice and where (as well as in the gorgeous Village Pub next door) she accommodated so many of her wedding guests when she married Arun Nayar. The hotel was once the home of Prince Charles's friend Rosemary Verey, and her outstanding gardens are very much part of the attraction. Excellent food, too.

Price: rooms from £295, including breakfast.

HOTEL

Cotswold Water Park Four Pillars Hotel

Lake 6, South Cerney GL7 5FP
☎ **01285 864000**
www.four-pillars.co.uk/cotswoldwaterpark

This newly opened hotel has merged nature, landscape and contemporary design to make sure guests get the most from its wonderful position: ask for a lake view if you want to derive maximum benefit from staying.

Price: double rooms from £75.

CAMPSITE

Hoburne Cotswold

Broadway Lane, South Cerney GL7 5UQ
☎ **01285 860216**
www.hoburne.com/cotswold_main.asp

Even families that don't normally favour camping should take a look at this top-quality accommodation, with plenty of facilities, based around four lakes (with fly fishing and boats) teeming with wildlife. There are holiday caravans, lodges, chalet, touring and camping pitches and an outdoor heated swimming pool.

Price: pitches from £14.40 per night; lodges (two-bed for up to four people) from £343 a week.

SELF-CATERING

Watermark Club

Isis Lakes, Spine Road, South Cerney GL7 5TL
☎ **01285 869181**
www.watermarkclub.co.uk

The Watermark is a select second-home complex over six lakes and 500 acres of land, with its own dedicated fishing lakes, a water-ski club, cable ski tow, sailing lakes, tennis courts and a health and fitness club. The lodges are New England-style and some will accept pets. Short breaks, weekly booking and longer, on request, are available.

Price: from £383 for a short break.

Log House Holidays

Poole Keynes, Cirencester GL7 6ED
☎ **01285 770082/07792 836279**
www.loghouseholidays.co.uk

This is your chance to relax in traditional Finnish Log Houses and wooden lodges set on a private, secluded 100 acre lake in the Cotswolds. The property is a Site of Special Scientific Interest because of its outstanding conservation interests. Each house comes with its own rowing boat and life jackets. Home-cooked meals by arrangement.

Price: from £600 to £1800 a week.

Mill Cottages

Fairford GL7 4JG; ☎ **0845 268 0785**
www.english-country-cottages.co.uk

The Ernest Cook Trust, dedicated to preserving English country houses and their estates, now owns Fairford Park, where it lets out two mill cottages sleeping six and seven, idyllically situated by the River Coln. Both form part of a 17th-century Grade II listed mill house. Just a short walk away lies Fairford's historic market square, with its shops, inns and restaurants.

Price: from £503 per week; short breaks available.

The best... FOOD AND DRINK

▶ Staying in

An unusual company is **The Country Monkey** in South Cerney. It produces delicious breakfast cereals made from local and organic ingredients. There's also a 'Trail Mix' which is ideal to take out when walking or biking as a quick and healthy energy snack. You can shop online (www.thecountrymonkey.co.uk; ☎01285 860333) or buy at many local farm shops.

There are some top farm suppliers of meat around, including **Great Farm** in Whelford near Fairford with its free-range chicken, guinea fowl and duck available from local butchers or directly from the farm. Email via the website at www.greatfarm.co.uk. **The Butts Farm** in South Cerney (GL7 5QE; ☎01285 862224; thebuttsfarmshop.com) – mentioned in the 'What to do with the children' section, above – is a top destination for rare-breed meat, poultry and eggs. It's run by Judy Hancox and Gary Wallace: their combined knowledge of food, cooking and master butchery really shine through.

For the best way to cheat peruse the gorgeous list from the **Cotswold Pudding Company** at Fairford, with their traditionally made sticky puddings, free from artificial additives and preservatives. They include chocolate, toffee and pecan, lemon, and ginger, and they all have one thing in common – plate-licking stickiness! They're for sale at Stroud Farmers' Market each Saturday and local shops including Burford Garden Company. For more information, see www.cotswoldpuddingcompany.co.uk.

Numerous **country markets** also take place each week around the Cotswolds – they're cooperatives, which bring together local people who love to cook to the highest standards. Fairford has one in the Palmer Hall in London Road (GL7 4AQ), selling baked goods, preserves, eggs, honey, garden produce and crafts, on a Wednesday morning, 9–11am. For more information about this, and other Country Markets, log onto www.country-markets.co.uk.

A good way to get hold of local meat is to buy in from some of the individual shops in the local towns, such as **Cutler and Bayliss**, the traditional family butcher and greengrocer at 4 Oak Street in Lechlade (GL7 3AX; ☎01367252451; cutlerandbayliss. co.uk) – plus, don't miss out on the hand-made sausages and home-cured bacon.

EATING OUT

FINE DINING

Allium
**1 London Street, Market Place,
Fairford GL7 4AH**
☎ **01285 712200**
www.allium.uk.net

Husband and wife team, James and
Erica Graham are passionate about
food, and they choose suppliers who
feel the same way. A set menu features
dishes such as rump of English rose
veal with local veg and Madeira sauce
(just under £40); more modest options
available in the week.

RESTAURANT

The Wild Duck Inn
**Drakes Island, Ewen,
Cirencester GL7 6BY**
☎ **01285 77031**
www.thewildduckinn.co.uk

This is the kind of place that any local
'foodie' will tell you about at the drop
of a hat (though they'd probably rather
keep it to themselves.) It's a byword for
good food, great atmosphere and lovely
setting. Choose burgers, sophisticated
dishes, or traditional fare, such as
Gloucester Old Spot ham salad at
under £10.

The Village Pub
Barnsley, Cirencester GL7 5EF
☎ **01295 740421**
www.thevillagepub.co.uk

Elizabeth Hurley and Arun love the
'VeePee' (as it's known) with its
flagstone and oak floors, exposed
beams, open fireplaces and local real
ales. Best of all is the food, praised by
critics from Jay Rayner to Matthew Fort.
Try the twice-baked double Gloucester
soufflé, if it's on, at around £10.

The Swan
Southrop GL7 3NU
☎ **01367 850205**
www.theswanatsouthrop.co.uk

This 17th-century Cotswold inn is run by
Sebastian and Lana Snow, a protégé
of Antony Worral Thompson. Kelmscott
pork and Southrop lamb rub shoulders
with continental escargots Bourgogne.
Three courses come in at around £30.

The Old Boathouse
**Lake 6, Spine Road East,
South Cerney, Cirencester GL7 5FP**
☎ **01285 864111**
**www.cotswoldwaterparkhotel.co.uk/
the-old-boathouse-_94**

Plenty of glass means you can fully
enjoy the lake this restaurant stands
beside; with its boathouse styling, you
could almost believe you're afloat.
There are no gimmicks with the food,
however, which is home-cooked and
contemporary. Enjoy the burger with
Cotswold blue cheese for around £11.

EATING OUT

Colley's Supper Rooms
**High Street, Lechlade-on-Thames
GL7 3AE
☎ 01367 252218
www.colleyssupperrooms.co.uk**

Guests are encouraged to spend the
entire evening savouring excellent
food, and options for each course
are presented to you at your table
– often by the head chef. The *pièce de
résistance* is the famous 'parade' of
home-made desserts. Four-course prices
vary midweek/weekend, but start from
around £25–£30.

Chilli Pepper
**Broadwell, Near Lechlade GL7 3QS
www.chilli-pepper.net**

Fresh, organic, seasonal and supplied
daily: that's the only description you
need of the ingredients that go into the
food at this 16th-century inn, tucked away
in a small village. Mains from around
£15–£20 are rich and delicious.

TEAROOMS

The Black Cat Tearooms
**High Street, Lechlade GL7 3AD
☎ 01367 252273**

Enjoy a traditional Cotswold cream tea
here with homemade scones, jam and
clotted cream, or snack lunches and
sandwiches. This is also the perfect
place to gather goodies for a picnic on
the banks of the River Thames.

EAT IN/TAKEAWAY

The Wheatsheaf Inn
**Oaksey SN16 9TB; ☎ 01666 577348
www.thecompletechef.co.uk**

Excellent food is on the daily changing
blackboard menus at this inn, which also
serves fantastic fish and chips to eat in
or take away on a Friday, 5.30–7.30pm.
It's a place of intriguing extremes
and has won awards for Britain's best
burgers.

Born to be wild

Are you after a good, old-fashioned bit of meat? Then try something new-fangled: wild boar. *'It's a flavour from the old days: traditional, slow, delicious,'* says farmer Simon Gaskell, who runs The Real Boar Company.

In an England of more than 300 years ago, boar would have been a common sight in the wild. But their downfall lay in being such fun to catch and even more fun to eat, and they were more or less hunted out of existence... Or were they? There are some who think that boars – Britain's largest mammal – never truly disappeared from the forest. No one is quite sure how many there are living in the wild today, but they're spotted in ever increasing numbers. They're known to have settled happily into the Forest of Dean, particularly around Cinderford. Groups of more than 20 have been observed, with sows and boarlets.

They live similarly on Simon's farm, just over the border in Wiltshire. He keeps 30 female boar in two family groups – or sounders (the collective name for wild boar) – each with a good strong male in charge. Julian is one; Sparky is the other.

The Fat Duck at Bray has a regular order for Simon's wild boar salami. Cured in red wine and interwoven with peppercorns, it has the feel and flavour of the finest quality charcuterie. You can also buy the usual cuts – chops, loin, fillet and so on – but boar meat has its own unique and delicious flavour, quite different from pork. It's also high in protein, low in cholesterol and fat. For local stockists and mail order check the website (www.therealboar. co.uk) or ring 01249 782861/ 07889 154002.

🍸 Drinking

You don't get many pubs like the **Red Lion at Ampney St Peter** (GL7 5SL; ☎01285 851596) – it's one of a dying breed. For one thing, the term 'drinking pub' is one hundred percent accurate here – no food is served. Conversation and good beer are both on the menu instead; and this is a landlord who knows how to keep beer in perfect condition.

In an area such as this, defined by its rivers and lakes, unsurprisingly there are numerous places to while away holiday time. At the **Old George** in the centre of South Cerney (GL7 5TR; ☎01285 869989; www.oldgeorgeinn.co.uk), you can even play a game on the boules court. Families will enjoy the **Baker's Arms** at Somerford Keynes (GL7 6DN; ☎01285 861298) with its low beamed ceilings, inglenook fireplaces and mature gardens, while the trendier **Railway Inn** in Fairford's London Road would probably appeal to young couples (GL7 4AR; ☎01285 712284). The 13th-century **Trout Inn** at St John's Bridge in Lechlade (GL7 3HA; ☎01367 252313; www.thetroutinn. com), by the weir pool to St John's Lock, the first lock on the River Thames, is well known for live jazz nights.

ⓘ Visitor Information

Tourist information centre: Cirencester Visitor Information Centre, Corinium Museum, Park Street, Cirencester GL7 2BX, ☎01285 654180, www.cotswold.gov.uk/go/tourism, Mon–Sat 10am–5pm, Sun 2–5pm and bank holidays.

Hospitals: Cirencester Hospital, Tetbury Road, Cirencester GL7 1UY, ☎01285 655711; Great Western Hospital in Marlborough Road, Swindon SN3 6BB, ☎01793 604020; (both 24-hrA&E).

Supermarkets include: Waitrose, Sheep Street GL7 1SZ, ☎01285 643733; Tesco, Farrell Close GL7 1HW, off Castle Street, ☎0845 6779183; Tesco Extra, Cricklade Road GL7 1NP, ☎0845 6779160; Cirencester, Londis, Burford Street, Lechlade GL7 3AP, ☎01367 252202.

Sports: Find a full list at www.waterpark.org, including Head 4 Heights, Keynes Country Park GL7 6DF, ☎01285 770007, www.head4heights.net (simulated parachute jumps, pole climbs, trapeze jumps, etc.); The Watermark Club in Station Road, South Cerney GL7 6TH, ☎01285 860606, www.WMSki.com (waterskiing, wakeboarding, cable ski tow and fun inflatable rides); South Cerney Riding School, Cerney Wick Farm, Cerney Wick, Near Cirencester, ☎01793 750151, cerneyridingschool.com.

Bike, wetsuit and boat hire: Boats, bikes, wetsuits and accessories from Go By Cycle, Hire & Sales Centre, Somerford Keynes GL7 6DS, ☎07970 419208, www.go-by-cycle.co.uk.

Taxis include: Cirencester Radio Cars ☎01285 650850; CT's Lechlade Taxi Service ☎01367 252575.

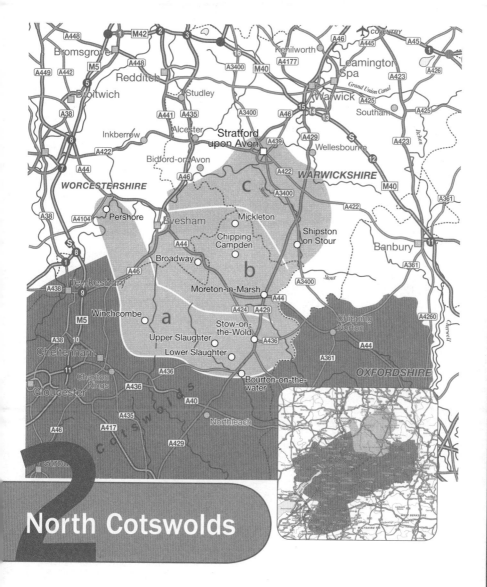

North Cotswolds

a. Bourton, Stow and Winchcombe
b. Moreton, Broadway and Chipping Campden
c. Stratford-upon-Avon

Unmissable highlights

01 Walk from Upper Slaughter to Lower Slaughter, two of the most gorgeous villages in England, and decide whether even Walt Disney could have done a better job, p. 147

02 Mix with the racing crowd from the surrounding well-known yards, at the Hollow Bottom pub in Guiting Power, and dream of riding your own winner, p. 164

03 Try some of Simon Weaver's organic Brie, made from the milk of cows grazed on fields by the River Dikler, p. 162

04 Pay your respects to Henry VIII's last queen, Katherine Parr, buried in a chapel in the romantic grounds of Sudeley Castle, p. 150

05 Enjoy a panoramic view over 13 counties from the top of Broadway Tower, 312m above sea level, once the country retreat of Arts and Crafts pioneer William Morris, p. 169

06 Marvel at the treasure trove that is Snowshill Manor; its eccentric owner stuffed it with 22,000 objects, including suits of 19th-century Samurai armour, p. 174

07 Go quad biking through the Cotswold countryside around Moreton-in-Marsh on a daring activity day (while the kids ride the mini-quads), p. 176

08 Discover what owls really get up to and watch a birds of prey flying display at the Cotswold Falconry Centre, p. 176

09 Visit the Shakespeare houses at Stratford-upon-Avon – followed by a drink with the actors at the famous Dirty Duck, p. 187

10 Weave some magic spells at the Creaky Cauldron in Henley Street and see if you can stay the course at one of Stratford's creepiest museums, p. 190

NORTH COTSWOLDS

For some people, the north is what the Cotswolds are all about. The unique warmth of the buildings, the wide valleys with their streams that gently undulate, and the views that seem hardly to have changed over centuries. You don't need a map to distinguish the north Cotswolds – just an eye for colour. For look at the houses in the towns and villages north of Northleach, and you'll see stone that could have been fashioned by bees: 'honey' is the word people the world over use to describe those distinctive mellow tones.

This limestone is not just found in the Cotswolds, though it's particularly characteristic of the region. Indeed, stone from local quarries was used in part of the construction of some of England's most lovely buildings, including St Paul's Cathedral and the Houses of Parliament. But it's been used to perfect effect in places such as Broadway, with its wide main street, and Chipping Campden, where the curved terraces of the High Street have been described as the most perfect in England. It's true of many of the smaller villages, too. Guiting Power idles around an iconic English green; Stanton's picture-perfect quality has been used to advantage in a plethora of films, and there's Blockley, built on the silk trade. Blockley's cottages that once housed humble weavers would now be every merchant banker's dream.

Further north, right at the extreme tip of the Cotswolds, is Stratford-upon-Avon, which produced the region's most famous son. William Shakespeare is everywhere in this delightful town, which can be approached by road or by water. You can see the house where he was born and the site of the house where he breathed his last. There's the farm on which his mother lived; the impressive cottage where his wife, Anne Hathaway, spent her childhood, and the houses his daughter and granddaughter called home. And yet somehow it escapes all traces of tackiness.

It would be hard to claim you'd had the full Cotswold experience without a visit to the likes of Chipping Campden, Broadway and Stow-on-the-Wold. And, anyway, why on earth would anyone want to miss out on idylls such as these?

BOURTON, STOW AND WINCHCOMBE
INCLUDING THE SLAUGHTERS

If Walt Disney had decided to build a Cotswold film set, he simply couldn't have bettered the backdrop of the Slaughters. These gorgeous villages, where the gentle waters of the River Eye run clear, bring visitors in their thousands from as far away as Japan – and they're not disappointed: the reality is every bit as picturesque as the scenes they dreamed over in their magazines and travel books.

Besides views, walks, villages and towns providing enjoyment for free, there are also attractions that will suit every member of the family. The fantastic Cotswold Farm Park is run by BBC TV presenter Adam Henson and conserves some of the rare breeds that helped shape the very Cotswold landscape. One of the Cotswolds' few castles, Sudeley, is in Winchcombe, packed full of historical tales and associations. There's also the breathtakingly beautiful and very lived-in Stanway House, which is as unlike a museum as you could imagine. You can take a steam train, explore the woods that inspired Tolkien, see one of Bill Bryson's favourite spots or even visit Brum, that superhero car, at the Cotswold Motor Museum. There are surprises too. One of the best restaurants in the area – 5 North Street – is in Winchcombe; and there's fantastic local produce on offer, such as Simon Weaver's Cotswold Brie.

It was of one of the villages in this area that Edward Thomas nostalgically wrote, '*I remember Adlestrop...*' And certainly, if ever there was an area where the words 'chocolate box' should be employed, this is it.

WHAT TO SEE AND DO

Bourton-on-the-Water

Bourton-on-the-Water is one of those places that simply has it all: beauty, attractions, historic architecture and, the lovely Windrush river meandering through its heart. There are some Cotswold hotspots where you just know you're going to be battling your way (at certain times of year particularly) through coach parties. But there again, there are some places where the effort is worth it, and this is one of them.

Bourton has been described as the Venice of the Cotswolds. There's plenty to do here, but first spend a little time simply looking at the five famous bridges that picturesquely ford the Windrush: the 17th-century Mill Bridge, Narrow Bridge, Paynes Bridge built in 1776, New Bridge and Coronation Footbridge.

There's also plenty of enjoyment to be had in admiring the buildings – both private and public. Some of the cottages date back to Elizabethan times, and the church of St Lawrence has a 14th-century chancel and Georgian tower. And if you enjoyed your first look round, then why not take a second tour – in miniature that is. Bourton's **Model Village** is a one-ninth size replica, perfect in every detail – including the fact that it has its own model model village! Opened on Coronation Day in 1937, it took eight craftsmen four years to build it in local Cotswold stone.

Also in the High Street is the **Model Railway Exhibition** and traditional toy shop. There's plenty of inspiration here for model

The riverside in Bourton-on-the-Water

> THE MODEL VILLAGE: The Old New Inn, High Street, Bourton-on-the-Water GL54 2AF; ☎01451 820467 Entry: adults £3.25, seniors £3, children £2.75 (under-3s free); open daily except Christmas Day, winter 10am–3.45pm (last admission), summer 10am–5.45pm.

rail enthusiasts – though bear in mind this fantastic 500sq ft of towns, bridges, countryside and stations, with more than 40 trains, has been built up over 25 years plus. The shop specialises in British and Continental model trains and accessories.

One wonderful thing about Bourton is that you can do without your car – at least for a while. A short walk from the centre of the village is **Birdland Park and Gardens**, where you'll find more than 500 birds from all over the world, including the only King Penguins in England (watch them taking afternoon tea at 2.30pm every day). There are parrots, falcons, pheasants, hornbills, toucans, touracos, pigeons, ibis and many more, with tropical, desert and toucan houses for the more delicate species.

Bourton's model village

Right by Birdland is the **Dragonfly Maze**, which combines a traditional yew hedge maze with a rebus puzzle. Find your way to the centre to see if you can

> BIRDLAND PARK AND GARDENS: Rissington Road, Bourton-on-the-Water GL54 2BN; ☎01451 820480; www.birdland.co.uk Entry: adults £5.50, children £3.30, seniors £4.50, family £16; open daily except Christmas Day, Apr to Oct 10am–6pm, Nov–Mar 10am–4pm.

discover the secret hiding place of the golden dragonfly – and enjoy the fantastic automated sculptures created by artist Kit Williams of *Masquerade* fame. In the summer, it's open from 10am to 5pm, though winter times may vary. It's best to ring before you go (☎01451 822251).

The superhero car Brum has found a home at the **Cotswold Motoring Museum & Toy Collection,** based in an 18th-century corn-mill, and which motors through 20th-century driving history. There are more than 30 cars, caravans, motorcycles and lots of bicycles – but the fun is equally in all the motoring paraphernalia – old garage equipment, petrol pumps, an AA box, radio sets, gramophones and knitted swimsuits. The collection has a charm and nostalgic sense that draw in even those with no interest in cars or mechanics.

Bourton is green in every sense of the word, as you'll see if you visit the organically run show garden at **The Living Green Centre**, Kevinscot in the High Street (next to the bus stop). Open every day (weather permitting) except Sundays from 10am to 5pm, the shop – which encompasses all sorts of products –and the show garden are packed with ideas for sustainable 21st-century living. Entry is free though donations are welcome (☎01451 820942).

> **BOURTON MODEL RAILWAY:** Box Bush, High Street, Bourton-on-the-Water GL54 2AN; ☎01451 820686; www.bourtonmodelrailway.co.uk. Entry: adults £2.50, children and seniors £2, family £7.50; exhibition open Jun to Aug 11am–5pm daily, shop open daily 9.30am–5.30pm and Suns 1am–5.30pm; Sept to May (excluding Jan) exhibition open weekends only 11am–5pm, shop open Mon/Tues/Fri/Sat 9.30am–5pm, Sun 11am–5pm.

> **COTSWOLD MOTORING MUSEUM & TOY COLLECTION:** The Old Mill, Bourton-on-the-Water GL54 2BY; ☎01451 821255; www.cotswold-motor-museum.co.uk. Entry: adults from £3.80, children £2.60, family £11.50; open daily 10am–6pm from Feb half-term to the first Sun in Dec; shop.

The only King Penguins in England are found at Birdland at Bourton-on-the-Water

During the early summer – May to July being the best months – wild orchids, ragged robin and other flowers are in bloom at **Greystones Farm Nature Reserve** on Greystones Lane, off Station Road (www.gloucestershirewildlifetrust.co.uk). The meadows are unimproved wet grassland, a fearsomely endangered habitat; they run along the banks of the Rivers Eye and Dikler where water voles and otters live.

The Slaughters

Ask outsiders to name their quintessential Cotswolds villages and the chances are they'll come up with **Upper and Lower Slaughter**, barely 2 miles from Bourton-on-the-Water and only a mile apart from each other. Strange names, one might say, for such havens of beauty and tranquillity; in fact, the name 'Slaughter' derives from the Old English word 'slohtre', meaning a muddy place. Today, that mud has been swept aside, for even the waters of the River Eye run clear, and the Old Mill, open from 10am to 6pm daily, houses a tea shop and a separate handmade organic ice cream parlour, craft shop and museum (☎01451 820052; www. oldmill-lowerslaughter.com). With

Visit Brum at the Cotswold Motoring Museum

its restored water wheel and red brick tower, it's an easy building to spot.

The River Eye, which makes its way through **Lower Slaughter** towards the Windrush, is only really a stream, spanned by two footbridges. As it passes cottages

The village of Lower Slaughter

covered with roses, the lovely church of St Mary, and the admiring tourists it meets along its way, you can see why it's in no particular hurry. Next to the church is the manor house, built in the 17th century by Valentine Strong for the grand sum of £200. Valentine's skill as a stonemason shines through, for this is one of the loveliest houses for many a mile. Now a country house hotel, (☎01451 820456), Lower Slaughter Manor still retains some original fittings, such as the stone fireplace in the lounge, and the drawing room ceiling, resplendent with fruit, flowers, angels and birds.

Just over a mile away by road, but closer still by footpath, is **Upper Slaughter**, a so-called 'thankful' village, meaning none of its inhabitants died in the First World War: quite a rarity. The village basks in its Cotswold stone houses, few newer than 100 years old – and many much more ancient. Here the river is so shallow, the road runs through it by means of a picturesque ford. Each summer, the village holds a fantastic fête, usually featuring a duck race to the ford. Two hundred years ago, the rector in Upper Slaughter was F E Witts, Lord of the Manor, and author of *The Diary of a Cotswold Parson*. This wonderfully observant writer brings back to life the lost world of 18th- and 19th-century Gloucestershire. Nowadays, Witts' former home has been transformed into the Lords of the Manor hotel (☎01451 820243).

The medieval almshouses around the Square were restored by Sir Edwin Lutyens, the well-known Arts and Crafts architect, in the early 20th century. At Eyford Park in the village, John Milton is supposed to have written *Paradise Lost*. There can be no doubt that Upper Slaughter is an historic settlement – though little remains of the motte and bailey castle that once guarded its portals. But the parish church of St Peter is still a stronghold, dating back to Norman times.

Stow-on-the-Wold

Travel some four miles north along the Fosse Way (or call it the A429 if you insist on being unromantic), and you'll find Stow-on-the-Wold. Even on the outskirts, the buildings are honey-coloured, mellow and shout the word 'history'. It's simply a lovely town from the moment you lay eyes on it.

'Stow-on-the-Wold, where the winds blow cold and the cooks can't roast their dinners,' goes the rhyme. To be fair, the town is the highest in the Cotswolds, sitting as it does on an 800ft hill on the Roman Fosse Way. But the warmth of its stone, the friendliness of its welcome and the pleasure to be found among its individual shops and restaurants more than make up for any vagaries of the weather.

Stow-on-the-Wold's long been a prosperous and busy market town (hence all the roads) and, indeed, at its heart is a distinctive market square. Many remark on its Italian ambience. Once fairs were held here, particularly during the heady days of the wool trade. The many alleyways that run between the buildings were used to herd sheep; on one occasion in the 19th century, it's said that 20,000 sheep changed hands.

Overlooking the square is **St Edward's Church**, once used to confine prisoners during the Civil War. In fact, the town was the site of the famous Battle of Stow of

Typical Cotswoldian houses in Stow-on-the-Wold

1646: the streets, they say, were so full of blood that the ducks bathed in it, hence the name of Digbeth – Ducks' Bath – Street. The church houses a leather-bound book commemorating the individual stories of 59 men who died in the First and Second World Wars, and whose names are listed on the war memorial on the tower wall. Outside, you may find flowers placed at the memorial stone to the dead of the Civil War. And don't miss the back door of the church – with yew trees growing around the base and an old lantern: pure Tolkien.

A A Gill, famous for his professionally vituperative comments, was (outrageously and unreasonably, Cotswoldians would say) rude about the town. He's welcome back any time: Stow's stocks in the square date from Victorian times and are still used today – though mainly for photo opportunities by visitors.

Winchcombe

Winchcombe, over to the west, has much history attached to it. In Saxon times, Kenulf, King of Mercia, had his palace here. The tale is told that Kenulf sent his 7-year-old son, Kenelm, to his sister, Quendrida, who was instructed to educate the boy; instead she had him murdered to ensure her own succession to the throne. But from the boy's decapitated body flew a dove with a message for the Pope: '*In Clent cow-pasture under a thorn; of head bereft lies Kenelm, king-born.*' The Pontiff duly discovered Kenelm's remains and arranged for them to be taken back for burial at Winchcombe Abbey, where the lad was created a saint.

The saddest part of this story is that it's not true – at least not according to spoilsport historians. What is undeniable is that thanks to Kenelm's legend, the abbey became a hotspot for pilgrims and, as a result, a wealthy institution indeed. It was finally shut down by good King Hal in 1539, and subsequently plundered for its stones by townsfolk with their own building projects in mind. As a consequence, little remains today apart from the wall on one side of Abbey Terrace. What you can see in its stead is the historic parish church of **St Peter**, built in the 15th century and renowned for its 40 gargoyles, ostensibly created to take rainwater from the roof.

SUDELEY CASTLE: Winchcombe GL54 5JD; visitor centre ☎01242 604244 (10am–5pm), recorded visitor information ☎01242 604357; www.sudeleycastle.co.uk Entry: adults £7.20, concessions £6.20, children £4.20, family £20.80 open March–end Oct; pheasantry, play area with zip wire, restaurant and shop.

The church also has on show an altar cloth, embroidered by Henry VIII's first wife, Catherine of Aragon. In spite of her unhappy life, cast off by her husband in favour of that hussy Anne Boleyn, there are no reports of Catherine still stalking the streets. Nor, indeed, of her successor, Henry's last wife, Katherine Parr who lived at the town's magnificent stately home, **Sudeley Castle**, and is buried in a chapel in the grounds. Nevertheless, Winchcombe is fêted in some quarters as one of the most haunted places in Britain. A black dog, a 'white lady' and a mysterious monk are all alleged to wander the historic narrow lanes, each trapped in their own ghostly tragedies.

Winchcombe is also great walking country, being at the intersection of the Cotswold Way, the Gloucestershire Way, the Wardens' Way, the Windrush Way, the Wychavon Way and Saint Kenelm's Way. In the fields outside the town, you can explore the Neolithic burial chambers of **Belas Knap** – one of the finest long barrows in Gloucestershire. It's

Sudeley Castle, home of Henry VIII's last wife Katherine Parr

Sudeley at grass roots level

Sudeley Castle is deservedly known as the most romantic castle in England, its golden beauty crowned by a series of marvellous gardens of all descriptions, as well as a pheasantry and wildfowl area. It's where Elizabeth Hurley and Arun Nayar got married. (Well, it is the family home of her best friend, Henry Dent-Brocklehurst.) It's also the place where Lady Jane Grey spent some of her happiest moments, and where Cromwell's vengeful soldiers – 300 red-coated musketeers, four companies of Dragoons and eight cavalry – once raged against a hopelessly outnumbered garrison of just 60.

The beauty of the gardens is very much down to Henry Dent-Brocklehurst's mother, Lady Ashcombe. She has helped to create different gardens throughout the award-winning 14 acres which reflect the castle's history and glorious situation. There are areas such as the intricate Knot Garden, the Queens' Garden, filled with the scents of old-fashioned roses and herbs, the White and the Secret Gardens, all fashioned with help from leading landscapers.

It's a pursuit that not only adds value to the castle, but which brings Lady Ashcombe closer to previous occupants. *'In one of her diaries, Lady Jane Grey says some of the happiest moments of her life were spent walking in the gardens of Sudeley with Queen Katherine. Katherine Parr was her guardian, a sort of tutor, who had her here to stay. When the Victorians came, they found the foundations from the Tudor parterre; that must be where they walked. The main message I have to give to my children is that they have to stay on top of the garden and not take it for granted.'*

situated on the hillside near the wonderfully titled Honeybee Woods, which were once beloved of *Lord of the Rings* author J R R Tolkien. The Roman villa at Spoonley Woods on the Sudeley Estate is mentioned in Bill Bryson's *Notes From a Small Island*. *'On a hill above Winchcombe, you see, there is a little-visited site so singular and wonderful that I hesitate even to mention it,'* he says of this tranquil spot.

The best place to discover more about the history of the town throughout the ages is at the **Winchcombe Folk and Police Museum** in the Town Hall (☎01242 609151; www.sunloch.demon. co.uk/museum.htm). It has a folk, a police and a family and local history collection and is open Monday to Saturday from April to October and there's a small charge. **Winchcombe Railway Museum and Garden** is a must for all rail enthusiasts. Children can clip tickets and experience being a signalman; gardening enthusiasts can enjoy the old and rare plants; and there's also a large display of line-side notices and signalling equipment.

WINCHCOMBE RAILWAY MUSEUM AND GARDEN: Gloucester Street; ☎01242 609305; www.rag-mag.co.uk/museum.htm Entry: adults £2.25, accompanied children 50p, concessions £1.75; open Easter to end Sept, 1.30–5pm, Wed–Sun; daily during Aug.

Surrounding villages

Just 3 miles up the road from Winchcombe is Toddington Station, home to the **Gloucestershire Warwickshire Railway** (www.gwsr.com; ☎01242 621405) an all-volunteer steam and diesel heritage railway with over 10 miles of line and stations at Winchcombe and Cheltenham Racecourse. Catch a train on the scheduled service or enjoy one of the galas, enthusiast and family events, including Santa Specials and Paddington Bear. Toddington village is where the artist Damien Hirst bought the huge gothic manor in 2005, which he plans to turn into a museum of art

Gloucestershire Warwickshire Steam Railway

Also close by is the 13th-century Cistercian **Hailes Abbey**, once a celebrated site of pilgrimage. Though now a ruin, its very lack of inhabitants over the years has merely added to its untouched beauty. The tale goes that Richard, Earl of Cornwall, was at sea when a terrible storm blew up.

HAILES ABBEY: Winchcombe, GL54 5PB; www.english-heritage.org.uk. Entry: National Trust members free, adults £3.80, concessions £3.20, children £1.90; open daily 1 Apr to 1 Nov: 10am–5pm Apr to Jun; 10am–6pm Jul to Aug; 10am–5pm Sept; 10am–4pm Oct to 1 Nov.

13th century Hailes Abbey

Stanway House, in the hamlet of Stanway

Fearing for his life, he vowed to found a monastery if God were to spare him. On his safe return, he relayed the story to his brother, Henry III, who granted him the manor of Hailes. Work began on the project in 1246, and the finished abbey was consecrated in 1251 in a ceremony attended by Henry, his Queen, Eleanor of Provence, and 13 bishops who walked there from Winchcombe, 2 miles away. Incidentally, it's a very good place for conkers.

Stanway House, in the little nearby hamlet of Stanway boasts a 300ft fountain in its water garden, the tallest fountain in Britain and the tallest gravity fountain in the world, fed by a reservoir 580ft above the canal. The house itself is built from soft mellow stone (known as Guiting Yellow). The oldest part is Elizabethan, which includes the Great Hall – a light and airy room with full height bay windows. Once upon a time, manorial courts were held here, and you can see the raised platform they would have used at one end. And then there's the magnificent gatehouse, built in 1630, and a 14th-century tithe barn built for Tewkesbury Abbey, its roof supported by massive timbers.

> STANWAY HOUSE: Stanway, Cheltenham, Gloucestershire, GL54 5PQ; ☎01386 584469; www.stanwayfountain.co.uk Entry: adults £6, concessions £4.50, children £1.50, family £14; open Jun, Jul and Aug, Tues/Thurs, 2–5pm, fountain plays 2.45–3.15pm and 4–4.30pm (subject to weather).

Very few rooms are barred – and certainly none of the ones downstairs. '*I often sit in the library next door and people will poke their heads round and say – Oh, I'm sorry! – and go away. And I'll have to shout after them to come back,*' owner, Lord Neidpath, says. The writer J M Barrie was a frequent guest at the house. In the church on the estate, there's a little fairy on a weathervane that various people have claimed was the inspiration for Tinkerbell. But the truth is Barrie wrote *Peter Pan* long before he ever visited Stanway.

If you enjoy gardens, look out for **Abbotswood** near Stow-on-the-Wold, which opens under the National Gardens Scheme (www.ngs.org.uk). Sir Edwin Lutyens himself designed the gardens – and how delightful they are. A stream and pools combine with woods filled with rhododendrons; terraces, formal gardens and a water garden add to the picture: some of the most stunning to be found in private ownership in the country.

What to do with children...

BBC TV *Countryfile* presenter Adam Henson runs the outstanding **Cotswold Farm Park** at Guiting Power, between Bourton and Winchcombe. It's both sheer entertainment and education at the same time. Adam's father, Joe, helped found the national charity, the Rare Breeds Survival Trust, established to ensure the continued survival of all the endangered rare breeds in British farm livestock.

COTSWOLD FARM PARK: Guiting Power, Cheltenham GL54 5UG (follow the brown signs as postcode leads to dead end); ☎01451 850307; www.cotswoldfarmpark. co.uk. Entry: adults £6.75, children £5.50, seniors £6.25, family £22; open around mid-Mar to early Sept daily; weekends to end Oct 10.30am–5pm.

PARK HOUSE: THE TOY & COLLECTORS MUSEUM: 8 Park Street, Stow-on-the-Wold, GL54 1AQ; ☎01451 830159; www. thetoymuseum.co.uk. Entry: adults £2.50, children, concessions and seniors £2, family £5; open every day 10am–4.30pm (but please phone first, if you're coming any distance).

You'll find many of those rare breeds here, including sheep, cattle, pigs, goats, horses, poultry and water birds. Even if it's your first visit, you might have seen the farm park before – it's often featured on television programmes such as *The Really Wild Show* and *Absolutely Animals*. One of the best things about the park is the sheer number of activities children can join in, from the adventure playground and animal touch barn to the mini tractors and farm safari rides. Keep a lookout for seasonal events such as lambing, shearing and milking.

In Stow-on-the-Wold, children of all ages will enjoy **Park House: The Toy & Collectors Museum**, which has one of the best collections of toys in the country. There are three large showrooms and lots of cases packed with interest – books, trains, lead soldiers, planes, toy sewing machines, and much more.

Farmer Adam and his daughter with some of the animals at the Cotswold Farm Park

Park House: The Toy & Collectors Museum in Stow-on-the-Wold

For a sheer letting-off-steam session, it's hard to beat **Fundays** at Unit 8 in Bourton's Industrial Estate (GL54 2HQ; ☎01451 822999; www.fundaysplaybarn.com), especially if it's raining. The indoor soft play fun is designed for children 12 years and under, with ball ponds, rope bridges and general opportunities for bouncing!

✖ ... and how to avoid children

The **Cotswold Perfumery** in Victoria Street, Bourton-on-the-Water (☎01451 820698; www.cotswold-perfumery.co.uk) is a shop and perfumery with factory tours and perfume courses under the watchful nose of perfumer John Stephen. One-day courses, held throughout the year, include science, history, fun and hands-on attempts to create your own personal scent in a bottle. *'Smell is a heavily neglected sense,'* John says. *'You can only taste four basics: salt, sweet, sour, bitter; but you can smell more than 10,000 things from birth.'*

The Cotswold Perfumery Shop

CELEBRITY CONNECTIONS

The market town of Pershore, just on the edge of the Cotswolds, lies on the River Avon in Worcestershire. It has various celebrity connections, including the fact that it inspired the great British poet John Betjeman who honoured it in *Pershore Station*.

The novelist **Nicholas Coleridge**, who is also Managing Director of Condé Nast in Britain (the magazine publishing house that includes *Vogue*, *Glamour*, *GQ*, *Tatler* and *Vanity Fair*) moved here with his writer wife, Georgina after falling in love with an 18th-century Queen Anne house he saw in *Country Life*. '*My wife took a lot of persuading*,' he said. '*... But then, eventually, she saw how much I wanted to move*.' The family now love their Cotswold Life.

And right in the middle of town lives the fine actress and one-time queen of punk, **Toyah Willcox** with her husband, the rock legend **Robert Fripp** of King Crimson. '*Our neighbours are fantastic*,' Toyah says. '*Everyone has the time to say, "Hello, how are you?"*'

Entertainment

'Sublime to the ridiculous' sums up the events on offer in this area. And why not start with the ridiculous... While tourists might stare in awe at the loveliness of the River Windrush, the residents of Bourton-on-the-Water treat it with more familiarity. Every August bank holiday, the famous **Bourton Water Game** takes place – a football match played in the Windrush itself by two teams from the village. No one quite knows when it began, but it has got to be around 100 years ago. There are photographs from some of the first games, which show buildings that don't exist any more, and that has helped villagers to date it.

Guiting Music Festival (www.guitingfestival.org), started by villagers in the 1970s, features classical music and jazz, all within the lovely unspoilt village of Guiting Power. Past festivals have featured such outstanding musicians as Joanna MacGregor, who is now festival president, Jacqueline Dankworth and R&B king Georgie Fame.

The **Gypsy Horse Fair** at Stow-on-the-Wold is held twice a year – in May and October – in accordance with dates set more than 500 years ago. Visitors can have their palms read, buy horses or simply find a decorative cushion or a painting from the many stalls that set up for the event. Gypsies the length and breadth of the country come here to trade horses and to meet up with friends and relatives. For definite dates, ring Stow's tourist information centre on 01451 831082.

Poetry fans will undoubtedly want to visit Adlestrop, between Stow and Chipping Norton, which holds a summer open day once a year (www.adlestrop.org.uk). The village was immortalised in Edward Thomas's poem, '*I remember Adlestrop...*'

LOCAL KNOWLEDGE

Perfumer **John Stephen** owns the Cotswold Perfumery in Bourton-on-the-Water. As well as his own range of scents, he creates bespoke perfumes for businesses and individuals; he has worked for London Perfume Houses, French Perfume Houses and even the Queen: on request, John created White Windsor and Royal Musk especially for her.

Favourite restaurant: The Dial House Hotel in Bourton: excellent cuisine and very consistent. We use this hotel for all the lunches provided for participants of perfumery courses and people are always impressed by the standard. Combine this with very professional and pleasant staff and you have a winner.

Best view: There is a small bench that overlooks Bourton village. It is tucked away at the top of Clapton Hill on left side of the Sherborne road.

Best walk: From the old Gas Works in Bourton to Sherborne. The walk is very varied and covers everything from ploughed fields to woodland, and once past the first couple of fields where dogs are walked, it is incredibly quiet. Normally you can walk the six miles and meet no-one. The peace and tranquillity allow you to think and the journey has provided the inspiration for many a perfume.

Best picnic spot: By the river between Lower and Upper Slaughter. On a summer's day it can't be beaten.

Quirkiest attraction: The Bourton Maze. The classic maze is large, confusing and a little daunting for most people. The Bourton Maze is small but it comes with a twist – there is a puzzle to solve and finding the answer changes the experience totally.

Best-kept secret: I may be biased here, but I'm going to say Perfumery Courses held at the Cotswold Perfumery! This small family business has managed to produce a range of courses that are not available anywhere else in the world – and participants travel from all over the world to participate. They are not exactly a secret but I doubt if most local people are aware of quite how rare they are.

157

commemorated with a Millennium Mural in the village hall. Jane Austen often stayed in the Old Rectory, opposite the medieval church, when her uncle was rector there. Richard Phillips has his racing stables in the village (www.richardphillipsracing.com).

Sudeley Castle (www.sudeleycastle.co.uk) in Winchcombe has an impressive events calendar. Plays and open-air concerts are held in the summer; there are Hallowe'en and Christmas events; and perennially popular are the spectacular medieval and jousting weekends.

All the fun of the circus

The legendary **Giffords Circus** is based at Folly Farm, Bourton-on-the-Water during the winter months, where they prepare for their summer season touring the village greens and commons of the Cotswolds. It's traditional, it's musical, it's arty, it's polished; it's enormous fun – even the family geese do a turn.

You'll see incredible horsemanship in the ring, acrobatics, juggling – all performed with dazzling skill – and a clown to out-clown all clowns: he's both beguilingly clever and genuinely funny.

The circus is the brainchild of Nell and Toti Gifford. Nell was brought up in the Cotswold village of Minety. Both before and after graduating from Oxford, she took a series of jobs in circuses all over the world, and became convinced she'd one day like to run her own. She and her husband, Toti, spent hours talking and planning their dream, but not much happened until Nell was invited to the Hay-on-Wye Literary Festival to talk about her autobiographical book, *Josser*. To liven it all up, Nell described their 'circus' in such vivid detail that, much to her own surprise, she secured a booking.

'*It was quite a stupid thing to do!*' Nell laughs. '*They asked how much it would be,*

Tweedy the Clown from Giffords Circus

so we just scribbled down figures, which came to about 100th of what it actually cost. And we got a deposit, so we were committed.' But Giffords has been a hit from the start. It sets out to recapture the spirit of 1930s showmanship, which appeals so greatly to audiences, they even seem temporarily to adopt some of the values.

'*It's wonderful to see the way people respond to it,*' Nell says. '*It's quite a curious thing that the circus can have an old-fashioned impact. People come on their horses; they walk here; they bicycle here. They meet their friends and bring picnics with eggs and things from their gardens.*' For more information, including latest tour dates, visit www.giffordscircus.com or phone 01451 820378.

🛒 Shopping

The Cotswold Pottery (☎01451 820173; www.cotswoldpottery.co.uk) is a small family-run studio started in 1973 by John and Jude Jelfs, in Clapton Row, Bourton-on-the-Water. The pottery is all made in the studio, entirely by hand. John makes mostly wheel-thrown studio pots, while Jude's work is hand-built and more sculptural. Both have exhibited world-wide at leading galleries.

Stow-on-the-Wold is a wonderful place for specialist **antique shops and art galleries**. Sean Clarke, for example, runs Christopher Clarke Antiques in Stow-on-the-Wold with his brother, Simon (☎01451 830476). Their shop is one of the few that specialises in campaign and travel furniture and effects. These items were mainly made for the British army, and for the colonists and administrators who flourished under the British Empire – but the stock also includes memorabilia used by early tourists. You'll find other unusual antique shops, as well as galleries selling beautiful Cotswold paintings – among other treasures.

Scotts of Stow, the mail order home, kitchen and garden company really is based in Stow. Instead of wandering through a catalogue, you can visit its stores in the square.

Winchcombe Pottery (GL54 5NU; ☎01242 602462; www.winchcombepottery.co.uk), just a mile out of Winchcombe on the Broadway Road, is one of the longest-running craft potteries in the country, and makes some of the finest and most practical domestic pottery you can buy. All of the beautifully-fired products from the kiln are on sale in the shop.

The best... **PLACES TO STAY**

HOTEL

Lords of the Manor

Upper Slaughter GL54 2JD
☎ 01451 820243
www.lordsofthemanor.com

Quite simply a gorgeous place to unwind, set in more than 8 acres of garden, lake and parkland. But when you're in such an idyllic rural setting, that's a bonus anyway. Once a rectory, and home to the Witts family for 200 years, it also offers an excellent restaurant.

Price: B&B from £195 per room.

Dial House Hotel

The Chestnuts, Bourton-on-the-Water GL54 2AN; ☎ 01451 822244
www.dialhousehotel.com

In the centre of Bourton, with attractions within walking distance, the 17th-century Dial House is the perfect bolt-hole. Enjoy a roaring log fire in winter, or lunch in the walled garden in summer.

Price: B&B from £120 for a double.

B&B

Isbourne Manor House

Castle Street, Winchcombe GL54 5JA
☎ 01242 602281
www.isbourne-manor.co.uk

Part-Georgian, part-Elizabethan, the gardens of this charming house border the River Isbourne. Inside, you'll find a combination of antiques and modern comforts. Guests benefit from private parking, and reception rooms.

Price: from £90 for two with breakfast.

Postlip Hall Farm

Winchcombe GL54 5AQ
☎ 01242 603351

This family-run sheep and beef farm guarantees peace and tranquility in a fantastic rural setting – lambing time, between February and April, is particularly popular. The hamlet of Postlip, with its 14th-century manor house and tithe barn, is a mile-and-a-half from Winchcombe. This property has a prestigious Visit Britain Gold Award.

Price: from £60 for a double room.

SELF-CATERING

Park Farm Holiday Cottages

Maugersbury, Stow-on-the-Wold
☎ 01451 870568
www.parkfarmholidaycottages.co.uk

Five minutes from Stow, there's an all-weather tennis court and games lawn for table tennis and badminton, plus interesting collections of old agricultural implements. The cottages are comfortably furnished and very well equipped.

Price: from £302 for a cottage for two.

Sudeley Castle

Winchcombe GL54 5JD
☎ 01242 602308
cottages.sudeleycastle.co.uk

These cottages lie on the edge of the estate, midway between the castle and Winchcombe. Set around a central courtyard with landscaped gardens and ample parking, each cottage has its own individual charm.

Price: from £270 per week for a 3 or 4 person cottage.

The best... FOOD AND DRINK

▶️ Staying in

Hayles Fruit Farm is one of the few remaining commercial fruit farms in Gloucestershire. It was planted by Lord Sudeley in 1880 – and there's still an original Bramley tree. It produces all sorts, including asparagus, strawberries, gooseberries, red and blackcurrants, raspberries, plums, apples, pears, cobnuts, stickbeans, apple juice, pear juice and the famous Badger's Bottom cider. The farm is between Toddington and Winchcombe off the B4632, next to Hailes Abbey. There's also a farm shop, a tea room, and pick-your-own (☎01242 602123; www.hayles-fruit-farm.co.uk).

If you're Stow way, then go and buy the fresh and smoked trout from **Donnington Trout Farm's** shop at Upper Swell (GL54 1EP; ☎01451 830873). The spring water they live in means they're some of the tastiest in the country. You can buy fresh trout, whole or filleted, or smoked trout and pate from the farm shop, as well as fly fish on the small, secluded lake. In Digbeth Street in Stow, there's **Hamptons Fine Foods**, selling gourmet foods and hampers (☎01451 831733; www.hamptons-hampers. co.uk). In the villages, locals swear by **Watson's**, the baker in Church Lane, Guiting Power (GL54 5TX; ☎01451 850310).

Other great producers include **Rushbury Meats** (GL54 5AE; ☎01242 673510; www. rushburymeats.co.uk) where cattle and sheep roam the grasslands in this beautiful protected area around Winchcombe. You can buy directly from the farm shop. **Sudeley Hill Farm** (GL54 5JB; ☎01242 602877 or 07850 597820; www.meatdelivered.co.uk) is a family-run farm in the same area, where three generations work together. They deliver all over the country – so you can continue to enjoy the taste of the Cotswolds, even when you're back home.

And there's fantastic beef at **Tagmoor Farm**, Bourton (GL54 2LF; ☎01451 810198; www.lovemycow.com), which has been in the MacCurrach family since just after the Second World War. Back then it consisted of about 80 acres. Today it is farmed by James and his father, Martin and now extends to approximately 500 acres – including a pair of holiday cottages and a caravan site that are run alongside the arable and beef enterprises.

🍺 Drinking

One of the most popular beers at Christmas from **Goff's Brewery** is Black Knight. This family-run micro-brewery, in Isbourne Way, Winchcombe also produces the well-known Jouster, twice voted one of CAMRA's champion British beers. You can visit buy from the website (www.goffs.biz) or call on ☎01242 603383, or sample their brews at local pubs.

Stanway Brewery (www.stanwaybrewery.co.uk; ☎01386 584320) is based at the beautiful Cotswold manor Stanway House, detailed in the 'What to see and do' section above. Its age-old brewery has been resurrected by brewer Alex Pennycook and is one of only two log-fired breweries in the country. It produces Stanney Bitter, Cotteswold Gold and Lords-a-Leaping sold at various pubs including **The White Hart** in Winchcombe and **The Pheasant Inn** in Toddington.

In 1865, the Arkell family began a brewery in a 13th-century watermill at Donnington near Moreton-in-Marsh (GL54 1EP; donnington-brewery.co). In the 21st century, the Arkells at Donnington still produce their beers by much the same recipe, drawing spring water from beside the mill pond, with the mill wheel driving some of the machinery used in the process. The brewery has 15 pubs, including the **Black Bear Inn in Moreton**, and the **Black Horse Inn in Naunton**. If you visit the latter, then stop to look at the dovecote beside the River Windrush in the village. It's around 500 years old and has been used as a mill and a hen house. It now belongs to a trust after villagers rallied round to buy it to preserve it for posterity.

Brie – the Cotswold way

Simon and Carol Weaver produce **organic brie** at Kirkham Farm (on the roadside between Upper Slaughter and Lower Swell). This is a farm where the ridges and furrows show that farmers worked the same land back in the Middle Ages; where even the fields have names, the origins of which are lost in time: Black Nell, The Hangings, The Marshes, Kingcups; and where, down by the River Dikler, no plough has ever touched the land.

'We want our product to reflect where we come from and contribute to the Cotswolds,' Simon says. Alongside the original soft, buttery brie, they make organic Cotswold blue-veined brie and a herb variety, and a new smoked brie. It's a time-consuming process, but one that is receiving just recognition. In little over a year, the cheeses scooped top prizes in the Taste of the West Food and Drink awards, and the Organic Cotswold Blue-Veined Brie won Best Organic Product at the World Cheese Awards in 2006.

Kirkham Farm produces an organic Cotswold brie

You can buy Simon Weaver's cheeses at various farmers' markets, including Bourton-on-the-Water (fourth Sunday), and Stow; from local farm shops and delis; or direct from the creamery door at Kirkham Farm, Monday to Friday, 9am–5pm. At other times, ring 01451 870852 or visit www.simonweaver.net.

EATING OUT

HOTEL

Fosse Manor
Fosseway, Stow-on-the-Wold GL54 1JX
☎ 01451 830354
www.fossemanor.com

One of the pleasures in eating here is the fact that the restaurant not only serves local produce, but its staff are knowledgeable and enthusiastic about it. They regularly go out to visit the producers. So whether you choose a supreme of Cotswold chicken or a beef steak burger with Single Gloucester cheese, you'll know you're getting local fare; costs between £12 and £15 for most mains.

Lower Slaughter Manor
Lower Slaughter GL54 2HP
☎ 01451 820456
www.lowerslaughter.co.uk

This beautiful manor house has a dining room that matches the quality of its supreme surroundings and head chef David Kelman always comes up with the goods. Luxury mains – around £20 – might be a seasonal loin of local venison with foie gras or a superb fillet of brill with a leek and bacon tartlet.

RESTAURANT

5 North Street
Winchcombe GL54 5LH
☎ 01242 604566

Top food critic Matthew Fort isn't the only person who loves this place. Kate and Marcus Ashenford have gained a fantastic reputation for skill and quality in their small but pretty much perfect restaurant. Marcus was just 25 when he first gained a Michelin star. Set menus are at £34, £39, and a £44 option based around lobster, scallops and venison.

The Old Butchers
Park Street,
Stow-on-the-Wold GL54 1AQ
☎ 01451 831700
www.theoldbutchers.com

Indeed, this once used to be the old butchers shop in Stow – but now it's an excellent restaurant. Expect modern British food in contemporary surroundings. You'll pay around £26 for three courses, which might include a Middle White pork chop, fennel, garlic and parsley, followed by panna cotta with almond caramel.

TEAROOM

Juri's – The Olde Bakery Tea Shoppe
High Street, Winchcombe GL54 5LJ
☎ 01242 602469
www.juris-tearoom.co.uk

Iwao and Junko Miyawaki and their daughter Juri – a Cordon Bleu-trained cook – opened Juri's in 2003. And not only have they taken on the English at their own game – they've beaten them! For they were named the 2008 top tea shop in Britain by The Tea Guild. A superb afternoon tea is available between 3pm and 5pm for under £15 (minimum two).

EAT IN/TAKEAWAY

Roman Court Hotel
Fosseway, Stow-on-the-Wold GL54 1JX
☎ 01451 870539
www.romancourthotel.com

This Italian restaurant has an eclectic menu offering European-style food. You can also get well-made take-away pizzas. There's lots of choice, from pastas at £10 to steaks at £20, but you can't miss out on one of those pizzas...

The Donnington brewery is based in a 13th century watermill

Naunton is a horse-lovers' paradise. Racing has replaced farming as the centre of the community, and there are a lot of yards – professional and point to point – on the doorstep: Nigel Twiston-Davies; Marcella Bayliss; and the Egans. A little further north is the legendary Jackdaws Castle, home to Jonjo O'Neill's yard. If you want to mix with the racing crowd, then visit the **Hollow Bottom** in Temple Guiting (GL54 5UX; ☎01451 850392); or the **Plough Inn at Ford** (GL54 5RU; ☎01386 584215).

Other great country pubs include:

- **Halfway House** – Kineton GL54 5UG; ☎01451 850344
- **Fox Inn** – Lower Oddington
- **Horse and Groom** – Upper Oddington GL56 0XH; ☎01451 830584
- **The Plough** – Cold Aston GL54 3BN; ☎01451 821459
- **Fox Inn** – Broadwell GL56 0UF; ☎01451 870909.

Broadcaster and journalist Sybil Ruscoe lives in Stow; she says the **Queen's Head** (☎01451 830563) in the Square is the perfect local. Another interesting venue is **The Royalist Hotel** (☎01451 830670) in Digbeth Street, Stow-on-the-Wold with the **Eagle and Child** pub next door. The Royalist dates back to AD947, built by the Cornish Duke Aethelmar, and is listed in the *Guinness Book of Records* as the oldest hotel in the country. Crime queen Agatha Christie is said to have visited the **Mousetrap Inn** in Bourton (GL54 2AR; ☎01451 820579).

ℹ️ Visitor Information

Tourist information centres: Bourton-on-the-Water Visitor Information Centre, Victoria Street GL54 2BU, ☎01451 820211, www.bourtoninfo.com, www.cotswolds.com, open 9.30am-4pm Mon-Fri and 9.30am-4.30pm Sats; Stow-on-the-Wold Visitor Information Centre, Hollis House, The Square, Stow-on-the-Wold, ☎01451 831082, open Mar to Oct, Mon–Sat 9.30am–5.30pm, Oct to mid-Nov, Mon–Sat 9.30am–5pm, Dec to Feb, Mon–Sat 9.30am–4.30pm, www.stow-on-the-wold.info; Winchcombe Tourist Information Centre, the Town Hall, High Street, Winchcombe, ☎01242 602925, www.visitcotswoldsandsevernvale.gov.uk; www.winchcombe.co.uk and www.winchcombe.info, open Apr to Oct, Mon–Sat 10am–5pm, Sun 10am–4pm, Nov–Mar, Sat/Sun 10am–4pm.

Hospitals: Cirencester Hospital, Tetbury Road, Cirencester GL7 1UY, ☎01285 655711, 24-hr A&E; Winchcombe Hospital, Cheltenham Road, Winchcombe GL54 5NQ, ☎01242 602341 (minor injuries and illness unit); Cheltenham General Hospital, Sandford Road, Cheltenham GL53 7AN, ☎08454 222222, 24hr A&E.

Supermarkets include: Co-op, Station Road GL54 2EP, ☎01451 821858; Somerfield, the High Street, Bourton-on-the-Water GL54 2AQ, ☎01451 820375; Tesco, Fosse Way, Stow-on-the-Wold GL54 1BX, ☎0845 6779630; for Winchcombe, Cheltenham's supermarkets, around 8 miles away, are listed in the Cheltenham section of this book.

Sports: The Avenue Leisure Centre, Bourton-on-the-Water GL54 2BD, ☎01451 824024; Cotswold Leisure Centre, Tetbury Road, Cirencester GL7 1US, ☎01285 654057; Leisure@Cheltenham, Tommy Taylors Lane, Cheltenham GL50 4RN; Cirencester Golf Club, Cheltenham Road, Bagendon GL7 7BH, ☎01285 653939; Naunton Downs Golf Club, Stow Road, Naunton GL54 3AE, ☎01451 850092, www.nauntondowns.co.uk; coarse fishing: Lemington Lakes, Todenham Road, near Moreton-in-Marsh, ☎01608 650872, www.lemingtonlakes.co.uk; Woodlands Riding Stables at Glebe Farm, Wood Stanway near Winchcombe GL54 5PG, ☎01386 584404, between 8am and 6pm, www.woodstanway.co.uk; Bourton Vale Equestrian Centre, Fosseway, Bourton-on-the-Water GL54 2HL, ☎01451 821101, www.bourtonvaleequestrian.co.uk.

Taxis include: Limozena Taxis Service ☎01451 820972; K Cars ☎01451 822578; Bourton-on-the-Water, Taylor Private Hire, Winchcombe, ☎01242 603651.

MORETON, BROADWAY AND CHIPPING CAMPDEN

It's no accident that Moreton-in-Marsh, Broadway and Chipping Campden are idyllic: they're a reflection of the ground on which they rest (and there are some drop-dead gorgeous villages in between, too).

When glaciers blocked the Severn estuary around 12,000 years ago or more, the rain and melt-waters needed to find another exit. Instead of being able to run off south through the Bristol Channel, they went north and broke through at Moreton-in-Marsh. On their unstoppable journey, they sliced between great swathes of land, cutting the beautiful Evenlode Valley. And standing proudly at the head of that valley is Moreton.

It's a superb little market town, charming in every respect. And things get even better from here on. The story of how Broadway, a little further north, got its name will become obvious the minute you step into its wide high street. Make your way up Fish Hill (once used by monks to store fish, so it's said) and you'll come to a room with a view: Broadway Tower, the favoured summer home of William Morris, from the top of which you can see 14 counties. And then there's Chipping Campden, where the broad, curved terraces of the High Street have been described as the most perfect in England.

There are some wonderful and unusual attractions to be seen: the extraordinary Sezincote – a little bit of India in the Cotswolds; and Snowshill Manor, a very English piece of eccentricity, packed with a collector's ephemera. But there are also some great fun events, so make sure you go at the right time of year. From opera in a garden at Longborough to shin-kicking at the Cotswolds' own 'Olimpick Games', you need to plan your diary carefully.

WHAT TO SEE AND DO

Moreton-in-Marsh

The market town of Moreton-in-Marsh is a wonderful place to meander, look at the shops, browse. And it's long been so. There are still those who remember the days of the Mitfords, whose family seat was originally at nearby Batsford, where the arboretum is now open to visitors. David Mitford – Lord Redesdale – was the father of the six beautiful Mitford sisters who took the early 20th century by storm, thanks to character as much as looks (see the Oxfordshire chapter for more). The Redesdale Market Hall, built in 1887, commemorates the family's role as great benefactors of the town. They also gave the name to the Redesdale Arms back in 1886, when the former coachman and cook to Earl Redesdale took it over. The **Curfew Tower**, on the corner of High Street and Oxford Street, still has its original bell, dated 1633, which was rung every day until 1860. A local worthy, Sir Robert Fry, gave money for its maintenance after it once guided him home through fog. It continued to be used even later to summon the fire brigade (though local lore says you had to keep the fire going if you wanted it still alight by the time they got there).

Reminders of Moreton-in-Marsh's past are all around the town – in fact, you can still see displayed a list of tolls charged back in 1905. The town was first granted a charter in 1227, but even in the 21st century, it remains one of the main market towns of the north Cotswolds. One of England's most famous and popular street markets takes place here every Tuesday, teeming with all kinds of stalls.

One reason for the town's importance has always been its accessibility. The Four Shires Stone, 2 miles east of the town, marks what was the meeting place of Gloucestershire, Warwickshire, Worcestershire and Oxfordshire (though the Worcestershire boundary has now moved). The Fosse Way, that old Roman road, runs through the broad high street with its 17th- and 18th-century buildings; indeed, the town is on the old London to Worcester coach road, which accounts for its excellent and historic inns. In the Civil War, Moreton was a centre for Royalist cavalry, and the White Hart Royal can boast that King Charles stayed here on his final march from his headquarters at Oxford.

One of the earliest railway stations in the country was built here: the Moreton to Stratford tramway opened in 1826, followed by the London to Worcester main line, via Oxford, in 1853. For such a delightful rural town, it has another unusual boast – it hosts a Fire Service College, the largest training centre of its kind in Europe. During the Second World War, an RAF station was developed to the east of the town as an airfield to train bomber crews. In fact, some say it was the inspiration for the name of the radio show *Much Binding in the Marsh*. There's now a small museum in the town dedicated to all who passed through RAF Moreton-in-Marsh, with a vast range of artefacts from the war years and beyond.

> **WELLINGTON AVIATION MUSEUM**: British School House, Broadway Road, Moreton-in-Marsh GL56 0BG; ☎01608 650323; www.wellingtonaviation.org. Entry: £2; open Tues–Sun 10am–12 noon and 2–5pm; closed Mon and Christmas Day.

Described as a collection of 'Royal Air Force jewels', the **Wellington Aviation Museum** holds many rare Wellington and other aircraft artefacts, photographs and records from the base; plus a range of paintings, prints, aircraft sculptures, books and videos for sale.

Broadway

Just a little further north, over the border into Worcestershire, is Broadway. It shouldn't come as a surprise to hear that there are some outstanding art galleries here: this Cotswold village, with its wide main street, has long been associated with artists. The phenomenon of fashionable outsiders moving into the Cotswolds goes back to the 19th century, when artists and writers flocked here. The American illustrator and painter Francis Davis Millet started the ball rolling. He fell in love with Broadway's quaint tranquillity and moved into Abbots Grange with his family, a decaying medieval house he rescued from dereliction. Around him, he gathered such celebrated souls as John Singer Sargent, Edmund Gosse and Henry James, who pronounced, '*Broadway and much of the land about it are in short the perfection of the old English rural*

Batsford Arboretum

Batsford Arboretum, a mile and a quarter west of Moreton, is one of the largest private collections of trees and shrubs in the country, and attracts thousands of visitors each year.

It owes its origins to Bertie (pronounced Barty) Mitford, grandfather of the Mitford sisters. Bertie, who was first cousin to the poet, Swinburne, was an extremely well-travelled diplomat. He'd spent more than three years working for the Foreign Office in Japan where he developed an admiration for the samurai culture, not dissimilar in structure to the chivalric ways of England's Middle Ages. A fluent Japanese speaker, he'd been one of

Daffodils at the Batsford Arboretum

the few Westerners to witness a traditional hara-kiri – honourable suicide – ceremony.

In 1886, Bertie inherited the Batsford Estate, near Moreton-in-Marsh, where he created a wild garden inspired by the Japanese landscape, and planted one of the foremost bamboo collections of the time; some of these are still alive. The collections on view at Batsford cover a wide range of plants from around the world but with an emphasis on the Far East. There are over 3,000 labelled specimens including about 1,600 different trees, shrubs and bamboo. (And if the children aren't convinced by all this, just remind them that Radiohead worked on *Kid A* and *Amnesiac* at Batsford House.) There's also the **Cotswold Falconry Centre** at Batsford, detailed under the 'What to do with children' section of this chapter.

BATSFORD ARBORETUM: Batsford Park, Moreton-in-Marsh GL56 9QB; ☎ 01386 701441; www.batsarb.co.uk Entry: Feb to Nov, adults £6, concessions £5, children £2; Dec/Jan adults £5, concessions £4, children £1; open Feb to Nov, daily 9am–6pm; Dec/Jan, daily 9am–4pm except Wed in Dec and Jan and Christmas Day.

tradition.' Over the years, it became home to such composers, artists and writers as Elgar, J M Barrie, Vaughan Williams and William Morris. Millet, by the by, was last seen helping women and children into the lifeboats on the *Titanic*; his body was later recovered.

A more recent artist was the renowned 20th-century furniture designer Sir Gordon Russell, who was greatly influenced by the Arts and Crafts Movement. He founded a firm in the Broadway workshops that grew to employ more than 200 skilled craftsmen. The **Gordon Russell Museum**, opened in 2008 by Sir Terence Conran, has on display original design drawings, photographs, a unique collection of furniture including

Tea room in Broadway

Arts and Crafts machine production and 1930s modernism, plus filmed interviews with Sir Gordon.

It's easy to see why artistic souls were drawn to the village: the broad sweep of the High Street – one of the longest in England – is strikingly lovely, lined with historic buildings in distinctive stone. The great architectural expert Pevsner called it the '*show village of England*'. Archaeologists have evidence that the village could be one of the first sites in the UK to be partially settled by hunter-gatherers. The area certainly has a long provenance: coins from the reign of the Roman Emperor Tiberius, who died in AD37, were discovered nearby, and a sixth-century Anglo-Saxon cemetery was unearthed near **Broadway Tower**.

Broadway Tower viewpoint, known as the 'highest little castle in the Cotswolds', rises 65ft on ground 312m above sea level. As a result, you can see 13 counties from the top. It was built on the site of an ancient beacon by James Wyatt in around 1799 for the wife of the sixth Earl of Coventry. She used it as a signalling device between their Springhill and Croome Court Estates. Later, it became the favourite country retreat of the renowned Socialist writer, painter

> **GORDON RUSSELL MUSEUM:** 15 Russell Square, Broadway WR12 7AP; ☎01386 854695; www.gordonrussellmuseum.org Entry: adults £3, concessions £2.50, children 12–16 £1; open Nov/Dec/Feb (closed Jan) 11am–4pm Tues–Sun and bank holiday Mons; and Mar to Oct, 11am–5pm, Tues–Sun and bank holiday Mons.

> **BROADWAY TOWER:** Broadway WR12 7LB; ☎01386 852390; www.broadwaytower.co.uk Entry: adults £4, children £2.50, family £11; open Apr to Oct 10.30am–5pm daily, and at weekends during Nov–Mar 10.30am–4pm (all subject to weather).

and craftsman William Morris and his Pre-Raphaelite contemporaries. Inside, attractions include a William Morris Room; outside, they include a red deer enclosure (with 'Bambies' from mid-June), country walks, wildlife, wild flowers and a barn restaurant.

Chipping Campden

Some 6 miles east of Broadway and back into Gloucestershire, you'll come to Chipping Campden,

Broadway Tower offers a view of 13 counties

a village that truly necessitates an intake of breath. Here lies perfection.

'Have nothing in your house that you do not know to be useful, or believe to be beautiful,' counselled the great 19th-century high priest of the Arts and Crafts Movement, William Morris. And it's as if Chipping Campden has taken those very words to its metaphorical bosom. For it excels both in beauty and usefulness – as indeed you might expect of a town with such a noble Arts and Crafts heritage.

The broad, curved terraces of Chipping Campden High Street – sometimes described as the most perfect in England – offer the architecture aficionado the best of building styles to study, starting with the grand houses commissioned by the newly wealthy woollen merchants of the 14th century. From the town's oldest home – the exquisite 14th-century Grevel's House, with its wonderful carved windows, sundial and gargoyles – to the arched 17th-century Market House, here are treasures aplenty. And there are more: Elizabethan, Georgian, Jacobean, Regency and Victorian buildings are all to be found in its fascinating streets. But perhaps most of all, it's the thatch-roofed cottages that provide the heart-stopping moments with their gracefully flowing lines. And useful? Well even the Almshouses, built for £1,000 by Sir Baptist Hicks in 1612, are still inhabited by 12 of the town's pensioners.

In the 1300s, Campden had its own Bill Gates: one William Grevel of the eponymous Grevel's House. When he first appears in literary sources in 1341, he's a man of modest property, married, and on his way up. But by the 1390s, he's lending King Richard II himself 200 marks (£135) on the surety of repayment the following Easter – no mean feat for a man who started life as a small-scale merchant. Some even think him the model for the merchant in Chaucer's *Canterbury Tales*. Astonishingly, his descendants went on to become the Earls of Warwick and he is described as '*The flower of English Woolstaplers*' on his tomb in the 15th-century **St James's Church**, considered by many to be the finest wool church in the Cotswolds. But don't think that Campden's lot has always been defined by wealth and privilege.

When the architect **C R Ashbee** arrived in Chipping Campden in the early 20th century, its heritage as a wealthy wool town had long grown threadbare. Ashbee needed to move his Guild of Handicraft out of London and this rural backwater, as it was then, was the perfect location. Modelled on the old idea of a Medieval Guild, his altruistic organisation worked as a cooperative for skilled craftsmen, and provided a training school for apprentices.

Ashbee and his 150 East End workers set up shop in the Old Silk Mill, which they renamed Essex House. At first, locals were suspicious of the incomers; indeed, they had no compunction about overcharging these more highly paid invaders. But the Londoners finally won the day, organising plays and lectures for townsfolk, and even running classes in keep-fit, gardening and cookery. Still working in the Old Silk Mill today is gold and silversmith, David Hart, whose grandfather was one of the original 150 East Enders. Also in the same building is a new cooperative of more than a dozen artists and artisans who moved into The Guild Workshops in July 2005, bringing a variety of contemporary and traditional craftspeople together.

> THE GALLERY@THE GUILD: Ground Floor, The Old Silk Mill, Sheep Street, Chipping Campden GL55 6DS; ☎07870 417144; www.thegalleryattheguild.co.uk. Entry: free; open daily 10am–7pm.

Called **The Gallery@The Guild**, they hold free exhibitions, which change every four to six weeks, featuring work by artists, calligraphers, ceramicists, designers, furniture makers, photographers, sculptors and stone carvers.

There's more information on the Arts and Crafts Movement and its legacy in Chipping Campden at the **Court Barn Museum** in Church Street (☎01386 841951; www.courtbarn.org.uk), which has a permanent exhibition of silver, jewellery, ceramics, sculpture, industrial design, bookbinding, printing and stained glass, and includes exhibits lent by the Victoria and Albert Museum and the National Portrait Gallery. The museum is open April to September, 10.30am–5.30pm Tuesday to Saturday, and 11.30am—5.30pm on Sundays; and October to March, 11am to 4pm, Tuesday to Saturday and 11.30am to 4pm on Sundays, with admission £3.75 for adults, concessions £3 and free for children under 16.

Sir Baptist Hicks can be thanked for many of the buildings in Chipping Campden, including Old Campden House. Not only was he responsible for commissioning it, he can also take the credit for burning it down during the Civil War. A close friend of Charles I, he declared he'd rather raze it to the ground than let those Parliamentarians get their filthy hands on it. All that's left now are the East and West Banqueting Halls, open on special days throughout the year (www.landmarktrust.org.uk).

The **Ernest Wilson Memorial Garden** (just off the High Street in Leysbourne) is dedicated to one of the world's greatest plant collectors, born in the town in 1876. It's planted with some of the 1,200 trees and plants he discovered. Admission is free and it's open all the year round. And the 102-mile **Cotswold Way** starts (or finishes) in Chipping Campden, with the other end in Bath (www.nationaltrail.co.uk/Cotswold).

Outstanding gardens

An Arts and Crafts masterpiece, the grounds at **Hidcote Manor Garden** near Chipping Campden are considered to be among the finest in the world. They were designed by

Hidcote Manor Garden near Chipping Campden

Major Lawrence Johnston, who died in 1957, as a series of outdoor rooms, each with its own character.

So what is an Arts and Crafts garden? Head gardener at Hidcote Glyn Jones explains: *'The principle is to use natural, locally available materials. Close to the manor, you have quite rigid formality both in the structure and the style of planting. The further away you get, the more fluid it becomes until, finally, the garden and the countryside merge into one. There are 24 different garden areas here, and each one needs its own plan, which is a huge challenge. But because it's in these smaller areas, people can relate to the garden and take ideas away with them, even if it's simply a particular plant combination.'*

HIDCOTE MANOR GARDEN: Hidcote Bartrim, near Chipping Campden GL55 6LR, ☎01386 438333; www.nationaltrust.org.uk/hidcote. Entry: adults £8.50, children £4.25, family £21.20; Mar to Jun/Sept, 10am–6pm Mon–Wed and Sat/Sun; Jul/Aug, 10am–6pm Fri–Wed; Oct, 10am–5pm Mon–Wed and Sat/Sun; shop, restaurant, plant sales.

The celebrated diarist and country house expert James Lees-Milne wrote, *'Papa drove me to Hidcote to tea with Laurie Johnston who took us round his famous garden. It is not only beautiful but full of surprises. You are constantly led from one scene to another, into long vistas and little enclosures, which seem infinite. Yet the total area of this garden does not cover many acres. It is also full of rare plants brought from the most outlandish places in India and Asia.'*

Hidcote's one-time owner Lawrence Johnston also advised on the design and planting of his neighbour's gardens at **Kiftsgate Court**, Chipping Campden

LOCAL KNOWLEDGE

Julian Linley is editor of celebrity, gossipy *Heat* magazine, famed for its insights into famous lives and its delicious sense of humour. An old boy of Chipping Campden comprehensive, he grew up in Draycott, near Moreton-in-Marsh, surrounded by a close-knit family. It was, he says, a *Just William* childhood: '*In all my memories, I appear to be running through a meadow.*'

Favourite pub: I have two. One is the Crown in Blockley because it's the local pub with local people and that's where I go with my friends. And similarly the Fox in Broadwell. I had a really wonderful Christmas Eve there last year. It's a real old-fashioned pub – not gastro – where they serve Donnington ale and I had an amazing time chatting to friends by the blazing fire.

Best hotel: The Cotswold House Hotel in Chipping Campden, where I celebrated my 18th birthday.

Can't-live-without-it shop: Blockley's new village-run shop. The last time I was in there, the back door was propped open and you could see straight through to the **churchyard behind it:** a postcard moment. It reminded me of being a kid and queuing up in the butcher's on a Saturday. I also love the fact that I can go to Warner's Budgens in Moreton and find an amazing selection of produce.

Best Cotswold read: *Cotswold Life* magazine. Like *Heat*, it's an escape from the world. The brilliant thing about *Cotswold Life* is you get to see inside people's houses you wouldn't normally see inside; you get to listen to what other people in the Cotswolds think. It draws back the net curtains.

Favourite view: I've got it on my phone. I love walking Buster, my dog, and one of the best things about coming home is taking him on a walk around the back of Draycott into Blockley. The views are wonderful.

Best thing about being in the Cotswolds: I can be who I am. I wear a battered old pair of jeans, a sweatshirt and t-shirt and old trainers with the sole falling off, and my glasses. I don't wash my hair and I walk the dog!

(☎01386 438777). Three generations of women from the same family created this beautiful series of interconnecting gardens: Heather Muir in the 1920s, Diana Binny from 1950, and Anne Chambers today. The gardens are home to the famous Kiftsgate rose, the largest in England.

It's also worth spending an hour or more at the beautiful Cotswold watermill **Mill Dene**, which dates back to Norman times. This 2.5 acre award-winning garden has a mill pool stream, grotto and rose walk (not recommended for toddlers).

> KIFTSGATE COURT: Chipping Campden GL55 6LN; ☎01386 438777; www.kiftsgate.co.uk Entry: adults £6.50, children £2; open daily May/Jun/Jul 12 noon–6pm, except Thurs/Fri: Aug daily 2–6pm except Thurs/Fri; Apr & Sept open 2–6pm Sun/Mon/Wed.

> MILL DENE: School Lane, Blockley GL56 9HU; ☎01386 700457; milldene.co.uk, 3 miles north-west of Moreton off the A44 Entry: adults £5, seniors and students £4.75 and children £1, with free garden trail; open Apr 1 to Sept 30, Wed–Fri 10.30am–5pm; bank holidays 2–5pm.

Wet weather

West of Moreton is the village of Snowshill, famous for **Snowshill Manor**, once owned by the eccentric collector, Charles Paget Wade. This house is stuffed full of 22,000

CELEBRITY CONNECTIONS

Julian Lloyd Webber, one of the world's greatest cellists, lives in a small village in the North Cotswolds, in one of the prettiest cottages imaginable. But the attraction isn't just the honey-coloured stone: it's the fact that this area rubs shoulders with the Malverns, which inspired one of his great heroes, the composer Edward Elgar.

'I was always fascinated by – and loved – Elgar's music. And the more I got interested in his music, probably when I was around 16, the more I became interested in the part of the world where he lived,' he says. He's owned his north Cotswold cottage since 1989. 'I try to get here as often as I can. I'm often on tour, or I have to be in London for one reason or another, but what I find is I can come up here and get through a fantastic amount of work, cooped up quietly and concentrating; it's reassuring to know I can do that.'

That move to the Cotswolds not only brought him tranquillity and privacy, but an even deeper understanding of the effects of surroundings on musicians. 'Any musician who has seen where Elgar lived is at a huge advantage,' he says. 'The chief characteristic of Elgar's music is that it is very influenced by the countryside and landscape: I'm absolutely convinced of that. And I think if he had not been brought up around Worcester and Malvern and had not spent his youth walking on the Malvern Hills, his music would be very different.'

miscellaneous objects he amassed over his lifetime. In the Green Room stands his collection of 26 suits of 19th-century Samurai armour, made from silk brocade, lacquered metal, bear skin and human hair – one of the most surreal sights in the Cotswolds. There are ancient bicycles, sedan chairs, children's toy trains, bunches of heavy keys, pictures, vases, clocks galore, tapestries and carvings. In fact, Wade's aim was to preserve excellent craftsmanship from any age and culture.

Even during his collecting days – from 1900 to 1951 – Wade had already acquired a certain amount of fame. Queen Mary visited and declared that the most fascinating thing was Wade himself. Virginia Woolf took a less favourable view: she was irritated by the fact that none of the many clocks in the house told the right time – as a result, she nearly missed her train. Outside, the charming organic garden houses more objects and Wade's final lodging – in an outbuilding.

Garden at Snowshill Manor

SNOWSHILL MANOR: Near Broadway, WR12 7JU; ☎01386 852410; www.nationaltrust. org.uk/snowshillmanor. Entry: adults £7.30, children £3.70, family £18.60; manor open Mar to Nov 12–5pm, Wed–Sat; garden open Mar to Nov 11am–5.30pm Wed–Sun; shop, restaurant, grounds open Mar to Nov 11am–5.30pm Wed–Sun; and from 12–4pm Sat/Sun Nov/Dec.

What to do with children...

The wonderful thing about the **Cotswold Falconry Centre** is the lack of gimmicks: this is not a circus act but a centre that focuses on conservation and education, where you'll have an amazing experience seeing birds in their natural habitat. The centre is home to up to 100 birds of prey: falcons, hawks, eagles, owls, vultures and caracara are all here. Other attractions include daily flying displays, a gift shop and the Owl Wood Project, where the secret life of owls is revealed. There are also regular owl evenings, three-day falconry course and eagle days.

The Domestic Fowl Trust at Honeybourne in Worcestershire (WR11 7QZ; ☎01386 833083; www. domesticfowltrust.co.uk), 5 miles from Broadway, consists of 20 acres in which to see duck, geese, turkeys, bantams and rare-breed farm animals (bring wellies when wet). There are indoor and outdoor play areas and tearooms in the summer. It also has a very useful shop for anyone who wants to keep domestic fowl. The trust is open every day bar Christmas and Boxing Days from 9.30am to 5pm, adults £4.50, children £3, concessions £3.75 and family £13.50.

From seven years upward and adults of all ages, an ultimate treat has to be a session with **Rob Ireland Activity Days**, just outside Moreton-in-Marsh. Supervised by professional instructors, there are mini and adult quad bikes, clay pigeon shooting, archery, 4 × 4 off-roading and fly fishing, to name but a few – and all amidst beautiful Cotswold scenery (☎01386 701683; www.robireland.co.uk).

> **COTSWOLD FALCONRY CENTRE:** Batsford Park, Moreton-in-Marsh GL56 9AB; ☎01386 701043; www.cotswold-falconry.co.uk Entry: adults £6, concessions £5, children £2.50, family £15; open Feb to Nov.

... and how to avoid children

> **SEZINCOTE:** Moreton-in-Marsh GL56 9AW; www.sezincote.co.uk. Entry: garden only, adults £5, children £1.50; £8 for house tour/garden; garden open Jan to Nov, Thurs, Fri and bank holidays Mon 2–6pm; house open May to Sept, Thurs/Fri/bank holidays 2.30–5.30pm; tea and home-made cake served in the Orangery.

Is it Sezincote or Shimla? In fact, the house at **Sezincote** near Moreton-in-Marsh is thought to be the only Moghul building to survive in western Europe. It was commissioned in 1810 by Charles Cockerell, who had worked out in India, with the help of his brother, the architect Samuel Pepys Cockerell, as well as Thomas Daniell, the painter of Indian architectural scenery, and the landscape designer Repton. That Indian influence continues into the garden over a bridge adorned by statues of bulls, through formal borders guarded by stone elephants, and a temple to the Hindu sun god. Sezincote was the inspiration for Brighton Pavilion.

It's also worth checking out the short courses on offer at the fascinating **Stanton Guildhouse** a beautiful hand-built stone manor house in the village of Stanton overlooking the Vale of Evesham, and now home to a wide range of thriving artistic and creative projects (www.stantonguildhouse.org.uk).

Entertainment

Special events

One of the Cotswolds' premier agricultural events takes place here: **Moreton Show** (www.moretonshow.co.uk). Organised by Moreton-in-Marsh and District Agricultural and Horse Show Society on the first Saturday in September each year, the show originated in the 1940s, when agriculture was still a big employer. The show is built up in the traditional way, with marquees and hurdle pens giving a true country show atmosphere. Competitions are held for horses, ponies, cattle, sheep, goats, poultry, dogs, homecrafts, flowers, vegetables and even scarecrows, plus there are around 250 tradestands.

In Chipping Campden, Robert Dover will never be forgotten. Another former Londoner, this colourful lawyer invented the **Cotswold Olimpicks** – long before the modern Olympic Games (www.olimpickgames.co.uk). The first great festival of sport and pageantry was held in 1612, during the reign of James I, on Dovers Hill, high above the town. While competitive shin-kicking and 'jumping on bags' might lack

Opera in a garden

Martin Graham and his wife Lizzie are the creators of **Longborough Festival Opera**, which takes place at their Longborough home every summer. The dream began after a visit to Glyndebourne 20 years ago, when Martin decided he wanted to found his own equivalent festival. Since then he's had built in his garden overlooking the Evenlode Valley a 480-seat opera house, complete with grand Palladian façade, complete with orchestra pit. All this is even more of a success story, when you learn that Martin's a local lad who's lived in Longborough almost all his life.

Longborough Opera House

'It all came about after a visit to Glyndebourne,' he says. 'I wrote to George Christie (the late John Christie's son) a bit tongue-in-cheek, and said "the wife" was quite keen to start our own country house opera on account of her liking Wagner and so on. I daresay he receives letters from all sorts of lunatics, and certainly his reply was cautious and ran something like, "I think you need help"; a delicate way of telling me either to go and see a psychiatrist, or to get myself an architect. He recommended someone – a theatre designer. When the building work started, I fancy locals thought, "What's he up to now?"; but at the same time, the music world was watching saying, "How exciting". That was very gratifying.'

Longborough Festival Opera is at Longborough near Moreton-in-Marsh GL56 0QF, 01451 830292, www.lfo.org.uk.

the decorum of more traditional sporting events, the games attracted up to 30,000 people in their heyday. Taking place in late May/early June, the Olimpicks' weekend includes the Scuttlebrook Wake, with races, dances, a fair and the crowning of the Scuttlebrook Queen in the square. In 2012 – when the modern Olympiad is held in London – the Cotswold Olimpicks will be 400 years old. And the town's tradition of altruism lives on in many forms, including that of wine merchant, Charlie Bennett. A one-time student at the Royal College of Music, his dream of running a prestigious classical music festival in the town finally came true in 2002 and is now an annual event (www.campdenmusicfestival.co.uk)

🛒 Shopping

Snowshill Lavender Farm at Hill Barn Farm, Snowshill (WR12 7JY; ☎01386 854821; www.snowshill-lavender.co.uk) not only looks gorgeous, it smells pretty good, too. It's a third-generation farm in the heart of the Cotswolds, which is perfect country for this sort of venture: lavender loves free-draining limestone. The crops are steam-distilled on the farm and made into a unique range of lavender toiletries including soap, shower gel, bath oil, balms and many other lavender gifts. It's all open from the second May Bank Holiday to August Bank Holiday Monday from 10am to 5pm daily, £2.50 for adults and £1.50 for children.

The best... PLACES TO STAY

BOUTIQUE

Dormy House Hotel

Willersey Hill, Broadway WR12 7LF
☎ **01386 852711**
www.dormyhouse.co.uk

This is a 'get away from it all' country house. Once a farmhouse dating back to the 17th century, the team is friendly and able to put you at your ease while still providing a top-notch experience. It's adjacent to Broadway Golf Course.

Price: doubles from £170, including breakfast.

Cotswold House Hotel

Chipping Campden GL55 6AN
☎ **01386 840330**
www.cotswoldhouse.com

Set in a lovely Regency townhouse, this hotel is renowned for its luxurious, warm, comfortable feel and extremely good food. The rooms are individual, with DVD, state-of-the-art television and free broadband connection. The townhouse garden is one of the finest in Chipping Campden.

Price: from £150 for a double; £325 for a deluxe king, £500–£600 for suites.

The Manor House Hotel

High Street, Moreton-in-Marsh GL56 0LJ
☎ **01608 650501**
www.cotswold-inns-hotels.co.uk

The famous Gloucestershire floods gave this classic hotel an excellent opportunity to do a complete renovation. Right in the middle of town, it's full of character, with helpful staff and a superb restaurant, with a three-course dinner costing £37.50.

Price: from £145 for a double; from £190 for a four-poster room.

HOTEL

Lygon Arms Hotel

Broadway WR12 7DU; ☎ **01386 852255**
www.barcelo-hotels.co.uk

Right in the heart of Broadway is The Lygon Arms, rich in history and charm. Never one to take sides – Cromwell and Charles I both stayed here (though not at the same time), it's also a favourite of Bill Bryson. It has 3 acres of ground (including croquet and floodlit tennis), a spa and impressive restaurant.

Price: double room with breakfast from £145.

SELF-CATERING

The Big Cottage Company

Stapenhill Barn, Blockley GL56 9LJ
☎ **01386 700980 www.bigcottage.com**

Gorgeously luxurious and ideal if you're part of a large group of people. They're idyllically situated with every conceivable luxury. Extra services include a chef, pampering and country pursuits, and they're set well away from the madding crowd.

Price: from £1,995 for a weekend or from £2,995 for a week for 16 people.

Brew House

Bourton-on-the-Hill, Moreton-in-Marsh GL56 9AE; ☎ **01386 701177**
www.ruralretreats.co.uk

The Brew House sits in the courtyard of Bourton House, surrounded by its magnificent gardens. Magazines such as *Hello* and *The Week* nominated it as a perfect honeymoon cottage. With its 16th-century charm and antiques, it's certainly romantic.

Price: from £258 (min two nights' stay).

The best... FOOD AND DRINK

▶ Staying in

Food writer, restaurateur, caterer, cookery-school founder and businesswoman Prue Leith lives in a village near Moreton-in-Marsh and loves Cotswold produce – despite some odd early experiences. *'When I first came to the Cotswolds, the local farmer delivered two buckets of food for me. One was full of sheeps' balls and the other was their tails. I had no idea this was a wind-up; in fact, I was absolutely thrilled, though I didn't know what to do with them. I thought the testicles looked most like sweetbreads so I looked up glands, and treated them as such: they were unbelievably delicious. As for the tails, I boiled them to get the woolly bits off – it smelt like socks because of the lanolin – then marinated and griddled them. They were the most wonderful crunchy little things, rather like pork scratchings, which the children adored. I was looking forward to a bucket of these every year, but I never got another.'* For more conventional fare, she shops at **P G Checketts**, the butcher in the High Street, Moreton-in-Marsh. In the same high street is the **Cotswold Cheese Company** (www.cotswoldhcheesecompany.co.uk), named Britain's best new delicatessen for 2006/7 by the British Cheese Awards, and also highly praised by *Country Life* magazine. It's the place to buy a lunchtime baguette.

By late April, the early young shoots of asparagus are ready for cutting. This plant, nicknamed 'white gold', has the shortest of seasons – Shakespeare's Birthday to Midsummer's day. As devotees will tell you, half the pleasure lies in the rarity value.

'There's an old saying: there are two things that kill asparagus. One is weed and the other is greed,' says William Haines, who runs the 2,000 acre Haines Farm in Chipping Campden with his brother, Martin. *'If you cut too late, the crown doesn't have chance to recover for next year.*

'You can't beat English asparagus. It's slightly slower growing – not so full of water – and so it's far better on taste,' William says. Look out for Haines asparagus at branches of Sainsbury's and Waitrose.

Warner's Budgens (www.warnersbudgens.co.uk), with stores in Russell Square, Back Lane, Broadway and Moreton-in-Marsh High Street (as well as Bidford-on-Avon, Tewkesbury and Gloucester) is an independent supermarket group with a difference: it has a passion for local foods. Around 10–15 percent of its sales consist of local products, and it's a huge supporter of local schools and community projects. One favourite Warner's Budgens producer is **Simple Suppers** from Moreton-in-Marsh (www. simplesuppers.co.uk, ☎01608 650399): David Graham gave up flying for British Airways in the 1970s and, with his wife Gill, started to produce naturally reared pork, where the animals were stress-free. Gill put her culinary skills into action and created a range of meals, pies, snacks and desserts.

Spot Loggins Ice Cream is made by the Applebys from their own milk at their farm at the foot of the north Cotswolds in Bretforton. The cows are kept organically and, wherever possible, they use local fruit to enhance the natural flavourings (www. spotloggins.net, ☎01386 830831).

Farm shops include the Old Farm at Dorn near Moreton (GL56 9NS, ☎01608 650394, www.oldfarmdorn.globalinternet.co.uk), where sheep, cattle and pigs are bred on the farm itself.

EATING OUT

RESTAURANT

Buckland Manor
Buckland, near Broadway WR12 7LY
www.bucklandmanor.co.uk

A real 'English' treat. This exquisite manor house nestles next to the church in as fine a setting as you could hope for. The cuisine makes the most of the fertile Vale of Evesham next door: predominantly English with European influences. Many mains, such as an oven-roasted fillet of pollock with a sweet potato puree, braised shallots and roast jus, will be around £30.

Russell's of Broadway
20 High Street Broadway WR12 7DT
☎ 01386 853555
www.russellsofbroadway.com

The 16th-century building was once the headquarters of famed furniture maker Gordon Russell; it's a blend of interesting history and great food with a contemporary twist. A grilled ox tongue with Parmesan mash, a poached duck egg, roasted beetroot and pumpkin and date chutney will make your mouth, but not your eyes, water at around £14.

PUB

The Ebrington Arms
Chipping Campden GL55 6NH
☎ 01386 593223
www.theebringtonarms.co.uk

Hot on the heels of the recent Cask Marque award for serving the perfect pint of ale, The Ebrington Arms near Chipping Campden was awarded an AA Rosette for its food. It was praised for its care, skill and good-quality ingredients. The varied menu (around £12 for mains) has good veggie options and traditional favourites such as beer-battered cod, minted pea purée, tartare sauce and home-cut chips.

Horse & Groom Inn
Bourton-on-the-Hill, Moreton-In-Marsh GL56 9AQ
☎ 01386 700413

Fabulous homemade food has made a name for this inn. It's a passion for good produce that drives the menu here, in a combination of traditional favourites and modern innovations. If the fish pie is on the menu – organic salmon, smoked haddock, mussels, spinach and egg – then do try it. Mains tend to be around £12.50.

Three Ways House and The Pudding Club
Mickleton, Chipping Campden GL55 6SB
☎ 01386 438429
www.puddingclub.com

You can enjoy all courses at this hotel, but it's most famous as the home of The Pudding Club, founded here in 1985 to prevent the demise of the traditional great British Pudding. Don't miss a Pudding Club evening (do book), where you'll be guaranteed a traditional dessert such as jam roly poly or spotted dick. You can enjoy them as part of a set menu at around £30.

TEAROOM

Tilly's
18–19 High Street, Moreton-in-Marsh GL56 0AF

Tilly's in Moreton-in-Marsh serves proper, old-fashioned, WI-type cakes. It's rare people have time for teas nowadays, but when you're on holiday in the Cotswolds, this is the kind of tea shop you hope to come across.

🍸 Drinking

There are some first-class pubs in this area, and everyone seems to have their favourite. MC Beaton, creator of the Agatha Raisin series of detective stories set in the fictional Cotswolds village of Carsely, favours the **Black Bear** on Moreton's High Street (☎01608 652992). (No crime here but there is an active poltergeist called Fred.) Real ale enthusiasts' hangouts include the **Red Lion** (GL55 6AS; ☎01386 840760) and the **Volunteer Inn** (GL55 6DY; ☎01386 840688), both at Chipping Campden, the latter also being popular with walkers because of its proximity to the start of the Cotswold Way; and the **Inn on the Marsh** (GL56 0DW; ☎01608 650709), a charming pub that started life as a bakery. And as well as a range of draught beers, you'll find regular folk music nights at the **Bakers Arms**, Broad Campden (GL55 6UR; ☎01386 840515).

Many of the villages boast an inn, and there's no better way of discovering them than simply touring round and stopping at the most picturesque spots:

- **Mount Inn** – Stanton WR12 7NE; ☎01386 584316; has panoramic views (and exciting woodlice races)
- **Fleece Inn** – Bretforton WR11 7JE; ☎01386 831173; a 600-year-old National Trust owned inn
- **Farriers Arms** – next to the old village smithy in Todenham GL56 9PF; ☎01608 650901
- **Churchill Arms** – Paxford GL55 6XH; ☎01386 594000; named after George Spencer Churchill.

Or check out one of the old pubs in Mickleton, the northernmost village in Gloucestershire – you won't be disappointed.

The popular microbrewery in this area is **North Cotswold Brewery** at Ditchford Farm at Stretton on Fosse on the Gloucestershire/Warwickshire border (GL56 9RD; ☎01608 663947; www.northcotswoldbrewery.co.uk). You can sample wines, ciders, perry and soft drinks at the **Barnfield Winery and Cider Mill** on the Broadway Road at Broadway (WR12 7HB; ☎01386 853145; www.barnfieldcidermill.co.uk). This family-run business uses a 1920s wine press to make cider from local apples and perry. It's open daily from 10am to 6pm.

ⓘ Visitor Information

Tourist information centres: Moreton Area Centre, High Street, Moreton-in-Marsh GL56 0AZ, ☎01608 650881, Mon 8.45am–4pm, Tues–Thurs 8.45am–5.15pm, Fri 8.45am–4.45pm, Sat in summer 10am–1pm, Sat in winter 10am–12.30pm, closed Sun; The Old Police Station, High Street, Chipping Campden GL55 6HB, ☎01386 841206, www.visitchippingcampden.com, Mon–Sun (except Christmas Day, Boxing Day and New Year's Day) 10:00am–5:30pm in summer and 10am–5pm in winter; Broadway Tourist Information Centre, Russell Square, High Street, Broadway WR12 7P, ☎013386 852937, www.visitbroadway.co.uk, open 1 Mar to 22 Dec, Mon–Sat 10am–1pm and 2–5pm.

Hospitals: Cirencester Hospital, Tetbury Road, Cirencester GL7 1UY, ☎01285 655711, 24-hr A&E; Winchcombe Hospital, Cheltenham Road, Winchcombe GL54 5NQ, ☎01242 602341, minor injuries unit; Cheltenham General Hospital, Sandford Road, Cheltenham GL53 7AN, ☎08454 222222, 24-hr A&E; Stratford-upon-Avon Hospital, Arden Street CV37 6NX, ☎01789 205831, minor injuries unit.

Supermarkets include: Warner's Budgens supermarket, an independent that stocks many local products, Russell Square, Back Lane, High Street, Broadway WR12 7AP, ☎01386 842870; Moreton-in-Marsh High Street, ☎01608 651854; Tesco Express, Manchester Court, 13, High Street, Moreton-in-Marsh GL56 0BY, ☎0845 0269414.

Sports: Chipping Campden Sports Centre, Cider Mill Lane, Chipping Campden GL55 6HU, ☎01386 841595; Broadway Golf Club, Willersey Hill, Broadway WR12 7LG, ☎01386 853683, www.broadwaygolfclub.co.uk; Durham's Farm Riding School at Chastleton near Moreton-in-Marsh GL56 0SZ, www.cotswoldriding.com; Cotswolds Riding, The Vine, Stanton, near Broadway WR12 7NE, ☎01386 584250/584777, www.cotswoldsriding.co.uk.

Taxis include: Anthony's Cotswold Taxis, Moreton, ☎07710 117471; QB Cabs in Broadway ☎07850 888565; Chipping Campden Cars ☎01386 840111/07751 334696.

STRATFORD-UPON-AVON

It goes without saying: you can't talk about Stratford-upon-Avon without mentioning Shakespeare. But you could still have the time of your life in this beautiful market town were it stripped of every single Shakespeare attraction. First, a river runs through it; and not only a river, but a canal too. What the Stratford-upon-Avon Canal lacks in size – it runs for only 25 miles from the suburbs of Birmingham to join the Avon in Stratford – it makes up in beauty. For its short path takes it through the pride of England's countryside: the aged oaks of the Forest of Arden, rolling hills, fey wildlife and ancient water meadows, to the Stratford Basin in the heart of town.

Stepping onto dry land, one of the first things you might notice is the straight streets. This is a town that the planners got right – the medieval planners, that is. For more than 800 years after it was laid out as a new town – in 1196 – the simple grid system still makes it an eminently pleasant place to stroll.

WHAT TO SEE AND DO

There's a whole variety of ways to see Stratford, including an hour-long **open-top bus tour**, which allows you to hop on and off at your convenience. It leaves from the tourist information office at the bottom of Bridge Street at regular intervals and tickets are valid for 24 hours. As well as a tour commentary in different languages, there's a children's version (☎01789 299123; www.city-sightseeing.co.uk). You can get your ticket from the driver. Combined tickets to the Shakespeare houses are available as part of a package, as well as a river cruise, weather permitting, with possible savings of around 10 percent.

Stratford operates a **Park and Ride scheme** (www.warwickshire.gov.uk/stratfordparkandride) from Bishopston Lane near the roundabout with the A46 and the A3400 Birmingham Road: follow the signs. Parking is free and the bus costs £1.30 per adult with up

CITY SIGHTSEEING: STRATFORD-UPON-AVON: bus tour: adults £11, concessions £9, child £5.50, family £27; buses leave from the Pen and Parchment Inn at 9.30am every day (except Dec 25/26 and Jan 1) every 60 minutes winter weekdays and every 30 minutes winter weekends; Easter to autumn, buses run every 20 minutes.

Open-top bus tour of Stratford

Stratford-Upon-Avon

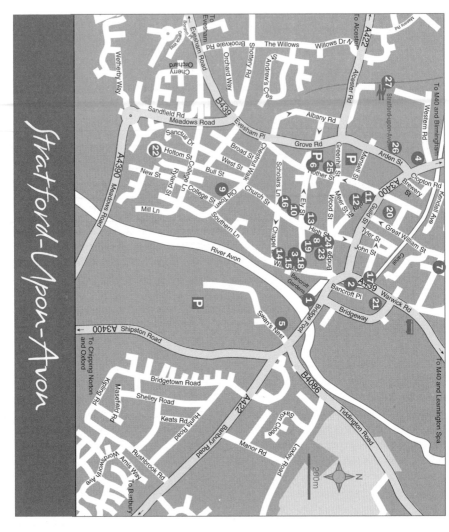

Things to see and do
1. Avon Boating
2. Bancroft Cruisers
3. Brass Rubbing Centre
4. Bus tour
5. Butterfly Farm
6. Civic Hall and town council
7. Hardwick House
8. Harvard House and the Museum of British Pewter
9. Holy Trinity Church and Shakespeare's grave
10. Nash's House and New Place
11. Shakespeare's Birthplace
12. Creaky Cauldron

Entertainment
13. Courtyard Theatre (RSC)
14. Royal Shakespeare Theatre
15. The Falstaff's Experience

Places to stay
16. Mercure Shakespeare Hotel

Eat and drink
17. Cox's Yard
18. Dirty Duck
19. Hathaway Tea Rooms
20. Marlowe's Restaurant
21. Thai Kingdom
22. West End
23. The Oppo
24. The Vintner

Shopping
25. Rother Street Markets

Visitor Information
26. Hospital
27. Railway Station

See Stratford from the river Avon

to two children under 16 travelling free. Buses are every 10–15 minutes to the town centre and attractions.

You can also view it all from the river. **Avon Boating** offers regular river-cruise departures from the Bancroft Gardens next to the theatre, and from the Boat House in Swan's Nest Lane, where you can hire rowing boats, punts and self-drive motor boats by the hour (☎01789 267073; www.avon-boating.co.uk); **Bancroft Cruisers** also runs river cruises from its landing stage at The Holiday Inn hotel (☎01789 269669; www.bancroftcruisers.co.uk), five minutes' walk from the car parks.

Both sides of the River Avon also offer easy **walks** on level footpaths.

Shakespeare's Stratford
A walk down Henley Street will begin to show you why Shakespeare couldn't keep away from his birth-town. Its charm, in some places little-changed from Elizabethan times, is evident. Indeed, even after Shakespeare fled to London from poor old Anne Hathaway, he'd frequently return to visit family and friends, and eventually became a Stratford property owner himself. This is the street of **Shakespeare's Birthplace**, where the Bard was born in an upper room, and where he grew up. You'll be following in a long line of distinguished tourists:

> SHAKESPEARE'S BIRTHPLACE: Henley Street, Stratford-upon-Avon CV37 6QW; ☎01789 204016; houses.shakespeare.org.uk Entry: adults £9, concessions £8, children £4.50, family £24, admission includes entry to Hall's Croft and Nash's House; open Mon–Sat 9am–5pm (10am–4pm Nov to Mar) and Sun 9.30am–5pm.

Charles Dickens, John Keats, Walter Scott and Thomas Hardy all left their mark after visiting the house.

Shakespeare's Birthplace has long been a popular destination for tourists, from Dickens to Hardy

The **Stratford Town Trail** (www.visit-stratford.co.uk) is an easy way to explore present-day attractions and history in one. It will lead you through picturesque spots such as Bridge Street, where once stood a market hall where Shakespeare's father sold the gloves he made. And there's Church Street with the grammar school – still thriving – that Shakespeare is said to have attended. The school usually opens its doors to visitors in September, during Heritage Open Days (www.heritageopendays.org.uk).

Shakespeare's Church, otherwise known as **Holy Trinity**, Stratford, hosts a thriving worshipping community, but it also receives thousands of visitors a year who come to see the place where Shakespeare was baptised, served as a lay rector, and lies buried in the chancel. Although there is no record of his birth, the original register still exists showing his baptism on 26 April, 1564 (which is the date used to estimate his birthday), and his burial 52 years later (almost to the day).

HOLY TRINITY: Old Town, Stratford-upon-Avon CV37 6BG; www.shakespeareschurch.org Entry: free, requested donation of £1.50 to see the grave; open year round but can be closed for funerals etc.; guided tours: £2/£1 adults/students ☎01789 266316; www.stratford-upon-avon.org; Jun to Aug, Wed/Thurs at 2.30pm.

As Bill Bryson points out in his book *Shakespeare,* the great man's grave and memorial leave almost as many unanswered questions as does his life. Among the puzzles are the fact that, although Shakespeare is buried with members of his family (though in curious order), no one knows the identity of Francis and Anne Watts who lie with them. And why does the message on his life-sized bust – on the north chancel wall – refer to Shakespeare as being 'Within this monument' when he's clearly buried elsewhere in the church? In fact, these lines have led scholars to speculate that the monument contains not the Bard's body but the body of his work – his manuscripts.

The five Shakespeare houses in and around the town not only offer a glimpse into the Bard's life, they also boast some peaceful and beautiful gardens. Not to be missed are the springtime blossoms at **Anne Hathaway's** orchard at nearby Shottery, the Elizabethan knot garden at **Nash's House & New Place**, and the lovely walled garden at **Hall's Croft**.

Nash's House was once owned by Thomas Nash, the first husband of Shakespeare's granddaughter, Elizabeth. Inside, you'll see much of the original 16th-century timberwork, as well as displays on the history of Stratford. It also houses the Complete Works of Shakespeare Exhibition, which tells the story of this great tome.

Equally interesting is the bit that isn't there: **New Place**, the site of the house – long destroyed – to which Shakespeare retired in 1610. He bought it while working in London for the princely sum of £60 in 1597. Indeed, it was an impressive house: the second largest building in the town. This was the place where he died (some say after an evening carousing with Ben Jonson and Michael Drayton, though it seems clear he had known he was dying for at least a few weeks beforehand).

Monument to Shakespeare within Holy Trinity Church

NASH'S HOUSE AND NEW PLACE: Chapel Street, Stratford-upon-Avon CV37 6EP; ☎01789 292325; houses.shakespeare. org.uk. Entry: adults £9, concessions £8, children £4.50, family £24, admission includes entry to Shakespeare's Birthplace and Hall's Croft; open Mon–Sat 10am–5pm (11am–4pm Nov to Mar) and Sun 9.30am–5pm.

The Elizabethan knot garden at Nash's House

A later owner of the property – the 18th-century eccentric, the Reverend Francis Gastrell – grew tired of the constant tourists who came to view the Bard's former home and razed it to the ground. All that remain today are the foundations and a well. But on the site of its orchards and kitchen gardens is the Shakespeare Memorial Garden – probably an area where Shakespeare himself liked to relax and spend time – in the form of a formal Elizabethan garden. In the centre of the lawn is a mulberry tree, rumoured to be from the cutting of a tree planted by the man himself.

The final house in the town centre associated with Shakespeare (the two others lie outside) is **Hall's Croft**, where Shakespeare's daughter, Susanna, lived with her husband, Dr John Hall. On view is Dr Hall's consulting room, with interesting medical artefacts and a first edition of his medical notes, published in 1657. Some

HALL'S CROFT: Old Town, Stratford-upon-Avon, CV37 6BG; ☎01789 292107; houses.shakespeare.org.uk. Entry: adults £9, concessions £8, children £4.50, family £24, admission includes entry to Shakespeare's Birthplace and Nash's House; open Mon–Sat 9am–5pm (11am–4pm Nov to Mar) and Sun 9.30am–5pm.

Shakespeare: just outside Stratford

Anne Hathaway's Cottage, in the hamlet of Shottery about a mile from the town centre, is where Shakespeare's wife spent her childhood. If we know little about Shakespeare, we know even less about Anne. Sadly, the fact most quoted is that her husband left her his 'second-best bed' (along with the bedclothes) in his will. Do feel free to speculate on the implications – many others have. Certainly, her early home is a beautiful thatched farmhouse of no mean size, indicative of the fact that she came from a relatively well-to-do family.

The gardens at Anne Hathaway's cottage are not to be missed

of the herbs he might have used in his curative potions are grown here, beside an ancient mulberry tree. And if you do happen to visit during April blossom time, you'll have the added pleasure of the annual festivities surrounding Shakespeare's birthday. Every year, a programme of activities runs in the days up to (and including the nearest weekend to) **Shakespeare's birthday** on 23 April. You can find the annual programme at www.shakespeare.org.uk/birthday.html or call 01789 204016.

ANNE HATHAWAY'S COTTAGE: Cottage Lane, Shottery, Stratford-upon-Avon CV37 9HH; ☎01789 292100; houses.shakespeare. org.uk. Entry: adults £6, concessions £5, children £3, family £15.50; open Mon–Sat 9am–5pm (Nov to Mar 10am–4pm), Sun 9.30am–5pm.; regular garden tours in summer; gift shop, and tea garden opposite.

Three miles from the town centre is **Mary Arden's Farm**. This is a Shakespeare attraction that younger children will enjoy, too. Here, they can discover what it was like to live on a 16th-century farm, as Shakespeare's mother, Mary Arden, did. This is a living history experience: visitors can see a Tudor family making bread over an open fire and tending to the farm in an authentic way. You can wander through the orchard and wild flower meadow and meet rare breeds including Cotswold sheep and Gloucester Old Spot pigs.

MARY ARDEN'S FARM: Station Road, Wilmcote, Stratford-upon-Avon CV37 9UN; ☎01789 293455. Entry: adults £8, concessions £7, children £4, family £21; open Mon–Sun 10am–5pm (Nov to Mar Mon–Sun 10am–4pm) gift shop and seasonal café.

Meet Cotswold sheep at Mary Arden's Farm

☂ Wet weather

Stratford has one of the largest **butterfly farms** in the UK. Watching hundreds of the world's most spectacular and colourful butterflies spreading their wings in the tropical garden is a unique pleasure – and you can meet some fearsome spiders in **Arachnoland** as well as visiting **Insect City** and the **Caterpillar Room**. It's a great place to visit in the rain, as well as when it's nippy – it's pretty warm in here!

See hundreds of butterflies at The Butterfly Farm

If it's raining, then use a fine weather spell – and the best place to find that would be the **Creaky Cauldron** in Henley Street. It's one of Stratford's creepiest museums and visitor experiences, but a pretty magic one, too. There are three

THE BUTTERFLY FARM: Swan's Nest Lane, Stratford-upon-Avon CV37 7LS; ☎01789 299288; www.butterflyfarm.co.uk
Entry: adults £5.75, seniors and students £5.25, children £4.75, family £16.75 (2 adults, 2 children; extra child £2.75); open 10am–6pm in summer and 10am–dusk in winter.

THE CREAKY CAULDRON: 21, Henley Street, Stratford-upon-Avon, CV37 6QW; ☎01789 290969; www.seekthemagic.org
Entry: daytime entry adults £5, seniors and students £4, children 8–16 £2.75 (under-8s free), family £12; open 10.30am–5pm every day except Christmas Day and New Year's Day.

enchanting floors filled with spellbinding facts that will delight every hardy soul from 6 years onwards. Visit the website for details of creepy evening events, ghostly theatre and overnight vigils…

👫 What to do with children

An unusual place to visit is **Stratford's Brass Rubbing Centre** at the Avon Bank Gardens in Southern Lane (CV37 6BA; ☎01789 297671; www.stratfordbrassrubbing. co.uk).Engraved brass plaques are often to be seen in medieval churches across the country, depicting family stories, medieval dress, armour, trades and professions. This centre has copies of medieval and Tudor brasses for visitors to do their own rubbings, including fine local brasses, and some modern ones of Shakespeare. The centre's free to look around, but it costs from £1.95 to £19.95 to do a rubbing, depending on the size of brass. There are also some unusual gifts for sale.

Children will love the interactive learning zone at **Harvard House and the Museum of British Pewter** (☎01789 204507; www.shakespeare.org.uk). This is an elegant example of an Elizabethan town house, with a museum that explores the story of

LOCAL KNOWLEDGE

John and **Helen Hogg** run the Stratford Town Walk. John is a member of The Magic Circle and adds a little magic into the ghost walks that take place on Mondays Thursdays and Fridays. They also run a Ghost Cruise in liaison with Bancroft Cruisers, which operates from Easter to Hallowe'en. You can find out more on ☎ 07855 760377 or at www. stratfordtownwalk.co.uk

Favourite restaurants: We love **The Oppo** in Sheep Street; the Vintner just up the road; and **Marlowe's Restaurant** and **Hathaway Tea Rooms** in the High Street. Marlowe's is believed to be haunted by a maid who burned to death in a serious fire during Shakespeare's time. At Hathaway Tearooms, be careful not to sit at the table sometimes occupied by 'Mabel', possibly the ghost of a previous employee!

Favourite activity: Take a 45-minute Bancroft Cruise alongside the Tiddington Road; pass under the 14 arch Clopton Bridge, hardly changed since it was built in the 1400s; and take in the Shakespeare theatres and Holy Trinity Church.

Best view: Standing on the Tramway Bridge, built to carry horse-drawn trams to Moreton-in-Marsh, and quietly contemplating the majestic River Avon meandering through tree-lined banks, past the theatres and church, on its long journey to the River Severn.

Favourite haunt: Sitting outside the Courtyard Theatre café/restaurant, with a strong cup of Americano, and people-watching: the actors, the ever-attentive autograph hunters, the theatre enthusiasts discussing the latest play, and the sudden exodus and hubbub of an excited audience after a performance.

Best picnic spot: The secret garden hidden behind Nash's House. Most of the garden was Shakespeare's from his 'retirement home', New Place; it is beautifully maintained, has flowers all year round, topiary hedges, and an amazing series of bronze sculptures representing Shakespeare's plays – an ideal spot for a peaceful picnic or to spend some quiet time.

pewter. Children can try their hands at the decorative pewter craft of repoussé, take a virtual reality tour and become a pewter detective. It's in the High Street and costs £3.50 for adults (children with accompanying adult free); it's also free if you're a multiple 'Shakespeare' house ticket holder.

Entertainment

It's a given, isn't it? If you're going to Stratford, you have to see a **Royal Shakespeare Company** (RSC) play. The company doesn't solely focus on Shakespeare: it also puts on plays by other Renaissance dramatists and contemporary writers. Come in 2010 and you'll find the finest modern playhouse for Shakespeare anywhere in the world. That's when work is due to finish on its main performance space, the Royal Shakespeare Theatre, which it's currently extending and updating. Until then, the RSC will continue to perform in the 1,000-seat Courtyard Theatre. For information about shows and to book tickets, visit www.rsc.org.uk or ring the ticket hotline on ☎0844 800 1110.

The RSC offers **free theatre tours** that last approximately 45 minutes, taking visitors behind the scenes. There are several tours in the week and two on a Sunday, but times vary according to performance schedules. To find more or to book a place, call 0844 800 1114 or visit The Courtyard box office.

For a less highbrow, but great fun Shakespeare fix, visit **The Falstaff's Experience** at The Shrieve's House and Barn in Sheep Street. By day (generally 10.30am–5.30pm, though winter can vary), this is a waxworks museum offering an historic tour of Stratford through the eyes of people who once lived here. Adult tickets cost £4.75, concessions £3.75, children (7–15) £2.25 and families £10.75. But by night, this building shows why it's been called one of the most haunted in England. Lantern-lit ghost tours of the building are held every evening from 6pm, and there are various paranormal and psychic events held regularly (☎0870 3502770; www.falstaffsexperience.co.uk).

Concerts and other performances take place in the **Civil Hall** in Rother Street in the centre of town (☎01789 207100; www.civichall.co.uk); while at **Cox's Yard**

Where for art thou, audience?

Apocryphal or not, the story goes like this: a few years ago RSC staff noticed that on a certain day of the week the occupants of a block of theatre seats would change during the interval. After investigation, they discovered that a coach operator was dividing American tour groups in two. The first half would go to the RSC, while the second half had dinner. Then they'd swap over at interval time. The reason, one of the Americans helpfully explained, was that the RSC was on their list of 'must sees', and this was a way of ticking that off without having to go through the inconvenience of a whole performance... The conversations afterwards must have been good. 'Have you seen *Two Gentlemen of Verona*?' 'No, just the one.'

(www.coxsyard.co.uk), next to Bancroft Gardens, the Playbox Theatre Company performs regularly in the Attic Theatre, and there's live music at The Music Room, the only dedicated live music venue in Stratford. In Victorian times, the warehouses and wharves here would have been at the heart of a busy river industry.

And there are the races. Steeplechasing has taken place at **Stratford Racecourse** since 1755; now 18 meetings are held each year, mostly in the summer months. The racecourse has a glass-fronted grandstand and is one of Britain's leading smaller courses. It's at Luddington Road (CV37 9SE; ☎01789 267949; www.stratford racecourse.net) a mile or so out of town.

Shopping

In spite of the half-timbered buildings, the almshouses, and the unusual 'weeping chancel' of Holy Trinity where Shakespeare is buried, you mustn't let history blind you to today's pleasures – indeed, let the past and present merge into one. For although the old glove-maker's market is long gone, there are still markets in Rother Street every Friday and a farmers' market on the first and third Saturdays. And the individual shops alone make the town worth visiting. Antiques, elegant fashion, crafts, bookshops galore for once threaten to eclipse the high street chains that loiter – many squeezed into old-fashioned charm by their anachronistic housing. You don't have to buy a ticket to browse in the various gift shops in the Shakespeare houses, where you'll find some fun and unusual mementos to take home.

The best... **PLACES TO STAY**

HOTELS

Mercure Shakespeare Hotel

**Chapel Street,
Stratford-upon-Avon CV37 6ER
☎ 01789 294997; www.mercure.com**

The RSC uses this half-timbered hotel in the heart of the town. Each of the 74 rooms is individually decorated and named after a Shakespeare character or play. You can choose to eat at the David Garrick Restaurant, or more informally in Othello's Bar Brasserie.

Price: double (room only) from £100.

The Stratford Hotel

**Arden Street,
Stratford-upon-Avon CV37 6QQ
☎ 01789 271000; www.qhotels.co.uk**

The Stratford is also regularly used by the RSC due to its central location and recently refurbished interior. Comfortable yet contemporary, it has free parking and a state-of-the-art mini-gym. Quills restaurant offers a mouth-watering menu that has earned an AA Rosette. Q Hotels was awarded AA Hotel Group of the Year 2008-09.

Price: doubles from £99 per night, including breakfast.

Ettington Park Hotel

**Alderminster,
Stratford-upon-Avon CV37 8BU
☎ 0845 072 7454
www.handpicked.co.uk**

Set in the green Stour Valley six miles from Stratford, this is country house luxury at its best. Inside, there are antiques, fine paintings, and historic friezes; outside, there are 40 acres of ground on which stand a 12th-century church. The genuine warmth and hospitality of the staff ensure it's a relaxing experience.

Price: from £125 for double room with breakfast.

B&B

Penryn Guest House

126 Alcester Road, Stratford-upon-Avon CV37 9DP; www.penrynguesthouse.co.uk

This popular guest house has won awards for its high standard of accommodation, and local produce breakfast. It's within walking distance of Anne Hathaway's cottage, the town centre and the railway station.

Price: doubles including breakfast from £65.

Hardwick House

**1 Avenue Road,
Stratford-upon-Avon CV37 6UY
☎ 01789 204307
www.hardwickstratford.co.uk**

Named as one of the top 20 B&Bs in the country by *Good Housekeeping* magazine – How's That? – there's an added bonus for cricket enthusiasts. Owner Simon Wootton used to play professional cricket for Warwickshire and Gloucestershire. It's a quiet location, with parking, a five-minute walk to the town, and a couple of minutes to the Welcombe Hills & Clopton Park nature reserve.

Price: from £42/£70 for a single/double.

SELF-CATERING

Shakespeare Holiday Cottages

**Arden Hill Farm, Birmingham Road, Pathlow, Stratford-upon-Avon CV37 0ES
☎ 01789 293046
www.shakespeareholidaycottages.co.uk**

A five-minute drive from the centre of Stratford, these cottages are set in the heart of the Warwickshire countryside with accordingly magnificent views. Luxuriously furnished, equipped and decorated, the cottages can cater for from one to six people, plus an exclusive property sleeping up to 20, with hot tub.

Price: from £340 for a cottage sleeping up to five; for up to seven, from £360.

The best... FOOD AND DRINK

▶ Staying in

It goes without saying that the first port of call in Stratford should be the twice monthly **farmers' market**. This, the largest farmers' market in Warwickshire, has won many awards and takes place in Rother Street between 9am and 2pm on the first and third Saturdays of each month. Here, of course, you'll find producers from all over the region. From the Stratford area, there'll almost certainly be a sizzling pig roast from **Kirby Farm** at Whatcote near Shipston-on-Stour (☎01295 680525), which also sells sausages and bacon. And there's homebred beef and lamb from the Holdsworths of Little Meadows Farm in Pebworth (CV37 8XE; ☎01789 721114; www. littlemeadowsfarm.co.uk), which has its own farm shop. You'll also find some fine food outlets in the town itself.

Talton Mill Farm Shop and Delicatessen is a winner of Warwickshire Life's Farm Shop of the Year Award. Based at Newbold on Stour (CV37 8UG; ☎01789 459140; www.talton-mill.co.uk, this farm produces an unusually broad selection of fresh fruit, meat and vegetables, as well as stocking food from other local producers, such as Fosse Way Honey, Drinkwater's vegetables and Woodlands Farm yogurt. Their own chef produces first-rate ready meals.

Lower Clopton Farm Shop (CV37 8LQ; www.LowerClopton.co.uk) is another award winner, particularly for its pork sausages. Look out for news of the trail and picnic area this 211-acre farm is currently developing on the previously inaccessible and picturesque slopes of Meon Hill, where its animals graze. For a real summer treat (or any time of year you fancy it), visit **Henley Tea Rooms and Ice Cream Parlour** in the High Street at Henley-in-Arden (B95 5BS; ☎01564 795172; www.henleyIcecream. co.uk) where you can buy delicious ice cream made on local Midlands farms from whole fresh milk and double cream.

EATING OUT

RESTAURANT

Thai Kingdom
**11 Warwick Road,
Stratford-upon-Avon CV37 6YW
☎ 01789 261103
www.thaikingdom.co.uk**

The Crown Prince of Thailand has even held a private party here! In good weather, you can enjoy a meal in The Oriental Garden. A royal banquet menu, for a minimum of two, with multiple dishes such as hot and sour clear prawn soup, and duck with ginger, spring onions and mushrooms in a light soy sauce will be under £25.

PUB

The Baraset Barn
**Pimlico Lane, Alveston,
Stratford-upon-Avon CV37 7RJ
☎ 01789 295510
www.barasetbarn.co.uk**

This impressive foodie pub is popular for many reasons. Converted from an old barn, it combines historic features with striking contemporary design. The menu follows suit, with classic dishes, modern twists and daily seafood specials. For a real old favourite, there's a half-spit roast chicken with lemon and tarragon butter; many mains at £15 or less.

The Bell Inn
**Binton Road,
Welford-on-Avon CV37 8EB
☎ 01789 750353
www.thebellwelford.co.uk**

A 17th-century inn with exposed beams and flagstone floors, it's even supposed to have played a part in Will's demise.

The story goes that he met Jonson and Drayton for a drink in the Bell and caught pneumonia on the way home. He should have had some of the Bell's comfort food, such as the scrumpy beef and tomato casserole made to a traditional Warwickshire recipe… Plenty of choice at the £12 mark.

The Fox & Hounds Inn
**Great Wolford CV36 5NQ
☎ 01608 674220
www.thefoxandhoundsinn.com**

This is another pub where you can truly 'eat the view'. The menus feature Dexter beef from Chastleton and venison from Todenham as well as seasonal game from local shoots. Fresh herbs and vegetables come from the inn's garden, when possible, and wild mushrooms gathered from round about. Sausages, bacon, chutneys, pickles and condiments are made here in the kitchen. Local Kitebrook lamb loin, homemade black pudding, celeriac puree and braised puy lentils is hard to beat at around £16.

CAFÉ/TEAROOM

Royal Shakespeare Company
**The Courtyard Theatre, Southern Lane,
Stratford-upon-Avon CV37 6BB
www.rsc.org.uk**

This café bar serves a range of light meals including sandwiches and meat or vegetarian shareboards, freshly prepared using local ingredients (maybe brie and spinach tartlet with new potatoes and mixed salad at £7.95?). Sit here, eat, drink, enjoy, and watch famous actors come and go. Great for lunch, pre-show dining and supper.

EATING OUT

BOAT

Countess of Evesham
PO Box 179, Stratford-upon-Avon
CV37 6ZG, ☎ 07836 769499
www.countessofevesham.mistral.co.uk

Nicknamed Stratford's Orient Express, the Countess is a purpose-built 70ft restaurant cruiser that will take diners for a romantic supper along the floodlit banks of the Avon; there are lunchtime cruises, too. Prices and menus vary, according to the evening, but for around a set price of £30, you might dine off baked trout or pan-fried breast of chicken in a lemon and tarragon cream.

 ## Drinking

To experience another side of Stratford, join the 'luvvies' in the **Dirty Duck**. More properly known as the Black Swan, this pub is famous in theatre circles all over the world: a 15th-century building where resting actors drown their sorrows alongside their more successful counterparts – Peter O'Toole is fondly remembered for his speed-drinking prowess. There's a convention that after a show's opening night, the critics head for one end of the bar and the actors for another – absolutely forbidden to eavesdrop or cross the line.

Stratford is blessed with pubs, many of which are charming, and many of which serve local ales and good wines. The local branch of CAMRA has put together a Real Ale Trail, which includes the **Golden Bee** in Sheep Street, **the Squirrel** in Drayton Avenue and the **West End** in Bull Street. You can get hold of a copy from local railway stations.

Award-winning pubs include the 17th-century **Plough Inn** at Stretton-on-Fosse (GL56 9QX; ☎01608 661053), where you'll find quizzes, folk music, bridge and whist drives during the Sunday evening entertainment slot; and the good old-fashioned **Norman Knight** in the historic village of Whichford (CV36 5PE; ☎01608 684621).

The town of **Shipston-on-Stour** on the River Stour – which once saw some of the busiest sheep markets in the country – is another top pub location. With its Georgian buildings, 15th-century church, shops, restaurants and tearooms, it's a good place to visit full stop. The **White Bear Hotel** ('the Bear' to the locals) is a lively, traditional pub in the market square (CV36 4AJ; ☎01608 661 558). **The Black Horse** (CV36 4BT; ☎01608 662732), the only thatched building in the town, has a licence dating back to 1540 (though that didn't stop it brewing even earlier!)

ⓘ Visitor Information

Tourist information centre: Stratford-upon-Avon Tourist Information Centre, Bridgefoot, Stratford-upon-Avon CV37 6YY, ☎0870 160 7930, www.shakespeare-country.co.uk, www.visitstratforduponavon.co.uk, www.enjoywarwickshire.co.uk.

Hospitals: Warwick Hospital, Lakin Road, Warwick CV34 5BW, ☎01926 495321; Stratford-upon-Avon Hospital, Arden Street, Stratford CV37 6NX, ☎01789 205831, minor injuries unit.

Supermarkets include: Somerfield Stores, Town Square, Stratford-upon-Avon CV37 6JP, ☎01789 292604; WM Morrisons, Alcester Road, Stratford-Upon-Avon, CV37 9DA, ☎01789 267675.

Sports: Stratford Leisure and Visitor Centre, Bridgefoot, Stratford-upon-Avon CV37 6YY, ☎01789 268826, www.stratford.gov.uk; Stratford-upon-Avon

Golf Club, Tiddington Road, Stratford-Upon-Avon, Warwickshire CV37 7BQ, ☎01789 205749, www.stratfordgolf.co.uk; Welcombe Golf Club, Warwick Road, Stratford-Upon-Avon CV37 0NR, ☎01789 413800, www.menzies-hotels.co.uk/golf/welcombe; Ingon Manor Golf & Country Club, Ingon Lane, Snitterfield, Stratford-Upon-Avon, CV37 0QE, ☎01789 731857, www.ingonmanor.co.uk; Stratford-on-Avon Gliding Club, Snitterfield Airfield, Bearley Road, Stratford-upon-Avon, Warwickshire CV37 0EG, www.stratfordgliding.co.uk for more details.

Bike rental: Stratford Bike Hire, ☎07711 776 340, www.stratfordbikehire.com.

Taxis include: 007 Stratford Taxis ☎01789 414007, 01789 415888; A to B Taxis ☎01789 415225.

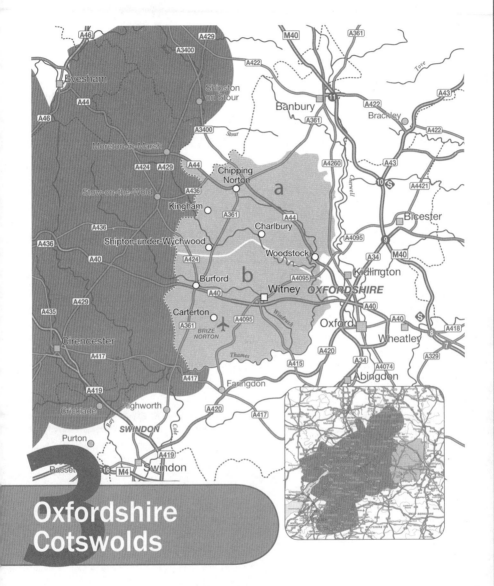

Oxfordshire Cotswolds

a. Chipping Norton and Woodstock
b. Burford, Minster Lovell and Witney

Unmissable highlights

01 Visit the fallen beauty of Minster Lovell Hall – one of the loveliest ruins in the country; but beware ghosts. A battle-scarred Lord and a young bride both died tragically here, p. 223

02 Watch the penguins being fed at the Cotswold Wildlife Park and Gardens, home to many endangered animals, p. 227

03 Take the children to Cogges Manor Farm, a unique working farm museum near Witney, p. 227

04 Take tea at Burford's most famous tearooms, Huffkins, in the High Street, p. 234

05 Try to count the mysterious Rollright Stones, megaliths that stand near the village of Long Compton. Legend has it you'll get a different answer each time, p. 202

06 Enjoy the vista at Blenheim Palace: Blenheim Lake, spanned by Vanbrugh's Grand Bridge. Lady Randolph Churchill (Sir Winston's mother) declared it *'the finest view in England'*, p. 206

07 Pay homage to Sir Winston Churchill, born at Blenheim Palace and buried just down the road in Bladon Churchyard, alongside his parents and his wife, Clementine, p. 207

08 Cool off in Chipping Norton Lido, with water slide, café, events and picnic grounds, p. 204

09 Shop at Daylesford Organic near Kingham, tagged 'Britain's poshest shop' by the national media, p. 212

10 Eat cheese that simply rocks: Little Wallop, made by Blur superstar Alex James and cheese guru Juliet Harbutt, who both live near Kingham, p. 214

OXFORDSHIRE COTSWOLDS

For many visitors, Oxfordshire is where it all begins, for Burford is known as the Gateway to the Cotswolds. Indeed, the Oxfordshire Cotswolds exemplify all that is wonderful about the region: beautiful landscapes, agriculture, busy market towns, and history by the bucket-load.

People have admired the area for a long time – we know that because there's evidence of more than 6,000 years of history to be found here. One of the earliest and most spectacular examples of early human life in the region is the mysterious Rollright stone circle, which probably dates back to the late Stone Age. That was the sort of period when farming first began – and it was farming that shaped this area. Even today, it's one of the least spoilt and most rural parts of England. The towns are small and individual – Burford, Chipping Norton, Witney and Woodstock – and the villages are some of the country's most idyllic: Minster Lovell, Great Tew, Churchill, the Wychwoods, and Swinbrook, where the famous Mitford sisters grew up.

There's plenty for all ages to do and enjoy. Youngsters will love Cogges Manor Farm, near Witney and the Cotswold Wildlife Park and Gardens, near Burford, where you can learn about the very real threats endangered animals face in the 21st century. In Woodstock, you'll find Blenheim Palace, where the gate with the lake and the house beyond was once described as '*the finest view in England*'. Landscaped by 'Capability' Brown, the palace has now drawn up a blueprint that will see the park exactly as it was planted in the mid-1700s. The Marquess of Blandford grew up in the magnificent surroundings of Blenheim Palace, the home of his father, the 11th Duke of Marlborough, and birthplace of Sir Winston Churchill. When asked what he particularly liked about the Oxfordshire Cotswolds, Lord Blandford replied, 'Individuality. The Cotswolds are full of interesting characters: woodcarvers, blacksmiths; all sorts of individual light industries.'

Indeed, individuality is what this region is all about.

CHIPPING NORTON AND WOODSTOCK

Mysterious, magical, mythical; this part of Oxfordshire resounds with strange tales and folklore, which are as much a part of the landscape as the hills themselves. For a start, there are the mysterious **Rollright Stones**, near the village of Long Compton in the north west of the area. Historians would tell you these are megaliths, dating back 5,000 years. But are they really stones, or rather a king and his warriors who dared to cross a witch...?

Chipping Norton is a charming town, full of individuality. Surrounded by beautiful walking and cycling country, it has a wonderful theatre, leisure centre, bookshops, art galleries, a museum, antique shops and great places to eat and drink. Nearby is **Rousham House** with its garden described by Monty Don as the best in Britain. Over to the east, **Woodstock** is dominated by the great **Blenheim Palace** a World Heritage Site. The town was named by top TV property hunters Kirstie Allsopp and Phil Spencer as one of the top 10 places to live in England, thanks to its low crime and low unemployment. The palace is probably one of the top places to live, too – but that's a privilege granted only to the Duke of Marlborough, whose ancestors began the mammoth task of constructing it more than 300 years ago.

WHAT TO SEE AND DO

Rollright Stones

You won't be surprised to hear that legends abound when it comes to the Rollright Stones outside Long Compton. One of the great mysteries from the late Neolithic period (2500–2000BC), these stones have defied explanation. Some say they were once human beings, the great army of a king, turned into stone by a witch. Another legend says if you visit at midnight on New Year's Day, you'll find them sipping the clear waters of the spring in Little Rollright spinney. Certainly, the stones date back to 3000BC and consist of three separate sites, all within five minutes' walk of the main parking area, which is free. There's a stone circle (**The King's Men**), which is likely to belong to the period of between 3000 and 2300 BC; the Whispering

The King's men

Once a steam-powered spinning mill, Bliss Tweed Mill

Knights, which are probably nearly 1,000 years older: although they have not been directly dated, by analogy this monument should date from around 3800-3600 BC; and The King Stone, probably an early Bronze Age cemetery marker, dating to c 1800 BC.

> **THE ROLLRIGHT STONES:** Just north of Chipping Norton, a mile south of Long Compton; www.rollrightstones.co.uk Entry: adults £1, children 9–16, 50p; you can also download an mp3 guided tour of the site from the website.

Chipping Norton

High on the wolds, 700ft up, is the Oxfordshire town of Chipping Norton. Approach it from the west, and the first sight you'll see will be **Bliss Tweed Mill**. Built by the wealthy cloth magnate, William Bliss, this extraordinary steam-powered spinning mill represented the most modern technological advances of the Industrial Revolution.

Bliss commissioned Lancastrian architect, George Woodhouse to create the effect of a great house rising up out of parkland. From Woodhouse's skilled sketches, a domed tower took shape, out of which rose a prominent chimney. Although originally industrial in intent, that design has come full circle; for the mill has now indeed been converted into luxury apartments. If you get really friendly with this busy Oxfordshire market town, you might be invited to call it by its more informal moniker of 'Chippy'. That indicates the affection residents feel for a place that seems to pack more than most within its boundaries, including excellent shops, pubs, tearooms and facilities. In *Tatler*, Harriet Compston rated it third best place to live in the country.

It's another place with a fascinating mix of history. You can go back 400 years to the time James I gave it a self-governance charter. Or to the 17th century when young James Hind threw in his job as apprentice to the town's butcher and made his way to London aged 15. Here, he hooked up with the notorious thief, Thomas Allen, and – as the Dick Turpin of his day – enjoyed a life of robbery and violence. In 1652, his career was brought to a full stop by the simple expedient of his being hung, drawn and quartered.

For almost 30 years – from 1971 onwards – there was a top recording studio in New Street, where The Bay City Rollers recorded *Bye Bye Baby*. Other bands to visit

The award-winning Chipping Norton Lido

and stay in the town included the Proclaimers, Doctor Feelgood, Duran Duran, Status Quo, Dexy's Midnight Runners, Fairport Convention and Radiohead.

The fine parish church of **St Mary**, built from the coffers of the wool trade, was given a three-star rating by Simon Jenkins in *England's Thousand Best Churches*, and there are fine almshouses beside it. There's also a medieval guildhall and lovely Georgian architecture. The town can boast some impressive celebrity connections.

THE CHIPPING NORTON LIDO: Fox Close, Chipping Norton OX7 5BZ; ☎01608 643188; www.chippylido.co.uk. Entry: peak times (public sessions at weekends and bank holidays), adults £4.14, concessions £2, children £2.60, family £11.95 (cheaper off-peak); check website for possible changes; open Apr to Sept.

Prison Break actor Wentworth Miller was born here while his father was studying at Oxford – as was actress Rachel Ward. The Who drummer Keith Moon once owned the Crown and Cushion Hotel in the High Street. And Top Gear's Jeremy Clarkson lives nearby.

Chipping Norton has a **museum** in the High Street, which is open from Easter until the end of October, Tuesday to Saturday and Bank Holiday Mondays from 2–4pm. For £1 (children free), you can see the history of the town, as well as farming, law and order, and Second World War displays (☎01608 641712).

If you fancy a dip, award-winning **Chipping Norton Lido** is heated to a minimum of 27°C, and is a wonderfully safe environment in grounds that invite a picnic. There's a water slide at the deep end, a toddler pool, a café, and events throughout the summer.

Picturesque villages

Kingham has been voted 'England's Favourite Village' by readers of *Country Life*. They loved every aspect of it, from architecture to the village green. Other local villages of note include **Enstone,** home to the Renault F1 motor racing team which is based at Whiteways Technical Centre in a former quarry; and **Churchill,** a small settlement with some lovely buildings, including All Saints Church of which the tower was admired by Sir John Betjeman. There's a free **heritage centre** here (☎01608 658603) which commemorates Churchill-born Warren Hastings (☎01732–1818), the first Governor-General of British India. It's easily found in the middle of the old graveyard – follow the brown signs. It's open at weekends, early April to late September, 2–4.30pm. You'll also learn about Churchill's other famous son, William 'Strata' Smith, known as the Father of English Geology. As a young lad growing up in 18th-century Oxfordshire, Smith became fascinated by the pound stones – also known as Chedworth buns – used by dairymaids to weigh butter. At the time, few recognised their true origins – as fossilised sea urchins; but Smith was to change all that. You can still find these beautiful stones in the fields around Churchill today.

In the 11th century, the Royal Hunting Forest of Wychwood covered most of West Oxfordshire. It gave its name to the Wychwoods, three attractive villages: **Ascott, Milton** and, the biggest, **Shipton-under-Wychwood.**

The Foxholes Nature Reserve, sloping down to the River Evenlode, is near the little village of Bruern. Once part of the Wychwood Forest, it's famed for its bluebells in spring, its birdlife throughout the year, and the fungi in autumn. It's not easy to find: you'd be better locating it on a Google map, or visiting Berkshire, Buckinghamshire and Oxfordshire Wildlife Trust's website (www.bbowt.org.uk/foxholes.html). The nearest postcode is OX7 6RW, and it can be approached from the B4450 via Foscot.

Chastleton House

On the outer edge of Oxfordshire, in the north-west, is Chastleton House, one of England's finest and most complete Jacobean houses; in fact, it's a 400-year-old time capsule. Croquet fans might know already that it was on the lawn here, in 1865, that the rules of the modern game were laid down. There's also a classic Elizabethan topiary garden.

The house was built by MP, lawyer and wool merchant, Walter Jones. He had bought the estate from the disgraced Robert Catesby, whose involvement with the Gunpowder Plot had led to his downfall. Inside there's a mix of rare and everyday objects, including tapestries, portraits and personal belongings. Next to the house is a 12th-century parish church (not National Trust).

Because the house is fragile, visitor numbers are restricted to 175 each day. So do book in advance if you wish to visit. There is no shop or tearoom on site.

Woodstock

The picturesque town of Woodstock is graceful and charming. In the 12th century, Henry I kept an exotic menagerie here, and his grandson, Henry II, held trysts in the royal manor with his mistress, Fair Rosamund; in fact, right up until Medieval times, England's kings had a home in Woodstock.

A walk around the town affords many glimpses into its fascinating past. There's the 16th-century Fletcher's House in the centre, named after the respected alderman who died in 1545, and now the county museum (see 'Wet weather'). Pass the old corn mill across the Causeway, and you'll get to Manor Farm, with its 13th-century chimney hiding behind the 17th-century façade. This is where the Black Prince is said to have been born in 1330.

The Jacobean Chastleton House

CHASTLETON HOUSE: Chastleton, near Moreton-in-Marsh, Oxfordshire GL56 0SU; ☎01494 755560 (infoline), 01608 674981 (booking line, open Tues–Fri, 10am–2pm); www.nationaltrust.org.uk. Entry: adults £8.25 Gift Aid (£7.50 standard admission), children £3.90 (£3.50 standard admission), family £20.25 (£18.40 standard admission); open Apr to Sept Wed–Sat 1–5pm and Oct/Nov Wed–Sat 1–4pm.

BLENHEIM PALACE: Woodstock OX20 1PX; ☎08700 602080; www.blenheimpalace. com. Entry: for 2009 palace, park and gardens, (main season) adults £17.50, concessions £14.00, children £10, family £46; (prices subject to change in 2010); open throughout the year (closed mid Dec–mid Feb, check website for details); palace/formal gardens closed Mon/Tues Nov/Dec. To purchase tickets online visit www.blenheimpalace.com/tickets.

Relationships between palace and town are close. The family are frequently seen – especially Lord Blandford, who readily confesses that one of his favourite places for a late breakfast is Harriet's Cake Shop. Other buildings bear witness to famous connections: the town hall built by architect Sir William Chambers; Chaucer's House, once owned by the famous poet's son, and Cromwell's House which allegedly owes its name to old Oliver himself lodging there in 1646 during the siege of Woodstock Manor.

Blenheim Palace

American-born Lady Randolph Churchill (Sir Winston's mother) was very impressed by her first visit to Blenheim Palace. What had particularly caught her eye was Blenheim Lake, spanned by Vanbrugh's Grand Bridge. She was to forge an even greater connection with the great house a few years later. It was during a visit in November 1874 that she went into premature labour and gave birth to the son who was to become the great British war-time leader – indeed, you can visit the very room where Churchill was born. He lies buried just down the road in Bladon Churchyard alongside his parents and wife.

Inside the palace, you'll see how the grandness of the project does not swamp the exquisiteness of detail in the hand-painted ceilings, the delicate carvings, the amazing porcelain collections, tape-stries and paintings. On the first floor, 'Blenheim Palace: The Untold Story' takes you through 300 years of history seen through the eyes of the household staff. Two exhibitions exploring the life and achievements of Sir Winston Churchill and his ancestor the 1st Duke of Marlborough are also available.

The library at Blenheim Palace

There are over 100 acres of glorious formal gardens to explore, including the Secret Garden, the majestic Water Terraces and Italian Garden, the Rose Garden, the

The Marlborough Maze at Blenheim Palace

A nation's gratitude

Among the many treasures at Blenheim Palace are the revered 18th-century tapestries that work the story of the origins of this great building in the form of exquisite and minute stitches. The masterpiece is the Blenheim tapestry, which weaves in rich threads the great and bloody battle of 1704 that catapulted the first Duke of Marlborough into the forefront of history.

The French leader, Count Camille de Tallard (who started this encounter with some 8,000 more men than the allies) hadn't counted on the tactics and intelligence of the British commander, the Duke of Marlborough. Thanks to the 'deserters' the Duke planted among the ranks of the enemy army, the French thought the British were in retreat. Far from it: in a daring move, the Duke attacked where they least expected it – at Blenheim, the strongest point of the whole French line. To express the nation's gratitude at his magnificent victory, Queen Anne, a friend of the Duke's wife, Sarah, granted the couple the royal manor of Woodstock the following year – along with a promise of funding for a magnificent palace. Sadly, the Duke was to learn an important lesson in life: get it in writing.

The result was that Marlborough spent £60,000 of his own money building Blenheim, and a further £25,000 bill came after his death. Sarah, naturally frugal, was not in favour of a palace she saw more as an uncomfortable monument than a practical family home; in fact, she so interfered with the building process that the architect, John Vanbrugh must at times have rued the day he ever clapped eyes on the project. The Blenheim Tapestry has recently been restored to its former glory, and can be seen by visitors today as part of a guided tour of the State Rooms.

Grand Cascade and lake. A miniature train takes you to the Pleasure Gardens with the Marlborough Maze, adventure play area, giant chess and the Butterfly House. There are five different shops – from gifts to food – and a choice of places to eat.

Wet weather

The **Oxfordshire Museum** in the centre of Woodstock has been redeveloped and has won awards for it. It's interactive, fun for all ages, and features collections of local history, art, archaeology, landscape and wildlife as well as a gallery exploring the county's innovative industries from nuclear power to nanotechnology – and there's a coffee shop, too.

The town of Charlbury is attractive, with an interesting history, much of

The gardens at the Oxfordshire Museum

The best of... COTSWOLDS THROUGH THE SEASONS

SPRING BEGINS WITH THE GREAT SNOWDROP GARDENS AND THE NODDING WILD DAFFODILS THROUGH THE ANCIENT WOODLANDS; THE SUMMER IS A WARM SUN ON HONEYED STONE; AUTUMN SETS THE TREES AGLOW WITH REDS, CRIMSONS AND ORANGES; AND WINTER CLOSES IN WITH ROARING FIRES INSIDE OPEN-BEAMED PUBS HAUNTED BY THE QUIET GHOSTS OF DRINKERS OF OLD.

Top: Bluebells at Westonbirt Arboretum;
Bottom: Shakespeare's birthplace, Stratford-upon-Avon

Top: Doorway surrounded by flowers in Cirencester; Middle: Ice cream seller in the village of Broadway; Bottom: The view from Elliott nature reserve at Swift's Hill, Slad, looking towards Stroud and the River Severn beyond

Top: Autumn in Bourton on the Water; Middle: Traditional red telephone box in autumnal Broadway; Bottom: Cyclist going past ivy covered cottage

Top: Misty morning over Keynes Park; Middle: Christmas lights in Witney; Bottom: Enchanted Christmas at Westonbirt Arboretum

which is well documented in **Charlbury Museum** (☎01608 810060), next door to the library. Artefacts and antiquities collected from around the region make up a museum that punches well above its weight. It's only open from Easter until the end of September, 10am–12 noon on Saturdays and 2.30–4.30pm on Sundays and bank holidays, or by arrangement (adults £1, accompanied children free).

What to do with children...

Wigginton Waterfowl Sanctuary and Children's Farm has been home, over the years, to many animals, including geese, ducks, bantams, rabbits, guinea pigs, goats, pigs, tropical birds, emus, terrapins, ostrich, chipmunks, donkeys, to name but a few. Sick, injured and neglected animals are cared for here; you

The Wigginton Waterfowl Sanctuary and Children's Farm

can also enjoy meadowland and wildlife ponds. Much native wildlife lives here, such as wild rabbits, birds of prey, frogs and newts. There's a cuddle corner and a licensed pet shop.

... and how to avoid children

Children under 15 and dogs are not allowed at **Rousham Park House and Garden**, around 9 miles north of Woodstock. It's a beautiful and early example of English landscape design: begun by Charles Bridgeman in the early 18th century, and continued by William Kent a few years later. It's pretty much untouched since the great man laid down his trowel and still has many 18th-century features *in situ*: classical temples, follies, statues, grottoes, cascades, ponds – very ancient Rome meets English countryside.

The house itself, built in 1635 by Sir Robert Dormer, is still in the ownership of the same family. They're determined not to commercialise this gem, which means you won't find guidebooks or a shop selling souvenirs. Bring a picnic.

See also the 'Drinking' section for tours of **Hook Norton Brewery**.

> ROUSHAM PARK HOUSE AND GARDEN: Tackley, near Steeple Aston, Bicester OX25 4QX; ☎01869 347110; www.rousham.org Entry: garden £5; the gardens are open daily all year round from 10am; the house is only open by prior arrangement to groups.

Entertainment

If music's what you're looking for, then this is an area of note. One of the best events on the contemporary scene is the annual July **Cornbury Music Festival** at Cornbury Park near Charlbury (OX7 3EH). Recent performers have included Paul Simon, Amy Winehouse and KT Tunstall. You can camp in the grounds for the weekend, or book one of the 'luxury' options, such as a podpad, bellepad or even a room at the fabulous Yurtel – all of which need to be reserved in advance. You can find out more at www.cornburyfestival.com.

Chipping Norton Music Festival is classically orientated. Held each March, it's one of the oldest festivals of its kind. Alongside classes in music and drama, there is a series of professional concerts, too (www.cnmf.org.uk). **Dean & Chadlington Summer Music Festival** offers an outstanding array of classical music stars and includes a hugely popular children's concert (www.chadlingtonfestival.co.uk). **Charlbury Riverside Festival** is a free contemporary summer music festival set on an 'island' in the River Evenlode on the edge of Charlbury (www.riversidefestival.charlbury.com).

Other musical events are held at Blenheim Palace each year, including festive music and carols in November and December, when the palace is decorated for Christmas. The palace hosts a full calendar of special events, such as jousts, classic car shows and craft fairs. Perhaps it's best known, however, for **Blenheim Palace International Horse Trials** in September, one of the world's premier three-star three-day events (www.blenheim-horse.co.uk). **Art in Woodstock** is an autumn festival promoting the visual arts in the town with exhibitions, workshops, competitions and other events for all ages: www.artinwoodstock.com.

Chipping Norton has its own **theatre** (☎01608 642350; www.chippingnortontheatre.co.uk), which offers a packed programme of shows, films, exhibitions, workshops, activities and youth theatre. Details of events in the area are constantly updated at www.oxfordshirecotswolds.org/site/events.

LOCAL KNOWLEDGE

Crime writer **Mark Billingham**, like many of his villains, leads a double life. His is split between a large Edwardian house in North London and a tiny thatched cottage in Great Rollright. With its low ceilings, it might not be the most practical option – *'I live with permanent concussion in the Cotswolds,'* he says – but he loves it.

Best pub: The Falkland Arms in Great Tew, where you can sit outside and enjoy the great views. Or the Chequers in Chippy: a very old-fashioned pub with a lovely sun-lit family area where you can have Sunday lunch.

Favourite tearoom: Jaffe & Neale, an independent bookshop and café in Chipping Norton. The people who run this bookshop love books – it sounds like an obvious thing to say, but not everyone does.

Which shop could you not live without? The cheese shop at Moreton-in-Marsh. I could live in there.

Most under-rated thing about the Cotswolds: One of the big misconceptions about the Cotswolds is that, if you're not into country pursuits, then there's nothing to do. I love Chipping Norton – there's a fantastic leisure centre where the kids will play badminton or go swimming. Or if it's a nice day, we'll go to the lido.

Favourite view: I adore the Rollright Stones. There is something weird about them. I'm told that you can never walk round them and count them accurately. I do love all that stuff: history and myth. Real life is always far stranger than anything I could dream up.

🛒 Shopping

The one Cotswold shop people country-wide seem to have heard of is **Daylesford Organic** at Daylesford near Kingham, which has achieved iconic status. The 'baby' of Lady Bamford, it's been tagged 'Britain's poshest shop' by the national media (or the Cotswold 'Harrods', if you prefer). Local people have a love/hate relationship with it. It's certainly not a place to get a bargain; but it is the place to do your organic shopping – from clothes to garden string. It's the food it's particularly famous for: vegetables fresh from the kitchen gardens; the best local artisan cheeses, plus those made in their own creamery; breads, cakes and biscuits from the bakery; dishes from their kitchens; and meat from their Staffordshire estate. There's an on-site organic café and restaurant.

Daylesford Organic

DAYLESFORD ORGANIC: Daylesford, Gloucestershire GL56 0YG; ☎01608 731700; www.daylesfordorganic.com Open Mon–Sat 9am–5pm, Sun 10am–4pm.

In Woodstock, you might well see the current Duke's daughter, Lady Henrietta Spencer-Churchill, at her interior design shop, **Woodstock Designs,** in the High Street.

The best... PLACES TO STAY

BOUTIQUE

The Feathers

Market Street, Woodstock OX20 1SX
☎ 01993 812291; www.feathers.co.uk

The Feathers is a country house
hotel right in the heart of Woodstock.
Excellent food and just the right sort
of attentive but discreet service will
characterise your stay here. Each of the
bedrooms and suites are individually
styled and furnished.

Price: from £169 double; from £279 suite.

HOTEL

The Bear Hotel

Park Street, Woodstock OX20 1SZ
☎ 0844 8799143
www.macdonald-hotels.co.uk

One of the best recommendations for
this hotel – which traces its origins back
to the 13th century – is that Richard
Burton and Elizabeth Taylor used it as
a loved up hideaway. With its ivy-clad
façade and old-world charm, it's the sort
of place where you can find both four-
poster beds and Sky TV.

Price: B&B from £75/£120, single/double.

FARMSTAY

Bould Farm

Bould, Near Idbury,
Chipping Norton OX7 6RT
☎ 01608 658850; www.bouldfarm.
co.uk

This 400 acre sheep, cattle and arable
farm, set in a small Cotswold hamlet, is
run by Gwyn and Lynne Meyrick and son
Robert. The 17th-century farmhouse is
surrounded by garden and has beautiful
views over the countryside. There's a
nature reserve adjoining the farm with
lovely walks.

Price: from £45/£65, single/double.

B&B

The Forge

Church Road, Churchill, Chipping
Norton OX7 6NJ; ☎ 01608 658173
www.theforge.co.uk

This friendly B&B is situated in Churchill.
The Forge, once the village blacksmith's,
is nearly 200 years old. Well equipped,
there's even free internet access; two of
the five rooms have Whirlpool baths.

Price: from £68 for a double.

SELF-CATERING

Bruern Holiday Cottages

Redbrick House, Bruern,
Chipping Norton OX7 6PY
☎ 01993 830415
www.bruern-holiday-cottages.co.uk

The biggest property, Weir House,
accommodates 10 to sleep and 30 for
a dinner party (with an on-hand chef).
All cottages have terraces or gardens;
all share a games room, glorious
Wendy houses, and a gorgeously warm
swimming pool. Dogs are allowed on
site but must sleep in the car. Bikes are
available free of charge.

Price: from £907 for cottage sleeping
four (£1,171 for one sleeping six).

Bluewood Park

Kingham, Chipping Norton OX7 6UJ
☎ 01608 659946
www.bluewoodpark.com

Perfectly placed in a small bluebell
wood, Bluewood Park is just outside
Kingham. The luxury lodges on this
complex have their own decks with
sunken outdoor hot tub. There's a
fishing lake – and riding, cycling, walking
and golf within easy reach.

Price: from around £500 for a week.

The best... FOOD AND DRINK

▶ Staying in

There's a winter treat waiting for you in this area – one you'd expect from somewhere with a forest as ancient and venerable as this: **Wychwood Forest Deer** produces venison between September and April (and antler products in autumn). It's sold at farmers' markets, including Chipping Norton, Charlbury, Witney and Woodstock. Cook it as you would beef, but remember, that there's very little fat; in other words, don't overcook it – and it's extremely good for you!

Coldronbrook Meats is based at a family farm in Spelsbury (OX7 3JR; ☎01608 811118; www.coldronbrookmeats.co.uk). At the heart of this farm is the beef produced from its own free-range Dexter cattle, all raised as nature intended. The pork and chicken it sells is also sourced as locally as possible.

It's a Cotswold tradition that if anyone dies in a house which has a hive in the garden, the oldest occupant of the house must walk round each hive three times, thrice repeating the name of the deceased – otherwise, the bees will flee. **Halcyon Honey Farm** in Charlbury (☎01608 810260) produces liquid and set honey, honeycomb and polish and candles, which they sell at local farmers' markets, as well as in food outlets in Charlbury itself – such as the **Good Food Shop** in Sheep Street. Among other things, the shop sells local vegetables – well worth a visit.

Other fine shops include **Chadlington Quality Foods** (☎01608 676675; chadlington. com), saved from closure by the villagers of Chadlington themselves. It's now a first-class emporium of local cheeses and vegetables, beer, clotted cream from up the road in Upper Norton, cured meats, home-baking (savoury and sweet), as well as excellent foods from elsewhere in the country. This is how village stores all used to be, in the good old days. **Slatters** the fine butcher is next door.

You can buy Alex James and Juliet Harbutt's wonderful goats' cheeses (see Celebrity connections) from **The Cotswold Delicatessen** in Middle Row, Chipping Norton (☎01608 642843; www.cotswolddelicatessen.co.uk)which sells a huge selection of British and European farmhouse cheeses, plus hams, charcuterie, speciality breads, pies, sausages, and many other artisan foods. Other local cheeses are produced by **Karen and Roger Crudge** – soft and semi-hard varieties made with raw cow, goat and sheep's milk. You can catch them at Chipping Norton, Woodstock and Stroud Farmers' Market, Daylesford Organic, or directly from The Green in Kingham, call 01608 658125.

Find out more about farmers' markets in this part of Oxfordshire – as well as the producers who take stalls there – at the Thames Valley Farmers' Market Cooperative website (www.tvfm.org.uk).

CELEBRITY CONNECTIONS

When Blur bassist **Alex James** moved to a farm outside Kingham in the summer of 2004, he couldn't stop talking – or writing – about it. His witty, wry and self-deprecating Great Escape column in *The Independent* is the monologue version of how this one-time naughty city boy – who blew a million on champagne, and once lived for a week under the snooker table at the Groucho Club – swapped the rock lifestyle for one of bucolic domesticity.

Where once he dealt with flocks of groupies, now it's rooks that swarm uncontrollably round him. The Groucho has given way to Kingham British Legion club. And the only things pickled in the James family kitchen at 9am on a weekday morning are vegetables in jam jars, gathered from the patch in the garden, and turned into chutney by Alex's wife, Claire Neate. '*When you come from London, you have preconceptions about the country – that everyone sits around looking at their vegetables – but I'm busier than I've ever been,*' Alex says. He's certainly busy making cheese. He and Juliet Harbutt – the founder of the prestigious annual British Cheese Awards – produced their first cheese in 2007. It's called Little Wallop, a fresh goats' cheese, washed in local cider brandy and wrapped in vine leaves. It is, foodies say, a thumpingly good cheese. They've since added Farleigh Wallop into their repertoire, a little goat camembert with a spring of thyme pressed into the rind; and the square (in shape not taste) Blue Monday.

Even in the days of manic stardom, Alex had cheese on his mind. '*Blur struggled until we were making* Parklife, *which was our third album – we didn't have any money. When we went to Japan, we were told we had to tell the fans over there what we liked because they would buy it for us. So we spent ages trying to think how we could extract the most value. We thought of saying we liked diamonds and gold because we were really poor at the time. In the end, I said I liked cheese. We got mobbed and had cheese thrown at us.*'

EATING OUT

RESTAURANT

Kings Arms Hotel
19 Market Street, Woodstock OX20 1SU; ☎ 01993 813636
www.kings-hotel-woodstock.co.uk

Centrally placed in Woodstock, the Atrium is a relaxed bistro-type restaurant within the Kings Arms Hotel. There's an extensive à la carte and bar menu, as well as daily specials. Expect a relaxed bistro atmosphere and classic English cooking with a contemporary twist. Main courses cost from £12.

GASTRO PUB

The Black Prince
2 Manor Road, Woodstock OX20 1XJ
☎ 01993 811530

This lovely pub has a garden on the banks of the River Glyme. It's quiet and relaxing, and serves good food at reasonable prices. One of the most popular dishes is the homemade burger using local beef. The average main course price is £8.50.

The Kingham Plough
Kingham, Chipping Norton OX7 6YD
☎ 01608 658327
www.thekinghamplough.co.uk

Since Emily Watkins (ex of Heston Blumenthal's Fat Duck) came to work her magic, the Plough has combined expert cuisine with impeccable local sourcing. A rare treat. A particular favourite – rich and comforting – is the Evenlode lamb pudding, served with heaps of curly kale. Three courses cost around £25.

The Bell at Charlbury
Church Street, Charlbury OX7 3PP
☎ 01608 810278
www.bellhotel-charlbury.com

This stylish and cosy 18th-century hotel offers modern British cooking with European influences where the menu – and ingredients – is put together with great care, and frequently changed to reflect the best local produce according to the season. There's a very good wine cellar too – and you take a turn in the acre of grounds afterwards. Mains generally well under £15.

The King's Head Inn
The Green, Bledington, Chipping Norton OX7 6XQ
☎ 01608 658365; thekingsheadinn.net

In the 16th century – this was a cider house; it's certainly kept its reputation for fine ales. But the food is also superb nowadays, with simply presented top produce. The setting is fabulous too: on the edge of the village green, with a babbling brook running beside it. Perhaps a spicy a crayfish and rocket linguine with shaved Parmesan? A three-course dinner will cost around £25.

Swan at Ascott
4 Shipton Road, Ascott-under-Wychwood OX7 6AY
☎ 01993 830345;
www.swanatascott.com

The best of comfort food is on offer at the Swan – fresh, local fare that combines hearty casseroles and home-made pies with puddings that will have you breaking any diet in a jiffy. It's traditional food, exceptionally well done, sometimes with a gourmet twist. Mains under £12.

🍸 Drinking

Hook Norton Brewery in the north of the area is popular and award-winning. Started by John Harris, a farmer and maltster 150 years ago, this acclaimed brewery is still being run by his descendants today. Beer is brewed in the building erected by John Harris's son-in-law, Alban Clarke, using some of the original equipment, including a steam engine – possibly the last one in England still used daily for its original purpose. See the brewing process in the museum, and buy the beer in the Visitor Centre. Brewery tours by prior booking.

THE HOOK NORTON BREWERY: Brewery Lane Hook Norton OX15 5NY; ☎01608 730384; www.hooknortonbrewery.co.uk Entry: tours at £9.50 per head (no children under 12); 2 hours; book by phone, online, or at the Visitor Centre; shop/museum open Mon–Fri 9am–5pm, Sat and summer bank holidays 9.30am–4.30pm.

The Cotswold Brewing Company (☎01608 659631), south of Chipping Norton at Foscot, is relatively new to the scene: established in 2005 by Richard and Emma Keene. Housed in an old Cotswold stone farm building on a working farm, the brewery gets its inspiration from continental Europe with its strong tradition of producing lager of the very highest quality in the heart of small communities. You can find out where to drink and buy their Cotswold lagers from the website – but the Village Shop at Hook Norton isn't a bad place to start. (www.cotswoldbrewingcompany.com).

Some favourite locals include the mainly 15th-century **Shaven Crown Hotel** (OX7 6BA) in Shipton-under-Wychwood, which was once a guest house run by the monks at nearby Bruern Abbey (but dissolved by Good King Hal in the 16th century). The pub, which overlooks the village green, is one of the 10 oldest in the country. Drinkers also love the **Falkland Arms** at Great Tew (OX7 4DB) – a real traditional English pub, which has regular music nights and an annual beer festival in the summer. A real intimate local is the **Red Lion** in Albion Street, Chipping Norton. It's a fun pub with a heart – regulars raise thousands of pounds for charity with events such as Chippy's Giant Vegetable Competition. It also serves good Hooky beer, as does the wonderfully named **The Gate Hangs High** at Hook Norton itself (OX15 5DF). South of Chippy at Nether Westcote (OX7 6SD) is the **Westcote Inn**: beautifully scenic.

Woodstock's houses of refreshment have many a tale to tell. **The Feathers Hotel** reaches back into the 17th century (look – or listen – for the hotel parrot in the hotel lobby); the **Marlborough Arms** dates from before 1730; the **Bear Hotel** has a doorway depicting two battling bears and, along Park Lane, there's **The King's Head**, distinguished as probably the oldest pub in town.

ⓘ Visitor Information

Tourist information centres: Woodstock Visitor Information Centre, The Oxfordshire Museum, Park Street, Woodstock OX20 4SN, ☎01993 813276, open Mar to Oct, Mon–Sat 9.30am–5.30pm, Sun 2–5pm, Nov to Feb, Mon–Sat 10am–5pm, Sun 2–5pm, www.chippingnortontown.info, www.wakeuptowoodstock.com, www.oxfordshirecotswolds.org.

Hospitals: Witney Community Welch Way, Witney OX28 6JJ, ☎01993 209400, minor injuries unit open 10am–10.30pm daily, ☎01993 209456/8; John Radcliffe Headley Way, Headington, Oxford, OX3 9DU, ☎01865 741166, 24-hr A&E.

Supermarkets include: Co-op, High Street, ☎01608 642672; Somerfield Stores, Market Place, ☎01608 641287; Chipping Norton Co-op, Spendlove Centre, Charlbury OX7 3QR, ☎01608 810815; Co-op, High Street, Woodstock, ☎01993 811493.

Sports: Chipping Norton Leisure Centre, Burford Road OX7 5DY, ☎01993 861951; Carterton Leisure Centre, Broadshires Way, Carterton OX18 1AA, ☎01993 861981; Chipping Norton Lido (summer), Fox Close OX7 5BZ, ☎01608 643188; Woodstock Swimming Pool (summer), Shipton Road, Woodstock, OX20 1LW; Chipping Norton Golf Club in Southcombe OX7 5QH, ☎01993 642383; Wychwood Golf Club, Lyneham OX7 6QQ, ☎01993 831841; Carterton Cycle Hire, 4 Mansell Place, Carterton OX18 3RX, ☎01993 844937/ 07799 605560, www.cartertoncyclehire.com (will deliver and collect from holiday accommodation); Pigeon House Equitation, Church Hanborough OX29 8AF, ☎01993 881628 (hacks for competent riders age 16 and over).

Taxis include: Ambassador Taxis, Chipping Norton, ☎01608 644015/ 07932162503; Townhouse Executive Travel, Woodstock, ☎07766 743081.

FURTHER AFIELD

Oxford

Although Oxford is not in the Cotswolds, you can't get this far and not visit this most wonderful of English cities. Urbane, clever, beautiful, small enough for intimacy, architecturally almost perfect, full of the hopeful young and the wise elderly – Oxford really is an absolute gem. The first tip is either to use one of the highly efficient park-and-rides (www.oxford.gov.uk/transport/park-and-ride.cfm) which, from the Cotswold end, will probably be Pear Tree. Or else fix your bikes to the back of the car – cycles are an excellent way to get around. Pack your copy of Evelyn Waugh's evocative *Brideshead Revisited*, and prepare to immerse yourself in a very different world. The city is said to divide itself on town and gown lines because of the mix of permanent residents and students studying at its famous university – and that's a good way to visualise and explore it.

The shopping is good – of course, with students all around, the bookshops are as superb as you would expect – and there are some great places to eat, such as **Brown's** and **Quod**. But the real joy lies in the beauty of the colleges, many of which you can visit. **Magdalen College**, for example, is within walking distance of the centre, yet is situated within 100 acres of woodlands, riverside walks and lawns; and there's **Christ Church**, the largest college in Oxford, refounded in 1546 by King Henry VII – the only college in the world with a cathedral within its walls.

In Oxford you can:

- climb to the top of **Carfax Tower** to see the 'dreaming spires' in panoramic form
- do a ghost walk
- go for a punt on the **River Cherwell**
- see the famous Oxfordshire dinosaurs at the **University Museum of Natural History**
- visit the **University of Oxford Botanic Garden** – the oldest botanic garden in the UK
- see modern art
- enjoy the **History of Science Museum**
- see the wonderful **Ashmolean Museum**.

Plan your visit first by exploring one of the websites on the town, such as www.visitoxford.org and www.oxfordcity.co.uk. You can also ring or visit **Oxford Tourist Information Centre** at 15–16 Broad Street, Oxford, OX1 3AS (☎01865 252200), open Monday to Saturday 9.30am–5pm (Jul/Aug, Thurs–Sat 9.30am–6pm), Sundays and bank holidays 10am–4pm.

BURFORD, MINSTER LOVELL AND WITNEY

If you asked 50 people to name the four corners of the Cotswolds, you'd probably get 50 different answers. The truth is, there's no hard and fast definition of where they begin and end. But that doesn't stop **Burford** calling itself the 'Gateway to the Cotswolds' and, to be fair, few would quibble with that title. Certainly, the view from the top of its steep high street down towards the River Windrush, with its medieval triple-arched bridge, is one of the great Cotswold 'classics'. What's more, it offers another regional speciality: wonderful and varied architecture, reflecting prosperity over a considerable period of time. Burford was the first town in the Cotswolds to be granted a market charter, in the 12th century; 500 years later, lovers Nell Gwyn and Charles II were planning trysts in the old priory – and the town is still a delightful place for lovers and others to browse and explore today.

This area is **Mitford** country – the place where those six extraordinary sisters grew up, who took the 20th century by storm with their wit, charm and (sometimes) outrageous actions. Indeed, four of them are buried in the village of Swinbrook, just a few miles from Burford. Their connections are not advertised, but you'll recognise many of the landmarks from their writings – and to be sure, the intensely rural quality they describe is still apparent today.

Travelling east towards Witney and Oxford, you'll come across the pretty village of **Minster Lovell**, by the River Windrush, where lie the extensive ruins of the 15th century Minster Lovell Hall and Dovecote. Pretty and romantic they might be, but beware: their story is more sinister than outward guise would have you believe...

Witney is a far bigger town than Burford, famous since the Middle Ages for the blankets it once manufactured. Some attributed the high quality of these blankets to the water used in the process, drawn from the River Windrush. Although, sadly, blankets have ceased to be made since the closure, a few years back, of Early's, the last remaining factory, the town thrives in other ways. It's a good place to do your shopping, and the **Cogges Manor Farm Museum** is first rate for children. Besides which, David Cameron is the local MP, meaning it's never in danger of being forgotten.

WHAT TO SEE AND DO

Burford
Smaller even than some of the villages round about, this market town has a population of just a smidgeon more than 1,000: in other words, it boasts a tight-knit community, where people actually know each other. That quiet attractiveness has been drawing people to it for many hundreds of years. Lying just 20 miles west of Oxford itself, Burford was once second only to Newmarket as a horse racing centre, when Burford

Races were held on the downs beyond Upton. James I and Charles II came for the racing and the Prince Regent kept his own horses here.

Among the half-timbered buildings, you'll find the town's museum, **The Tolsey**, an early Tudor building on stone pillars with a meeting space beneath. Now a memorial to time past, it was once at the hub of contemporary life where the wool merchants would gather and conduct their financial transactions. There are two small rooms of exhibits, which tell a particularly good tale of the trades that once flourished here, from bell-founding and brewing, to leatherworking and clarinet-making.

THE TOLSEY: 126 High Street, Burford, OX18 4QU; ☎ 01993 823196
Entry: free; open Apr to Oct.

The parish church of **St John the Baptist** has a peaceful atmosphere today – but grant a thought to Anthony Sedley who carved his own signature into the rim of the baptismal font. He was one of the 340 Levellers, rounded up and imprisoned in the church by Cromwell during the Civil War in 1649. Three of the leaders were executed in the churchyard; though their ghosts might now rest quietly, you can still see bullet holes from that historic siege. Tony Benn had a memorial plaque placed on the wall, and each year there is a 'Levellers' Day' of celebration – the Saturday nearest 17 May, the date they died.

Interestingly, it was a visit to the church in 1876 that inspired Arts & Crafts founder William Morris to establish the Society for the Preservation of Ancient Buildings. He was horri-

The Tolsey, an early Tudor building

fied to find the priest in charge cleaning off medieval wall paintings. '*This church, sir, is mine, and if I choose to, I shall stand on my head in it*,' the vicar told him. Thankfully, some of those paintings still survive.

The 'wool-bale' tombs in the churchyard are not just moving memorials – they were useful too. Once upon a time, when the Wychwood Forest covered the land, poachers would lift the tops off and store illicit deer carcasses inside.

It's worth just taking a moment to look up to the roof-line of Burford: a fascinating, complex and beautiful jumble, with no two houses the same. The old tilers had special names for the different-sized roofing slates they used, such as Muffetties, Long Wyvetts and (the most difficult to fit) 'Cursoms'! A couple of miles from Burford is the village of **Swinbrook**, once home to the Mitford sisters. The six sisters – Nancy, Pamela, Diana, Unity, Jessica and Deborah – with their one brother, Tom, were raised in the Cotswolds by their parents Lord and Lady Redesdale. The children's rural isolation and education mainly by their mother (a series of governesses fled the family one after the other) meant they relied on each other for companionship, inventing their own private language.

Lord Redesdale had inherited his title in 1916 and moved from London, which he hated, to a new 100-room mansion his father had built at Batsford, near Moreton-in-Marsh (see the north Cotswolds section). Nancy Mitford based the early part of her semi-autobiographical novel *The Pursuit of Love* on the family's time here. But soon after the First World War, the estate had to be sold to cover death duties, and the family moved to the more manageable Asthall Manor in Oxfordshire, before finally settling in

Church of St John the Baptist in Burford

nearby Swinbrook. Nancy's portrait of Sydney, her mother, was as the vague, other-worldly Aunt Sadie. In real life, Sydney was a woman who had to face up to tragedy. Her only son, Tom, was killed in Burma in 1945. And for many years she devotedly nursed her daughter, Unity, whose love for Hitler led to a suicide attempt that left her brain-damaged. Diana, of course, caused a scandal when she left her first husband, brewing heir Bryan Guinness, for the fascist leader, Oswald Mosley. Nancy, Pamela, Diana and Unity are all buried in the church graveyard at Swinbrook.

Minster Lovell

Don't be fooled by the small amount of space allocated to this village on a map; what it lacks in size, it makes up for 10-fold in its picturesque mix of Cotswold stone and thatched houses. St Kenelm's Church, built around 1450, contains a tomb thought to belong to its founder William, 7th Baron Lovell. But the real beauty of the place

The ruins of Minster Lovell Hall

lies in the most atmospheric of ruins; the fallen beauty of **Minster Lovell Hall**, lazing beside the slow-flowing river. (It's also a good place to look for lobster-like crayfish.)

> THE HERITAGE CENTRE: 130 Burford Road, Minster Lovell OX29 0RB (on the B4047); ☎01993 775262; www.minsterlovell.com Entry: adults £2, children free; open Mon–Fri 10am–1pm, 2–5pm.

The tragedies of Minster Lovell Hall

The 7th Baron William, who built the church, also constructed the once-elegant stately home of Minster Lovell Hall on family lands – but that family was soon to be torn apart. The 9th Baron Lovell, Francis, fought for Richard III at the Battle of Bosworth, in spite of the fact that his late father had been a staunch Lancastrian. Two years later, he fought unsuccessfully again, this time to put Lambert Simnel on the throne in place of Henry VII. After this second defeat, Francis disappeared without trace.

Time now shifts to the 18th century when workmen at the hall discovered an underground room. They entered its gloomy depths, so the story goes, to the most horrifying of sights: a skeleton, sitting at a table, surrounded by books and pens. Indeed, it belonged to no less a personage than Lord Lovell himself, who is supposed to have hidden himself in a secret chamber after the battle, and died there of starvation.

Nor is that the only tragic tale associated with the house. During the 16th century, a young bride, who was to be married to a Lovell suitor at Christmas time, went missing there on her wedding day, following a game of hide and seek. When she couldn't be found, her family accused the bridegroom's kin of foul play – but nothing was ever proven. Years later, workmen moving a rarely used lead-lined box found it heavier than they'd expected. When they prized the lid off, they discovered a body in a wedding dress. The poor girl had climbed in and suffocated.

You can wander round the ruins for free any day of the year. You can also look around the outside of the medieval dovecote nearby. Both are owned by English Heritage (www.english-heritage.org.uk).

The village has its own **Heritage Centre,** in one room of a picture-framing workshop. The owner, Graham Kew, is not only an artist, but also a tour guide and storyteller, who'll sing you the ballad of *The Mistletoe Bough*, telling the story of the tragic Lovell Bride.

Witney

Witney isn't as obvious a tourist town as Burford – you will find high-street multiples here; but it's both a useful and pleasant place to visit, with some interesting corners. One of Witney's best-known streets is **West End**, often described as one of the best-preserved in England. Many of the buildings are listed, dating back to the 17th and 18th centuries and associated with the town's former trade of blanket-making. In fact, it inspired the popular early 20th-century song, *'There's an old-fashioned house in an old-fashioned street/In a quaint little old-fashioned town'*. West End has a website with more information (witneywestend.com).

The Buttercross and town hall in Witney

The town certainly has a long history. You can see the remains of the 12th-century Bishop of Winchester's Palace here, near the church on Church Green, which was one of 24 grand houses in the diocese, discovered in the early 1980s. There's a small interpretation centre, open from Easter to the end of September on Saturday and Sunday afternoons (2–4pm); or you can see the site each weekday from 10am–5pm. Other landmarks include the Buttercross in the High Street market square where people from all around would gather to trade butter and eggs from the Middle Ages onwards; St Mary's, another fine wool church; and the 17th-century town hall which locals claim (though cannot prove) was designed by Sir Christopher Wren. There are also buildings associated with the blanket industry, such as the Blanket Hall in the High Street, built in 1721 by the Company of Blanket Weavers. You can find out more about the blanket industry which sustained the town for more than 300 years at www.witneyblanketstory.org.uk.

WITNEY & DISTRICT MUSEUM: Gloucester Court Mews, High Street, Witney OX28 6JF; ☎01993 775915; www.witneymuseum.com Entry: children free, adults £1.50; open Apr to Oct Wed–Sat 10am–4pm and Sun 2–4pm.

Witney & District Museum in the High Street features all the trades associated with the town, including glove making and brewing; and there's a reconstruction of a 1950s kitchen and a Victorian schoolroom.

Within a mile of the town centre is **Witney Lake** (☎01993 704614; also known as Duck and Ducklington Lake), a former gravel pit which is now part of a nature reserve. There's a good path round the lake (though take wellies in inclement weather) where you can see lots of wildlife – black-headed gulls, Canada geese, coot, heron, cormorant, great-crested grebe and kingfishers; you might catch a common tern plummeting into the water after a fish, or a common sandpiper, tail bobbing as it runs or long bill delving into the mud for food. At Standlake near Witney, you'll find Hardwick Parks (OX29 7PZ; ☎01865 300501; www.hardwickparks.co.uk). Although ostensibly a camping and caravan site, it does welcome outside visitors to the **water sports centre** where you can waterski (for complete beginners up to slalom training), wakeboards and kneeboards. Children will love the ringo rides.

Around 4 miles north-east of Witney is the **North Leigh Roman Villa** in East End near North Leigh (www.english-heritage. org.uk). A short walk from the main road, the remains of this villa – once owned by a wealthy Roman – are open every day with no admission charge. You can see the almost complete red and brown mosaic floor, thought to have been made by craftsmen from Cirencester. For something a little different, the **Oxford Bus Museum** is a couple of miles further on at Long Hanborough. There are more than 40 buses on display, as well as all sorts of other vehicles from fire engines to bikes. On the first Sunday of the month,

OXFORD BUS MUSEUM: Incorporating the Morris Motors Experience, Old Station Yard, Long Hanborough, Witney OX29 8LA; ☎01993 883617; www.oxfordbusmuseum. org.uk. Entry: adults £4, concessions £3, children £2, family £9; open Sun/Wed/bank holidays, 10.30am–4.30pm daily; Sat from Easter to end Oct.

The North Leigh Roman Villa

The Witney & District Museum

from April to October, you'll get a free ride in a vintage bus, as well as on special event days, including Easter Sunday and Santa days in December. Entrance includes the **Morris Motors Experience**, on the same spot, which tells the story of the cars and commercial vehicles produced at Cowley, Oxford, by William Morris (Lord Nuffield).

COMBE MILL MUSEUM: Blenheim Palace Sawmill, Combe, Long Hanborough OX29 8ET; ☎01865 379402; www.combemill.org Entry: adults from £4, children and concessions £2.50; open and 'in steam' on the 3rd Sun of Mar/Apr/May/Jun/Aug/Oct, 10am–5pm.

In the next village **Combe Mill Museum** is an industrial museum demonstrating what went on behind the scenes of the old Blenheim Palace Estate timber mill and workshops. Volunteers operate the machinery and demonstrate lost skills, and the waterwheel can also be seen turning. There's a craft table and a quiz for children, a lovely picnic area by the river, and a shop with refreshments.

Wet weather

One of the most fascinating places to visit in the Cotswolds is the **Cotswold Woollen Weavers** at Filkins, three quarters of a mile off the A361 between Burford and Lechlade. '*The smell of wool oil and the clack of the shuttles welcome visitors who tour our traditional 18th-century woollen-mill set in the beautiful English Cotswolds,*' proclaims the website. This mill shop, where you can watch age-old craft skills, is run by one of the most knowledgeable couples around, Richard and Jane Martin. '*In medieval times, this area was the great centre for the growing of wool, none of which was used here – because it wasn't encouraged. The King made his money by taxing the wool as it was exported: that's why they used to say "half the wealth of England rides on the back of sheep"; it's why the Lord Chancellor sat on a woolsack – to show the power of wool,*' Richard says.

COTSWOLD WOOLLEN WEAVERS: Filkins, Lechlade GL7 3JJ; ☎01367 860491; www.naturalbest.co.uk. Entry: free; open daily.

You can find out more at the small on-site museum, with its age-old pictures of black-clad 19th-century workers; artefacts; models; and even a replica of a shepherd's hut. But one of the most glorious sights is the shop itself, with its piles of cloth of the most superb quality, and the racks of clothes, designed by Jane, that attract so many customers each year; there's also an interiors section with rugs, cushions and throws.

What to do with children…

One of the most exciting Cotswold days out for children is to be found at Burford in the form of the **Cotswold Wildlife Park and Gardens**. Over 160 acres of gardens and parkland, set around a listed Victorian manor house, are home to animals from all over the world at the park, which has a tropical house, reptile house and insect exhibition. Many are endangered and in the IUCN's (International Union for the Conservation of Nature) Red Data Books; others are still relatively numerous in the wild, but offer a great educational encounter. There's a lot to see, including penguins, which have regular feeding times, lions and leopards, and farmyard animals; there's a narrow-gauge railway, and a special brass-rubbing centre. Picnics are permitted, and there is an adventure playground and café.

Another superb family day out is provided by **Cogges Manor Farm**, a unique working museum depicting life in the Oxfordshire countryside as it would have been lived in Victorian times. Set in an historic manor house and Cotswold farm buildings, you can talk to farm hands and dairy maids and watch them as they work, and meet animals in the children's farm

Canadian Timber Wolf at the Cotswold Wildlife Park

area, such as piglets, lambs, two cows, a donkey, chickens and ducklings, and even two farm cats called Lucy and Annie, if you can find them hiding around the farm. Regular activities and events encompass

COGGES MANOR FARM: Church Lane, Witney OX28 3LA; ☎01993 772602; www.cogges.org. Entry: adults £6, children £2.50, concessions £5, family £15; open end Apr to Aug Tues–Fri 10.30am–5pm; Sat/Sun/bank holidays 11am–5pm.

COTSWOLD WILDLIFE PARK AND GARDENS: Burford OX18 4JP; ☎01993 823006; www. cotswoldwildlifepark.co.uk. Entry: check the website, but currently, adults £10.50, children and over 65s £8; open daily 10am–4.30pm (earlier in winter).

demonstrations of hand-milking, feeding the pigs and butter-making. The farm is under threat because of funding difficulties so do go and see it – it's a fantastic place, and the more visitors who discover this, the more secure its future will be.

... and how to avoid children

Take a tour of the **Wychwood Brewery** in Witney, named after the ancient forest of Wychwood. This independent brewery produces a range of award-winning traditional craft-brewed beers; in fact, it's one of the UK's top producers of organic beers. The guided tour lasts around 45 minutes (plus an extra 45 minutes for

A Cask worker at the Wychwood Brewery

WYCHWOOD BREWERY: Eagle Maltings, The Crofts, Witney OX28 4DP; ☎01993 890800; www.wychwood.co.uk. Entry: £6.50 per person includes the tour, beer sampling and a souvenir Wychwood Brewery glass; brewery tours every Sat and Sun afternoon; prebooking essential, preferably via the website.

tasting and shopping) and takes you through the brewing process from raw ingredients to finished product; plus, of course, you're allowed a few samples of the flagship Legendary Hobgoblin and the range of Wychwood and Brakspear bottled beers. The brewery shop is an old building so it's not suitable for anyone with walking difficulties.

Entertainment

Burford Festival takes place every other summer (on odd year numbers) with music – blues, folk, jazz and classical – barn dancing, garden fetes and a banquet; it also features the famous **Burford Dragon**. The origin of this symbol is probably from a great battle fought in the town in the 8th century when Aethelhum, the Mercian standard bearer who carried the flag depicting a golden dragon, was killed by a Saxon warrior. In 1814, a sarcophagus was discovered at Battle Edge, near Sheep Street, by workmen. The skeleton inside wore a leather cuirass studded with metal nails. Was it the body of Aethelhum? It was certainly, in all likelihood, a victim of that original battle, who is now reburied in the church. For more information visit www.burford festival.org.

The village of Ducklington, just over a mile south of Witney, celebrates its 10 acre meadow of snakeshead fritillary every April with a **Fritillary Sunday**. The flower has been adopted as the symbol of Oxfordshire, and Ducklington is one of the very few places it can be seen in abundance. The village has its own **Morris dancers** who perform ancient Ducklington dances (see www.ducklingtonmorris.org.uk).

Bampton Classical Opera, based 5 miles south of Witney in the village of Bampton is renowned for its relaxed and informal quality performances. It stages annual open-air summer performances at Bampton and at Westonbirt near Tetbury. For more information, contact 020 7222 1173 or 01993 851876, or visit www. bamptonopera.org.

The Royal Forest of Wychwood, which once covered much of what is now West Oxfordshire, is celebrated each summer with the renowned **Forest Fair**. The location of the fair changes each year, moving within the former forest boundaries. In a tradition that goes back to the 18th century, revived in 2000, the fair includes stalls, a fun fair, nature trail, Morris dancing, local food, books, arts and crafts and other entertainment. The fair is organised by local conservation group The Friends of Wychwood and publicises the work of the Wychwood Project, which is helping restore habitats and recreate some of the Wychwood woodlands. There is an entry fee, check www.wychwoodproject.org. In the heart of the Wychwood, a large remnant of the original ancient woodland remains, extending to 870 HA, and is now owned by the Cornbury Estate. The central part of this forest is now a national nature reserve near Leafield, north west of Witney, with more than 360 species of flowering plants and ferns: log onto www.english-nature.gov.uk and search for 'Wychwood NNR'.

🛒 Shopping

Burford was chosen as the Antiques Shopping Street of 2003 by *Homes & Antiques* magazine – and it's certainly retained a reputation for being a delightful place to window shop (and buy!). It's also home to the oldest pharmacy in England. Apothecary Nicholas Willet began trading at 124 High Street on 16 July 1724, and that tradition has continued right up to the present day. Reavley's, established in 1918, dispenses there today. You can also browse at the **Burford Garden Company** on the Shilton Road (OX18 4PA; www.burford.co.uk), one of the biggest independents in the UK.

Fashion expert Tania Llewellyn, married to garden designer Roddy, holds wonderful sales – **Affordable Chic** – in April and October each year in the ballroom of Asthall Manor, where the Mitfords once lived. As well as designer clothes, which include excess stock and samples at a good third less than the normal price, there's jewellery and shoes (☎01608 661947).

Children will adore the famous **Teddy Bears of Witney** at 99 High Street (www. teddybears.co.uk), with three of the world's most famous bears on display: Alfonzo, Aloysius (from Brideshead Revisited) and Theodore, Peter Bull's pocket companion.

A great place for gifts to take home is the **Aston Pottery**, 5 miles south of Witney. Based in farm buildings and surrounded by a delightful garden, the pottery has a gift shop and tea room. You can see how mugs, jugs and teapots are made and decorated, using traditional methods of slipcasting and stencilling.

West Ox Arts Association is a similarly good place to find unusual arts and crafts. On the first floor of a Grade II listed building in the village of Bampton, it's a registered charity which holds regularly changing exhibitions. (And you could combine your visit with a look-see into the village church at nearby Black Bourton, with its 13th century wall paintings.)

ASTON POTTERY & TRADING COMPANY: The Stable, Kingsway Farm, Aston OX18 2BT; www.astonpottery.co.uk. Entry: open Mon–Sat 9am–5pm, Sun/bank holidays 10.30am–4.30pm.

WEST OX ARTS: Town Hall, Market Square, Bampton OX18 2JH; ☎01993 850137 Entry: free; open Tues–Sat 10.30am– 12.30pm, 2–4pm; Sun 2–4pm.

The best... **PLACES TO STAY**

BOUTIQUE

Burford House Hotel

99 High Street, Burford OX18 4QA
☎ **01993 823151**
www.burford-house.co.uk

This is the kind of hotel people visit the Cotswolds for. A 17th-century town house, it's brimming with character and replete with personal touches. The eight bedrooms have oak beams and luxury bathrooms.

Price: doubles from £150.

Bay Tree Hotel

Sheep Street, Burford, OX18 4LW
☎ **01993 822791**
www.cotswold-inns-hotels.co.uk

This is another corner of old England, with 21st-century comfort. Once a row of houses which included the courthouse, this historic building epitomises country house style. The 21 bedrooms are all different; the Bay Tree Restaurant, which overlooks the rose and herb garden, is regarded as excellent.

Price: from £119/£165/£215 for a single/double/suite.

HOTEL

Witney Four Pillars Hotel

Ducklington Lane, Witney, OX28 4TJ
☎ **01993 779777**
www.four-pillars.co.uk

Traditional in style but up-to-the-moment as far as facilities are concerned: that's one way to sum up this hotel a short walk from the centre of Witney. The leisure club incorporates a swimming pool, and there's a splash pool especially for children.

Price: double rooms from £70.

FARMSTAY

Potters Hill Farm

Langley Leafield, Burford OX29 9QB
☎ **01993 878018**

The converted coach house at this family farm has three comfortable en suite B&B rooms. It's set in 15 acres of peaceful, mature parkland, supporting lots of different birds and other wildlife. It's the attention to detail that helps make this a lovely place to stay – plus the owners offer excellent advice on the area.

Price: from £65 for two, including breakfast.

B&B

Upham House Bed & Breakfast

Upham House, The Lanes, Bampton, OX18 2JG
☎ **01993 852703 or 07946 625563**

This award-winning B&B is a 10 minute drive from Witney. A comfortable and well appointed place to stay, plus there's always a warm welcome from the owner. Rates are reduced for more than three days' stay.

Price: doubles from £70, including breakfast.

SELF-CATERING

Oxfordshire Narrowboats

Heyford Wharf, Station Road, Lower Heyford Bicester OX25 5PD
☎ **01869 340348**
www.oxfordshire-narrowboats.co.uk

Oxfordshire Narrowboats has a base at Racot, 9 miles from Witney. From here you can head to Lechlade or Oxford. Boats are from 2-12 berths, and you can hire for a week or a short break (Friday to Monday)

Price: from £539 for a short break.

The best... FOOD AND DRINK

▶ Staying in

You can't get a better or more genuine outlet than **Foxbury**, the family-run farm shop just off the A40 at Brize Norton (OX18 3NX), which produces meat *par excellence*, including beef, reared via their own suckler herd, lamb from their own flock, and Gloucester Old Spot pork. You can also buy chicken and duck from here. Although not organic, they employ a free-range method of the highest quality. The shop sells Foxbury Fast Feast Ready Made Meal range, using Foxbury meat and locally grown English vegetables with fresh herbs. It's open Tues 9am–5pm, Wed–Sat 9am–6pm and Sun 10am–2pm (☎01993 867385; www.foxburyfarm.co.uk).

Upton Smokery at Hurst Barn Farm, Burford (OX18 4TH; ☎01451 844744; www. uptonsmokery.co.uk) sells a broad range of oak and beech-smoked meat, game and fish sourced, wherever possible, from local suppliers and game from Cotswold estates. The traditional process uses only pure salt, water and natural smoke. **Callows Farm Produce** at Stonesfield near Witney (OX29 8EG; ☎01993 891967/891172) is another good farm shop selling local goods: meat, fruit, vegetables, cakes, bread, preserves and cheeses, and open Monday–Wednesday 8am–5pm; Thursday and Friday 8am–6pm and Saturday 8am–2pm. There's also **Palace Cuisine** in Witney (☎01993 702942), a family baker which using traditional methods to hand make bread and pastries. Master baker Tim Bennett is the last producer of Banbury cakes from a unique 17th ·century recipe.

Witney Farmers' Market takes place 8.30am–1.30pm in the Market Place on the third Wednesday of each month. There you'll find **Shaken Oak Products** (☎01993 868043), producing a range of handmade mustards and other products, using the finest ingredients, as many as possible bought locally. Award-winning cookery writer **Sophie Grigson,** who lives in Oxfordshire, is a passionate advocate of the local farmers' markets. '*So many people in England today shop entirely in supermarkets – and that means they're missing out on where food comes from,*' she says. '*I can't pretend that I don't go to supermarkets myself, but if that's constantly where you buy from, you lose that sense of what food is. Whereas, if you go to a farmers' market, you can talk to stall holders about the seasons, about where the food comes from and how to cook it. At the moment, we are in danger of de-skilling the consumer and the sales person.*'

The truth about goats

Windrush Valley goats' cheese might be one of the Cotswolds' most iconic products – but don't be surprised to hear its artisan makers speaking with New Zealand accents! Renee and Richard Loveridge moved to the pretty village of Windrush, near Burford, from the other side of the world just over eight years ago; but in a remarkably short space of time, they've established themselves as award-winning local goat cheese makers. Some goat cheeses have a strong flavour, which can put people off. But those who've tasted the Loveridges' version will testify it's delicious, fresh and mild. They make cheese every day and pasteurise it, which makes it safe for everyone, including pregnant women and tinies.

Richard and Renee are, understandably, big goat fans, who are keen to dispel some of the myths about these misunderstood animals. For one thing, goats won't chew the washing on your line! *'Actually, they tend to be quite particular about what they eat,'* Richard says. *'We feed them on haylage (high quality forage) and a concentrate. They're very intelligent animals, so they don't like to be tethered, which is also how people think of goats. One of the nice things about them is their character – they're lovely with our children.'*

You can buy Windrush Valley products, which include fresh, soft cheeses, probiotic yogurt, baked cheesecakes, and milk, at local farmers' markets, farm shops and delis, or ring the Loveridges at Pinchpool Farm, Windrush (☎01451 844828).

 EATING OUT

FINE DINING

Angel at Burford
14 Witney Street, Burford OX18 4SN
☎ **01993 822714**
www.theangelatburford.co.uk

The Angel offers food people have taken time to prepare and select, enhanced by an extensive wine list. The menu changes regularly, though you'll always find regular favourites at this 16th-century former coaching inn. Mains around £16, such as medallions of venison with sautéed new potatoes and blackberry and gin sauce.

HOTEL

Witney Lakes Resort
Downs Road, Witney, OX29 0SY
☎ **01993 893000**
www.witney-lakes.co.uk

At this resort, you'll find a golf course and a restaurant all rather attractively set beside a lake with food served on the terrace in summer. It's a good excuse to eat an aged Oxfordshire sirloin steak with creamed spinach, peppercorn sauce and roasted vine tomatoes, followed by cheeses from Roger Crudge and Simon Weaver: three courses for around £20.

EATING OUT

INN

The Lamb Inn
Sheep Street, Burford OX18 4LR
☎ 01993 823155
www.cotswold-inns-hotels.co.uk

This perennially-popular inn serves contemporary English cuisine with strong traditional influences. Carpaccio of beetroot with apple and walnut beignet to begin? Followed by pavé of salmon with braised cabbage, saffron poached potato, with a warm anchovy dressing, perhaps. Three courses for around £35.

Inn for All Seasons
The Barringtons, Burford, OX18 4TN
☎ 01451 844324
www.innforallseasons.com

Log fires, beams and Cotswold stone: this inn offers a local experience, combined with excellent food. Specialising in fresh fish and shellfish from Devon and Cornwall (around £16 for a main), it also sources game, pork, poultry and lamb from around the area – plus the best Scottish beef.

The Trout Inn at Tadpole Bridge
Buckland Marsh, Faringdon SN7 8RF
☎ 01367 870382; www.trout-inn.co.uk

Surely the name alone is enough to persuade you this is an inn worth visiting! It's hard to know which looks better – the menu or the setting. As well as the fine main menu, try the 'Sausage Club', with temptations such as hog's pudding – a white pudding made with pork – Thursdays at £10.50.

The Plough
Clanfield OX18 2RB; ☎ 01367 810222
www.theploughclanfield.co.uk

You'll find Cotswold produce in abundance on the menu – hare, venison, pigeon, pheasant and rabbit – at this 16th century Elizabethan Manor. Perhaps you'll be tempted by a selection of charcuterie meats with grilled artichoke, mozzarella, roast peppers and tomatoes. You'll average £14 for a main course.

Café Messina
1 Langdale Court, Market Square, Witney OX28 6FG; ☎ 01993 706845
Cafemessina.co.uk

Eat at this traditional Sicilian café and you'll have two holidays in one – because for a few moments, you'll really believe you've been transported to the Med. It serves the best pasta around and is great value: you'll find lots of main meals from under £10.

TEAROOMS

Huffkins
98 High Street, Burford OX18 4QF
☎ 01993 822126; www.huffkins.com

From its craft bakery in Burford, the revered Huffkins produces its own speciality breads, cakes and confectionery. You can take away fresh sandwiches and soups at lunchtime, or enjoy a fast and casual meal – if you want it – in the café. Traditional Sunday lunch is at Witney's Huffkins only (£15 for three courses) and needs to be booked (☎01993 703540).

🍷 Drinking

The Cotswold Arms in Burford's High Street (☎01993 822227) is one of the friendliest pubs – especially for children. People know it from miles around for its famous garden model railway; and in summer, there's live children's entertainment from Lego the clown.

The Fleece (☎01993 892270) is a very pleasant place to sit outside and enjoy a drink in summer. Overlooking Witney's Church Green, it's supposed to have been a regular for Dylan Thomas when he lived in South Leigh. For a long time, it was believed that the poet had written *Under Milk Wood* in the town of Laugharne, Carmarthenshire, in the Boat House – now a museum – by the River Taf. But Thomas's friend, the actor and comedian Harry Locke who also lived in South Leigh, confirmed that much of the play was written here in this rural Oxfordshire village. Another literary connection in this area is to be found in Finstock. It was in the village Methodist church that the poet **T S Eliot** was received into the Church of England in 1927.

Real ale lovers would do well to visit somewhere such as **The Royal Oak in Ramsden**, just off the B4022 between Witney and Charlbury, which likes to feature unusual beers from microbreweries. It's good for food and wine, too. There are plenty of other good pubs: the

· **Windrush Inn**, Burford Road, Witney, OX28 6DJ; ☎01993 702612 – lovely views
· the unpretentious **Woodman Inn**, North Leigh OX29 6TT; ☎01993 881790
· **The Lamb and Flag**, Hailey OX29 9UB; ☎01993 702849 – ideal for families
· **Clanfield Tavern** OX18 2RG; ☎01367 810223 – has great food and, so it's said, the best Bloody Mary in the Cotswolds
· **Fox Inn** at Great Barrington, near Burford OX18 4TB; ☎01451 844385 – riverside setting
· **The Boot Inn**, Barnard Gate, just off the A40 between Witney and Eynsham OX28 6DJ; ☎01993 702612 – bizarrely, the Boot lives up to its name and boasts a collection of footwear donated by the stars, including Gary Lineker, Stanley Matthews, Henry Cooper and Jeremy Paxman.

Wherever you go, don't forget to try a pint from Witney's Wychwood Brewery.

ⓘ Visitor Information

Tourist information centres: Witney Visitor Information Centre, 3 Welch Way, Witney OX28 6JH, ☎01993 775802, Mon–Thurs 9am–5.30pm, Fri 9am–5pm and Sat 9.30am–5pm, www.oxfordshirecotswolds.org; Burford Visitor Information Centre, The Brewery, Sheep Street, Burford OX18 4LP, ☎01993 823558, Mar to Oct Mon–Sat 9.30am–5.30pm, Nov to Feb, Mon–Sat 9.30am–4pm.

Hospitals: Witney Community Welch Way, Witney OX28 6JJ, ☎01993 209400, minor injuries unit open 10am–10.30pm daily ☎01993 209456/8; John Radcliffe Headley Way, Headington, Oxford OX3 9DU, ☎01865 741166, 24–hr A&E.

Supermarkets include: Waitrose, 25 Woolgate Centre, Market Square OX28 6AR, ☎01993 778411; Sainsbury's, Witan Way, Witney OX28 6FF, ☎01993 776038; Co-op, Black Bourton Road, Carterton OX18 3HQ, ☎01993 847702.

Sports: Windrush Leisure Centre in Witan Way, Witney OX28 4YA, ☎01993 202020; Carterton Leisure Centre, Broadshires Way, Carterton OX18 1AA; ☎01993 861981; Burford Golf Club, Swindon Road, Burford OX18 4JG, ☎01993 822583, www.burfordgolfclub. co.uk; Witney Lakes Resort (golf), Downs Road, Witney, Oxfordshire OX29 0SY, ☎01993 893000, www.witney-lakes. co.uk; Carterton Cycle Hire, 4 Mansell Place, Carterton OX18 3RX, ☎01993 844937/ 07799 605560, www. cartertoncyclehire.com (will deliver and collect from holiday accommodation); Pigeon House Equitation at Church Hanborough OX29 8AF; ☎01993 881628, hacks for competent riders age 16 and over.

Entertainment: Screen at the Square, 19 Market Square, Corn Exchange; Witney, www.screenwitney.co.uk, bookings taken on ☎01865 880645.

Taxis include: MJ Taxis, Witney, ☎07876 752586.

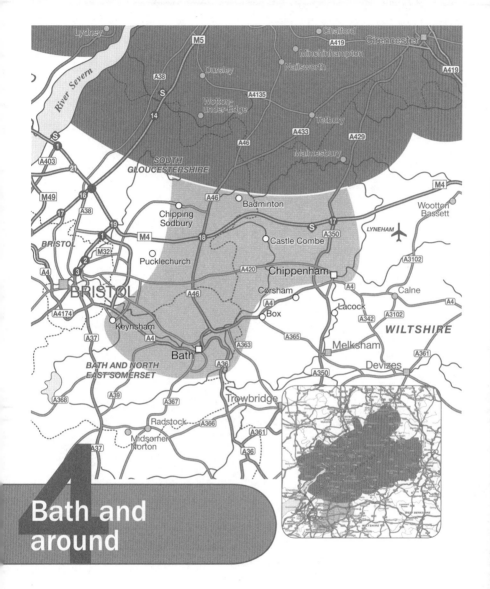

Bath and around

a. Bath, Castle Combe and the Sodburys

Unmissable highlights

01 Visit the Roman Baths – among the most splendid in Britain – where the natural spring produces more than a million litres of water a day at 46°C, p. 243

02 Experience life above and below stairs at Number One Royal Crescent, John Wood's masterpiece of Palladian design, magnificently restored and authentically furnished, p. 244

03 Join a Jane Austen walking tour round Bath, taking in the places she lived, visited and shopped, as well as the settings for her novels, p. 246

04 Experience Hogwarts for a day: National Trust property **Lacock Abbey** was turned into classrooms for the Harry Potter films, p. 249

05 Tuck into a Sally Lunn Bun from Sally Lunn's in North Parade passage, the famous tea and eatery which occupies the oldest house in Bath, p. 259

06 Sip tea in the Pump Room, the social heart of Bath for more than 200 years, p. 261

07 Promenade in one of Bath's beautiful parks, such as Royal Victoria Park, beneath Royal Crescent, with its nine acres of botanical gardens, p. 246

08 Admire the view from the Packbridge in Castle Combe, a picture-perfect English village little changed over the centuries, p. 264

09 Join the throngs at Badminton Horse Trials each May: this three-day event is one of the elite of the equestrian world and attracts the largest crowd of any paid-entry sporting event in the UK, p. 255

10 Cook a great roast with the award-winning rare-breed lamb from Langley Chase Organic Farm, beloved of food writers such as Tom Parker Bowles, p. 260

BATH AND AROUND

All too often in England, 'city' is a dirty word – one that conjures up ubiquitous high streets; hectic feet scurrying to the next destination; soulless concrete and filthy pavements. Bath, with its glorious Georgian architecture, is different. Elegant and cultured, it envelops visitors in its sophistication. Nor is it a fast-paced, rushed affair; on the contrary: it invites you to take your time and explore the many well-thought-out attractions and famous sites it has to offer.

Indeed, the whole of this southern area seems imbued with the same kind of genteel charm. The countryside that surrounds the city is breathtaking and varied. Depending on which direction you take, you might find yourself in the Midsomer Valleys to the south, the lakes of the Chew Valley, west with the River Avon; or you could stroll alongside the Kennet and Avon Canal through Limpley Stoke. And then there are the open spaces of west Wiltshire and the ancient secrets of the Mendips. Or, of course, you could head north towards the heart of the Cotswolds once again. Choose the latter option and you'll pass through some of the loveliest of villages, whose inns and taverns promise relaxing respite from the outside hustle and bustle. Here, you'll enter Beaufort Hunt country, that traditional world exemplified by the drumming of hooves, the baying of hounds, and riders in their distinctive livery: the Huntsman and Whippers-In wearing green and the subscribers a bluecoat with buff facings.

Bath is the start (or finish) of the Cotswold Way, the 102-mile national trail that leads walkers though the heart of the Cotswolds, right up to Chipping Campden in the north. If ever there were a way to see the changing face of this wonderful region, this has to be it.

BATH, CASTLE COMBE AND THE SODBURYS

If you've never seen the golden rays of the setting sun gilding the mellow stone of Bath, then you've missed out on one of the most beautiful sights in England. Bath truly is a unique city – a fact that's acknowledged in its status as a World Heritage Site. It's also a manageable city; because it's neither huge nor sprawling, it's somewhere you can quickly get to know – like the lords and ladies who once fashionably flocked here to take its spa waters, you feel you can truly make its acquaintance.

As for the village of Castle Combe, if you've seen the film *Stardust*, you'll already have been introduced, for the village took a starring role as a perfect backdrop for this modern-day fairytale. It also has a pacier side, for it's home to Castle Combe Circuit, providing some of the best motor racing in the country. Near to Bath is the fascinating National Trust property Lacock Abbey. This medieval cloistered former abbey provided a backdrop to another series of famous films – the Harry Potter movies. The cloisters and side rooms became Hogwarts classrooms – particularly fitting considering Harry's creator, the author J K Rowling, was born at nearby Yate near Chipping Sodbury, some 15 miles north of Bath.

WHAT TO SEE AND DO

Pop into a bar in Bath, and you might just find yourself sitting next to Robbie Williams, Will Young, Johnny Depp or Orlando Bloom: they're known to adore the city's pubs. And if you fancy a bit of shopping in an exclusive boutique afterwards, you might discover you're flexing your credit card beside the likes of Geri Halliwell or Camilla, Duchess of Cornwall.

Not that this celebrity spotting is anything new. For Bath has been a society magnet since the 18th century. Indeed, the Georgian era was the city's heyday. Before Queen Anne came to visit in 1702, Bath had enjoyed a quiet life as a simple market town, little changed from medieval times. But thanks to that initial royal patronage, its importance grew so rapidly that, within a century, its population had swelled from 2,000 to 30,000.

The reason for Queen Anne's visit was the alleged restorative power of Bath's hot springs. This life-long invalid was far from the first to put her faith in the healing potential of the city's sulphurous waters. As long as 7,000 years ago, pilgrims were throwing flint tools into the steaming spring and later, in Celtic times – when the spring was surrounded by an oak tree grove – druids would worship the goddess Sulis here. But it was when the Romans colonised the city, naming it Aquae Sulis ('the waters of Sulis') that Bath's fame spread wide.

Discovering Bath

Some of Bath's historic characters seem reluctant to leave – and who can blame them? There's the Man in the Black Hat who frequents the Assembly Rooms, and the beautiful singing lady who still thinks of Royal Crescent as her home. It's only polite to call on these well-known figures, if you're in the area; and the best way to do it is via a **ghost walk** (☎01225 350512; www.ghostwalksofbath.co.uk). One of the most popular ways of seeing the city is the **Bizarre Bath** walk – a hilarious and irreverent view of the city. It leaves the Huntsman Inn, North Passage Parade every evening at 8pm from April to the

> BIZZARE BATH WALK: ☎01225 335124; www.bizarrebath.co.uk
> Price: adults £8, students £5 – no pre-booking required.

end of October, and lasts for around 90 minutes. There's also a **free walk** provided every day except Christmas Day (Sun–Fri 10.30am and 2pm; Sat 10.30am), leaving from outside the main entrance to the Pump Room. From May to September, there are additional tours on Tuesday and Friday at 7pm. Tours last approximately two hours and no pre-booking is necessary for individuals (☎01225 477411).

The **Bath Bus Company open-top sightseeing tour** is available in seven languages with the latest sound technology. You can buy a ticket from the driver (adults £11,

The Roman Baths, founded on a sacred spring

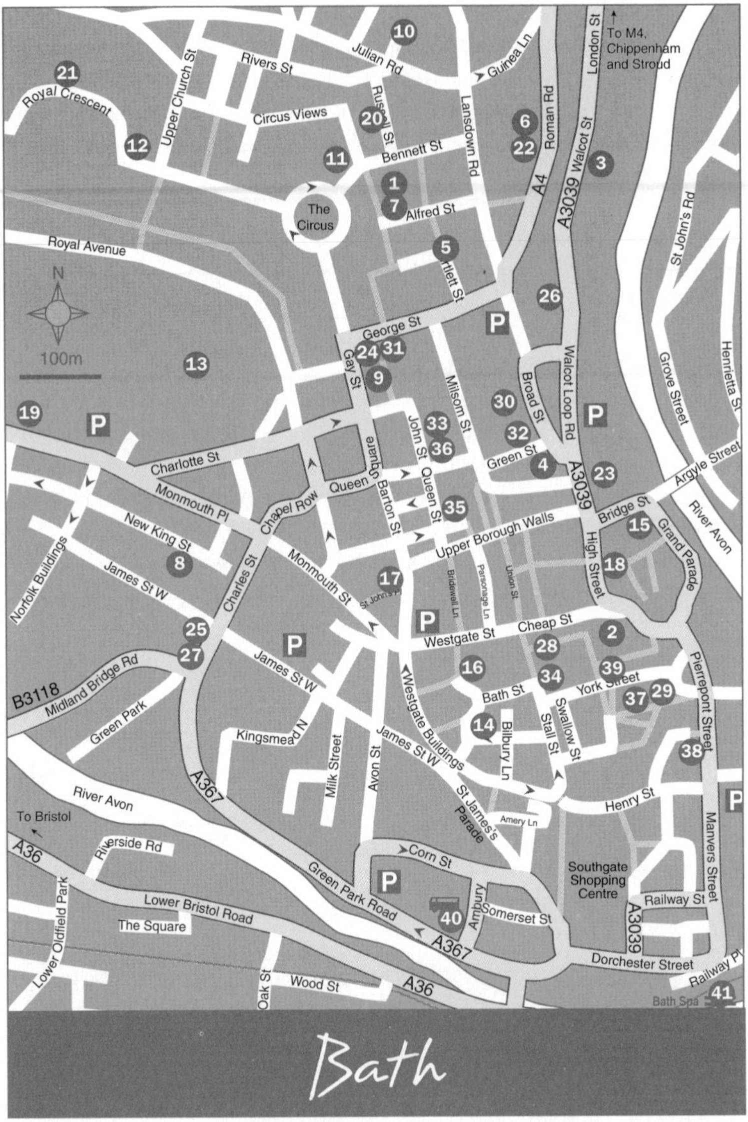

Bath

Things to see and do
1. Assembly Rooms
2. Bath Abbey/Vaults Heritage Museum
3. Bath Aqua Theatre of Glass
4. Bath Postal Museum
5. Bertinet Kitchen
6. Building of Bath Museum
7. Fashion Museum
8. Herschel Museum of Astronomy
9. Jane Austin Centre
10. Museum of Bath at Work
11. Museum of East Asian Art
12. Number 1 Royal Crescent
13. Royal Victoria Park
14. Thermae Bath Spa
15. Victoria Art Gallery

Entertainment
16. Little Theatre Cinema
17. Theatre Royal

Shopping
18. Guildhall Market

Places to Stay
19. The Bath House
20. Queensberry hotel
21. Royal Crescent hotel

Eat and Drink
22. Abbey Ales
23. Arabesque
24. Chandos Deli
25. Farmers' Market at Green Park Station
26. Fine Cheese Company
27. Green Park Brasserie
28. House of Minerva Chocolaterie
29. Huntsman Inn
30. Jamie's Italian
31. Moles Club
32. Old Green Tree
33. Paxton & Whitfield
34. Pump Room Restaurant
35. The Raven
36. The Salamander
37. Sally Lunn's House
38. Yak Yeti Yak

Visitor Information
39. Tourist Information Centre
40. Bus station
41. Railway Station

children £6, concessions £9, family with up to three children £25). All the main locations are included on the 45-minute trip, but you can get on and off at any stop, and presenting your ticket will mean discounts at certain attractions. Tickets are valid for two days, and you can also use them for the Bath Skyline tour, which goes further out. Download maps – with bus stops marked – from the website (www. bathbuscompany.com; ☎01225 330444).

Historic Bath

The major part of the Romans' time in Bath lies buried 2m below the Georgian streets. Not only are these remains among the most splendid in Britain, but here was one of the finest thermal spas of the ancient world. There are four main elements to the **Roman Baths:** the Sacred Spring, the Roman Temple, the Roman Bath House and the Museum which houses numerous finds, including objects which were thrown into the Sacred Spring as offerings. Apart from thousands of coins, there's a gilded head of Sulis Minerva on display, which was stumbled upon by workmen at Stall Street in the city in 1727. Experts think the head once stood in the goddess's temple, which was ransacked by Christians in the sixth century. Her sacred spring still produces more than a million litres a day at a temperature of 46°C. These Roman remains are one of the reasons Bath has earned itself a place as a World Heritage City, ranking it alongside famous cousins such as Edinburgh and Liverpool. Look out for special events, such as the Roman Baths by torchlight.

> ROMAN BATHS: Abbey Church Yard, Bath BA1 1LZ; ☎01225 477785; www. romanbaths.co.uk. Entry: adults £11 (£11.50 Jul/Aug), children £7.20, concessions £9.50, family £32; open daily (including evenings until 9pm throughout Jul/Aug). You can get a saver combined ticket with the Fashion Museum.

If you want to know who to thank for the Georgian elegance you see around you, you can discover more about the city's principal architect at the **Building of Bath Museum**. It celebrates the achievements of John Wood the Elder (see box), son of a humble builder. He was responsible for many of the glorious buildings and streets that define the town, such as the **North and South Parades**, **Queen Square**, **The Circus** and **Prior Park**; he also designed the **Royal Crescent**, which his son, John Wood the Younger, went on

> BUILDING OF BATH MUSEUM: The Countess of Huntingdon's Chapel, The Vineyards, The Paragon Bath BA1 5NA; ☎01225 333895; www.bath-preservation-trust. org.uk/museums/bath. Entry: adults £4, children £2, concessions £3.50; open Easter weekend to end Oct, Sat/Sun/Mon (including bank holidays) 10.30am–5pm.

> 1 ROYAL CRESCENT: Bath BA1 2LR; ☎01225 428126; www.bath-preservation-trust.org.uk/museums/no1 Entry: adults £5, children £2.50, concessions £4, family £12; open Feb to Dec Tues–Sun 10.30am–4/5pm; closed Good Fri and Easter Mon, open bank holidays.

to build. His son designed and built the 'new' **Assembly Rooms**.

Of course, everyone is free to walk around the outside of these stunning buildings. But if you want an intimate glimpse of life in 18ᵗʰ century Bath, then visit **Number One Royal Crescent,** the first house to be built in Royal Crescent, a masterpiece of Palladian design. Take a look inside and see how its early residents would have lived.

Bath Abbey in the centre of the city dates back to 1499, though worship has taken place on this same site for more than 1,000 years. You can take a guided tour of the tower which, with its 212 steps, offers a panoramic view of the city, generally every hour from Monday to Saturday, 10am–3pm. Tickets cost £5 (children 5–14 £2.50) from Bath Abbey Shop. On the south side of the abbey is the **Vaults Heritage Museum**: 18ᵗʰ-century cellars, which host a presentation detailing the church's history alongside an exhibition of objects dating back to Saxon times. They're open Monday to Saturday, 10am-3.30pm.

Another fascinating attraction is **The Jane Austen Centre** in Gay Street, put together with advice from the Jane Austen Society. The perennially popular novelist paid two long visits here towards the end of the 18ᵗʰ century, and used the city as a setting for *Persuasion* and *Northanger Abbey*. 'Oh! Who can ever

The entrance to the Assembly Rooms

Bath Abbey dates back to 1499

THE JANE AUSTEN CENTRE: 40 Gay Street, Queen Square, Bath BA1 2NT; ☎01225 443000; www.janeausten.co.uk Entry: adult £6.95, child £3.95, concessions £5.50, family (up to four children) £18; open every day in summer 9.45am–5.30pm (and until 7pm Thurs–Sat Jul/Aug); Nov to Mar Sun–Fri 11am–4.30pm, Sat 9.45am–5.30pm; **Walking tours**: adults £6, concessions £5; 11am weekends/bank holidays year round (not Boxing Day or New Year), additional walks in Jul/Aug on Fri/Sat; walks last 90 minutes.

be tired of Bath?' one of her characters asks. Then from 1801 to 1806, Bath was her home. If the truth be known, Jane didn't much enjoy life here, preferring her subsequent move to Clifton and, later, the Hampshire village of Chawton. By the time she arrived in Bath, it had become

The Circus designed by John Wood the Elder

Building Bath

John Wood the Elder, born in 1704, the son of a Bath builder, was destined to create the very fabric of Britain's greatest Georgian city: here was the man who designed North and South Parades, Queen Square, The Circus and the sweeping curve of Royal Crescent. Look at those buildings today, and you'll see the epitome of sanity and intellectualism: classical architecture, drawing heavily on the ideas of the ancients, full of Doric, Ionic and Corinthian influences. But behind that façade lay a deeply eccentric mind. Wood worked according to his own highly complex theories, bizarrely bound up with legend: specifically, the legend of Bladud, founder of Bath.

The story goes that Bladud, son of a British king, was cast out when he contracted leprosy. Exiled to the life of a swineherd, the boy was devastated when his pigs also contracted the disease. Wandering in despair, he stumbled across a rural spring, which his animals delightedly wallowed in. To the prince's astonishment, they emerged from the waters cured. Thus was discovered Bath's healing spring, allowing Bladud to return home whole again. Finally, as King, he returned to the spot and founded the city. Not only did Wood believe implicitly in this wholly apocryphal tale; he also embellished it. He conjectured that Bladud travelled to Jerusalem, where he witnessed the construction of the second Temple of Solomon, and that he took this art back to the Druids of Britain. By this complicated process, Wood effectively 'Christianised' pagan architecture.

By the time he was 21, this maverick had completed a full architectural plan for Bath, determined by this philosophy. Having given the Druids a pseudo-Christian root, he felt justified in resurrecting their temples – and so Royal Crescent was a recreation of a pagan Temple of the Moon; and The Circus, a Temple of the Sun. The latter is not so much based on The Colosseum as Stonehenge. Wood sent his grand plan to another poor-boy-made-good, Ralph Allen. A talented entrepreneur, Allen had made a fortune by redesigning and improving the English postal system, saving the Post Office a colossal £1,500,000 over 40 years. Together, Wood and Allen began to create a city that would take its place as one of the most spectacularly beautiful in the world.

less of a fashionable epicentre and more a home for the genteel retired. For a full Jane Austen experience, take a **walking tour** of the places she lived, visited and shopped, and used as the settings for her novels.

The Jane Austen Centre situated in Gay Street where the author lived

Bath's museums

So many attractions does Bath have, they're too numerous to detail. Among the best of the rest include the **American Museum in Britain** at Claverton Manor (☎01225 460503; www.americanmuseum. org), showing how Americans lived from the time of early settlers to the American Civil War (open March to October, closed Mondays). **Beckford's Tower & Museum** in Lansdown Road (BA1 9BH; ☎01225 422212/460705; www.bath-preservation-trust.org.uk) houses a collection of art and books amassed by the 19th-century eccentric William Beckford (and it also offers wonderful views).

Another interesting character was the astronomer William Herschel who, with his sister Caroline, lived in Bath in the last part of the 18th century. You can see his astronomer's workshop, the original kitchen and music room, and the Georgian garden he once owned at the **Herschel Museum of Astronomy** at 19 New King Street (☎01225 446865; www.bath-preservation-trust.org.uk). The **Museum of Bath at Work** in Julian Road looks at the city's working heritage since Roman times, and features a reconstructed ironmongers' shop, Victorian engineering works and a mineral water factory (☎01225 318348; www.bath-at-work.org.uk).

There's also lots for the art lover. One of the more unusual collections, with artefacts from China, Japan and South East Asia is the **Museum of East Asian Art** at 12 Bennett Street (☎01225 464640; www.meaa.org.uk). While the **Victoria Art Gallery** in Bridge Street (entry free) houses work by Gainsborough, Sickert, Zoffany and many other leading artists from the 15th century to the present day (☎01225 477232; www.victoriagal.org.uk).

Bath's parks and gardens

If the sun's shining, there's plenty of free fun to be had outdoors. Bath has a whole host of parks and gardens in and around the city centre. There are the 57 acres of the **Royal Victoria Park**, beneath Royal Crescent, with their nine acres of **Botanical Gardens** – beautiful trees, shrubs, rock gardens and pool, scented walk and roses; while **Sydney Gardens** behind the Holburne Museum (currently closed for refurbishment) at the end of Great Pulteney Street, is Bath's oldest park and a former Georgian Pleasure Garden. You can find a full list of parks at www.cityofbath.co.uk.

LOCAL KNOWLEDGE

David Baldock is Director of the Jane Austen Centre in Gay Street, Bath. He opened the centre in May 1999 after discovering, to his amazement, that the city at that time did little to advertise its connection with the great novelist. The centre attracts more than 50,000 visitors each year, runs a hugely successful Jane Austen Festival every September, operates a Regency-themed tea room and organises walking tours.

Favourite restaurant: I really like the Green Park Brasserie in the old booking hall of Green Park Station. There's always a good atmosphere, sometimes live music; the staff are great and the food is always good.

Secret tip for lunch: The Lebanese restaurant, Arabesque, in the Podium is brilliant. The lunch mezze offers some really unusual and extremely tasty dishes.

Favourite takeaway: I don't really do traditional takeaways but the sandwiches and rolls at the Chandos Deli in George Street are the best around.

Favourite pub: St James Wine Vaults in St James Square, where I run a monthly blues club. It's a great pub with a fantastic landlord who has good music on all week.

Best view: Without doubt, the view of Bath from Beechen Cliff. Just go up to Alexandra Park and take a look – Jane Austen was a frequent visitor and remarked on the view.

Best walk: I love my walk to work every day over Lansdown with great views. The trip uphill back home is not so pleasant.

Quirkiest attraction: The Building of Bath Museum is in a lovely building and has wonderful models showing construction techniques. It's a bit of a hidden gem.

Best thing about living here: There are so many good things about Bath, and all those elements contribute towards the unique atmosphere of the City. They say that Bath is the graveyard of ambition... What do I care! I have achieved my ambition and I live here!

Best-kept secret: The walks along the canal and by the train track in Sydney Gardens and on into town. Spectacular!

Palladian bridge in Prior Park Landscape Garden

PRIOR PARK LANDSCAPE GARDEN: Ralph Allen Drive, Bath BA2 5AH; ☎01225 833422; www.nationaltrust.org.uk/priorpark Entry: adults £5, children £2.80, family £12.80; open Mar to Oct Wed–Mon 11am–dusk; Nov to Jan Sat/Sun 11am–dusk.

Just outside Bath, but with beautiful views over the city, lies **Prior Park Landscape Garden**. This 18th-century joy was designed with advice from poet Alexander Pope and the legendary Capability Brown, and contains one of only four ornamental Palladian bridges in the world. It's a lovely place to picnic and walk, and to see plenty of wildlife. If you haven't brought a car, you can get there by public transport. The house itself is now a school and not open to the public; but it's a building worth studying. John Wood the Elder and Ralph Allen constructed it as an advertisement for the quality of Bath stone: *'To see all Bath, and for all Bath to see'*.

Corsham Court, Lacock and Dyrham Park

CORSHAM COURT, CORSHAM: Wiltshire SN13 0BZ, ☎01249 712214; www.corsham-court.co.uk Entry: house and garden, adults £7 (gardens only, £2.50), seniors £6 (£2), children £3 (£1.50); guided tours £2 extra per person; open Mar to Sept Tues–Thurs and Fri–Sun (also bank holidays) 2–5.30pm; Oct to Mar, weekends only 2–4.30pm; closed Dec.

The most beautiful stately homes lie within easy drives of Bath. **Corsham Court**, which sits within a park designed by Capability Brown, is famed for its art, one of the most distinguished collections of Old Masters in the country. The estate is still privately owned, and today is home to James Methuen-Campbell, one of the eighth generation of the Methuens to live there. The present house was built in 1582, though magnificent state rooms were added in Georgian times.

For Harry Potter fans, a trip to **Lacock Abbey** is a must – indeed, visitors come from all over the world to see this atmospheric location. But it's not just the abbey; the village of Lacock itself had a starring role. For the sixth film, *Harry Potter and the Half-Blood Prince*, local roads were closed between 5pm and 5am for three nights of filming, and game locals agreed to black out their windows.

LACOCK ABBEY AND FOX TALBOT MUSEUM: Lacock, near Chippenham, Wiltshire SN15 2LG; ☎01249 730459; www.nationaltrust. org.uk/lacock. Entry: abbey, museum, cloisters and grounds adults £10, child £5, family £25.50; museum open Feb to Nov, 11am–5.30pm daily; Nov to Jan Sat/Sun only; cloisters/grounds open daily Mar to 2 Nov 11am–5.30pm; abbey open Mar to Nov daily (except Tues) 1–5.30pm.

The abbey was also used as the gardens, cloisters and rooms of Whitehall Palace for *The Other Boleyn Girl*. When you visit, you'll instantly realise why this is such a popular film location. The medieval abbey was founded in the 13th century, before being turned into a country house 300 years later. You can see the cloisters, a sacristy and chapter house which look much as they always have. In the 19th century, it was owned by William Henry Fox Talbot, a pioneering photographer who invented the negative/positive process. **The Fox Talbot Museum**, also on site, is dedicated to his achievements. His first successful image – a tiny photograph the size of a postage stamp – featured the abbey's oriel window in the south gallery.

Not that photography was his only interest: Fox Talbot was also devoted to botany, a passion reflected in the abbey's woodland grounds, full of flowers and interesting

Lacock Abbey was used as a location for *Harry Potter* films

Dyrham Park and Gardens

DYRHAM PARK: Dyrham, near Bath SN14 8ER; ☎0117 937 2501; www.nationaltrust.org.uk/dyrham Entry: adults £10, children £5, family £25; garden and park only, adults £4, children £2, family £8.90; open Mar to Nov 12–5pm, Fri–Tues; garden/shop/tearoom open Mar to Jun, Sept/Oct; 11am–5pm Fri–Tues; Sat/Sun Nov; park open daily all year round 11am–5.30pm.

trees, and the botanic gardens. It was Talbot's descendants who donated the abbey and the 13th century village to the National Trust in 1944. Because of this legacy, Lacock is uniquely preserved: full of limewashed, half-timbered and stone houses.

Dyrham Park, 8 miles north of Bath, is so unchanged, you can almost imagine yourself back 300 years or more watching its one-time owner William Blathwayt furrowing his brow, advising William III on affairs at home and abroad. Indeed, the house was built between 1691 and 1702 for Blathwayt, who was the King's Secretary at War and Secretary of State. He furnished it in true 17th-century fashion, with a passion for all things Dutch, and recorded the details in a housekeeper's inventory, which still exists. The mansion is beautifully positioned, within a Gloucestershire valley, with stunning views towards Bristol. There's an ancient deer park, elegant formal gardens, woodlands and lakes to explore.

Wet weather

Not only can you while away a morning while it rains – you can also discover what the gentry of Bath would have worn on wet (and sunny) days at **Bath's Fashion Museum**.

Here you'll find a world-class collection of contemporary and historical dress, with 150 dressed figures to illustrate the changing styles in fashionable clothes from the late 16th century to the present day. All in all, the museum owns 30,000 original items. And if you're a glutton for punishment (but certainly not a glutton), there's a special 'Corsets and Crinolines' display where visitors can try on reproduction garments. Breathe in!

Historical dress at Bath's Fashion Museum

FASHION MUSEUM: Assembly Rooms, Bennett Street, Bath BA1 2QH; ☎01225 477173; www.fashionmuseum.co.uk Entry: adults £7, children £5, concessions £6.25, family £20, a saver combined ticket with the Fashion Museum; open daily, 10.30am–5pm (4pm in winter) with exit an hour later.

On the same site, **The Assembly Rooms** themselves are open to view when not in use for booked functions, with hours as for the Fashion Museum. Call ☎ 01225 477173 to check availability.

Beau Nash

At the same time as Queen Anne was taking Bath's sulphurous waters, a new name was gaining currency in the corridors of the rich and powerful – that of **Richard 'Beau' Nash**. A people-person of genius, Nash was to be elemental in shaping Georgian society. Born in Wales, Nash had spent time in the army before making his way to London where he mixed with the highest of society, gaining a reputation as an extravagant master gambler. Following Queen Anne's visit, he moved to Bath where he started to organise the very fabric of the emerging society there.

According to his strict diktats, no one could entertain at home; all partying had to be done in the public arenas of the city, and certainly not behind private closed doors. He imposed a curfew, which meant that balls ended at 11pm; he outlawed swords. He even decided what people should wear – a smart move in more ways than one, for he himself bucked the trend; as the only person in the city to sport a black wig when others wore white, he became its symbol. Most extraordinarily of all, he was the antithesis of a snob. Instead of the usual social apartheid, he insisted the rich strata of England should all mix together, from the grandest of lords to the lower middle classes.

Surprisingly little is known about this influential character – but perhaps part of his appeal was his very enigma. How he made his money is also rather shrouded in mystery. For sure, he was an inveterate gambler, who undoubtedly took a cut from many of the tables. Under his tutelage, Bath out-Vegas-ed Las Vegas.

⚡ What to do with children...

BATH POSTAL MUSEUM: 27 Northgate Street, Bath BA1 1AJ; ☎01225 460333 Entry: adults £3.50, seniors £3, children £1.50; open Mon–Sat 11am–4.30pm (5pm in summer); closed Sun/bank holidays.

THE AVON VALLEY ADVENTURE AND WILDLIFE PARK: Pixash Lane, Keynsham, Bristol BS31 1TP; ☎0117 986 4929; www.avonvalleycountrypark.com. Entry: adults £7, children and concessions £6.50; open daily Apr to Nov 1, 10am–6pm.

WOOKEY HOLE CAVES: Wells, Somerset BA5 1BB; ☎01749 672243; www.wookey.co.uk Entry: adults £15, children and concessions £10, family £45, open daily Apr to Oct 10am–5pm; Nov to Mar 10am–4pm.

CHEDDAR CAVES & GORGE: Cheddar, Somerset, BS27 3QF; ☎01934 742343; www.cheddarcaves.co.uk Entry: caves & gorge explorer tickets, adults £16, children £10, family (up to three children) £42, seniors £9 including refreshments; tickets for outdoors only, adults £4.50, children £3; tickets for adventure caving or climbing and abseiling, adults and children £17, or £32 for both activities; open 10am–5pm (10.30–4.30pm winter).

In Bath itself, **Bath Postal Museum**, which was involved in research for *Lark Rise to Candleford*, has games, quizzes, videos and computer challenges for younger visitors. Everyone's able to perforate their own sheet of stamps.

And you can easily enjoy an hour at the **Victoria Falls Adventure Golf** in the Royal Victoria Park, in the centre (☎01225 425066), a miniature golf course open daily from 10am to dusk, popular with adults and children (adults £4, concessions £3.50, children under 12 £3, family £12). The **Avon Valley Adventure and Wildlife Park** covers 50 acres of beautiful countryside alongside the River Avon, around 6 miles from Bath, and has an adventure playground, indoor play barn, nature trail, children's assault course, pets' corner, mini quad bikes, trampolines, steam train rides, boats, fishing, falconry display weekends, picnic and barbeque areas, cafés and a gift shop. You'll even find plenty to do when it's raining!

The **Avon Valley Railway** at Bitton Station (BS30 6HD) isn't just for children, of course. Adults can take a course on how to drive a steam engine, and there are monthly Sunday lunch trains. But the kids will love the regular Teddy Bears' Picnics, days out with Thomas, and the Christmas Santa Specials. The talking timetable is on ☎0117 932 7296 or you can visit www.avonvalleyrailway.org.

Close to each other – around 30 minutes' drive from Bath – are **Wookey Hole Caves** at Wells, and the **Cheddar Caves and Gorge**. Wookey Hole features large illuminated caverns, underground lakes, stalactites and stalagmites, and Britain's last handmade paper mill, plus many other attractions including indoor play areas, a mirror maze, Valley of the Dinosaurs and a fairy garden. Older children will enjoy Cheddar Gorge, which also includes two illuminated caves. For 11-year-olds upwards, there's adventure climbing and abseiling on offer.

CELEBRITY CONNECTIONS

There are two legendary authors connected with this area, both beloved by children the world over: **Dick King-Smith** and **Allan Ahlberg**.

Dick King-Smith lives in the village of Keynsham, a hop, skip and a jump from Bath, in a cottage 3 miles from where he was born. The countryside has not only been a companion all his life; it's provided inspiration for so many of his books, which now number more than 100 titles, translated into 20 languages including, most recently, Faroese. His story of Babe, the heroic pig who trained as a sheep-dog, was even snapped up by Hollywood.

This farmer-turned-writer has drawn on much of his South Gloucestershire life for his books. Such as the very first one, *The Fox Busters*, published in 1978, which tells the tale of three brave chickens, Ransome, Sims and Jefferies, who are determined to rid their farm of foxes. *'One morning, during my 20 years of farming, I was having breakfast, while outside around two dozen of my very handsome cockerels were strutting about,'* Dick recalls. *'It was daylight and I heard nothing, but I came back to a massacre: a lot of corpses, some headless. And I suppose I thought: one day I'll write a story where instead of the strong vanquishing the weak, the chickens will beat up the foxes. And eventually I had a bash!'*

Allan Ahlberg and his late wife Janet are the creators of stories such as *Funnybones* and *Burglar Bill*. Indeed, Burglar Bill's life of crime has paid off. Among other things, it's helped buy Allan a beautiful Georgian home within walking distance of Bath. *'I like the idea of living in a place you can see the edges of,'* Allan says.

Each year in September, there's **Bath Children's Literature Festival** where you'll have the chance to meet many of the top writers and illustrators working today. For more information, visit www.bathkidslitfest.co.uk.

... and how to avoid children

For a thoroughly modern (and sensuous) experience of Bath's warm waters visit the **Thermae Bath Spa**, Britain's only natural thermal spa, which opened in 2006. It's a fabulous new facility: the main spa has two natural thermal baths, an open-air rooftop pool, large steam room and treatment facilities. The whole complex is a blend of old and new. It sits mainly

THERMAE BATH SPA: Hetling Pump Room, Hot Bath Street, Bath BA1 1SJ; ☎0844 888 0844; www.thermaebathspa.com
Entry: from £22 for 2-hour session, or refer to website for other spa packages; open daily 9am–10pm, including bank holidays except Christmas Day, Boxing Day and New Year's Day.

Britain's only natural thermal spa, the Thermae Bath Spa

in a contemporary glass cube building designed by Sir Nicholas Grimshaw, interlinked with historic sites such as the Hot and Cross Baths. More than 50 spa treatments are on the menu, offering a combination of health and relaxation benefits.

Alternatively, recapture that romance at **Bath Boating Station**, a Victorian boating station offering punts (as well as canoes and rowing boats) by the hour, on a lovely stretch of river out to the old toll bridge at Bathampton (☎01225 312900; www.bathboating.co.uk; from £7 per adult). At **Bath Aqua Theatre of Glass**, you can book a course where you'll be taught how to blow your own paperweight with the help of a professional glass-blower. Based at 105–107 Walcot Street (BA1 5BW; ☎01225 428146; www.bathaquaglass.com), it's a great place to buy an unusual going-home gift. (It's also a working museum.) Or take a cookery class at **The Bertinet Kitchen**, run by French chef and baker Richard Bertinet in St Andrews Terrace. The choice is dazzling and for all abilities, from Indian entertaining to jam-making (☎01225 445531; www.thebertinetkitchen.com).

Entertainment

Festivals

The annual **Bath International Music Festival**, now more than 60 years old, takes place over 17 days each late May/early June and features orchestral, chamber and contemporary classical music, contemporary jazz, world music, folk and electronic (www.bathmusicfest.org.uk). **Bath Mozartfest** (www.bathmozartfest.org.uk) in November showcases performances of the works of Mozart and related composers.

Bath Literature Festival in early spring is another calendar highlight, attracting top names from the world of literature, politics, science and other fields (www.bathlitfest.org.uk). But Bath, being Bath, isn't satisfied with run-of-the-mill subjects for its festivals. There's also **Bath Film Festival** in the autumn (www.bathfilmfestival.org); **Bath Comedy Festival** (in April, of course) (www.bathcomedyfestival.co.uk) and **Bath Fringe Festival** (www.bathfringe.co.uk), among others. And, inevitably, Miss Austen has her own, dedicated set of celebrations. The **Jane Austen Festival** each September includes a costumed promenade along the Georgian terraces, outdoor festivities, dancing, music, workshops and a grand Regency ball (www.janeausten.co.uk/festival).

Theatre and cinema
There's plenty on at Bath's **Theatre Royal** (www.theatreroyal.org.uk); **Bath Abbey** hosts concerts and other events; and alongside the more conventional Apollo cinema, there's **the Little Theatre Cinema** (www.picturehouses.co.uk) in St Michael's Place, showing quality cinema from around the globe.

Sports
And, of course, no mention of the city would be complete without paying homage to **Bath Rugby Club** (www.bathrugby.com); founded in 1865, it's one of the oldest in existence. Bath plays at the Recreation Ground (known as 'The Rec') in the centre of the city, beside the River Avon. **Castle Combe Circuit** (SN14 7EY; www.castlecombecircuit.co.uk) provides some of the best motor racing in the country. Not only can you see top drivers performing – you can also have a go yourself! There's the opportunity for customers to try the circuit in their own cars or on motorcycles, or hire a racing car, sports car or high performance saloon around the 1.85-mile circuit. Book in advance on ☎01249 782417.

Bath Racecourse (www.bath-racecourse.co.uk), perched on Lansdown Hill, is the highest in Britain, and known for its relaxed air of friendliness. There's a variety of weekday, weekend and evening fixtures and two excellent restaurants. There are races all through the summer flat season. If you enjoy the races, the chances are you'll also want to visit **Badminton Horse Trials**. An elite of the equestrian world, this three-day event takes place each year

BADMINTON HORSE TRIALS: Badminton, Glos GL9 1DF; ☎01454 218272 (horse trials office); www.badminton-horse.co.uk Entry: held over four days in early May; for pre-booking and prices, consult the website.

at Badminton House, the seat of the Duke of Beaufort, and attracts the largest crowd of any paid-entry sporting event in the UK. The house is not open to the public.

This, of course, is Beaufort country and home to one of the oldest and largest fox-hunting packs in the country. The earliest records of hounds being kennelled at Badminton date back to 1640 when the Marquis of Worcester hunted mainly deer, but hare and fox as well. Hunting usually occurs four days a week during the season (www.beauforthunt.com).

Badminton horse trials

When Great Britain hosted the 1948 Olympics, the 10th Duke saw the British equestrian team make rather a pig's ear of the games. Positive action was needed, and he decided to invent a new horse trials as a means of getting his country's riders up to speed. Not wanting to undersell the event, the Duke billed the first **Badminton Horse Trials** - which took place a year later – as the 'most important horse event in Great Britain'. Although, at that time, this was more a prophecy than a promise, it turned out to be self-fulfilling. Socially, the event's now up there with Wimbledon, Henley and Ascot. These days, the Saturday commands the biggest one-day sporting crowd in Europe, and the third biggest in the world. Over the four days of the competition, that makes for around 200,000 people flooding through the gates. And just to complete the picture, in case you wondered, there *is* a connection with the game of Badminton too, which was first given social kudos when played at a lawn party held in 1873 by the then Duke of Beaufort.

Shopping

Bath isn't huge, but proportionately it has the number and quality of shops many bigger metropolises can only dream of. And if you're after that rare gift – that luxury item – it would be a surprise if you couldn't discover it amongst the specialist emporia that abound: nearly half of all its shops are independent. There are department stores – one of them is Jolly's, the oldest in the country.

There are six main shopping areas, all with their own distinct character: **around the abbey**; **Pulteney Bridge**; the **central area** of SouthGate, Stall Street and Union Street; **the Milsom Quarter** with Milsom Street (one of the city's main shopping streets), Milsom Place, New Bond Street and Broad Street (www.milsomplace.co.uk); **Upper Town** at the top of Bath – Bartlett Street, George Street and Margaret's Buildings; and the **Artisan Quarter** in Walcot Street with its independent craft and curio shops. Each has its own character. Pulteney Bridge, designed by Robert Adam, is one of only four bridges in the world lined with shops. The most exclusive area of all is probably Milsom Place (www.shiresyard.co.uk), full of sophisticated shops and designer stores – Armani, Nicole Farhi, Alessi, MaxMara, Prada, Gucci, Marilyn Moore and many more.

You'll find two great markets – the **Guildhall Market**, located within a Grade II listed building in the High Street; and **Green Park Station** (www.greenparkstation. co.uk) – the first farmers' market in the UK – set in a beautifully restored Victorian railway station two minutes' walk from the city centre. In December, look out for the magical **Bath Christmas Market** next to the abbey – beginning with the switch-on of the lights – which boasts musicians and magicians as well as diverse stalls housed in traditional wooden 'chalets' (www.bathchristmasmarket.co.uk).

Cricketing legend Jack Russell is a talented artist. Born in Stroud, he now has his own **Jack Russell Gallery** in Chipping Sodbury's High Street (www.jackrussell.co.uk). Always good at technical drawing at school, he decided to try his hand at painting after being stuck in the pavilion one rainy summer day. '*My thoughts were: if Rembrandt can*

Shops line both sides of Pulteney Bridge

do it, then so can I!' he jokes. In fact, his pictures are, quite simply, superb, whether it's the Ozleworth Valley or the forge at Badminton; a powerful rhino or one of the soldiers he hero-worshipped as a lad (*We Will Remember Them*, a work commissioned by the Royal Regiment of Fusiliers, hangs in the Tower of London). *'I just enjoy painting what's in front of me. It doesn't matter if it's a steam train or cricket – it all excites me. That way you stay fresh with it,'* he says.

The best... **PLACES TO STAY**

BOUTIQUE

Queensberry Hotel

Russel Street, Bath BA1 2QF
☎ **01225 447928**
www.thequeensberry.co.uk

Tucked away in a tranquil corner just off the Circus, the Queensberry Hotel is within perfect walking distance of just about everything. It also has the qualities you would expect of a boutique hotel. Set in a town house, it offers a personal welcome, comfort and service and a fabulous restaurant.

Price: from £120 for room only.

HOTEL

Manor House Hotel and Golf Club

Castle Combe, Wiltshire, SN14 7HR
☎ **01249 782206**
www.manorhouse.co.uk

Unashamed, decadent luxury; this country house hotel, in lovely Castle Combe, has it all – including a golf course. There's even a 'pillow' menu, as well as lavender biscuits and hot milk brought to your room each night, to help guarantee a great night's sleep! The restaurant is excellent; and the 365 acres of gardens and woodlands, including the golf course, are the icing on the magnificent cake.

Price: B&B from £180.

The Royal Crescent Hotel

16 Royal Crescent, Bath BA1 2LS
☎ **01225 823333**
www.royalcrescent.co.uk

The name's a giveaway: this hotel, with its 45 individual, luxury bedrooms, is situated in one of Europe's finest 18th-century masterpieces – the Royal Crescent. There's a renowned spa and gym, fine restaurant, and beautiful gardens in which to enjoy alfresco dining.

Price: B&B from £195.

FARMSTAY

Corston Fields Farm

Corston, Bath BA2 9EZ
☎ **01225 873305**
www.corstonfields.com

This 17th-century farmhouse is a blend of old and new: stone mullioned windows on the one hand; heated by renewable energy on the other, plus all mod cons. This is an award-winning conservation farm, and there's a farm trail designed especially for guests.

Price: B&B from £90 for two.

B&B

The Bath House

40 Crescent Gardens, Bath BA1 2NB
☎ **07711 119847/01179 374495**
www.thebathhouse.org

This luxury B&B is a few minutes' easy walk to all that central Bath has to offer. Breakfast is served in your own spacious en-suite bedroom, plus numerous facilities such as Wi-Fi, LCD TV with freeview, hairdryer, fan and a generous hospitality tray with fresh milk, and email and web access.

Price: B&B from £79 for two.

GUEST HOUSE

Tasburgh House

Warminster Road, Bath BA2 6SH
☎ **01225 425096**
www.bathtasburgh.co.uk

This is the best of both worlds: close to Bath, yet with the feeling of being in the countryside. Tasburgh House is a Victorian mansion in seven acres of garden and meadow park, bordering the Kennet & Avon Canal. Ample parking, gourmet breakfasts, friendly welcome and service and Broadband wireless connection throughout. By the way, you might have seen it on the *Hotel Inspector*!

Price: from £110 for two.

The best... FOOD AND DRINK

▶ Staying in

There are some foods synonymous with Bath, of course – and top of the list has to be the **Bath Bun**. From the early 18th century onwards, Bath's healing springs turned the city into the urban equivalent of paracetamol – to be taken when aches and pains demanded it. In fact, at one time it was so full of invalids and beggars hoping for cures that the Bath Acts had to be introduced, effectively banning visitors who didn't have money in their pockets and a doctor's note legitimising their stay in the city. It wasn't just the patients who benefited, of course. Dr Oliver was one of the most eminent of 18th-century doctors – in fact, along with John Wood and Beau Nash, he helped found the Royal Mineral Hospital, one of the oldest working hospitals in the country. He's credited with the invention of the Bath Bun, originally a sort of brioche topped with crushed caraway seeds. However, Dr Oliver's patients discovered they had a side effect: vastly increased girths. Which is why the less-fattening Bath Oliver had to be hurriedly concocted in its place!

Bath buns today are made from sweet yeast dough, sprinkled with sugar and often with a sugar-lump centre. Don't confuse these with **Sally Lunn Buns**, available from Sally Lunn's in North Parade passage. It's the oldest house in Bath, and the museum there shows the actual kitchen used by the young Huguenot baker, Sally Lunn herself, when she came to the city as a refugee more than 300 years ago. The Sally Lunn bun is larger than the Bath bun and served with sweet or savoury accompaniment. Don't ask for the recipe – it's a closely guarded secret. You might also have heard of **Bath chaps**, the lower part of a pig's cheek, cured like bacon. Despite being somewhat fatty, they're served cold, like ham, and often with eggs. And just to balance the scales with

A Sally Lunn bun

a healthy alternative, there are the **Beauty of Bath apples**, first grown by Mr Cooling near Bath in 1864. They're sharp, sweet and juicy and appear early in the season.

Bath also has some fantastic food shops, such as **The House of Minerva**, a chocolaterie in Abbey Churchyard where the Belgian (what else?) owners Thierry and Philippe tempt passers-by with irresistible confectionery. Another specialist is **The Fine Cheese Company** on Walcot Street, stocking dozens of British cheeses – and it has its own coffee shop next door where you can enjoy your favourite variety made up into a sandwich with Hobbs House bread, and a glass of red wine. **Paxton & Whitfield** also has a charming cheese (and more) shop at 1 John Street. Whichever cheese shop or deli you're in, ask for the fine artisan produce of the **Bath Soft Cheese Company**, producing handmade organic cheese from their own herd. Bath Soft Cheese is full fat white-mould ripened and distinctively square in shape! It's made at Park Farm in Kelston, just outside the city, by Graham Padfield, a third-generation farmer. He began back in 1993, but used a traditional British recipe dating back to Admiral Lord Nelson who, in 1801, was sent some by his father as a gift. They also make Kelston Park, Wyfe of Bath and Bath Blue (☎01225 331601; www.parkfarm.co.uk).

Other excellent producers have stalls at **Bath Farmers' Market**, at Green Park Station in central Bath every Saturday, 8.30am–1.30pm (www.bathfarmersmarket. co.uk). Nearby **Keynsham** also has its own farmers' market on the second Saturday of each month (www.sfmdirect.co.uk/markets). Five miles east of Castle Combe is **Langley Chase Organic Farm**, which has won top awards for its lamb. They sell Manx Loaghtan, a distinguished primitive rare breed sheep, high in flavour and far lower in fat and cholesterol than commercial breeds. Food writer Tom Parker Bowles is a big fan! You can buy from the farm shop at Kington Langley (SN15 5PW; ☎01249 750095; www.langleychase.co.uk).

Chipping Sodbury has its own farmers' market on the second Saturday and last Thursday of each month, from 9am to 1.30pm. The town's High Street also is home to **Hobbs House Bakery**, one of Rick Stein's 'Super Heroes'. The range of breads, using locally milled flours, includes rye, spelt, soda and fig and walnut, which all run alongside standard wholemeal and harvester breads. All the handmade cakes are produced from scratch.

EATING OUT

FINE DINING

The Bath Priory Hotel & Restaurant
Weston Road, Bath BA1 2XT
☎ **01225 331922**
www.thebathpriory.co.uk

The Bath Priory is fine dining indeed – but that doesn't mean to say it's at all stuffy or intimidating. Head chef, Chris Horridge works closely with head gardener, Chelsea medal-winner, Jane Moore. How about some Norton St Philip spring lamb or a slow-poached beef and banana shallot with comfrey? Around £60 for dinner.

Lucknam Park
Colerne Chippenham SN14 8AZ
☎ **01225 742777**
www.lucknampark.co.uk

If you want to head out into the country to dine, try Lucknam Park, a listed Palladian mansion in 500 acres of parkland, 6 miles from Bath. The emphasis is on organic, local, and herbs from the garden. Go in season and try the game. From £65 for three courses.

RESTAURANT

Jamie's Italian
Milsom Place, Bath BA1 1BZ
☎ **01225 510051**
www.jamieoliver.com/italian

Jamie Oliver's flagship restaurant has opened in Milsom Place: dry-cured meats from a family company in Milan, free-range Devonshire Red chicken, and sustainable squid caught by a day boat on the South Coast of England. Main courses from the £10 mark.

Sally Lunn's House
4 North Parade Passage,
Bath BA1 1NX
☎ **01225 461634**
www.sallylunns.co.uk

Open for morning coffee through to dinners, Sally Lunn's is rich in local cuisine and authentic dishes, including the trencher dinner: a thick slice of bun topped by meat or fish and accompanied by seasonal veg and potatoes – a great value meal for around £10.

TEA ROOM

The Pump Room Restaurant Bath
Abbey Church Yard, Stall Street,
Bath BA1 1LZ
☎ **01225 444477**
www.romanbaths.co.uk

It's a rite of passage to take tea in the Pump Room, for this has been the social heart of Bath for more than 200 years. Traditional afternoon teas, with a trio playing violin, cello and piano in the background, can cost around £20, but you will feel spoilt!

EAT IN/TAKEAWAY

Yak Yeti Yak
12 Pierrepont Street, Bath BA1 1LA
☎ **01225 442299**
www.yakyetiyak.co.uk

A family-run Nepalese restaurant specialising in freshly cooked authentic food, freshly prepared: you can eat on traditional low tables with floor cushions, or more conventionally. The Yak Yeti Yak beef marinated in their own special blend of spices, then stir-fried with onion, sweet pepper and tomato comes highly recommended. Eat well for under £20.

🍷 Drinking

Cider, of course, is *the* Somerset drink, thanks to the wonderful apples grown in its orchards: Dabinett, Kingston Black, Yarlington Mill and Harry Masters. At one time, every large house or farm worth its salt would have produced cider. In fact, at one time it would have formed part of a labourer's pay, and farms with a reputation for tasty cider would have had the pick of the workforce. Pubs such as **The Raven** in Queen Street (BA1 1HE) and **The Salamander** in John Street (BA1 2JL), just off Queen Square serve a fearsome pint of local brew.

In the city itself, **Abbey Ales** (www.abbeyales.co.uk) proudly announces itself the first and only brewery in Bath for more than 50 years. It produces the city's top-selling cask bitter, Bellringer, made with hops from Worcester. Again, the choice of bars that serve this amber-coloured ale provide a great choice of drinking: perhaps try the Star Inn ('No games machines, no music, no pool table and no cordon bleu food menu to distract the taste buds') at The Vineyards, Off the Paragon (BA1 5NA) or the ancient Old Green Tree in Green Street (BA1 5NA), almost unaltered (to its credit) since its last 'makeover' in 1923!

The annual **Bath Ales Race day and Beer Festival** at the racecourse in August, is run by Bath Ales, a brewery in Warmley, Bristol, 10 miles north-west of Bath (www.bathales.com). It owns several pubs in the area, including the aforementioned Salamander, and a traditional country pub – The Swan – at Swineford (BS30 6LN). **Wickwar Brewing Company** (GL12 8NB; www.wickwarbrewing.co.uk), 5 miles north of Chipping Sodbury, is Gloucestershire's largest independent brewery. It uses the fresh Cotswold water in its hand-crafted process to produce an award-winning range of beers – Bob, IKB, Cotswold Way, Station Porter and Mr Perrett's traditional stout are particularly popular.

There's even a vineyard a few miles east of Bath, overlooking the Avon valley: **Mumfords** at Shockerwick Lane in Bannerdown (BA1 7LQ; ☎01225 858367; www.mumfordsvineyard.co.uk). The name derives from one-time landowner in the area, the great Simon de Montfort. One of the few vineyards in the AONB, it produces red and white wines, available from its winery (but ring first), as well as other local outlets. Madeleine Angevine and Kerner are two excellent dry white wines.

For a venue that's far from traditional, head underground – to the **Moles Club** in George Street (BA1 2EN; www.moles.co.uk). An irresistible blend of live music and DJs, it has played host to the likes of Oasis, Blur, The Cure and Snow Patrol. Meander about the area, and you'll spend plenty of happy hours discovering some local gems. There's the **Bell Inn at Lacock**, a multiple winner of the local CAMRA (Campaign for Real Ale) award (☎01249 730308), the sociable **Old Royal Ship** at Luckington, the **Portcullis Inn** in the High Street at Tormarton, Badminton (GL9 1HZ), among any others. And don't miss out on a fine pint of Adam's Ale – or water, as it's better known! **Cotswold Spring Pure English Water** at Dodington Ash near Chipping Sodbury BS37 6RX (☎01454 312403; www.cotswold-spring.co.uk) is water from the source of the River Boyd, a tributary of the Avon – the only natural bottled water the region has to offer. The water is naturally high in calcium and low in sodium. The water is also used to produce beers for the **Cotswold Spring Brewery**, on the same site (☎01454 323088). You can buy straight from the brewery, or through the website (www.cotswoldbrewery.co.uk).

ⓘ Visitor Information

Tourist information centres: Bath Tourist Information Centre, Abbey Chambers, Abbey Churchyard, Bath BA1 1LY, open Oct to May, Mon–Sat 9.30am–5pm, Sun 10am–4pm and June to Sept Mon–Sat 9.30am–6pm, Sun 10am–4pm, ☎0906 711 2000 (50p/min) or ☎+44 (0)844 847 5257 from overseas, www.visitbath. co.uk; The Sodbury Three Parishes Tourism Group, The Clock Tower, High Street, Chipping Sodbury, Bristol, Avon BS37 6AH, ☎01454 888686; Chippenham Tourist Information Centre, The Yelde Hall, Market Place, Chippenham SN15 3HL, ☎01249 665970.

Hospitals: Royal United Hospital Bath (A&E) Combe Park, Bath BA1 3NG, ☎01225 428331; Bristol Royal Infirmary (A&E), Upper Maudlin Street, Bristol BS2 8HW, ☎0117 923 0000.

Supermarkets include: Waitrose, The Podium, Northgate Street, Bath BA1 5AL, ☎01225 442550; Sainsbury's, Green Park Station, Green Park Road, Bath BA1 2DR, ☎01225 444737; Morrisons, York Place, London Road, Bath BA1 6AE, ☎01225 789617; Morrisons, Station Road, Yate BS37 5PW, ☎01454 311674; Tesco, 12, East Walk, Yate BS37 4AS, ☎0845 6779756.

Sports: Wellow Trekking Centre, Little Horse Croft Farm, Wellow, Bath BA2 8TE, ☎01225 834376/07860838788, www.wellowtrekking.com; Hacks for experienced riders: Equestrian Centre, Lucknam Park, Colerne near Chippenham, ☎01225 740556, www.lucknampark.co.uk; Lansdown Golf Club, Bath BA1 9BT, ☎01225 422138/420242, www. lansdowngolfclub.co.uk; The Park (golf) Resort, Wick, Bath BS30 5RN, ☎0117 937 1800, www.theparkresort.com; Manor House Golf Club, Castle Combe SN14 7JW, ☎01249 782982, www. manorhousegolf.co.uk; Bath Sports & Leisure Centre, North Parade Road, Bath BA2 4ET, ☎01225 486905, www. aquaterra.org/BathNES/BathSAL.

Park and ride: Newbridge, Lansdown, Odd Down to City Centre, ☎01225 394041, www.bathnes.gov.uk/ BathNES/transportandstreets/Parking/ parkandride/default.htm.

Bike rental: Bath & Dundas Canal Company, Brass Knocker Basin, Monkton Combe BA2 7JD, ☎01225 722292, www.bathcanal.com; History on your Handlebars, The Barn, Notton Park, Lacock SN15 2NG, ☎01249 730013, www.historyonyourhandlebars.co.uk.

Taxis include: Bath Taxis ☎01225 650018; V Cars ☎01225 464646; Yate Taxis, Chipping Sodbury, ☎01454 324747.

FURTHER AFIELD

Castle Combe

Lacock can recognise itself as a backdrop in the Harry Potter films, but **Castle Combe** isn't far behind. When the makers of *Stardust* wanted a picture-perfect English village of fairytale proportions, they picked breathtakingly lovely Castle Combe. With its 19th-century Butter Cross (used as a mounting block for horse riders) and old water pump, the stone cottages with leaded lights, and clematis-clad walls, it slipped seamlessly into the role. Once upon a time, the gentle Bybrook, crossed by the Packbridge, powered numerous mills – the village's wealth came from wool, and many of the pretty cottages were once inhabited by weavers. Today, the bridge is a lovely place to stand and watch a quieter world go by. Right at the end of the main village is the Roman Bridge (with a ghostly centurion who's said to haunt it); cross here and follow the path for a delightful walk through the **Bybrook Valley** to the village of Long Dean a couple of miles away. You can find out more about the village's history at the small but delightful **Village Museum** halfway up the hill between the public car park at the top and the old village at the bottom, which is manned by knowledgeable locals.

CASTLE COMBE VILLAGE MUSEUM: The Hill, Castle Combe, SN14 7HU; ☎01249 782250; museum.castle-combe.com. Entry: free but donations appreciated; open Easter to Oct 2–5pm Sun/bank holidays; please use the public car park, especially during busy times.

About half a mile north of the old Manor House – now an hotel – lie the remains of Castle Combe's castle. It's overgrown, but you can still see the earthworks on a promontory overlooking the Bybrook Valley.

The village of Castle Combe was used as a location for the film *Stardust*

The Sodburys

Ten minutes' or so drive from Castle Combe are **the Sodburys** – Little, Old and Chipping Sodbury. Lacock has the film but Chipping Sodbury can claim the author herself – well, almost. Joanne Rowling (her middle name doesn't exist; the publishers wanted to disguise the fact that she was a woman) was born in the former **Chipping Sodbury** Maternity Hospital – though it happens to be located in the next-door town of Yate. The town can also boast the widest working high street in Europe. Its elder cousin (hence the name) is **Old Sodbury**, with its Iron Age hill fort offering excellent views of the Severn Vale. It's north of the village and can be reached via a footpath from the A46. The church of Saint John the Baptist is noteworthy for its 13th- and 14th-century carved effigies of knights, and for the old bale-tombs for rich merchants in the churchyard. **Little Sodbury** is the third of the villages. In the early 16th century, William Tyndale, who translated the Bible into English, worked at the manor house as a tutor and chaplain. He's said to have started work on the translation in his bedroom here.

Dodington Park, just south of the three, is a private country home now owned by James Dyson, inventor of the bagless vacuum cleaner.

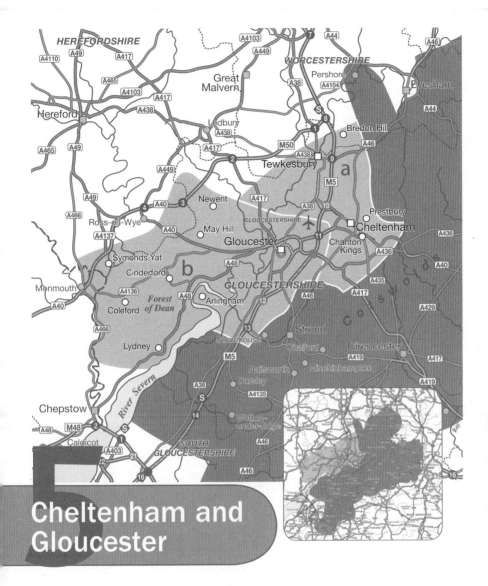

5 Cheltenham and Gloucester

a. Cheltenham and Tewkesbury
b. Gloucester and the Forest of Dean

Unmissable highlights

01 Enjoy a flutter at Cheltenham Racecourse – and hats off to you if you manage a win on Gold Cup day, p. 281

02 Considered one of the best restaurants in the country, dine at Cheltenham's Le Champignon Sauvage, owned by the Cotswolds' only two-star Michelin chef, David Everitt-Matthias, p. 290

03 Forget cider – down a pint of cyder made by Kevin Minchew at Aston Cross, Tewkesbury. '*Cyder is made from a single pressing of vintage fruit, rather like extra virgin olive oil*,' he says, p. 291

04 Experience the giddy heights of Cleeve Cloud on Cleeve Common, 3 miles north east of Cheltenham. It's Gloucestershire's highest point and a wonderful place to stroll, p. 276

05 Pay homage to Tewkesbury Abbey, a magnificent 12th-century building, saved from the purges of Henry VIII by the locals who bought it from him for £453–5s-2$^1/_2$d, p. 277

06 Stand on the banks at Stonebench, wait for the birds to fall silent and the very air to quieten around you – then listen, amazed, as the Severn Bore tidal wave rushes up the river like an express train, p. 297

07 Shop, dine or take in the museums at Gloucester Docks: after all, the city is Britain's most inland port, p. 293

08 Admire Gloucester's wonderful cathedral: either for the glorious tomb of Edward II, or for the cloisters, which doubled as the corridors of Hogwarts in Harry Potter films, p. 299

09 Try Charles Martell's Stinking Bishop cheese. Like Marmite, you'll either love it or hate it. (If you've seen The Curse of the Were-Rabbit, you'll know that Wallace and Gromit love it), p. 314

10 Trek round the Forest of Dean on a llama, camel, mule or donkey with Severnwye Llama Trekking, p. 302

CHELTENHAM AND GLOUCESTER

Cheltenham and Gloucester dominate the west of the Cotswolds. Barely 10 miles apart, they're rival cousins; the former with breathtaking Regency charms – the polite, urbane sophisticate that knows all the right people, that offers flower-rich parks, top-class shops, and a spa that once attracted royalty – and the latter is the vibrant, multi-cultural rebel that's going places.

Indeed, Gloucester's docks, once the hub of a diverse shipping industry, are now leading a revolution in city life. The warehouses are being turned into chic apartments; there's an antique centre, shops, restaurants and the award-winning National Waterways Museum. The docks also house the Soldiers of Gloucestershire Museum, dedicated to the brave men and women who have brought such honour to the region. Down past Gloucester, the River Severn winds along its flat plain. Here in the vale, many of the apple varieties once grew in orchards along the banks. Arlingham Schoolboys, Longney Russet, the Flower of the West: apples ancient and distinctive, unlike the imported tasteless fruit sold in supermarkets; apples you can still buy from farmers' markets, freshly picked from the tree, or squeezed into delicious juices and cider.

Then there's the stunningly beautiful Forest of Dean. The towns and villages of this area are like a throwback to a different age – not a genteel Regency time, or a bucolic and romantic yesterday. But to England of 50 years back, stripped of sophistication but with a real sense of community. And there's so much to do here. The forest offers fantastic cycle paths, beautiful walks, a high ropes course and water-based activities.

Cheltenham's festivals are known throughout the world: classical music, literature, science, jazz, folk, and the famous Gold Cup, highlight of the jump racing calendar. As for Gloucester, if you've never watched grown adults racing Gloucester cheeses down a hill, you've simply never lived.

CHELTENHAM AND TEWKESBURY

Cheltenham sits snugly against the escarpment, the Cotswold hills on one side, and the Malverns stretching away on the other. It's a unique town in more ways than one. First, its Regency architecture sets it apart: distinctive balconies and verandas with their decorative ironwork, the painted stucco facades, wide streets, squares and terraces. Second, despite its sophistication, the countryside is right on the doorstep. The novelist Jane Bailey grew up in the town. *'When I was young, it didn't occur to me that other people weren't so privileged,'* she says. *'I took it for granted that if I walked one way, I'd end up among cows and pigs and sheep; yet if I turned and walked the other, I'd be able to go into this wonderful cultural centre.'*

The countryside around offers pleasures such as **Cleeve Common** with Gloucestershire's highest point – Cleeve Cloud, 330m above Cheltenham. Or Leckhampton Hill which looks out across the town and the Severn Vale. The town itself provides more culture than cities twice its size, with wonderful festivals of literature, science and music – and the Gold Cup, highlight of the jump racing calendar, at the racecourse. Because of that, you'll see famous faces galore at various times of the year. **Tewkesbury**, 10 miles north, is different again. One of the best medieval townscapes in the country, it lives and breathes history. As you head still further north out of this town, you'll find the beauty of Bredon Hill. The stone buildings become fewer, and the countryside less undulating. Not the edge of the universe, certainly; but a landscape that's no longer Cotswoldian.

WHAT TO SEE AND DO

Cheltenham town
Cheltenham is a gem of a town. It's tempting to describe it as a smaller Bath – but that wouldn't do it justice. For although there are similarities – lovely architecture, interesting shops, different 'quarters', pavement cafés, an unhurried air and a sense of history – it has its own unique character.

Once upon a time, Cheltenham was considered the home of retired colonels of the empire, a fact that is still evidenced by a high concentration of quality Indian restaurants, the military precision of some of the town's parks and the unusually high quality of Indian artefacts in the museum. In more recent times, employers such as GCHQ (colloquially known as the Government spy shop) began to draw in linguists and other professionals in droves. Now there's a lively intellectual contingent who support to the hilt the fantastic theatres, museum, art galleries, festivals and other cultural events.

Spies and doughnuts: GCHQ

If someone mentions 'doughnut' to you in Cheltenham, they might be talking in code. For the chances are they're not referring to a sugar-coated snack, but to the headquarters of GCHQ, the government's electronic spy centre.

The organisation used to work from a series of small buildings dotted around Cheltenham. But in 2003, it moved to a massive new £337 million state-of-the-art building on the edge of town: circular, with a hole in the middle, it doesn't take a genius to work out why it earned the nickname The Doughnut. It does take geniuses to run it, though. The code-breaking work they carry out in here means there's even an underground road for delivering secret documents.

The public are not allowed in, but the GCHQ website (www.gchq.gov.uk), with its code-breaking challenges, is great fun for adults and children.

With its charming town houses, its historic Promenade, the squares and terraces, Cheltenham is deservedly known as England's most complete Regency town. Again like Bath, it wasn't so very long ago in the grand scheme of things that Cheltenham was simply another little backwater, quietly minding its own business. But in the 18th century, it struck gold – or rather water. For when a landowner, one William Mason, happened to discover a 'healing' spring in his field, Cheltenham won the property equivalent of X Factor. Mason's son-in-law, Captain Henry Skillicorne was the man who really turned Cheltenham into a fashionable spa town (indeed, the tiny walled water garden just behind the Town Hall is called the Skillicorne Gardens.) When George III visited the town in 1788, its transformation into an English garden city began.

View across one of the many green spaces in Cheltenham

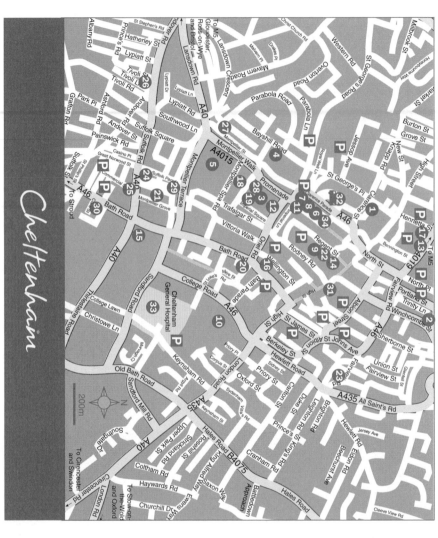

Things to see and do
1. Cheltenham Art Gallery and Museum
2. Holst Birthplace Museum
3. Imperial Gardens
4. Cheltenham Ladies College
5. Montpellier Gardens
6. Montpellier Gardens
7. Municipal Offices
8. Neptune's Fountain
9. Regent Arcade
10. Long Gardens
11. Sandford Park
12. St Mary's Church
13. Town Hall

Entertainment
14. Cineworld
15. Everyman in Regent Street
16. Cheltenham College
17. The Playhouse

Shopping
18. The Brewery

Places to Stay
19. Cheltenham Apartments
18. 32 Imperial Square

Eat and Drink
20. Bath Tavern
21. Beehive Inn
22. The Cheese Works
23. Curry Corner
24. Daffodil
25. Le Champignon Sauvage
26. Maison Chapais
27. Montpellier Chapais
28. Queen's Hotel
29. The Retreat
30. The Natural Grocery Store

Visitor Information
31. Beechwood Shopping Centre
32. Coach/bus station
33. Hospital
34. Tourist Information Centre

'Rarely have I seen such a place that so attracted my fancy,' Charles Dickens said of Cheltenham, and even today the eye rarely falls on anything but a harmonious sight, full of history, elegance and interest. Nor was Charles Dickens the only 'celebrity' to enjoy the delights of this fashionable Regency town. The Duke of Wellington, Queen Victoria, Lord Byron and Jane Austen all took the waters here.

Lewis Carroll is also associated with the area. He used to stay at a friend's house in **Charlton Kings** in the south-east 'quarter'. The three children of the family – Alice, Lorina and Edith – loved hearing the author's stories. It's still a private house but, if you were to be invited in, you'd see a large-framed mirror at the top of the stairs – the same that inspired Carroll's *Through the Looking Glass* and *What Alice Found There*.

In more recent times, **Michael Jackson** has been known to pop by. He's great friends with Mark Lester, the former child star of Carol Reed's film *Oliver!* Mark, now an osteopath, runs the Carlton Clinic in town.

One of the top public schools in the country, **Cheltenham Ladies' College**, is located in and around the Bayshill Road. The school has a great sense of tradition and history; its buildings are often on view to the public during Heritage Open Days each September. But it's also known for its innovations, such as the new Fauconberg Wing, a triumph of modern architecture. Incidentally, it's also rumoured that college girls are responsible for another phenomenon: the invention of the word Chav, supposedly shorthand for 'Cheltenham Average' – local lads with no chance of a date.

Pupils at Cheltenham Ladies College

The Promenade is a great place to shop – as well as to sightsee. At the bottom (or south end, to be precise), there's the dramatic **Neptune's Fountain**, modelled on the Trevi Fountain in Rome, showing the Roman god of the sea with sea horses and tritons. On very cold days the statue can grow some incredible icicles. Further up, outside the municipal offices, is a statue of Antarctic explorer Edward Wilson, sculpted by Robert Falcon Scott's widow Kathleen.

There is a permanent display featuring some of Wilson's work and personal effects (and a penguin!) at **Cheltenham Art Gallery & Museum in Clarence Street**. The museum also includes a collection of important Dutch 17th- and 18th-century paintings, rare Oriental porcelain and English ceramics. But it is best

CHELTENHAM ART GALLERY & MUSEUM: Clarence Street, Cheltenham; ☎01242 237431; www. cheltenhammuseum.org.uk Entry: free, donations welcome; open Apr to Oct 10am–5pm; Nov to Mar 10am–4pm; closed bank holidays; café and shop.

Edward Wilson, Antarctic explorer

Edward Wilson was born in Cheltenham at 91 Montpellier Terrace in 1872. As a day boy at Cheltenham College, he'd wander for hours in the fields around his mother's farm, The Crippetts, overlooking Leckhampton. It is said that he could not only distinguish bird calls, but that he knew exactly what the bird was doing when it made such a call.

After school, Wilson read zoology at Gonville and Caius College, Cambridge, before training to become a doctor in London. It was during a spell as a locum at Cheltenham General Hospital that he received the letter that was to change his life. Out of the blue, he was invited to apply for the post of Junior Surgeon and Vertebrate Zoologist for the forthcoming British National Antarctic Expedition. Under the command of Robert Falcon Scott, the expedition aimed to explore along the coast of the Ross Sea. Wilson got the job and spent much of his time away producing stunningly accurate art-work of Antarctic phenomena.

The next year, Wilson was one of the four men Scott picked to go with him to reach the South Pole. After terrible struggles, they got there on 17 January, 1912, only to find their great rival, the Norwegian Roald Amundsen, had got there a month before. At enormous personal expense, Wilson cared for his sick colleagues on the way back, including Lawrence 'Titus' Oates, who sacrificed himself to try to save his companions, with the words, '*I am just going outside and may be some time*'. All five died in their attempts to make it back to base, tragically just 11 miles short of 'One Ton Depot'.

In Scott's final letters, discovered by his side, there was one written to Wilson's widow, Oriana. It said, '*I should like you to know how splendid he was at the end – never a word of blame to me for leading him into this mess… I can do no more to comfort you than to tell you that he died as he lived, a brave, true man – the best of comrades and staunchest of friends.*' For more information on Edward Wilson, visit www.edwardawilson.com.

known for a world-famous Arts and Crafts collection. The Arts and Crafts movement was a reaction to the industrial revolution – it praised the craftsman, the handmade, and was inspired by nature and natural patterns. You can find out more at www.artsandcraftsmuseum.org.uk, and there's further information on p. 44.

Cheltenham's oldest building, unsurprisingly, is a church: the parish church of **St Mary's** in Clarence Street, to be exact. It dates back to the middle of the 11th century; but it also manages to include a spa theme. There's a royal coat of arms, commemorating George III's visit in 1788, as well as a memorial to Henry Skillicorne, who developed the first spa. For spa history, head for the **Pittville Pump Room** in Pittville Park (☎01242 523852). This grand-looking building owes its origins to the wealthy 19th-century entrepreneur, Joseph Pitt. You can still taste the waters here (though ring first to check it's open) via the original marble and scagliola (a paint effect) pump, though nowadays electricity powers their course from a well 80ft down. If you're feeling scrofulous, constipated or gouty the water may still do the job, but most people would recommend the nearby café instead. It serves light refreshments during the summer months (on Central Cross Drive).

The Pittville Pump Room in Pittville Park

There's a regular programme of all sorts of concerts here all year round, including during the Cheltenham Music Festival each July. It's a venue festival director Meurig Bowen rates highly: 'The acoustic of the Pittville Pump Room is a near-perfect combination of clarity and generosity of reverberation,' he says. The pump room lies within Pittville Park, where brass bands play in the summer, and which also has its own boating lake. It might not be Lake Como, but you can have huge amounts of fun, hiring a rowing boat or a pedalo.

Cheltenham takes its green spaces seriously – in fact, it's been described as a town within a park. It's a constant winner of Britain in Bloom titles for its beautiful and creative flower displays. As well as Pittville Park, there are: the **Montpellier Gardens**, in the town centre – originally one of the pleasure grounds for the spa - with tennis courts, skate ramps for skater kids, and a toddlers' play area; **Sandford Park**, off the Keynsham Road near the centre, where the River Chelt flows through; the tree-lined **Promenade** with its **Long Gardens**; and **Imperial Gardens**, by the Queen's Hotel, which boast magnificent bedding plants.

Around Cheltenham

Leckhampton Hill and **Charlton Kings Common** lie south and south-east of Cheltenham. You can park at Daisybank Road off Leckhampton Road and at Hartley Lane, near the top. Parts of the hill have been designated Sites of Special Scientific Interest because of its flora and fauna – foxes, stoats, badgers, reptiles, rare butterflies, buzzards and kestrels as well as wild flowers – and because of the fascinating geological features found there. Once these areas were worked as quarries; as a result, you'll find the thickest and most complete sections of Middle Jurassic rocks, all clearly exposed, with interpretation boards; you can also get leaflets published by the Gloucestershire

Local legends: the Devil's Chimney

The **Devil's Chimney** is a well-known local landmark – a geological feature shaped like a crooked chimney, standing on the edge of an old quarry at Leckhampton. Local legend tells that Old Nick himself once sat on this hill, throwing stones at the faithful on their way to church, until those very stones returned to bury him, trapping him beneath their vengeful weight. But if the devil isn't behind it, then perhaps mischief was. For another theory supposes it to be the creation of bored 18th-century quarry workers. If you prefer a scientific approach, the more prosaic explanation is that a tram road was cut behind it, to take stone down to the railway line.

Geology Trust (www.glosgeotrust.org.uk). You'll often find fossils too, such as the Devil's Toenail – more formally known as *Gryphaea arcuata* – an ancient oyster.

The romantically named Cleeve Cloud on **Cleeve Common**, 3 miles north-east of Cheltenham, is Gloucestershire's highest point. With its thousand acres, the common is the largest unenclosed 'wold' on the Cotswold escarpment, and the perfect place to walk – the long-distance trail, the Cotswold Way, runs across it. If you keep to the bridleways and tracks, you can ride and cycle here, and mountain boarding is even allowed on the steep front slopes above the B4632 (☎01242 251544; www.cleevecommon. org.uk).

The Devil's Chimney at Leckhampton

Take a trip in the opposite direction and, on the edge of the Cotswold escarpment is **Crickley Hill Country Park**, overlooking the Vale of Gloucester. On a clear and sunny day, it is possible to see as far as the Black Mountains. The visitor centre opens seasonally, but you can visit for free any time of year and enjoy five self-guided trails – an Iron Age hill fort trail, scrubs trail for natural history, scarp trail for geology, family trail and park trail. There are excellent walks for younger children through the woods, and a picnic/barbecue area (☎01452 425666 or ☎01452 863170). A couple of miles further on is **Great Witcombe Roman Villa** (www.english-heritage.org.uk). Beautifully positioned against the Cotswold escarpment, it's the remains of a large and luxurious villa built around AD250, with a bathhouse complex. Entry is free and it's open all year round.

Romantics should head for the village of **Coberley**, 4 miles from Cheltenham on the A435. Apart from being picturesque, its church of St Giles boasts some unique memorials, including Sir Giles de Berkeley's heart burial – the only one of its kind in the Cotswolds. This idiosyncratic knight was also allowed to bury his horse, Lombard, in the churchyard. Finally, just south of Coberley on the road to Cirencester is **Colesbourne Park** (GL53 9NP, ☎01242 870264; www.snowdrop.org.uk), named by *Country Life* magazine as '*England's greatest snowdrop garden*'. The garden was resurrected by Colesbourne's owner, Henry Elwes and his wife, Carolyn, from original plantings by an ancestor, the well-known Victorian botanist, also Henry Elwes. You can see the wonderful show of snowdrops every weekend throughout February.

Tewkesbury

Ten miles north-west of Cheltenham is Tewkesbury, famed for its medieval buildings and its place in history. In fact, the Council for British Archaeology listed it among 57 towns '*so splendid and so precious that the ultimate responsibility for them should be of national concern*'. Its timber-framed buildings, with carved

Tewkesbury museum, an example of the town's half timbered buildings

doorways, and a great maze of little alleyways behind the main street were once pits of poverty and overcrowding. Today, they're an historic delight.

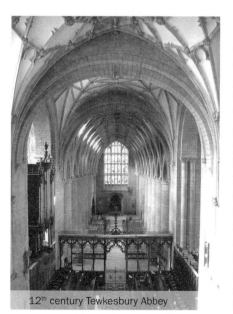

12th century Tewkesbury Abbey

In May 1471, Tewkesbury was caught up in one of the most significant battles of the **Wars of the Roses** and witnessed the fall of Henry VI and the rise of the house of York, culminating in the confirmation of Edward IV as the King of England. Inconveniently locked up in the Tower of London at the time, Henry was only present at the battle in spirit; but his poor son, another Edward, was very much there in the flesh – for a while at least. His mortal remains, slain on the battlefield, are buried in the glorious surroundings of Tewkesbury Abbey, a magnificent 12th-century building in the centre. It was saved from the purges of Henry VIII by the locals who bought it from him for £453–5s-2$^1/_2$d. They had taste: Pevsner later called its Romanesque tower 'probably the largest and finest in England'. After

The 12ᵗʰ century Tewkesbury Abbey

Westminster Abbey, Tewkesbury contains more medieval tombs than any other church in Britain. The abbey became the symbol of Tewkesbury during the summer floods of 2007 when it appeared as an island surrounded by rising waters.

OUT OF THE HAT: 100 Church Street, Tewkesbury GL20 5AB; ☎01684 855040; www.outofthehat.org.uk. Entry: adults £4.70, children £2.50, seniors £3.75, families (two adults and up to three children) £12.50 (price includes portable media players); open Mon–Sat 9.30am–5pm.

You can enjoy lovely riverside walks over the many bridges and along the banks. For a **walking information pack** (£5.95) and a **cycling companion** (£3.95), including routes, maps, and suggestions of refreshment stops call Tewkesbury TIC on ☎01684 855040. Back on dry land, there are some great places further to explore the history of the town. **Out of the Hat** is a new heritage and visitor centre, based in a beautifully restored 17ᵗʰ-century building. Learn about the life of a former owner, glove-maker Bartholomew Read – the first floor looks as it would have done in his time. The second floor

Heritage and Visitor Centre Out of the Hat

explores Tewkesbury's past. Keep watching the website, as there's a constant range of events on.

A short walk from Out of the Hat is the **Old Baptist Chapel**. Dating back to the 15th century, it's one of the oldest in England. Approaching the timber-framed building down a narrow alleyway is as near as you'll get to a medieval experience. You can request a tour round by contacting the tourist information centre on ☎01684 855040. William Hart Shakespeare, a descendant of the Bard himself, lies in the Baptist Burial Ground at the end of the alley.

A fascinating character was the author John Moore (1907–1967), a Tewkesbury man through and through whose novel *Portrait of Elmbury* was a fictionalised biography of Tewkesbury. An early environmentalist, he loved the countryside, and his life and work are celebrated in the **John Moore Countryside Museum** in Church Street. Housed in a row of 15th-century purpose-built shops, which had shutters that opened onto the street as counters, this museum includes a natural history collection with preserved mammals and birds. Part of the Alan R Jack collection of scrap-metal wildlife sculptures is also here.

> **JOHN MOORE COUNTRYSIDE MUSEUM:** 41 Church Street, Tewkesbury GL20 5SN; ☎01684 297174; www.johnmooremuseum.org. Entry: adults £1.50, students and seniors £1.25, children £1, family £4; open April to Oct Tues–Sat 10am–1pm/2pm–5pm.

Just along the road at number 45 is the **Merchant's House**, a 15th-century timber-framed building, showing how a Tudor merchant's shop and house would have looked. With the same opening times as the John Moore museum, it costs 75p per visitor.

Deerhurst

In the beautiful Anglo-Saxon church of **St Mary** in Deerhurst, you'll see carvings of the 'Deerhurst Dragon' – supposedly slain by local labourer John Smith in days of yore – at the feet of the arch at the church's western door and the chancel arch. This is one of the finest surviving and most complete buildings in England to predate the Norman Conquest, and

The John Moore Countryside Museum

much of it is believed to date back to the first half of the 9th century. A recent discovery is of a painted figure of a saint carrying a book in a veiled hand, high up in the east wall of the nave. Possibly dating back to the 10th century, it is believed to be the oldest wall-painting of any church in Britain. The font disappeared from the 12th century to the 19th century and was found being used as a cattle trough in the village. It was then married up with the base which was found at the local pub; they're now safely restored. You can find out more at www.deerhurstfriends.co.uk.

Deerhurst also has **Odda's Chapel**, built by Earl Odda in 1056, one of the most powerful Saxon nobles when Edward the Confessor was on the throne. A simple two-cell church, it's now partially incorporated into a farmhouse. Take particular note of the horseshoe arches curve in at the bottom, which is an early Anglo-Saxon feature and quite rare. It's free to visitors and open every day from 10am

The Saxon church Odda's Chapel

to 6pm in summer, and until 4pm from November to March (closed December 24/25 and January 1).

☂ Wet weather

A hidden gem is the **Holst Birthplace Museum**, dedicated to Gustav Holst, composer of *The Planets*. Holst was born in this house and lived here with his family until he was seven, when his mother died. As well as housing wonderful artefacts, such as Holst's piano, the museum includes a working Victorian kitchen and laundry, an elegant Regency drawing room and a charming Edwardian nursery. A great walker, Holst would regularly stroll from Cheltenham to Wyck Rissington where, at the age of 18, he was organist at St Lawrence's Church. Cranham, near Painswick, also featured in his life – it provided the title for the music Holst wrote for Christina Rossetti's poem, *In the Bleak Midwinter*.

THE HOLST BIRTHPLACE MUSEUM: 4 Clarence Road, Pittville, Cheltenham, GL52 2AY; ☎01242 524846; www.holstmuseum.org.uk Entry: adults £3.50, concessions £3, family £8; open 10am–4pm, Tues–Sat and some bank holidays; usually closed mid-Dec to mid-Jan; specialist CD shop.

🚸 What to do with children

Sandford Parks Lido is regarded as one of the top 10 lidos in Britain. Set in the four acres of Cheltenham's Sandford Park, it was built in 1935 and has been well restored. It's 50m long, with 10 lanes, two slides, a disabled access hoist, warm showers, café with ice creams, chips (and healthier stuff) and barbeque. It has a heated children's pool and a paddling pool, slides, its own little garden for tots and parents and baby-changing facilities.

The **Gloucestershire Warwickshire Railway** – an all-volunteer steam and diesel heritage railway – starts at the station at Cheltenham Racecourse in Prestbury (GL50 4SH) (as well as at Toddington or Winchcombe). GWR offers a 20-mile round trip through the Cotswolds, with on-train catering and special events for children and enthusiasts (☎01242 621405; www.gwsr.com). **Tewkesbury Borough Museum** in Barton Street (opposite the police station) is very child friendly, with lots of dressing-up clothes, work-sheets and quizzes. Among many other things, it tells the story of the Battle of Tewkesbury with a fine panorama of the battlefield – essential viewing before walking around the real thing.

SANDFORD PARKS LIDO: Keynsham Road, Cheltenham GL53 7PU; ☎01242 524430, www.sandfordparkslido.org.uk Entry: all-day prices adults from £3.80, concessions £2; families from £5.40 to £10, under-5s free; Apr/May to Sept open daily 11am–7.30pm, early swims in the main pool from 6.30am–9am Mon/Wed/Fri and 8–9.30am Sun.

TEWKESBURY BOROUGH MUSEUM: 64, Barton Street, Tewkesbury Gl20 5 PX; ☎01684 292901, www.tewkesburymuseum.org Entry: adults £1.50, children 75p, concessions £1, family £4; open Mar to Aug, Tues–Fri 1pm–4.30pm, Sat 11am–4pm, Sept–Oct Tues–Fri 12pm–3pm, Sat 11am–3pm, Nov to Mar, Sat and event days only.

Entertainment

Cheltenham's festivals are famous throughout the world for their imaginative programming, exciting formats and for the international 'stars' they attract as speakers. The year begins with jazz in May, followed by science in June, music in July and literature in October. Brochures are printed well in advance and are available online at cheltenhamfestivals.com. You do need to pre-book individual events on the box office number 0844 576 7979.

Horse racing

One of the biggest events of the equestrian calendar is held at **Cheltenham Racecourse**, the home of jump racing, each March: The Festival, featuring the legendary totesport Cheltenham Gold Cup. Over the course of the week, around 260,000 people attend and more than £500 million-worth of bets are made. Nor is the entertainment confined to the track. You'll find trade stands, music, food and drink aplenty. Cheltenham also hosts The Open each November, the first major meeting of the jump racing season.

CHELTENHAM RACECOURSE: Cheltenham GL50 4SH; ☎01242 513014; www.cheltenham.co.uk Entry: tickets for The Festival in Mar begin at £18, and for The Open in Nov from £8.

The racecourse couldn't have a more scenic location – in a natural amphitheatre just below Cleeve Hill. Edward Gillespie has been managing director here for more than a quarter of a century. Of the racecourse itself, he says, '*Everyone who comes here acknowledges it has a special vibe that works on the subconscious. I don't know whether it's to do with the hill or with things that have happened in the past; but there's a heartbeat about the place.*' The racecourse has a Hall of Fame, charting steeplechasing history from 1819, open Monday to Friday, entry free, all year round. Other events from concerts to antique fairs take place at the Centaur, the racecourse venue, throughout the year.

Other sports

Cheltenham Cricket Festival takes place each July/August at Cheltenham College, another of the town's public schools. This is the longest-running cricket festival in the world on an outground, and it's seen the likes of W G Grace, Wally Hammond and Gilbert Jessop playing during its illustrious past (☎0117 9108000; www.gloscricket. co.uk).

From spring through to autumn, visit **Prescott Speed Hill Climb**, (GL52 9RD; ☎01242 673136; www.prescott-hillclimb.com) just outside Cheltenham. Here you'll find one of the world's most prestigious motor racing venues in a glorious setting – on a 60 acre Cotswold estate. Major motor racing championships are held here, as well as a host of classic car and bike weekends.

One of the newest attractions takes place at Christmas when **Skate at Cheltenham** opens its indoor skating rink in Montpellier Gardens, under the cover of a large marquee. Prices for sessions, which run Tuesday to Sunday from late November to

Motor racing venue Prescott Hill Climb

early January, are £5 for children, £6 for adults and £15 for families, including skate hire. You can buy on the day or book in advance at www.skatecheltenham.co.uk.

Music and theatre

There are three theatres in Cheltenham: **The Playhouse** in Bath Road where talented amateurs regularly put on superb shows (☎01242 522852; www.playhousecheltenham.org); the **Bacon Theatre**, based at Dean Close School (GL51 6HE; ☎01242 258002; www.bacontheatre.co.uk); and the **Everyman** in Regent Street (GL50 1HQ, ☎01242 572573; tickets.everymantheatre.org.uk) stages ballet, opera, drama, dance, comedy, music events and traditional family pantomime throughout the year. The main auditorium is a Victorian architectural masterpiece, designed by Frank Matcham. Poet Pam Ayres is patron of the theatre's friends' organisation. *'It's circular, so when you stand on the stage, you feel as if you're being hugged,'* she says.

Cheltenham Town Hall provides a year-round entertainment venue

Other great entertainment venues include **Cheltenham Town Hall** and the **Pittville Pump Room**, which both offer year-round entertainment programmes, varying from stand-up comedy to classical music (☎0844 5762210; www.cheltenhamtownhall.org.uk). The website will also tell you about the town's annual **Folk Festival** in February.

Tewkesbury entertainment

-Tewkesbury recreates its historic battle in the form of a spectacular **Tewkesbury Medieval Festival** each July, the biggest of its kind in Europe, complete with medieval

Battle recreation at the Tewkesbury Medieval Festival

fair. And just to make absolutely sure in between times, the battlefield society puts on regular historical Battlefield Walks, showing all the important sites (www.tewkesburymedievalfestival.org). At the end of July, Tewkesbury Abbey hosts the **Musica Deo Sacra**, an annual celebration of religious choral music by choristers from all over the country (☎01684 850959; www.tewkesburyabbey.org.uk).

Tewkesbury's **Awaken Your Senses** in September is designed to tickle everyone's fancy with theatre, dance, music and light entertainment (www.awakenyoursenses.org).

Many of the events take place at the **Roses Theatre** in Sun Street (GL20 5NX; ☎01684 295 074; www.rosestheatre. org), which offers a year-round eclectic mix of live performances and arthouse cinema. It was in this theatre that comedian Eric Morecambe collapsed in 1984, after giving a charity performance. He died shortly afterwards in Cheltenham General Hospital.

The Tewkesbury Water Festival

Also in September, there's the **Tewkesbury Water Festival**, with events on the river, including an evening display of brightly lit boats, while in October, there's the **Mop Fair**, one of the oldest fairs in the country. Once a 'hiring' fair where people would try to find jobs, it's now a great excuse for a fun fair (www. tewkesburyfairsociety.co.uk). At Christmas, the town looks at its best, beautiful decorations brought to life in the **Festival of Lights**. Tewkesbury also has a festive **ice rink** at the Abbey Lawns Car Park in December; ring Tewkesbury Tourist Information Centre on 01684 855040 or log onto www.outofthehat.org.uk for all event details.

Fairground rides at the Mop Fair

LOCAL KNOWLEDGE

Donna Renney, who lives in the nearby village of Naunton where she was brought up, is chief executive of Cheltenham's festivals, which have gained international acclaim. The science festival each June has been described as the best in the world; the music festival in July is one of the oldest in Europe; while the October literature festival constantly breaks its own box office records, with high-profile speakers from Michael Palin and Ian Hislop to Helen Mirren and Robert Harris.

Best restaurant: The Daffodil in Suffolk Parade. The décor is so unusual and it's the kind of place where you can have an experience to suit the person you're with. If you want to be private, you can sit in one of the big seats upstairs; or you can choose to join in with everyone else. The Monday jazz nights are a particular favourite of mine.

Best thing about the area: Cheltenham Farmers' Market (on the second and last Friday of each month). I never saw a supermarket until I was 12! Food came from the village or we produced it ourselves. We made our own butter with milk from the house cow; we had our own lamb, and a big vegetable garden.

Best pub: The Beehive Inn in Montpellier Villas. It's got a really wonderful atmosphere – almost intellectual, though you certainly don't have to be an intellectual to go there!

Cheltenham's best-kept secret: The inside of the Town Hall, in Oriel Road – it's stunning. Someone once perfectly described it as being like a wedding cake. At the moment, you have to attend an event to get to see it, but I'd like to find a way of opening it up to everyone.

Most underrated Cotswold asset: Cheltenham Jazz Festival. People don't associate jazz with the Cotswolds, and British people in general are nervous of it; they think it's going to be difficult when, actually, it's one of the most accessible experiences.

Favourite takeaway: The Curry Corner in Fairview Road. You can dine in or out at this fantastic Bangladeshi restaurant.

🛒 Shopping

Even the arcades in Cheltenham seem to have character. In the Regent Arcade in Regent Street (www.regentarcade.co.uk) – just off the High Street – you'll find the **Wishing Fish Clock**, created by the artist Kit Williams who wrote the book *Masquerade*. A masterpiece of artistry and design (the working parts were made by local clockmaker Michael Harding), you'll find people stopping to stare every time it strikes: every half hour the fish blows bubbles (to the tune of *I'm Forever Blowing Bubbles,* of course). Further up the High Street is the **Beechwood Shopping Centre** with its cascading water features (www.beechwoodsc.co.uk).

There's a continental feel to Cheltenham, particularly in Montpellier and 'The Suffolks'. The former, with its street cafés and pubs, was originally designed to supply spa tourists with luxury goods. That tradition continues today with speciality shops and boutiques. Five minutes from the town centre, the buildings are distinguished by their Grecian charm: instead of pillars to support the shops of Montpellier Walk, the architects imaginatively employed Caryatids, female figures based on the Acropolis in Athens. The Suffolks, meanwhile, is unique, with its antique shops, crafts, shops and cafés, based around Suffolk Square complete with bowling green. Cosmo Fry (a descendant of the famous 'Fry's Chocolate' family) and his girlfriend, the designer Lulu Anderson, own Cheltenham's Big Sleep hotel: '*We love going to Brosh, a restaurant up in The Suffolks. That area of Cheltenham feels like Clifton in Bristol or Notting Hill: village-y, with interesting boutiques.*'

Cheltenham's newest area is **The Brewery** off St Margaret's Road (www.thebrewerycheltenham.co.uk) with shops, eateries and a Cineworld cinema (☎0871 2002000; www.cineworld.co.uk). Tewkesbury also has a good range of interesting shops you just won't find elsewhere, such as **JW Jennings**, the Oriental rug specialist in Church Street (www.jenningsrugs.co.uk). Clare Jennings not only travels the world to find the rugs, she also fundraises to help needy groups of people she comes across in the countries she visits, such as Pakistan.

The best... PLACES TO STAY

BOUTIQUE

Thirty Two

32 Imperial Square, Cheltenham, Gloucestershire GL50 1QZ
☎ 01242 771110
www.thirtytwoltd.com/stay

This boutique B&B has the 'Wow!' factor. Overlooking Imperial Gardens, it's one of a listed Regency terrace and provides a quiet and exclusive place to stay, yet all within two minutes' walk of the town's top shops, restaurants and bars.

Price: B&B and parking from £150 to £215.

HOTEL

Cowley Manor

Cowley, Cheltenham GL53 9NL
☎ 01242 870900
www.stayatcowleymanor.com

This quirky hotel's traditional exterior belies the humorous and contemporary interior. The hotel is out in the country, with 55 acres of grounds, and a great spa with indoor and outdoor pools. The 'posh comfort' food is organic and locally sourced where possible.

Price: B&B and spa from £250 per room.

The Greenway Hotel

Shurdington Cheltenham GL51 4UG
☎ 01242 862352
www.thegreenway.co.uk

The Greenway offers a luxury country house experience just a short drive from the town centre. Eleven of the bedrooms have undergone a full refurbishment, succeeding in capturing the historical spirit of The Greenway while injecting a taste of modernity and contemporary stylishness. This beautiful Elizabethan manor was a favourite stop-over of the late Queen Mother when she visited for Gold Cup Week.

Price: B&B from £145/£175, single/double.

Tewkesbury Park Hotel, Golf and Country Club

Lincoln Green Lane, Tewkesbury GL20 7DN
☎ 01684 295405
www.foliohotels.com/tewkesburypark

A Victorian manor house with an 18-hole golf club, set in 176 acres of parkland, this hotel is high on the hills above Tewkesbury, with lovely views. There are excellent facilities, including an indoor pool, spa pool, steam room, squash and tennis courts.

Price: B&B and dinner from £64 pppn.

SELF-CATERING

Cheltenham Apartments

16 Montpellier Spa Road, Cheltenham GL50 1UL; ☎ 01780 460407
www.cheltenhamapartments.co.uk

There are six fully furnished and equipped apartments, centrally located in Montpellier, two minutes' walk from the town centre. The apartments, which vary from one bedroom to three, have all the facilities you'd expect, including satellite TV and free WiFi.

Price: from £120 per night min stay, two nights.

Deerhurst Holiday Cottages

Abbots Court Farm, Deerhurst, near Tewkesbury GL19 4BX; ☎ 01684 275845
www.deerhurstcottages.co.uk

This 230-acre organic dairy farm lies on the banks of the River Severn in the historic village of Deerhurst. Created from the former cart shed, there are two fully equipped cottages, with patio and garden area.

Prices: from £220 for the cottage for two per week; and from £305 for the cottage for four

The best... FOOD AND DRINK

▶ Staying in

One of the best new farm shops on the block is **Primrose Vale Farm Shop and PYO** (GL51 4UA, ☎01452 863359, www.primrosevale.com) on the Shurdington Road just outside Cheltenham. Open daily, the shop stocks fruit and vegetables produced on the farm, and other local fare, including game, fantastic cheeses, and ready meals, soups, quiches and tarts made in the on-site kitchen. In season, you can pick your own strawberries raspberries, loganberries, currants and gooseberries, and vegetables including runner beans and sweetcorn, and pumpkins in the autumn.

At 150–156 Bath Road, Cheltenham, the **Natural Grocery Store** (GL53 7NG; ☎01242 243737; www.naturalgrocery.co.uk) offers the best natural and organic food (with home delivery, if required). You'll find an excellent range featuring Fairtrade, vegan, vegetarian, dairy-free and no-added-sugar products. Ranges include drinks, baby products, household, personal care and supplements. Cheltenham also has a choice of delicatessens and specialist food shops. **The Cheese Works** (5, Regent Street; ☎01242 255022; www.thecheeseworks.co.uk), owned by Masterchef finalist Ben Axford, is recognised as one the UK's finest cheesemongers, while **Maison Chaplais** (52 Andover Road (☎01242 570222; www.maisonchaplais.com) is run by Maurice Chaplais, is an internationally renowned master baker, as well as an expert on delicatessen produce.

Tewkesbury has long been famous for **Tewkesbury mustard**, a blend of mustard and horseradish, which made the town hot stuff in the 16th century. Shakespeare even mentioned it in Henry IV: '*his wit was as thick as Tewkesbury Mustard*'. Try a jar made by Cotswold company Kitchen Garden (www.kitchengardenpreserves. co.uk), which is based on a traditional recipe. It's well worth searching out the **1471 deli** at 101 Church Street, Tewkesbury (☎01684 291471) where the range of cheeses and meats shows how passionate the owners are about food. Also try the **asparagus** from **Bangrove Farm** at Teddington near Tewkesbury (GL20 8JBT; ☎01242 620697), which is ready from late spring onwards every year.

Tewkesbury's Food and Drink Festival

Both Cheltenham and Tewkesbury have their own **annual food festivals**. Cheltenham's is held in the summer in Montpellier Gardens (www.garden-events. com). There's also a farmers' market (www.cheltenham.gov.uk) from 9am to 3pm on the second and last Friday of the month (though December's can vary) by the Long Gardens on the Promenade. Tewkesbury's Food and Drink Festival is the largest and most well established in Gloucestershire. Taking place on the first bank holiday weekend in May, it includes a cookery theatre, food hall, craft hall, kids' cookery and more.

Bredon Hill

Beautiful **Bredon Hill** is a massive outcrop of Cotswold rock, standing on its own and peaked by a small tower named Parson's Folly – once a summer house for an 18th-century MP. Thanks to millions of years of erosion, it looks out of kilter to the rest of the land around it, in the flatter plains of the Vale of Evesham. It's now been designated a Special Area of Conservation and a National Nature Reserve because of its importance as one of the best wildlife sites in England.

Meadows Lamb at Home Farm in Bredon's Norton nestles on the slopes of Bredon Hill. The farm started with its renowned turkeys more than 50 years ago and have now added sheep, beef cattle and pigs. The farm shop opens Thursday to Saturday from 10am to 5pm (GL20 7HA; ☎01684 772322; www.meadowshomefarm.co.uk).

An excellent way to sample other foods produced on and around the hill is by visiting the website of **Bredon Hill Foods** (☎01386 710447; www.bredonhillfoods.co.uk). All the foods from wine to honey, which are available on line and mail order, are grown or made within a 15 mile radius. Lucy Rollett, who runs the business, also makes Nurses Cottage elderflower cordial and pressé at home from flowers picked on the hill. '*It grew from my passion for Bredon Hill,*' she says. '*People love walking up it; I wanted them to be able to taste it and take it home, too.*'

EATING OUT

FINE DINING

Le Champignon Sauvage
**24–26 Suffolk Road,
Cheltenham GL50 2AQ
☎ 01242 573449
www.lechampignonsauvage.co.uk**

Considered one of the best restaurants in the country, never mind Cheltenham, this is a place for people who are serious about their food. Heston Blumenthal and Gordon Ramsay are both fans of the Cotswolds' only two-star Michelin chef, David Everitt-Matthias, who runs the restaurant with wife, Helen. Expect to pay around £30 for a three-course lunch and around £50 for dinner.

Corse Lawn House Hotel
**Corse Lawn GL19 4LZ
☎ 01452 780771
www.corselawn.com**

Set in an elegant Queen Anne building, this hotel is owned and run by the Hine family of Cognac fame. All the food is homemade and English/French in style; and there's a choice between the popular bistro and relaxed restaurant. Corse Lawn majors in game, fish and local produce, with set menus between £20 and £35 for a three-course meal.

RESTAURANT

The Daffodil
**18–20 Suffolk Parade,
Cheltenham GL50 2AE
☎ 01242 700055
www.thedaffodil.com**

The cinema origins of this fantastic art deco venue are still apparent with interiors designed by Laurence Llewelyn-Bowen. It's hard not to be tempted by local fare such as Gloucestershire sirloin steak au poivre with hand-cut chips and roasted vine tomatoes. Many mains around £16; good value set lunch menus. Do catch one of the Monday Jazz Nights.

GASTRO PUB

Reservoir Inn
**London Road, Charlton Kings,
Cheltenham GL54 4HG
☎ 01242 529671
www.thereservoirinn.co.uk**

Run by Andrew and Susan Proctor, who've worked with Heston Blumenthal, and overseen by top chef Martin Blunos, the food is local and of the finest quality. Whether you're ordering bangers and mash or a wild game suet pudding, you'll find both excellent. Expect to pay £6 for a soup and sandwich or around £22 for a three-course meal.

TEAROOM

Queen's Hotel
**Promenade, Cheltenham GL50 1NN
☎ 01242 514754
www.mercure.com**

In the past, some famous names have stayed at this hotel, including Edward Elgar, Arthur Conan Doyle and various royals. The impressive Regency-style hotel is at the heart of the town, overlooking the Imperial Gardens at the top of the Promenade. Have a very English afternoon tea, with a perfect view from the windows.

EAT IN/TAKEAWAY

Curry Corner
**133 Fairview Road,
Cheltenham GL52 2EX
☎ 01242 528449
www.thecurrycorner.co.uk**

It might be tucked out of the way, but discerning diners know where to find this, one of England's oldest Bangladeshi restaurants. Carefully sourcing local ingredients to create authentic dishes, chef Shamsul Krori and daughter Monrusha use more than 16 types of freshly ground herbs and spices to create real masala. Dishes are from as little as £7.95

\boxed{} Drinking

Once upon a time, just about every landowner in the area – indeed, in the country – would make their own cyder. 'Cyder' refers to the drink you make with the first pressing of apples. It's when the pulp is re-pressed and mixed with water that you get 'cider' – and this is brew that would have been given to agricultural workers.

Kevin Minchew is a true cyder-maker who founded **Minchew's Real Cyder and Perry** in 1993 at Aston Cross, Tewkesbury. '*Cyder is made from a single pressing of vintage fruit, rather like extra virgin olive oil*,' he says. '*That first pressing gives a concentrated intense liquid*.' In other words, Kevin's award-winning drinks – that he creates on a simple second-hand press – come straight from apples newly picked from local orchards. You can ring Minchews on 0797 403 4331 (www.minchews. co.uk; visiting strictly by appointment), or buy the cyder and perry (made from pears) at various outlets, including the Beehive Public House in Montpellier, Cheltenham (GL50 2XE), as well as delis and farmers' markets. Other favourite Cheltenham drinking places include:

- **Bath Tavern** GL53 7JT; ☎01242 256122 – with its great atmosphere
- **The Retreat** GL50 2AB; ☎01242 235436 – a fun wine bar in Suffolk Parade
- **Montpellier Wine Bar** GL50 1SY; ☎01242 527774

To check out other top venues – especially for a night out – visit www.furryfeet.tv, an interactive video tour.

Battledown Brewery, Cheltenham's oldest working brewery, in Keynsham Street (GL52 6EJ), is open to the public for sales. Check out the beers on the website (www.battledownbrewery.com) or call them on 01242 693409/07734 834 104.

A favourite amongst real ale enthusiasts is the **Royal Oak at Prestbury** (GL52 3DL; ☎01242 522344). With its ghostly cavalier and spectral Black Abbot, Prestbury is said to be one of the most haunted villages in England – and the Royal Oak is situated in The Burgage – the oldest and most spooky street of them all. You'll find local rugby boys such as Mike Tindall enjoying a drink here. ...Further out, in Cockleford near Cowley, is the **Green Dragon** (GL53 9NW; ☎01242 870271), with its roaring log fires, beams, and stone-flagged floors. You'll get a very decent meal here, as well as a fine pint.

In Tewkesbury, drink in history alongside your tipple. **Ye Olde Black Bear Inn** (☎01684 292202), built in the High Street in 1308, is said to be the oldest inn in Gloucestershire, while the **Royal Hop Pole Hotel** (☎01684 293236) in Church Street was mentioned by Dickens in *The Pickwick Papers*. The 17th-century **Bell Hotel** (☎01684 293293), also in Church Street and once the guest house for the abbey, is positively youthful in comparison.

On the banks of the River Severn near Tewkesbury is **The Boat Inn**, Ashleworth (GL19 4HZ; ☎01452 700272). This pub – which can flood in winter – is an unspoilt, tranquil haven that has been in the same family since it was granted a licence by Charles II. Beers are served direct from the cask.

ℹ Visitor Information

Tourist information centres:
Cheltenham Tourist Information Centre, 77 Promenade, Cheltenham GL50 1PJ, ☎01242 522878, www.visitcheltenham.com, open Mon–Sat 9.30am–5:15pm, Wed 10am–5.15pm, public holidays 9.30am–1.30pm; Tewkesbury Tourist Information Centre, Out of the Hat, 100 Church Street, Tewkesbury GL20 5AB, ☎01684 855040 (24 hour answerphone), www.visitcotswoldsandsevernvale.gov.uk, open Mon–Sat 9.30am–5pm, Sun (Easter to Sept) 10am–4pm.

Hospitals: Cheltenham General Hospital, Sandford Road, Cheltenham GL53 7AN, ☎08454 222222; Tewkesbury Hospital, Barton Road, Tewkesbury GL20 5QN, ☎01684 293303 (nurse-led minor injury/illness cover with GP support when necessary, from 8am–8pm).

Supermarkets Include: Cheltenham: Waitrose Food and Home, Honeybourne Way GL50 3QW, ☎01242 241425; Sainsbury's, Tewkesbury Road GL51 9RR, ☎01242 222011; Tesco, Colletts Drive GL51 8JQ, ☎0845 6779161 and the High Street ☎0845 6779151; Morrisons, Up Hatherley GL51 4UA, ☎01242 862660; Tewkesbury: Tesco, 4–6 Bishops Walk GL20 5LQ, ☎0845 6779670; Morrisons, Ashchurch Road GL20 8AB, ☎01684 273261.

Sports: Leisure@Cheltenham, Tommy Taylors Lane, Cheltenham GL50 4RN, ☎01242 252515; Cascades Leisure Centre, Oldbury Road, Tewkesbury GL20 5LR, ☎01684 293740; Tewkesbury Sports Centre, Ashchurch Road GL20 8DF, ☎01684 293953; Cotswold Hills Golf Club, Ullenwood, Cheltenham GL53 9QT, ☎01242 515264, www.cotswoldhills-golfclub.com; Tewkesbury Park Golf & Country Club, Lincoln Green Lane GL20 7DN, ☎01684 272320; Hilton Puckrup Hall, Tewkesbury GL20 6EL, ☎01684 296200; Sherdons Golf Centre, Manor Farm, Tredington GL20 7BP, ☎01684 274782; Tennis courts, Montpellier Gardens and Pittville Park, Cheltenham, ☎01242 250019; Woodlands Riding Stables & Livery Yard, Glebe Farm, Wood Stanway, near Winchcombe, Cheltenham GL54 5PG, ☎01386 584404, www.woodstanway.co.uk.

Bike hire: Compass Holidays, Cheltenham Spa Railway Station, Queen's Road GL51 8NP ☎01242 250642, www.compass-holidays.com.

Taxis Include: Starline Taxis, Cheltenham, ☎01242 250250; Avonside Taxis, Tewkesbury, ☎01684 292580.

GLOUCESTER AND THE FOREST OF DEAN

Neither Gloucester nor the Forest of Dean is in the Cotswolds. But if you're going to explore the Cotswold region, then you're already on the doorstep of this interesting city and, let's face it, it could be considered simply rude not to call in. If you do take that courteous route, you'll find yet another set of reasons to curse '60s planners (why, oh why did they concrete over a magnificent historic city?); but you'll also discover a phoenix rising from its ashes.

Gloucester is the most inland port in Britain, with history dating back to Roman times. The docks area has been revitalised into shops, museums, restaurants, and a place to watch a bit of maritime action where you'd least expect it. The Norman cathedral is one of the most magnificent you'll see anywhere, and there are numerous other bits of history, if you only take the time to look for them. Glance at the main streets, and you'll see some hideous shop fronts; take a moment to look past them, and you'll be rewarded. Off Westgate Street, for example, is medieval Maverdine Lane, with a magnificent 16th-century merchant's house – the largest and finest timber-framed building in England, HQ to Colonel Massey during the Siege of Gloucester in the Civil War.

Around 10 miles from Gloucester begins the ancient Forest of Dean, first designated for hunting by the Saxons. When Norman kings moved their winter court to Gloucester, hunting in the nearby Dean was an important reason why. And thus the Domesday Book came to be ordered at Gloucester Cathedral. Occupying an area of more than 200sq miles, with 20 million trees, the Forest is sandwiched between the valleys of two great tidal rivers – the Severn and the Wye. It's a fantastic place to walk, cycle and ride. But there are also some more unusual pursuits on offer: canoeing, diving, caving, climbing, zip wire, archery and fishing, among others.

The River Severn, of course, defines this whole area: it has provided for Gloucester for centuries, and helped carve out the very countryside the city sits upon. It's famous for its bore – a great surge of a wave that's a truly exceptional natural phenomenon.

WHAT TO SEE AND DO

Gloucester docks

Stand on the streets of the city of Gloucester and look out across the Severn to the Forest of Dean, and you'll see a view identical to that which composer and poet Ivor Gurney saw as a cathedral chorister more than a century ago. In fact, if you were to take away the cars, the First World War poet would still feel a kinship and familiarity with the beautiful and ancient college green where his beloved Norman cathedral stands. But were he to be spirited back, Gurney would certainly be amazed by the

Gloucester

The revitalised Gloucester docks

sight of the modern-day **Gloucester Docks**. At the height of maritime trade, tall ships would wait patiently for hours to unload their cargoes of grain and timber. And their rag-tag crews of sailors from the world over would strain at the leash, desperate to explore the numerous alehouses the city had – and still has – to offer, including the haunted **New Inn**, where tragic Lady Jane Grey is said to have been proclaimed Queen of England.

The docks are the hive of a different type of industry today. Gone are the burly tattooed dock workers; in their stead are besuited young executives who've snapped up the warehouses as lifestyle apartments.

A good way to explore the docks is to take a **guided walk**, courtesy of Gloucester Civic Trust, with a qualified guide. Tours of the docks, which last around an hour, begin at the Mariner's Chapel and tours of the city centre from outside the tourist information centre in Southgate Street.

You can also enjoy a ghost walk exploring Gloucester's spookier side (www.gloucesterghostwalks.co.uk).

GLOUCESTER CIVIC TRUST GUIDED WALKS: ☎01452 396572; www.gloucestercivictrust.org.uk Entry: adults £2.50, children free; tours of the docks from mid-Jun to mid-Sept, as well as Easter (Fri/Sat/Sun/Mon) and Sat/Sun/Mon of the bank holidays on May Day, late spring and early summer, pre-booking not necessary; tours of the city centre from mid-Jun to mid-Sept – booking essential.

Foolish 1960s developers came close to ruining the historic city with their concrete monstrosities. Nowadays the sympathetic reworking of the docks represents what's

The award-winning National Waterways Museum

best in town planning. This area is leading a revolution where city life in Gloucester is newly chic. The warehouses have not only been turned into housing, but offices, an antique centre, shops, restaurants and the award-winning **National Waterways Museum**. Interactive exhibits, quizzes, and original canal boats tell the story of the UK's inland waterway network from the 18th century to the present day. There is also a café, and boat trips along the Gloucester & Sharpness Canal.

NATIONAL WATERWAYS MUSEUM: Llanthony Warehouse, Gloucester Docks, Gloucester GL1 2EH; ☎01452 318200; www.nwm. org.uk. Entry: adults £3.95, children £2.75, family £12; open Apr to Oct 10am–5pm (daily) and Nov to Mar 11am–4pm (Sat/Sun only).

The docks (www.gloucesterdocks.me.uk; gloucesterdocks.visit-gloucestershire. co.uk) house a shrine to the city's pride and joy; for the **Soldiers of Gloucestershire Museum** is dedicated to the brave men and women who have brought such honour to the region. It tells the story of these soldiers and their families in peacetime and war during the last 300 years, with life-size displays, sound effects, archive film and computer

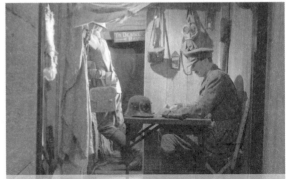

An exhibit at the Soldiers of Gloucestershire Museum

The Severn Bore

The Severn Bore is a tidal wave that sweeps up the river in an awe-inspiring wall of water on a good day – or in a barely perceptible ripple at other times. A bore works on a funnel effect. The Atlantic races up through the Bristol Channel, joining the Severn Estuary, which then gets narrower and narrower. As the leading wave flows in, the water behind is pushing up until, at Newnham, the proper bore is formed and continues for 10 miles to Gloucester.

The bore takes place a couple of days after the full or the new moon. To get a good one (around 6ft), three things have to be right: the barometric pressure; the wind force and direction; and the amount of water in the river. It has been known to reach 2m in height, and its average speed is 16kmph. The Severn Estuary experiences the second highest tide anywhere in the world (first is the Bay of Fundy in Canada), and the difference between the lowest and highest tide in any one day can be more than 14.5m.

Good bores are hard to predict, though March and October tend to be the best months. Keep your eye on bore predictions – the Environment Agency issues leaflets and there's a helpful website (www.environment-agency.gov.uk/regions/midlands/434823). As far as viewing is concerned, the safest place is Minsterworth, because it very rarely comes over the bank. Stonebench is the most spectacular: the road is lower than the river bank so, before you know it, the water is in your car!

There's a great website on the Severn by local expert Chris Witts at www.severntales.co.uk.

games. Discover why Gloucestershire was the only British regiment to have both front and back cap badges.

Historic Gloucester

Charles Dickens once described Gloucester as a '*wonderful and misleading city*', words that ring true today. It's easy to see the modern inroads life has made, with the high street chains that abound here – no-one can accuse Gloucester of a lack of shopping facilities. But look up, around, behind. Careful exploration reveals the roots of this historic city have not all been lost. Traces still remain of its time as a Roman fort, a Saxon town and a Norman stronghold.

To establish a town at Gloucester, Romans were encouraged to retire here, and old timber barracks – used by the invading army – were converted into shops and houses. These new colonists were given a plot of land in the countryside, as well as a house in the town. By the second century, Gloucester – or Glevum as it was known – had a forum, baths, and a basilica. Even today, the names of its main streets – Northgate, Southgate, Eastgate and Westgate – reflect the Roman layout of the town, for they were once gateways through the protective fortress walls.

> **SOLDIERS OF GLOUCESTERSHIRE MUSEUM:** Custom House, Gloucester Docks, Gloucester GL1 2HE; ☎01452 522682; www.glosters.org.uk. Entry: adults £4.25, concessions £3.25, children £2.25, family £13; open every day 10am–5pm (including bank holidays) mid-Mar to end-Oct and Tues–Sun 10am–5pm Nov to Feb.

Novel connections

Literary buffs come to Gloucester to explore its many 'novel' connections, including the fact that the fictional Tom Jones stayed at the Bell Inn, and Long John Silver was based on one-legged W E Henley, born in Gloucester in 1849. Henley's daughter, Margaret, was the inspiration for another famous character. The family was friends with *Peter Pan* author J M Barrie whom Margaret named 'my fwendy'. While the fictional Wendy grew up, Margaret died of cerebral meningitis aged just 5.

Harry Potter fans flock to the **Gloucester Cathedral** cloisters, which doubled as the corridors of the Hogwarts School of Magic for the recent films – a fact that delighted the pupils of The King's School, who were invited to appear as extras.

Gloucester was one of only three colonia in Britain, which was the highest rank of city, self-governing and with similar rights to those of Rome itself. You can see impressive Roman sculpture, including votive tablets, tombstones and an ornament that may have come from one of Gloucester's earliest theatres, at the **Gloucester City Museum and Art Gallery** in Brunswick Road, ☎01452 396131. It's open daily, admission free, from Tuesday to Saturday, 10am–5pm, all year round. While in an underground display outside Boots in Eastgate Street, you can see glimpses of the defences and the East Gate of the city, dating from around AD68.

GLOUCESTER FOLK MUSEUM: 99–103 Westgate Street, Gloucester GL1 2PG; ☎01452 396467; www.gloucester.gov.uk/museums. Entry: free; open Tues–Sat 10am–5pm.

Moving swiftly on in time, Westgate Street's **Gloucester Folk Museum**, in Tudor timber-framed buildings, provides an intimate glimpse into social history. Here lies the past, not seen through the eyes of kings and statesmen, but via the relics of the ordinary people who experienced its joys and discomforts, from the medieval shoemaker who once worked on this very spot, to the seed drills of the overburdened farm labourer. Gloucester has always been a good

Local legends: the real Scrooge?

At Gloucester Folk Museum, you can learn about notorious Gloucester folk such as **Jemmy Wood**, born in 1756, who took over the family business of the Gloucester Old Bank in Westgate Street. Wood was the richest commoner in England: when he died, he left an estate valued at £900,000. But he was such a miser, his clothes were valued at just £5. He once walked to Westbury-on-Severn, where he owned some land. When he began to fill a bag with his own turnip crop, he was beaten by a farm worker who mistook him for a tramp. He was so famous that he was the subject of Toby Jugs and cartoons. The story goes that some people would heat up coins if they knew he was coming, then spread them on the floor to see if he'd pick them up. It's even claimed that his miserly ways inspired Charles Dickens to create the character of Ebenezer Scrooge in *A Christmas Carol*.

place to seek employment – why Dick Whittington ever left is a mystery (Dick, of course, was born at Pauntley, just down the road).

Gloucester Cathedral (☎01452 528095; www.gloucestercathedral.org. uk), tucked away in College Green off Westgate Street, was founded 1,300 years ago. It's a haven – almost a parallel universe – miles away in spirit from the busy streets alongside. Among other treasures, you'll see medieval glass, and the tomb of Edward II, described by Pevsner as '*a work of genius*'.

There are other religious sites well worth seeing in the city, including the statue of **Bishop Hooper** in St Mary's Square: the martyr was held in what is now Gloucester Folk Museum and burned alive in front of his own cathedral for 'heresy' by Mary Tudor. There's **St Mary de Lode Church** on Archdeacon Street, with its Norman tower; **St Oswald's Priory** in St Oswald's Road, probably the oldest upstanding building in the city, built by the last

Gloucester Cathedral provided the setting for Hogwarts in the *Harry Potter* films

One of the most complete surviving friaries of the Dominican 'black friars'

Llanthony Secunda Priory

King of Mercia Aethelred II, and his formidable wife, Lady Aethelflaed in about 890; **Blackfriars** (www.english-heritage.org.uk), one of the most complete surviving friaries of Dominican 'black friars' in England, in Ladybellegate Street (open any reasonable time; entry free); and the **Llanthony Secunda Priory** in a park in Llanthony Road,

Defiant Gloucester

King Charles I was in confident mood in the summer of 1643 – indeed, it had been dubbed the 'Royalist summer' because of the run of successes he'd had. In fact, Charles seemed on the very point of victory in the bloody battle he'd started against his own Parliament. Soon after the fall of Cirencester, the Parliamentary stronghold of Gloucester was next on the King's list. This was a valuable port, with access to arms from abroad; and its fidelity would provide an easy route to his staunch supporters in Wales and Cornwall, as well as to the riches of the Forest of Dean with its timber and iron. But the King had miscalculated if he thought this would be another swift victory. He arrived outside the city on 10 August, 1643, and waited… and waited. The month before, the great city of Bristol had surrendered to him; surely Gloucester could not hold out?

The King hadn't reckoned on the defiance of the governor, Colonel Massey, who urged the citizens on to build up Gloucester's defences. 'And we imployed some time in lining of the house adjoyning to the north gate with earth, and in amending and strengthening the works about the Fryar's barne,' wrote John Dorney, the town clerk, in his diaries. While Charles and his army languished in the fields round about, there was help on its way for the besieged city. When the Earl of Essex and his men pitched up from London on 5 September, it wasn't a moment too soon: Massey had only three barrels of gunpowder left. Defeated, the King and his army slunk off to the Cotswold hills.

a ruined outer court of an Augustinian priory, now used for special events (www.gloucester.gov.uk).

Forest of Dean

The Forest is still Gloucestershire – but it's a very different Gloucestershire from the sophistication of Cirencester or Cheltenham. Its market towns – **Coleford, Cinderford, Lydney and Newent** – are faintly old-fashioned yet vibrant, at the same time. There have been relatively few incomers into the area – house prices have tended to stay far lower than elsewhere in this prosperous county; which means the locals are still very much in evidence. It's the natural beauty of the area that so captivates above all. Oak, beech, larch, ash, birch and holly trees abound, with sheep wandering freely, plenty of deer, and even wild boar (though it's rare to see them in the open in daylight).

You can walk, drive or cycle around the **Royal Forest Route** that takes you on a 20-mile tour through the heart of this country. For more details see www.royalforest.info, or phone 01594 812388 (Coleford Visitor Information Centre) for a copy of the map.

Beechenhurst Lodge, at Speech House Road near Coleford (GL16 7EG; ☎01594 822612), formerly the site of Speech House colliery is the ideal base for a family day out with walking trails, superb cycle rides, play area, and a recently extended restaurant, plus a new visitor information centre and shop, showcasing local produce and gifts. It's also the start of the Forest's **Sculpture Trail**, a free walk through the woods, open daily from dawn to dusk, featuring permanent works of art (www.forestofdean-sculpture.org.uk). Leaving from Mallards Pike (near Blakeney GL15 4JP), you can take a **trek,**

'Place' – a sculpture on the Sculpture Trail in the Forest of Dean

with qualified guide, by llama, camel, mule or donkey, who'll carry all your provisions and kit for the day. First, you'll be given a handling demonstration; then the route will take you from the lakes at Mallards Pike, through woodland glades and other picturesque spots (☎01291 621593/07929 372933; www.severnwyellamatrekking.co.uk). Or take an hour's carriage drive, pulled by a team

Trek through the Forest of Dean on a llama, camel, mule or donkey!

of mules, if you prefer (pre-booking essential). Mules were the traditional working animals of the Forest and, during industrial times, the area's main transport.

Whatever time of year you visit the Forest of Dean, you'll find something to enjoy outside. In spring, the woods are carpeted with bluebells; in summer, you can picnic at the **Cannop Ponds** outside Coleford, home to mandarin ducks and dragonflies; in autumn, the Forest is magical: golds, russets, oranges and browns beyond belief, along with fruits, fungi and berries. And in winter, without leaves to block the view, you can see, it seems, for ever.

Lydney Park Spring Gardens in Lydney Park (GL15 6BU) are particularly beautiful, with magnificent displays of rhododendrons and azaleas in this wood-land garden. There's an important Roman temple site, excavated in the 1920s by the eminent archaeologist Sir Mortimer Wheeler, who mentions JRR Tolkien as an advisor. Underneath the site were

Cannop Ponds, outside Coleford

tunnels and early open-cast iron mines which, after the Romans had left, local people thought were the homes of little people and hobgoblins, and they named it Dwarf's Hill. Some people believe it was this very hill that gave Tolkien the inspiration for *Lord of the Rings*. The gardens, Roman camp and Roman museum are generally open from late March until early June on Sundays, Wednesdays and bank holiday Mondays, plus Sunday to Thursday in May (adults £4, children 50p); other days are possible, but phone the office for details on 01594 842844.

The **Forest of Dean Model Village, Gardens and Adventure Play** is in the same area; visitors can see miniature versions of local attractions and model trains, beautiful gardens and sculptures, plus there's a play area with bouncy castle, play houses, picnic area and café. Look out for seasonal events, such as Easter egg hunts and Christmas Winter Wonderland.

Westbury Court Garden, owned by the National Trust, is the only restored Dutch water garden in the country. It's said to be home to England's oldest evergreen oak, along with many other 16th- and 17th-century trees and shrubs.

There are some particularly stunning viewpoints in the Forest: **Symonds Yat Rock** where in summer months the peregrine falcons nest among the cliffs, and where a ferryman pulls his passenger ferry across the river using an overhead rope, and **May Hill**, which heralds the dawn of May Day each year with a celebratory dance by Morris men. And there's the village of **Soudley**, south of Cinderford, with the **Blaize Bailey viewpoint**.

WESTBURY COURT GARDEN: Westbury-on-Severn GL14 1PD; ☎01452 760461; www.nationaltrust.org.uk/westburycourt. Entry: adults £4, children £2, family £10.50; open Mar to Jun, Wed–Sun 10am–5pm; daily in Jul/Aug 10am–5pm; Sept/Oct, Wed–Sun and bank holiday 10am–5pm.

FOREST OF DEAN MODEL VILLAGE, GARDENS AND ADVENTURE PLAY: Old Park, Lydney Park Estate, Aylburton GL15 6BU; ☎01594 845244. Entry: adults £5.95, children £4.95, family £16.95; open 10am–6pm (summer) and 10am–5pm (winter).

Westbury Court Garden

Dymock Poets

Between 1911 and 1914, a group of six poets – Lascelles Abercrombie, Rupert Brooke, John Drinkwater, Robert Frost, Wilfrid Wilson Gibson and Edward Thomas – would gather in the village of Dymock, 4 miles south of Ledbury, and walk and talk together, taking inspiration from places such as May Hill in the beautiful countryside surrounding them. Abercrombie, Frost and Gibson all lived in the area; the others were merely visitors. Yet their attachment to the landscape and the strength they drew from each other had an indelible impact on their work. They even published their own quarterly, *New Numbers*, which contained poems such as Brooke's *The Soldier*: '*If I should die, think only this of me:/ That there's some corner of a foreign field/ That is forever England*'.

There are two circular walks from Dymock that take in landmarks associated with these poets, including their houses (though they're not open to the public). There's another path you can follow leading through the area's wild daffodils, for which it is famous. The leaflet, *A Walk in Dymock Woods,* details these routes and is available from local tourist information centres. The village of Kempley holds a special **Daffodil Weekend** each March (www.greenway.clara.net/daffodils). It's also a chance to hear lectures about St Mary's Church in the village, which has 'the most complete set of Romanesque frescos in northern Europe'.

The University of Gloucestershire in Cheltenham keeps the Dymock Poets Archive, including manuscripts, letters and photographs. Visit www.glos.ac.uk/archives or call 01242 714851 for details.

Soudley is where you'll find the **Dean Heritage Centre**. It's an excellent place for the whole family. This museum, which details the history of the Forest of Dean, is situated by a millpond in a wooded valley, with woodland walks, an adventure playground and a picnic site. The museum specialises in social and industrial history, with a beam engine, forester's cottage, and mill pond with ducks.

Dean Heritage Centre

DEAN HERITAGE CENTRE: Camp Mill, Soudley, Glos, GL14 2UB; ☎01594 822170; www.deanheritagemuseum.com. Entry: adults £4.90, children £2.50, concessions £4.20, family £14; open daily including bank holidays Mar to Oct 10am–5pm; open daily including BHs Nov–Feb 10am–4pm except Dec 24-26; open New Year's Day 11am–4pm.

Clearwell Caves is a combination of a natural cave system and some of Britain's oldest mine workings, dating back well over 4,500 years. These impressive caverns were created by generations of Forest people who made their living by mining iron ore and ochre. There's a working blacksmith on site, and various events throughout the year: caving for all ages, including children; spooky Hallowe'en storytelling, and a fantastic annual Father Christmas experience.

CLEARWELL CAVES: Near Coleford GL16 8JR; ☎01594 832535; www.clearwellcaves.com Entry: adults £5.50, concessions £5, children £3.50, family £16; open Feb to Nov daily 10am–5pm; caves also open during Dec for 'Christmas Fantasy' – check the website for prices and other details.

A tour through Clearwell Caves

Families with slightly older children will revel in **Puzzlewood**, 1 mile south of Coleford on the B4228 (it's not accessible to buggies and pushchairs, nor are dogs allowed in). It's a unique experience with 14 acres of weird and spectacular scenery through which an intriguing maze was built during the 1800s. The surrounding land is a working farm with Highland cattle, miniature Shetlands, donkeys and wildfowl. There's an indoor maze for children, an adventure play area, tea room and gift shop.

PUZZLEWOOD: Perrygrove Road, Coleford, GL16 8QB; ☎01594 833187; www. puzzlewood.net. Entry: adults £4.80, children £3.40, family £15; open Easter–end Oct 10am–5.30pm, Oct 11am–4.30pm daily, also open Feb half term.

The intriguing maze of Puzzlewood

🌂 Wet weather

One thing you'll learn from the Dean Heritage Centre (see above) is the importance of mining: it's been carried out in the Forest for thousands of years – coal and iron ore. **Hopewell Colliery** is a coal mine that's now also a museum. You can take an underground tour with a former miner as a guide and experience life in the very colliery that William Smith, the father of geology, once oversaw. You might come across the term 'Free Miner' in the Forest: this was a right granted from the 13th century onward. To become a Free Miner, you had to be male, over 21 years old, born within the hundred of St Briavels and to have worked in a mine for a year and a day. Free Miners had the right to mine anywhere in the Forest, except under churchyards, gardens and orchards.

HOPEWELL COLLIERY: Speech House Road Cannop Hill, Coleford GL16 7EG; ☎01594 810706/832216. Entry: adults £4, children £3; open daily during school holidays from Easter to Sept 10am–4pm; café and shop.

Three miles north of Gloucester is the **Nature in Art Museum** at Twigworth, where you can see artists at work, enjoy the sculpture garden and relax in the café. It's the world's first museum dedicated exclusively to fine, decorative and applied art inspired by nature, all housed in a Georgian mansion. Beautifully situated, it's a treat for adults as well as artistically minded children.

NATURE IN ART: Wallsworth Hall, Twigworth, Gloucester GL2 9PA; ☎01452 731422; www.nature-in-art.org.uk Entry: adults £4.50, children and seniors £4, family £13; open Tues–Sun and bank holidays 10am–5pm, closed Dec 24–26.

CELEBRITY CONNECTIONS

Lady Edna Healey is long used to being passed over in favour of her famous husband: the extravagantly eye-browed former Chancellor of the Exchequer. Yet here is an Oxford-educated woman of no mean intellect; a teacher, lecturer and author of several outstanding biographies. Born in Coleford in 1918, Edna Edmunds – as she was then – was a child of the old Forest, a world defined and limited by the natural boundaries of the rivers Severn and Wye. Anyone from beyond was a 'foreigner'. It was a gritty place of rough reality, where miners would come home with the lines on their skin etched into bold relief by the dark artistry of coal dust; where the lavatories were outside and the Saturday night baths were in the kitchen. '*In my childhood, there was no drinking water laid on; it had to be brought in pails from a standpipe. Water for washing came from the iron pump over the stone sink in the back kitchen.*'

Of course, Edna and Denis have long been settled in East Sussex, but the Forest is never far from her thoughts. '*I was very lucky in that I've always had a deep sense of roots; and that means that you can go wandering wherever you like but your roots will hold you,*' she says, with great pride. '*The poet, Leonard Clarke, was a great friend. Once, when he came and had tea with me, I showed him my little London garden and I told him, "Underneath that apple tree, I'm going to plant daffodils, and I've got bluebells underneath there; and there's a bank with some violets..." 'And he looked at me and said, "And where are you putting the bracken?" He could see exactly what I'd done. I'd recreated the Forest of Dean.*'

⟋ What to do with children...

Gloucester

Start unlocking the city's secrets by following a quiz trail at www.gloucesterquest. info – a great fun way to enjoy a walk round. If the children get the answers right, they'll eventually come to the **House of the Tailor of Gloucester**: '*For behind the wooden wainscot of all the old houses*

> THE BEATRIX POTTER MUSEUM AND SHOP: 9 College Court GL1 2NJ; ☎01452 422856; www.tailor-of-gloucester.org.uk. Entry: free; open Mon–Sat 10am–4pm and Sunday, noon until 4pm.

in Gloucester, there are little mouse staircases and secret trap-doors; and the mice run from house to house through those long narrow passages...' wrote Beatrix Potter, in her famous story about the mice who helped a poor tailor.

Strangely for a city, there's plenty of 'wildlife'. In Albany Street, Tredworth (GL1 4NG), the heart of the city, there's **St James City Farm**, where children can experience hands-on contact with sheep, goats, pigs, rabbits, ducks and geese. Animals are fed throughout the day, and there are places to picnic. Entry is free, and the farm is open from the first Saturday in March until the end of November from 10am–4pm daily, except Sundays, when it's closed (☎01452 305728).

A little way out of Gloucester at Hempsted, is the **Barn Owl Centre** – a rescue centre, which also focuses on education and conservation, it has barn owls, falcons and hawks, all in need of a little tenderness. Based on a farm, it's currently being developed into a nature reserve. Although its only regular opening day is Sunday, there are special events throughout the year.

> THE BARN OWL CENTRE: Netheridge Farm, Netheridge Close, Hempsted, Gloucester GL2 5LE; ☎01452 383999; www.barnowl. co.uk. Entry: adults £5, children £3, concessions £4.50, family £10; open Sundays only 11am–5pm.

Two miles south of Gloucester, off the A4173, are an amazing 250 acres of countryside with wonderful walks and views: **Robinswood Hill Country Park** on Reservoir Road (GL4 6SX; ☎01452 304779). Local schoolchildren frequently come on trips here because it's such a good place to learn about the country with its waymarked nature, geology and horse trails. There's a proper working rare breeds farm on site where children can learn about farm animals. It's open every day of the year, and entry is free; the car park closes at dusk.

The Forest

The Forest is one big playground for families (though, of course, it should be treated with respect). There's a waymarked 17km circular **Family Cycle Trail**, which is traffic free. The trail is specially surfaced and suitable for all ages and abilities (it's a very gentle ride; for serious cyclists, there is a designated 4km single-track area behind the Pedalabikeaway cycle centre, GL16 7EH, with technical sections). As the family trail follows the (flattish) old railway line, you will see traces of the area's industrial history including former coal mines, collieries and railway stations. To hire cycles call Pedalabikeaway on 01594 860065 (www.pedaabikeaway. co.uk), where you can buy a route card for 60p or a more detailed map for more serious cyclists or those wanting to explore the Forest fully, at £2.99. (The route cards are also available from Beechenhurst Lodge (GL16 7EG) and the visitor information office in Coleford High Street (☎01594 812388).

Cycling in the Forest of Dean

The list of outdoor activities available is literally and metaphorically breathtaking. Parts of the Wye are swift enough for **white water kayaking**; there's **climbing**, **diving**, **caving**, **archery**, **paintballing**, **shooting**, and much more. For more information, visit www.active.visitforestofdean.co.uk or request a leaflet from Forest tourism (☎01594 812388). Especially popular are the **high ropes courses**, Go Ape! where you'll find rope bridges, Tarzan swings and zip slides up to 40ft above the forest floor. Under-10s or children under 1.4m are not allowed, and under-18s must be accompanied by a participating adult.

For toddlers and children up to the age of 10, the **Dick Whittington Farm Park** has indoor and outdoor fun, with soft play, aquarium and reptile room, small pets, a chicken shack, Shetland ponies, deer and animal farms, pedal karts and nature trails.

The National Birds of Prey Centre at Newent is one of the finest birds of prey centres in the country, home to some 170 birds of prey, including 25 species of owl and 22 species of eagle, hawk and falcon. It holds twice daily flying demonstrations, and has a coffee shop and picnic areas.

Other attractions include **Elton Farm Maize Mazes**, open daily from mid-July to

GO APE!: Mallards Pike Lake, near Blakeney, Forest of Dean, GL15 4HD (but check website for directions); ☎0845 643 9215; www.goape.co.uk. Entry: adults from £25, children (10–17) from £20; generally open Feb half term, Mar to end Oct, weekends throughout Nov but check website; last admission 3hrs before dusk; prebooking essential.

DICK WHITTINGTON FARM PARK: Blakemore Farm, Little London, Longhope GL17 0PH; ☎01452 831000; www.dickwhittington. org. Entry: adults and over 10s £5, seniors and children under 3 £4.50, children (3–10) £5.50; open daily 10am–5pm.

NATIONAL BIRDS OF PREY CENTRE: Newent GL18 1JJ; ☎0870 990 1992/01531 820286; www.nbpc.co.uk. Entry: adults £8.50, seniors £7, children £5.50, family £23; open daily 10.30am–5.30pm from Feb to end Oct (or dusk in winter).

Zip slide at Go Ape!

One of the steam railways in the Forest of Dean, the Dean Forest railway

early September, 10.30am–6pm. Each year has a different theme, such as pirates, and superheroes and villains (GL14 1JU; ☎079263 77110; www.eltonfarm-leisure. co.uk). There's also a mountain board centre on site (www.redhillextreme.co.uk).

There are two steam railways in the Forest, which both get visits from Santa at appropriate times of the year. **The Dean Forest Railway** can take you to Parkend for the Forest, to Lydney town, and to Lydney Junction from where you can walk to see the restored harbour. There's a 24-hour railway information line at ☎01594 843423 and a website: www.deanforestrailway.co.uk.

The Perrygrove Railway and Treetop Adventure is fun both on and off the rails. Set in 20 acres, there's an indoor village with secret passages and hidden treasure boxes, four stations, each with paths through ancient woods, and a riddle to solve. New for 2009 is a treetop adventure, suitable for all ages. There are plenty of places to picnic, and you can have as many rides as you like on the trains. Coleford centre has its own **Great Western Railway Museum** housed in a GWR goods shed of 1883 and open on Saturdays 2.30–5pm all year round for the museum and mini train ride (☎01594 833569; www.colefordgwr.150m. com).

PERRYGROVE RAILWAY & TREETOP ADVENTURE: Perrygrove Road, Coleford GL16 8QB; ☎01594 834991; www. perrygrove.co.uk. Entry: family ticket should be less than £20; open Sat/Sun from Easter to Hallowe'en and most days during local school holidays, but check website.

For a full list of attractions and activities, visit the Forest of Dean tourism website at www.visitforestofdean.co.uk, which will also supply brochures on request.

... and how to avoid children

Take a spin in a vintage biplane, such as a Tiger Moth or a modern aerobatic trainer, with **Tiger Airways** (☎01452 854141; www.tigerairways.co.uk). Flights allow you to experience flying the biplane for yourself. You'll take off from Gloucestershire Airport at Staverton (between Gloucester and Cheltenham), and flights cost from £95. Staverton was once the home of the famous Gloster Aircraft Company; its most famous employee was Frank Whittle, who developed the first jet engine. In fact, the first jet flight happened in Gloucestershire.

Entertainment

Held every Spring bank holiday, the **cheese rolling** at Cooper's Hill, Brockworth, just outside Gloucester is simply madness in cheese form. Crowds gather at the top of Cooper's Hill, which, from a spectator's point of view, has wonderful views; or, from a competitor's angle, a fearsome gradient: 1-in-2 in places and 1-in-1 in others. It's almost impossible to remain upright when running down it. And why would you? To chase a seven-pound Double Gloucester cheese, of course. At the end of this event of break-neck speed, the winners receive a cheese, while others receive neck braces from paramedics. But they still come back year after year.

No one is sure of the history of this event, though it possibly lies in fertility rites or hopes for a good harvest. It was certainly well established even in the early 19th century (www.cheese-rolling.co.uk). Cheese rolling isn't the only bizarre cheese custom practised in this area: there's **St Briavels Bread and Cheese Dole** at the church of St Mary the Virgin, St Briavels, in the Forest of Dean. After the evening service on Whit Sunday, small pieces of bread and cheese (or 'dole') are thrown into the air from large baskets, to be caught by waiting parishioners. Just don't ask for mustard. It's another historic custom, this time originating with King John.

Gloucester holds festivals throughout the year, including the **Gloucester Festival** with its carnival, free concerts, huge funfair in Gloucester Park and fireworks; and at Christmas, Kings Square in the city centre is turned into an **ice rink**. Find out more from the 'Freetime' pages at www.gloucester.gov.uk. Every three years, the **Three Choirs Festival** comes to Gloucester. It's an international classical music event the city shares with the cathedral cities of Hereford and Worcester. Each August, you'll find choral and orchestral music at its best, with varied programmes performed by world-class artists (www.3choirs.org).

For rugby fans, there's The Shed, Gloucester Rugby Club's famous home stadium in Kingsholm. As well as regular games, the club participates in a **Gloucester Festival of Rugby** each September (www.gloucester.gov.uk). Of the many country shows, the event held at Frampton-on-Severn is one of the best. Thousands of people flock to **Frampton Country Show** in September, with heavy horses, falconry, a clay shoot, fishing exhibitions and gun dogs (www.framptoncountryfair.co.uk).

The Forest of Dean has a plethora of events throughout the year. The popular **Coleford Carnival of Transport**, at Easter time, attracts all sorts of vehicles from classic cars to military vehicles (www.colefordcarnivaloftransport.co.uk), while the **Dean Outdoors Festival** provides local residents and visitors with the chance to sample some of the leisure pursuits and sports on offer throughout the Forest: archery, laser battlesports, caving, mountain biking, tree climbing, walking and more (www.active.visitforestofdean.co.uk).

Among Gloucester's theatres and other entertainment venues, the **Guildhall** in Eastgate Street has to be one of the most diverse and lively in the area, with cinema, concert hall, theatre, galleries, workshops and a café-bar (www.gloucester.gov.uk). There's a **Cineword cinema** at The Peel Centre, St Ann's Way, Bristol Road GL1 5SF (☎0871 2002000; www.cineworld.co.uk).

Shopping

Gloucester is changing. **Gloucester Quays** is a new £400 million designer outlet at Gloucester Waterfront plus a food store, bars, cafés, restaurants and leisure facilities open June 2009 (www.gloucesterquays.co.uk). Nearby, in the Victorian Docks, you'll find specialist and individual shops, including the five-storey **Gloucester Antiques Centre** in one of the old warehouses. Open daily, it hosts more than 100 different dealers (www.gacl.co.uk).

At 23 Westgate Street, there's the **Made in Gloucestershire** shop (madein gloucestershire.co.uk), where 95 different craftsmen and women from throughout the county sell their wares, from jams and preserves, pottery, wood, textiles and silver jewellery to decorative objects for the home and garden.

The Forest of Dean is particularly good for craft shops. **Harts Barn Craft Centre** is on the Monmouth Road, Longhope (GL17 0QD; ☎01452 830954). Formerly a Norman hunting lodge, it now houses an array of craftsmen and women such as a master stone carver and letter-cutter, a curtain-maker, blacksmith, jeweller, and an artist with gallery and studios. There's plenty of parking, plus the old dairy tea room which serves homemade cakes, Sunday lunches and more besides. **Taurus Crafts** at The Old Park, Lydney (GL15 6BU; ☎01594 844841; www.tauruscrafts.co.uk) is a social enterprise and a training and trading centre for the Camphill Village Trust, supporting adults with special needs. The craft shop offers an array of original crafts, designer gifts, home interiors, quality toys, jewellery and more. Visitors can even throw their own pot, which will be fired ready for collection later. In Newent is **Cowdy Gallery** (31 Culver Street, GL18 1DB; ☎01531 821173; www.cowdygallery.co.uk), one of the UK's largest independent glass galleries.

The best... **PLACES TO STAY**

HOTELS

Ramada Bowden Hall Gloucester

Bondend Lane, Upton St Leonards, Gloucester GL4 8ED; ☎ 0844 815 9095 www.ramadajarvis.co.uk

This Regency-style hotel is based in an 18th-century manor with 12 acres of woodland, country gardens and a lake. There's a good restaurant, a health club with pool and sauna, and the rooms have broadband internet access. Bikes are available for guests, and the hotel's 18-hole golf club and dry ski slope are 1.5 miles away.

Price: doubles from £70 including breakfast.

Speech House Hotel

Coleford, GL16 7EL; ☎ 01594 822607 www.thespeechhouse.co.uk

This hotel is simply one of the great Forest landmarks, and perfectly placed to make the most of the area. For hundreds of years, it has held the Verderers' Court (the last remnant of traditional Forest administration). Most rooms have lovely views of the surrounding area, and some have four-poster beds.

Price: B&B from £65/£98, single/double.

FARMSTAY

Dryslade Farm

English Bicknor, Coleford GL16 7PA ☎ 01594 860259 www.drysladefarm.co.uk

One of few B&Bs to earn an AA Highly Commended, Dryslade Farm is a 184 acre mainly beef cows and calves farm with 20 acres of woodland. Guests are welcome to wander around the buildings, fields and woodland, and the farm is close to forest tracks for walking and mountain bike rides.

Price: doubles from £30 per person.

B&B

Deanfield

Folly Road, Parkend, Lydney GL15 4JF ☎ 01594 562256

Once home to the local quarry master, this family B&B backs onto the lovely Nagshead RSPB nature reserve with its walking and cycle trails. It's also perfectly located to catch a steam train! You can stay B&B or there's a coach house here, too, for self-catering.

Price: doubles from £32 per person, including breakfast; coach house from £380 per week.

SELF-CATERING

The Coach House

Almshouse Road, Newland, Coleford ☎ 01594 832808; www.craigdam.net

The lovely village of Newland, whose 13th-century church is known as the Cathedral of the Forest, is the setting for this well-appointed coach house with open fire.

Price: from £375 per week.

UNUSUAL

English Holiday Cruises

Alexandra Warehouse, The Docks, Gloucester GL1 2LG ☎ 0845 601 7895/01452 410 411

For something a little different, English Holiday Cruises run a six-day trip on board the MV Edward Elgar, all the way up the River Severn from Gloucester to Stourport, which includes a trip on board the Severn Valley Railway. All meals are freshly prepared by the resident chef.

Price: full river cruises cost £495.

The best... FOOD AND DRINK

▶ Staying in

There's a wealth of produce available from this area. Cheeses, apples, plums, Gloucester sausage, Old Spot pork, and much more – make the most of it by calling in to delis, the village shops that sell local food, and the many farm shops whenever you see them, as well as using the farmers' markets – Gloucester's is every Friday in the city centre; in the Forest, there's one at Lydney on the last Wednesday of the month.

A great place to start is Rob Keene's **Over Farm Market** (GL2 8DB; ☎01452 521014; www.over-farm-market.com) – in fact, it's almost a day out. There are animals to visit, trailer rides, pick your own, as well as the shop itself. Much of the produce is grown on the farm, much of the rest is local. Susie Keenan runs **Shepherd's Farm Shop** at Three Shires Garden Centre, near Newent; ☎01531 828590; www.shepherdsfarmshop. co.uk. '*We're based in an area called The Scarr which, historically, has always been a real horticultural hotspot,*' she says. '*When the Forest miners came back from the war, the mines had gone, so the government gave many of them seven-acre plots around here. As a result, there grew up lots of market garden businesses. There are a couple of growers still based on The Scarr and they are supplying us. They bring their produce in to me every day – and I've other people who bring me in vegetables from their own gardens. So buying from here is as good as growing it yourself!*'

Another gem is **Hunter & Todd Delicatessen & Wine Shop** at Newnham-on-Severn (☎01594 516211; www.hunterandtodd.co.uk), with a great range of local and international produce.

When you think of the River Severn, however, there has to be one kind of food that springs to mind before all others – even if your reaction is to shudder! Elvers. Because of the high prices they now command, this local delicacy is mostly sold abroad. But a great way to experience fish at its best is to visit **Severn and Wye Smokery** in Chaxhill, Westbury-On-Severn (GL14 1QW; ☎01452 760190; www.severnandwye.co.uk), the home of smoked salmon. As well as Gloucestershire and Forest of Dean foods, you can buy fresh wild salmon, fresh farmed salmon, Scottish smoked salmon, organic salmon, smoked wild salmon, fresh fish, fresh seafood, smoked fish and smoked poultry. Watch the smoked fish being processed, and eat in the restaurant.

The Forest Food Showcase (www.visitforestofdean.co.uk) is the perfect way to catch local food producers in one place at the same time. Held in the autumn at the Beechenhurst picnic site in the heart of the Forest, it includes cookery demonstrations, talks, tasting sessions, a producers' marquee and music. More unusual is the **Newent Onion Fayre**, with roots dating back to the 13th century. It's the largest one-day festival in the county and (perhaps unsurprisingly) the only one in the world dedicated to onions. Held each September, it's a mix of music, dance, craft, funfair, entertainment and, of course, eye-watering onion-eating competitions

Stinking Bishop

It has been said of Charles Martell, 'his whole farm is a testament to the rich agricultural heritage of Gloucestershire' – but you're more likely to know of his cheese than the man himself. For Charles makes the famous **Stinking Bishop**, which was featured in the Wallace and Gromit film, The Curse of the Were-Rabbit. This award-winning cheese lives up to its name with its challenging aroma – you wouldn't want to take it too far in a car on a sunny day – but actually its title derives from the variety of pear used to wash the curds before they're ladled into moulds. This wonderful cheese is far from Charles's only achievement. When he moved to his farm in Dymock in the Forest of Dean in 1972, he already had a keen interest in Gloucester rare breed cattle. At that time, only 68 remained in the world. Thanks to his work over the next few years, he was almost single-handedly responsible for rekindling interest and getting the breed back onto a surer footing. Not only that: he and his first wife can take credit for resurrecting Single Gloucester cheese in 1978. Before then, it had become extinct.

Charles has also worked his magic on another native attribute: the region's ancient apple and pear varieties. In 1989, he set up England's National Collection of Perry Pears at Malvern's Three Counties Showground, and the Gloucestershire Apple Collection. This apple-tree collection is kept on land near Cheltenham owned by Gloucestershire County Council, but there are duplicates all over the place, including some on Charles's own farm.

So which achievement is he most proud of? 'Making Stinking Bishop: 90 percent of people think it's disgusting, but 10 percent of 60 million is enough for me.'

Charles Martell is patron of the Gloucester Cattle Society. For more information, visit www.gloucestercattle.org.uk

(www.forest-online.co.uk/newent.html). **Taurus Crafts**, mentioned in the shopping section, holds an annual **Living Food** celebration in autumn, where people are encouraged to reconnect with food and nature: book on to one of the fantastic mushroom hunting expeditions (www.tauruscrafts.co.uk).

Remember the insanity of the cheese rolling? Well, those cheeses are made by Diana Smart at **Smarts' Traditional Gloucester Cheese** at Old Ley Court, Chapel Lane, Birdwood, Churcham (☎01452 750225). She makes Double and Single Gloucester cheese traditionally, with milk from the farm's cows, using a recipe that's been handed down through a family for generations. She also makes 'Harefield', the Gloucester version of Parmesan. You can buy from various outlets or mail order from www. smartsgloucestercheese.com. Nor should you miss out on **Ruddle Court Cheese**, on a dairy farm overlooking the Severn. These soft cheeses are made with milk from their own Friesian cows at Newnham (GL14 1DY; ☎01594 516304; www.grovefarm-uk.com/cheese.html) and include a Gloucestershire Camembert. Among other outlets, you can buy directly from the farm by arrangement, which also offers bed and breakfast.

EATING OUT

RESTAURANT

Vinings Restaurant
Vinings Warehouse, Gloucester Docks, Gloucester GL1 2EG
☎ 01452 384455
www.viningsrestaurant.co.uk

This striking restaurant is located in the historic docks area; choose from a wide variety of starters, mains and puddings at set prices from a buffet-style range of Indian and Thai cuisine. On Friday and Saturday nights, a family of four can feast for less than £45 – other nights can be even more reasonable.

Comfy Pew Restaurant
11, College Street, Gloucester GL1 2NE
☎ 01452 524296
www.thecomfypew.co.uk

This restaurant is one of Gloucester's 'finds'– all the locals know about it – a hop, skip and a jump from the cathedral on an old cobbled street. The food is freshly cooked and delicious – the chicken and ham pie with chunky chips and salad at under £10 is a must. Limited dinner nights.

The Wharf House
Over, Gloucester GL2 8DB
☎ 01452 332900
www.thewharfhouse.co.uk

All profits go to the Herefordshire and Gloucestershire Canal Trust, and this is a great place to explore the canal basin and the visitor centre. Plenty for everyone, including the fish eater and vegetarian, as well as dishes such as pan-fried duck on a bed of orange and ginger couscous for around £18.

The Old Passage Inn
Passage Road, Arlingham GL2 7JR
☎ 01452 740547
www.theoldpassage.com

The Old Passage, gorgeously set on the River Severn, has a fantastic reputation for its fish. Dishes vary according to availability but there are always fresh lobsters, oysters, and the famous fruits de mer – one of its specialities. In fact, the restaurant won a 'Best British Seafood Restaurant' award, despite not being by the sea! Everything varies according to availability, but you could try a Cornish stew at around £17 – or splash out with lobster for a real treat.

Tudor Farmhouse Hotel and Restaurant
High Street, Clearwell, Coleford GL16 8JS
☎ 01594 833046
www.tudorfarmhousehotel.co.uk

An intimate award-winning restaurant within a 13th-century farmhouse, the menu makes the most of the wonderful local produce that abounds here, as well as food grown in their own garden. Staff are friendly and there's great attention to detail. There's a three-course dinner menu for just over £30, with desserts such as toffee panacotta with caramelised poached pear.

EATING OUT

The Ostrich Inn
Newland, Coleford GL16 8NP
☎ **01594 833260**
theostrichinn.com

This 13th-century inn is renowned for being one of the best places to eat in the area (and there are some pretty good beers served, too). Despite its excellent food, it's as unstuffy as they come. In winter, expect a log fire; in summer, enjoy the ambience of the garden. Dinners in the bar are simpler than the more sophisticated restaurant fare, but all equally good. Before you even get onto the mains, dwell on starters such as wild boar pate with rum and ginger served with apricot chutney and sour dough; two courses around £22.

CAFÉ

The Stables Café
Sandfield Bridge, Canal Bank, Saul GL2 7LN
☎ **01452 741965**
www.thestablescafé.co.uk

The Stables was once the building used for the horses that towed the vessels up and down the canal – and now it's a fine café with a menu based on local ingredients, run by the former bridge keeper's son. There are various seating areas, including an upstairs terrace overlooking the canal. They're expanding the menu all the time. You can enjoy a trip on the Perseverance on the Gloucester & Sharpness Canal at weekends and Bank Holidays, April to late September, from nearby Saul Junction (www.cotswoldcanals.com).

🍸 Drinking

Local producers

Let's begin with a wonderfully healthy option: **Jess's Ladies Organic Milk**. The ladies in question are a herd of cows living at Hardwicke Farm just outside Gloucester (☎01452 720343; www.theladiesorganicmilk.co.uk). It's fair to say they're pampered – they insist on dining on lush organic pasture – but it's also fair to say they deserve it. The milk they produce is nutritious, pure and totally traceable; nor is it homogenised. There's also a range of cream.

The dedication of local producers is staggering, and none demonstrate that more than Helen Brent-Smith and Dave Kaspar of **Day's Cottage Apple Juice** at Brookthorpe, 4 miles south of Gloucester (☎01452 8136020; www.applejuice.care4free.net). The couple once worked in London, but when they got the chance to take over part of the family farm, they jumped. They make fine juices, ciders and perry, using only unsprayed fruit grown in traditional Gloucestershire orchards – and it's thanks to people like them that old varieties are still available. Buy at farmers' markets such as Stroud's, every Saturday. Find out more about local fruit at Gloucestershire Orchard Group at www.orchard-group.uklinux.net/glos.

In this area are some of the best English wine producers. The **Three Choirs Vineyard** in Newent is England's most awarded single estate vineyard. Every current estate wine – white, red, rosé and sparkling – is sold in the well-stocked shop. Guided tours are available, with wine tasting, and there's an excellent à la carte restaurant (GL18 1LS; ☎01531 890223; www.three-choirs-vineyards.co.uk). Wine expert Oz Clarke is a fan – as well as of nearby **Strawberry Hill** (www.strawberryhillvineyard.co.uk), which offers day tours and tastings. For further alcoholic treats, there's **St Anne's Vineyard** at Wain House, Oxenhall near Newent (GL18 1RW; ☎01989 720313), producing fine English and country wines, with all the fruit grown on site or sourced from local producers. Varieties include summer fruits, elderflower, damson, strawberry, tayberry, special elderberry, rhubarb and ginger, and many more! Tours and visits are by prior arrangement; visitors are welcome during opening times: March 15 to October 15, Wednesday to Friday, 2–6pm, Saturday and Sunday 11am–6pm; October 16 to March 14, Saturday and Sunday only, 11am–5pm. **New Town Wines** at Newton Nurseries, Strawberry Hill, Newent (GL18 1LH; ☎01531 821847) produces grape and country wines, apple juice and cider, and raspberries, blackcurrants and red currants in season.

Cotswold Country Liqueurs, Arlingham, are homemade from a variety of natural seasonal fruits and fairly-traded sugar. Wild fruit liqueurs use fruits and flowers picked from local fields, away from polluted roads. Soft fruit liqueurs are made by steeping cultivated Gloucestershire fruits from local farms in various spirits. The range includes damson brandy, sloe gin, raspberry brandy, and blackberry liqueur (☎01452 740681; www.cotswoldcountryliqueurs.com). For local real ales, try **Freeminer's** range, named after the area's ancient miners, which uses quality ingredients for a fine product (☎01594 827989; website.lineone.net/~freeminer.brewery). At **Whittington Brewery** at the Three Choirs Vineyard the beer names revolve around Dick's famous cat, Puss! (www.three-choirs-vineyards.co.uk).

Pubs

In Gloucester itself, the **Fountain Inn** in Westgate Street is a well-established venue, while the 15th-century **New Inn** in Northgate Street is said to be haunted by Lady Jane Grey. Doors open and close when no one is there, followed by the sound of a coach and horses in the courtyard. Sometimes glasses and bottles move, and there's even talk of a figure in a long robe who walks through the Queens Suite. **Robert Raikes House**, once home to Mr Raikes, the father of Sunday Schools, is a beautifully refurbished pub in Southgate Street that really shows off its 16th-century roots.

Ten miles south of Gloucester lies Frampton-on-Severn with its manor house where 'fair' Rosamund Clifford was born, mistress to Henry II. Cricket is played on the Green, which is said to be the longest in England. Try the **Bell Inn** for a pleasant drink. You can also wander along and see the historic tithe barn, built in the early 1600s, 100 yards from the church. It's in the top 5% of the most important historical buildings nationally.

And there are simply oodles of good pubs in the Forest – **The Glasshouse** at May Hill, Longhope (GL17 0NN); the **Rising Sun** in the High Street in Bream (GL15 6JF). Another to look out for is the **Miners Arms**, New Road, Whitecroft near Lydney, with the steam railway passing just behind it. CAMRA recommends it for its real ales, but it's also passionate about cider and perry. A good place to eat or drink is the **Dog & Muffler** in Joyford, Coleford (GL16 7AS), but do book if you're after a meal: it's popular.

ⓘ Visitor Information

Tourist information centres: Gloucester Tourist Information Centre, 28 Southgate Street, Gloucester GL1 2DP, ☎01452 396572, www.visitgloucester.info, open Mon 10am–5pm, Tues–Sat 9.30am–5pm and Sun in Jul/Aug 11am–3pm; Coleford Visitor Information Centre, High Street, Coleford GL16 8HG, ☎01594 812388, open Mon–Sat 10am–4/5pm, Sat 10am–2pm in Oct, Feb, Mar and Sun/bank holidays, 10am–2pm in Jul/Aug; Newent Tourist Information Centre, 7 Church Street, Newent GL18 1PU, ☎01531 822468; Lydney has a tourist information point with leaflets at Unit 1, Newerne Street, Lydney GL15 5RF, ☎01594 844894; as does Cinderford at Bellevue Centre, 4 Bellevue Road, Cinderford GL14 2AE, ☎01594 823184.

Hospitals: Gloucestershire Royal Hospital in Great Western Road, Gloucester GL1 3NN, ☎08454 222222 (24-hr A&E).

Supermarkets include: Tesco, St Oswald's Road GL1 2SG, ☎0845 6779305; Asda, Bruton Way GL1 1DS, ☎01452 833000; Gloucester Budgens, Market Square, Newent GL18 1PS, ☎01531 828334.

Sports: GL1 Gloucester Leisure Centre, Bruton Way, Gloucester GL1 1DT, ☎01452 396666, www.gloucester.gov.uk; The Warehouse Climbing Centre, The Warehouse Health Club, Parliament Street, Gloucester GL1 1HY, ☎01452 30235, www.the-warehouse.co.uk; Gloucester Ski and Snowboard Centre, Matson Lane, Matson, Gloucester GL4 6EA, ☎01452 874842, www.gloucesterski.com; The Heywood Leisure Centre, Causeway Road, Cinderford, Gloucestershire GL14 2AZ, ☎01594 824008; Forest Leisure, at Five Acres, Berry Hill, Coleford GL16 7JT, ☎01594 835388; Newent Leisure Centre, at Watery Lane, Newent GL18 1PX, ☎01531 821519; Whitecross Leisure Centre, Church Road, Lydney GL15 5DZ, ☎01594 842383, www.forestleisure.org.uk; Cotswold Trail Riding Centre at Ongers Farm, Brookthorpe GL4 0UT, ☎01452 813344/07966 099 359.

Taxis include: Gloucester Taxis ☎01452 290031; First Associated Taxis, Gloucester, ☎01452 523523/07737 523 880; Acorn Cabs, Coleford, ☎01594 835010; KC Cars, Cinderford, ☎01594 823020; Crystal Travel Taxis, Cinderford, ☎01594 824846.

INDEX

A

B

C

L

Y

Z

This first edition published in Great Britain in 2009 by
Crimson Publishing, a division of Crimson Business Ltd
Westminster House
Kew Road
Richmond
Surrey
TW9 2ND

A catalogue record for this book is available from the British Library

ISBN: 978 1 85458 463 2

The author and publishers have done their best to ensure that the information in *The best of Britain: Cotswolds* is up-to-date and accurate. However, they can accept no responsibility for any loss, injury or inconvenience sustained by any traveller as a result of information or advice in this guide.

Printed and bound by Legoprint SpA, Trento

Series editor: Guy Hobbs
Layout design: Nicki Averill, Amanda Grapes, Andy Prior
Typesetting: RefineCatch Ltd
Cover design: Andy Prior
Picture editor: Holly Ivins
Production: Sally Rawlings
Town map design: Linda M Dawes, Belvoir Cartographics & Design and Angela Wilson, All Terrain Mapping, using source material from Ordnance Survey.
Regional map design: Linda M Dawes, Belvoir Cartographics & Design and Angela Wilson, All Terrain Mapping, using source material: © Maps in Minutes™/Collins Bartholomew, 2009.

This product includes mapping data licensed from Ordnance Survey® with the permission of the Controller of Her Majesty's Stationery Office. © Crown Copyright 2009. All rights reserved. Licence number 150002047.

Acknowledgements
My heartfelt thanks to all who have been interviewed, quoted and consulted in the writing of this book, particularly Alex James for the introduction; and Jilly Cooper and Emma Samms for their valued support. Great appreciation (as always), to Mike Lowe, Candia McKormack, Mike Charity, Mark Fairhurst, Rob Rees, Clare Gerbrands, Dean Boston, Jackie Aldridge, Charles Wilson, Claire Cunningham, Maurice Flynn, Emma Bradshaw, Vicky Hancock and Guy Hobbs. Local tourism offices and councils have been invaluable: Hayley Beer, Nicola Greaves, Isobel Milne, Carole de Lacroix, Anna Sanders and Samantha Snow especially. Ian, Ellie, Ed, Miles and Josh; Pam and Roy Wilson, and Yvonne Phillips were eternally patient. Above all, I have to thank Chris Dee for his constant advice, wisdom and (sometimes appalling) jokes.

Help us update
While every effort has been made to ensure that the information contained in this book was accurate at the time of going to press, some details are bound to change within the lifetime of this edition: phone numbers and websites change, restaurants and hotels go out of business, shops move, and standards rise and fall. If you think we've got it wrong, please let us know. We will credit all contributions and send a copy of any *The Best of Britain* title for the best letters. Send to: The Best of Britain Updates, Crimson Publishing, Westminster House, Kew Road, Richmond, Surrey TW9 2ND.

Cotswolds picture credits

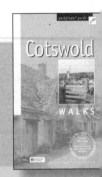